DÙTHCHAS

Landscape and Community
in Mull and Iona

GAVIN WIGGINTON

First Published in 2024 by AD ASTRA BOOKS, an imprint of Aviation Books Ltd, CF47 8RY, United Kingdom.

Also by Gavin Wigginton
Wig's Secret War
For Goodness Sake
Woods, Roos and Cougars
Don't Look Back

Cover Photograph: Benjamin Elliot on Unsplash. 'Isle of Mull Cliffs'.

Cover Design: Topics - The Creative Partnership
www.topicsdesign.co.uk

A CIP catalogue reference for this book is available from the British Library ISBN 9781915335371

The accounts of current organisations and the stories of current residents are presented in good faith, without prejudice, and with due regard for accuracy and sensitivities. Every attempt has been made to consult with the people concerned to obtain their consent and approval for the material presented. Some historical accounts involve conjecture and are based on published material as available. By the time of publication, some statements about current activities may have been overtaken by events.

CONTENTS

"*The law does punish man or woman, Who steals the goose from off the common, But leaves the greater villain loose, That steals the common from the goose.*"

Robert Louis Stevenson

This book is written as an inspiration
for the unacquainted, to visit and
appreciate the islands of Mull and Iona

*"The mark of a Scot of all classes is that he remembers
and cherishes the memory of his forbears, good or
bad; and there burns alive in him a sense of identity
with the dead even to the twentieth generation."*

Robert Louis Stevenson

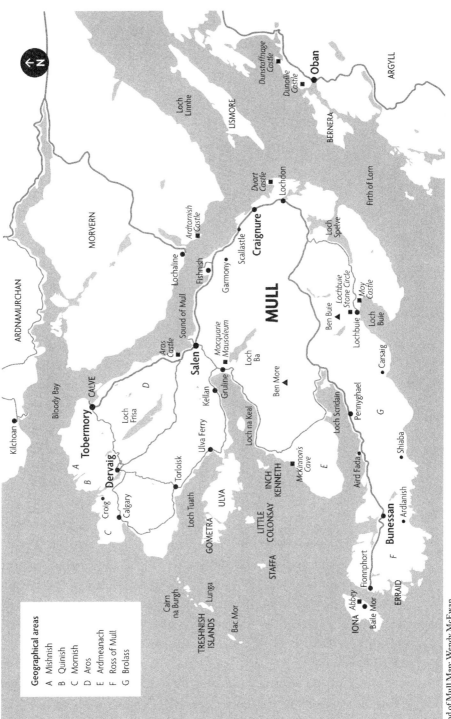

Island of Mull Map; Wendy McEwan

PREFACE

W hen I told friends and family about my plans to write a book about the Hebridean island of Mull, most people were a little incredulous. How could such a small bit of land warrant such a commitment of time and effort? In explaining myself, I am clear that my motivation derives from what has become an abiding attachment to the place and people. The rugged landscape of hills and lochs engenders a sense of wonder and inspiration, and the relatively small population are a vibrant example of the resilience and viability of small and diverse communities that flourish in relatively remote locations. The ability to thrive in challenging circumstances demonstrates the power that derives from the connection of place, identity and belonging. And Mull's story is a microcosm of the broader and relentlessly unfolding history of the formation and rebirth of the Scottish nation state.

I first became acquainted with this island more than fifty years ago. At the time, I was living in the Hillhead district of Glasgow and working at the Aero-Engine Division of Rolls Royce Ltd in Hillington. In those days, for someone from the south of Great Britain, moving to Scotland was a bit like going abroad. As a new arrival, one quickly learnt that this part of the British Isles was **not** England. It wasn't just that there was a need to develop an ear for English that was spoken in a very different way and with a distinctive vernacular.[1] The locals were quick to tell you that Scotland was once a separate country. And a little research (necessary for an Englishman raised on a diet of being British) revealed that, until the Act of Union in 1707, Scotland and England were indeed independent nation states. Although, in the 1960s, it no longer had its own parliament, a distinctly Scottish identity was demonstrated by separate legal, education and banking systems. There were also a whole set of customs into which I as a Sassenach was about to be initiated.[2] In Glasgow, this ranged from eating *haggis* and *neeps*, drinking ale that came in pints of "heavy" with a chaser of scotch, and becoming accustomed to people wearing kilts at formal events where bag pipes were *de rigueur!*[3] And while the Scots celebrated Christmas Day, it was back to work on Boxing Day, with Hogmanay taking pride of place as a public holiday at the end of the calendar year along with the custom of "first footing".[4] In my first few months, I also became aware of a radically different climate in a place so far from the equator. The nights in winter were long and cold and, in the days before central heating and duvets, I went to bed wearing a beanie and flannelette pyjamas snuggled under a great pile of woollen blankets! There was also an undercurrent of animosity between an established Presbyterian church and adherents of the "old religion", with people called Episcopalians sitting a little uncomfortably somewhere in between. This division in the Christian church between Catholic and Protestant extended not only to the football teams but several other organisations. To top it all, there were the folk with "separate nation status" on their minds, whose aspirations for "independence" were expressed through supporting what was then a nascent Scottish National Party.

The distinctive character of this *other* part of Great Britain manifested itself in many other ways. First of all, there was the topography. Despite living within a large city such as Glasgow, one was aware of the looming hills to the north, the vast and sometimes stormy waters of the Clyde estuary, and a rugged coastline sitting within easy reach to the west. And, in summer, when the twilight lingered long, one had the opportunity to drive north and west up the sometimes perilously winding and narrow A82 "trunk road". At first, and occasionally battling tides of weekend traffic, I ventured to Loch Lomond and the Trossachs hills. But then I travelled further afield, eventually arriving in a variety of locations on the western coast, including Mallaig which was the terminus of a spectacularly scenic Highland railway line from Glasgow, and Oban where I first heard people speaking Gaelic.[5] Once you reached those towns, you soon become aware of the places that lie beyond, and it wasn't long before I was taking the ferries to the Inner Hebrides, including the two largest islands, Skye and Mull.[6] I don't recall much from my first visit to Mull in the late 1960s, apart from the sweep of colourful houses along the sea front at Tobermory, the fishing vessels anchored in the harbour, and a somewhat derelict distillery.[7] But the seeds of attachment had been sown in a fertile mind.

In 1970, I left Scotland and I did not return for over thirty years. My career in industry took me south to various parts of England and, in the mid-1980s, I left the British Isles altogether to start a new life in Australia. But connection to land is never completely extinguished. And in the early 2000s my interest in Mull was rekindled when I visited the UK for a wedding. On this trip, I ventured north for a holiday, and again took the ferry across from Oban to Craignure for a stay of several days at the 17th century Bellachroy Hotel in Dervaig.[8] For the first time, I explored the island from north to south, taking in Iona. Smitten, on subsequent visits to the UK, a visit to Mull became a central feature of my time in the country.

So, what draws me to this island that stretches only 90 km by road from Tobermory in the north to Fionnphort in the south? And why should Mull be of interest to you? I think the answer to these questions begins with the landscape. The most outstanding physical features are ancient mountains formed by volcanic activity, massive headlands which have been shaped by the relentless pounding of the North Atlantic Ocean, and extensive sea lochs which have been left by the flow of rivers and glaciers since the end of the last Ice Age 15,000 years ago. This evidence of the Earth's changing geology and climate provide a stark reminder of the power of nature.

Although the island is a long way from the equator, with a climate influenced by the warm air of the Gulf Stream, the island is also blessed with an abundance of flora and fauna some of which are unique. The many species of bird include golden and reintroduced sea eagles, ospreys, and puffins. Sea life includes dolphins, seals, porpoises, and minke whales; and, on land, there are otters, four species of deer, highland cattle and sheep, and adder snakes. Then there are the numerous species of invertebrates including native bees and the inevitable midges which occasionally leave their mark on unprotected skin. This biodiversity retains many features that have been there for time immemorial, although deforestation and the elimination of the wolf have taken their toll not least in the preponderance of the red deer.

As regards the human species, there is evidence of man's existence on the island since the Hebrides were settled at least 8,000 years ago, and a rich history involving occupation by several waves of humanity. After the prehistoric period, Mull was untouched by the Roman occupation of Britain. But, in medieval times, the island and its smaller companions were occupied by a succession of migrant peoples, including the Scoti from Ireland who formed the Gaelic speaking kingdom of Dál Riata, and itinerant Vikings who established the Norse speaking Kingdom of the Isles.[910] Eventually, and after a period of autonomy as part of the Scottish *Lordship of the Isles*, in the 16th century the island was gradually integrated into the kingdom of Scotland. Subsequently, as Scotland experienced the Reformation, the Jacobite rebellions, consolidation of land ownership into relatively few remote hands, and the clearances associated with the agricultural revolution, the island then lost not only its autonomy and culture, but also many of its inhabitants. However, in more recent times, the population has recovered with a diversified community including many migrants from other parts of Scotland and England.

Because of this demographic churn, and the struggles by Scottish rulers to gain ascendancy over the island, Mull has contributed a great deal more to Scottish and British history than you might expect. In the process, it has accommodated several notable characters and produced a number of famous sons and daughters. Perhaps pre-eminently, there is the venerable St Columba who founded his mission on Iona in 593 to bring Christianity to the British Isles. In the Middle Ages, there was a succession of local chieftains who played important roles in the struggles to establish the Scottish nation, including Lachlan Mor Maclean. Also, the island's contribution to the spiritual life of the nation was complemented by several generations of leading physicians, with members of the Beaton family attending to the physical wellbeing not only of the local people but also of national leaders. In the 18th and 19th century, the tiny island of Ulva produced the colonial administrator Lachlan Macquarie, who became Governor of NSW in Australia, and was also the ancestral home of the missionary and explorer David Livingstone.

Mull has also become famous through people who figure in its history. Visitors include Felix Mendelssohn whose trip to the island of Staffa (to the west of Mull) inspired the composition of the *Hebrides Overture*, the lighthouse-building Stevenson family including Robert Louis Stevenson who lived on the island (and who based part of his book *Kidnapped* in Mull with references to the landscape of the 18th century that are evident to this day), the botanist Sir Joseph Banks who first documented Fingal's Cave, and Dr Samuel Johnson who visited the island and its neighbours in 1773 with his friend James Boswell giving rise to some interesting reflections in his diaries on the people and place of that time. More recently, there are several notable people associated with the island including Major-General Sir Colin Gubbins the head of the Special Operations Executive in World War II, the poet Sorley Maclean, and the historian Professor Sir Tom Devine to name but three.

Of importance for this book, Mull is also a place that has manifested, and continues to demonstrate, the meaning of community. In the later Middle Ages, like much of the Scottish highlands, local society was dominated by the clans. The families that prevailed in Mull for several centuries were the MacDougalls, the Macleans, the Maclaines, the Macquaries, and the McKinnons. In the days before land became an economic commodity, the clan system engendered a strong sense of collective governance and mutual interdependence which ensured the flourishing of a form of civil society that survived through war and peace, famine and feast. Mind you, for most of the time, the island was beholden to more powerful clans located on adjacent islands and the mainland. In the Middle Ages, the Macdonalds would dominate the leadership of the Inner Hebrides which withstood integration into the Scottish state until well into the 16th century. And, for 200 years commencing in the late 17th century, successive Earls and Dukes of Argyll (of the Clan Campbell) held sway during a time when Scotland became part of Great Britain.

Sadly, in the late 18th and the 19th centuries, the power of community took a major hit, with changes in land ownership and an agricultural revolution that led to the exit of many local people to congregate in hastily constructed crofting villages on the coast, and/or to migrate to the lowlands and overseas. However, more recently, and especially since a Scottish parliament was re-established through devolution from the British Parliament in Westminster in 1999, there has been a renaissance. Since 2000, the Scottish government has facilitated significant investment in local development through encouraging local community, enterprise and employment. And legislation designed to effect land reform and community empowerment has given local people the ability to reclaim ownership of parts of the island. In many ways, Mull is now a model for how community activism can reinvigorate a society to become vibrant and sustainable in a Scotland that embraces the kind of social democratic model of nationhood that prevails in northern Europe.

In summary, what makes Mull such an interesting place in the 21st century is that, despite the ravages of time, the island has retained an authentic culture, based on a largely unchanged landscape with an inclusive community that echoes its history whilst embracing the modern world. Indeed, far from undermining its values, the modern communications revolution has opened up opportunities for people to live in even the most remote corners of the island, and the advent of renewable energy is facilitating an increasingly independent and sustainable economy.

Finally, I should say something about belonging. For the young, this is not a concept that attracts much thought or consequence. Indeed, the drive of a free spirit to discover the nature of "other" people and place is an essential part of personal development that often ignores or discounts one's ancestry. This outward looking perspective on life enables us to appreciate that there are many versions of culture that bring value in a world of enormous diversity. However, as we get older, we begin to understand how our origins and early associations serve to define our identity. And, in Scotland, the character of some parts of the nation is deeply rooted in the ancient Gaelic spirit of *dùthchas* which reflects a sense of people belonging to place and community in a mutually supportive way.[11] That is why I have included this word in the title for this book, and it is a central feature of what I have to share with the reader. The word may be interpreted in many ways, but combines a rich combination of birthright and heritage, sense of native place and home, kindred affinity, mutual support, and connectedness with nature. I think that these are the characteristics which defined the civil society that developed in the Hebrides in medieval times. And, there is evidence that in the 21st century a modern version of this spirit has again become an intrinsic feature of life on the island, as a rich counterpoint to the philosophy of self-centred libertarianism that has gripped much of the western world in the early 21st century.

Gavin Wigginton

July 2024

ENDNOTES

1   Scots English developed as a separate language over a thousand years ago and exists today in a form known as "Standard Scottish English". Descended from the Anglo-Saxon family of dialects, the language encompasses many words from the other languages spoken across Scotland over the ages including Northumbrian English, Gaelic, Norse, Welsh, Pictish and the languages of significant trading partners such as the Dutch and French.

2   Sassenach is a Gaelic word for Saxon.

3   Neeps is a dish of mashed swede.

4   The word Hogmanay is said to derive from the French word hoginane meaning "gala day" and came into use in the time of the French speaking Queen Mary in the 1560s. The associated practice of first footing comes from the Gaelic practice of qualtagh with the first person to arrive after midnight being a harbinger of prospects for the year to come.

5   In Scotland, the word Gaelic is pronounced "Gallic".

6   Technically, I think that Skye has lost its island status. Traditionally, the main access was via a ferry from the Kyle of Lochalsh to Kyleakin. But, in October 1995, the island was connected to the mainland by the Skye Road Bridge, with a viaduct across Eilean Ban Island. The ferry crossing is now just a tourist trip.

7   The Tobermory Distillery is now very much back in business producing a range of peat flavoured Scotch whiskies as well as gins.

8   The Bellachroy Hotel is Mull's oldest inn, established in 1608 as a drovers' rest and arguably the island's finest hostelry. It pre-exists the village of Dervaig.

9   Scoti or Scotti is the Latin word for the Gaelic people, which came into use in the 4th century CE with a reference in the Nomina Provinciarum Omnium which dates to CE 312. It was first used as a term to refer to various native peoples in the British Isles but was eventually reserved for people living in Ireland.

10   In this book, Dál Riata is used to describe this kingdom. However, following the separation of the Irish and Scottish parts of this entity, the residual Scottish kingdom was known as Dalriada.

11   Dùthchas is a Gaelic word meaning association of a group of people with the homeland of a clan over which hereditary rights are exercised by a Chief.

DÙTHCHAS
LANDSCAPE AND COMMUNITY IN MULL AND IONA

INTRODUCTION

Sometimes, the motivation for writing a book can hit you unexpectedly. In 2017, I had just published a biography of my father and was thinking about where I should next focus my creative energy. I took a break by visiting one of my favourite haunts, the island of Mull, and ventured on a boat trip to Staffa and the Treshnish Islands. As we chugged our way past majestic cliffs, and indulged in some "puffin therapy" on the island of Lunga, inspiration hit me.[1] As the skipper of the good ship "Hoy Lass" Iain Morrison suggested later, it appeared that I had contracted what he called *island fever*. In truth, I was overwhelmed with a passion to record, and share with others, the spirit of a beautiful place and a vibrant community.

Once the germ of the idea had seeded, I determined that I would need to do a couple of things before beginning what might be a lengthy period of writing. The first was to complete an analysis of previous publications, and decide whether I had something new to add. The second was to spend some time living on the island, so that I could contemplate and draw inspiration from the landscape, and become properly acquainted with the community and culture of which I had only a superficial knowledge from visiting as a tourist.

My initial research of previous publications about the island revealed that there were already more than 250 books with significant references, including 90 that were exclusively about Mull and Iona. This veritable library of reading included general guidebooks, histories of human existence and endeavour, and specialist accounts of the physical and natural environment. Apart from mentions in ancient annals, the earliest sources appeared to be four books published in the 18th century, around fifteen in the 19th century, and some seventy between 1900 and 1970.[2] In the 1980s and 1990s, as interest in the Hebrides soared, there were then 90 publications in just twenty years and, since 2000, there have been yet another 50. This plethora gave me cause for thought. For whom was I writing this book, and was there a fresh and engaging perspective on the island and its people that would engage an unknowing public?

As regards the potential reader, it seemed to me that there were two groups of people with whom I wished to connect. As an Australian, I am very conscious of the long and rich history of migration to the Antipodes from the Highlands and Islands, and many ancestors of Scottish migrants are keenly interested in their heritage. Secondly, I am very conscious that many people visit Mull without any knowledge of the true nature of life in the past or in the present day. For both these groups, I thought there was a place for a book that would enlighten them not only about the history of the island but also the country of which it is a part.

The abundance of books about Mull reinforced the imperative to spend an extended period of time on the island. Finding somewhere to live for more than a few days was challenging. Convenient and comfortable as it would have been, I ruled out accommodation at the hotel where I had previously stayed on a number of holidays. More than anything, this was because I needed to escape the mindset of being a visitor. Fortunately, there is an organisation in Mull that facilitates the short term rental of property and, during my visit in 2017, I identified a suitable cottage in the centre of the island on the banks of Loch na Keal. Kellan Mill Lodge provides easy access to all parts of the island and commands inspiring views of the majestic Ben More.[3] On my return to Australia, I quickly discovered that bookings were made a year ahead, and this dictated a significant delay. So it was that I made a commitment to visiting for six weeks in 2019.

In preparation for this first extended visit, I did some research on current Mull society. This led me to join three organisations, the *Mull Historical and*

Archaeological Society ("MH&AS") which encourages interest and research into local history and archaeology, the *Mull Museum* which has a library with significant historical sources, and the *Mull and Iona Community Trust* ("MICT") which fosters and manages community-based development projects and services. Each of these organisations would prove to be invaluable in terms of access to the island's history and current society. Local people also proved to be generous in sharing their knowledge and experience and helping to arrange interviews with current islanders.

Given the delay in visiting the island, during the next twelve months, I put the project to one side. However, in April 2019 I flew from Australia to London where, before embarking on the long drive north, I met with a contact who has property on the island. David Fell was the source of much valuable local information and, during our lunch, he made a telling comment, suggesting that the project might require more than one extended visit. How right he was!

Shortly after taking up residence at Kellan Mill Lodge I commenced the first of a series of interviews, and visited the Mull Museum in Tobermory to review local documents covering many aspects of life in the Hebrides over the ages. I also travelled around the island at a more leisurely pace than when I had been a tourist. This enabled me to absorb the power and beauty of the physical landscape, encounter the ruins of previous habitation, and visit a number of sites of archaeological and historical interest. One evening, I also attended the AGM of the North West Mull Community Woodland Company in Dervaig, to learn about some significant community-based activity.

As I proceeded with this field work, a very strong theme began to emerge which would eventually become a central feature of the book. In particular, I was struck by both the very strong sense of community, identity, and belonging that existed within the current island society, and the remarkable achievements of a number of its residents through both individual and collective endeavour. The outcome was enhanced prosperity and well-being both for individuals and the wider society. It was also clear that this strong sense of community was not just a feature of the modern era. It almost seemed as if there was a kind of collective memory of the power of mutual inter-dependence in a remote place that derived from earlier times, albeit moulded by the tide of history and transformed by the influx of many outsiders who now formed the majority of the population.

In these early days, I also became aware of a dynamic tension in the modern community. In particular, it was evident that the island was not a homogenous entity. This was not just a matter of landscape, with a dividing line that seemed to stretch from somewhere south of Salen, through the central village of Gruline, and down the middle of Loch na Keal, with Ben More forming a kind of central pivotal axis. Alternative character and perspectives were clearly evident not only in different educational arrangements driven by logistics, but other more subtle differences reflecting local loyalties and demographics. However, this was not to deny a connectivity which linked together the communities of the whole island. The unifying elements included a number of institutions that reflected an all-of-island approach, the plethora of community Facebook pages, and periodic Mull-wide events such as the Highland Games, the Rugby Sevens competition, literary and culinary gatherings, music festivals, and a car rally.

During this formative period, through a conversation with local landscape painter and artist Angus Stewart, I was also introduced to a very knowledgeable local film maker and activist named Alasdair Satchel. Alasdair was undertaking a long-term oral history project in which he recorded conversations with local people, and produced podcasts and films based on his insightful interviews through a programme entitled *"What We Do in the Winter"*. He and his partner Georgia, who just happened to be the most helpful resident archivist at the Mull Museum, gave me some valuable insights into local society as well as useful literary and historical references.[4]

Whilst living on the island, I also had the benefit of being exposed to the Mull version of political activity, with local Council elections taking place in early May 2019. As it happened, the son of the aforementioned skipper of the *Hoy Lass* was also the local Convenor of the Scottish National Party. Through talking with Colin Morrison I obtained insights into the history of the island including the devastating effect of the "clearances", and an appreciation of the multi-cultural nature of the current population. Colin also informed me of the significant legislative programme of the recently restored Scottish Parliament that provided for land reform, community empowerment, and the regeneration of island communities; and he introduced me to what he called the "mosaic" of modern community activity.

Finally, during this relatively intensive period of engagement with the local community, I did allow myself some relaxation. One of the best things available on the island for locals and visitors is an institution called An Tobar and Mull Theatre. As their publicity says, the An Tobar cultural centre acts as "a creative beacon", providing exhibitions of arts and crafts and live concerts; and the Mull Theatre is a venue for live theatre, workshops, and visiting shows. I attended five events, with a range of music and entertainment including a memorable performance by the Fergus McCreadie Trio.

Eventually, my time on the island in 2019 came to an end, and I left with a real sadness. This first period of residence had been an enormously valuable experience, not only for gathering information, but also for thinking through exactly what I wanted to write about the island, and for whom. Interestingly, consumed with my project, when it came to leave I had not bothered to book my return journey to the mainland. In making enquiries, I discovered that the car ferry from Craignure to Oban was fully booked and, for a few days, I thought I might be marooned! However, local people soon told me that there was another way to get across to the mainland with a car ferry service operating from Fishnish on a first-come-first-served basis. This twenty minute trip takes you to the village of Lochaline (pronounced "lock-alan"), and you then have a long drive down mainly one-track roads to another ferry at Corran which connects with the A82 between Glasgow and Inverness. Apart from enabling a timely exit, this alternative route revealed a relatively obscure corner of Scotland that in earlier times figured strongly in Mull's history.[5]

Even before I had completed this first extended stay in Mull, I had already realised that six weeks was not nearly enough time to complete my field work. Accordingly, I scheduled a further visit in September 2020.

However, the world was then struck by the dreaded Covid-19 virus, forcing me to alter my plans. With a lengthy interruption to my personal life not to mention international travel, in the next couple of years I switched my attention to undertaking desk research, including an investigation into the operation of clan-based society, and the part played by the residents of Mull in Scottish history. In the process, I became aware of a whole new view of *British* history, seen for the first time through *Scottish* eyes; and, with a focus on the Hebrides, I was surprised to discover the strong influence of Irish and Norse heritage for those parts of Scotland which lie on the western and northern periphery. This revelation led me to appreciate how Mull had experienced a huge churn of multi-cultural influences from the original inhabitants of Celtic origin, through the influx of Gaelic speaking migrants from Ireland, the establishment of Norse Rule in the Kingdom of the Isles in the 9th century, the transfer of sovereignty to Scotland in the 13th century with the creation of the autonomous Lordship of the Isles, and finally the slow integration into the kingdom of Scotland after the abolition of the Lordship in 1493. It was also highly revealing to see how the subsequent Reformation, unification of the crowns of Scotland and England in 1603, eviction of the Clan Maclean by the Earl of Argyll in 1692, union of Scotland and England in 1707, and the failed Jacobite rebellions had been a slow burn for the erosion of community life on the island. This had culminated in attempts by the British government to completely eradicate clan culture and the Gaelic language, the recruitment of many highlanders into being the militant vanguard of British colonial armies, and the destruction of rural communities through the agricultural revolution in which the majority of the population was cleared from the land by absentee landlords. This long saga served to provide a poignancy for the return of the Clan Maclean in the 20th century and the re-birth of Scotland's community-based identity in the 21st century.

In making the concept of community and belonging a central focus of the book, I was mindful that a true sense of *belonging* is a function of connection to place. Consequently, I acquainted myself with the geological origins of the physical environment of Mull. I began with very little prior knowledge, naively assuming that the Hebrides were specks of elevated terrain that had at some stage parted company with the main land of the British Isles due to changes in sea level. As I would discover, nothing could be further from the truth. The reality was that the Western Isles and the associated north-west section of the mainland had almost literally attached themselves to the rest of the British Isles after a long journey around the surface of the planet, with a clash of tectonic plates that was reflected in the formation of the Great Glen that runs through the centre of Scotland and across the south eastern corner of Mull! Not surprisingly, one was left with the conclusion that, by a quirk of nature, the independent nature of the peoples of the Western and Northern Isles actually reflected the separate geography of the land on which they lived!

In April 2023, I returned to Mull to complete my field work and renew the associations I had made in 2019. I quickly rediscovered my love affair with the island, and completed 15 more interviews. I also undertook further research at the Mull Museum, with a focus on oral histories which are a particularly revealing source of culture. During this second period of residence, I reflected on some of the ideas I had developed about island communities and significantly adjusted my views. Hitherto, I had it in mind that the current society in Mull was in some way a continuation of the kinship that had existed in the clan based society in medieval times. However, an analysis of who currently owned the land, and the background of the current inhabitants, disabused me of this notion. In reality, most of the current major land owners, many of whom do not live in Mull, are people who have little ancestral connection with the island; and the wider population are a diverse set of people, few of whom can trace their ancestry back to the traditional residents. On the other hand, the current community do share with their forbears an affinity with the landscape, a strong bond of mutual inter-dependence that exists in many remote places, and the echoes of human history that abound in manifest signs of previous habitation.

By early June 2023, I had completed my field work and, again with great sadness, I left the island. As in 2019, my departure was stymied by problems with the ferries. This time, the ageing fleet of ships were out of action for essential maintenance. As before, I took a ferry from Fishnish to Lochaline, and took the long way back south. That afternoon in Hamilton I had a wonderful conversation with Professor Sir Tom Devine who provided very helpful insights into Scotland's modern history, and the Celtic Football Club![6]

Finally, I should say something about the structure of the book. After a reflection in the next chapter about the meaning of community and belonging, in *Part One*, I begin with an explanation of the physical landscape of the island, and a description of the climate and ecology which have shaped human existence. In *Part Two*, I trace the roots and history of humanity on the island, beginning with the fragile existence of peoples surviving in a harsh landscape in prehistoric times, through medieval times to the point where the Hebrides became part of the Scottish state. In *Part Three*, I explain how the clan system evolved and provide a brief history of the main clans who have occupied Mull as reflected in the lives of Chiefs. In *Parts Four and Five*, particularly as essential context for the non-Scottish reader, I provide a brief history of Scotland through to the present day, with references to Mull where it has played a significant part. In *Part Six*, there is an account of recent community development, including the legislative framework, and a description of three outstanding examples of successful community activism. Finally, in *Part Seven*, I give an account of the current community, economy and culture. The book concludes with a reflection on the prospects for community in the modern world.

The writing of the book has been a great adventure, and the journey has taught me much about what it is to be Scottish, as well as developing my own sense of identity which derives from the Scottish heritage of my mother. The project has also left me with the firm view that, if humanity is to survive for much longer, it will be because we acknowledge the need for connection to the physical environment within which we live and of which we are a part, and we understand and value the power of community in living together in peace and harmony for the achievement of a fruitful and prosperous life for all.

ENDNOTES

1   The expression "puffin therapy" is attributable to Iain Morrison who uses it in characterising the benefits of visiting the habitat of puffins.

2   The earliest book is entitled A Description of the Western Islands of Scotland Circa 1695 by Martin Martin, printed by Andrew Bell in Cornhill 1703. This is an account of a journey made in the late 17th century, and sheds light on the society that existed in Mull just after the Dukes of Argyll took ownership of Maclean lands, and before the failure of the Jacobite rebellions and the subsequent clearances altered Highlands and Islands society for ever.

3   Kellan Mill Lodge is located on the site of what was once a water-powered flour mill on lands once owned by the Clan MacQuarrie.

4   At the time of writing, Alasdair is close to completing some 100 of these interviews which contain amazing insight into the life and times of people living on the island over the last century.

5   In the 12th century, Lochaline in Morvern was the location of a fortress occupied by the ancestor of local clans, Somerled, and Ardtornish Castle was a Clan Donald home in the late medieval period.

6   Sir Tom Devine is emeritus Professor of Modern History at Edinburgh University.

DÙTHCHAS
LANDSCAPE AND COMMUNITY IN MULL AND IONA

COMMUNITY
AND BELONGING

In current times, "community" is a well-worn term used to describe many aspects of human existence. In this book, the word is used over 400 times and it's important to be clear about the meaning! The origins of the word include the Latin "communitas" meaning public spirit and "communis" meaning common and shared service. The traditional meaning refers to the sense of, and structures for, connection between people who share culture, social capital, and sometimes land; and in older cultures it is manifest in using other words such as the Gaelic *dùthchas*. Sadly, in the modern world of social media, where "community" means the "friends" with whom you exchange on-line messages, the word has become devalued. However, the older usage is still relevant, and the resurrection of a society which reflects a communion between people and their environment is vital for humanity's survival on a planet of finite resources and delicate eco-systems.

Over the last two centuries, there have been a number of theories about the nature of "community", with several schools of thought.[1] There are also many definitions of the word including the following:

"Community is a group of people who live in the same place, share similar values, and are committed to working together in pursuit of the common good."

This wording contains several phrases which reflect what it means to live in a civil society. Specifically, there is no reference to, and it is **not** about, "entitlement to property", "individual rights", and the "pursuit of personal interest". This is not to deny that in a healthy community, there should be a place for diverse individual rights and aspirations, and minority considerations. It must also be acknowledged that rights to land are a deeply ingrained feature of human existence. However, the successful operation of a civil society requires broad acceptance of the need for sharing through some form of social contract. This is not communism or socialism. It does not suggest a one party state, or the state ownership of property of the means of production. Nor does it deny that the human species is inclined to adopt some sense of hierarchy, and that people with different roles may be worthy of different rewards. However, it does imply a minimum standard of life to be experienced by all who share in the common good and a generosity of spirit towards the disadvantaged.

An understanding of what constitutes a "healthy" community warrants a brief explanation of the main schools of thought that underpin current thinking. Early theories of community development in the 19th century were built on the concept of what is known as "Social Darwinism". This theory suggested that social organisms evolve rather like flora and fauna and, according to Herbert Spencer, a society grows through *"acts of spontaneous cooperation by gregarious and social individuals who are displaying social self-consciousness".*[2] For Spencer, human populations become subject to actions and reactions within the community through a form of social osmosis. This provides that, over time, individuals adapt to each other, to the wider society, and to external conditions; and the changes made to the community and individual behaviour lead to further iterative adaptations to foster a joint sense of heritage. In the process, there is an inclination for the more "successful" characteristics to be inherited by future generations, and this is at the heart of "progress".[3]

Subsequently, sociologists have developed a range of other theories that fall into two main schools of thought – "conflict" and "functionalist". The *conflict* school, of which a notable proponent is Karl Marx, focuses on the idea that society evolves through competition between common interest groups for the use of limited resources including land, with social and economic institutions used as tools of the struggle. In *Das Kapital*, Marx suggests that this leads to an inevitable conflict between the proletarian working class and the bourgeois ruling class, which culminates in revolution. This certainly had meaning for the down-trodden serf who was subject to the feudalism of the Middle Ages; and the consequence of class-based tension in Europe, between the 17th and 20th centuries, was a series of revolutions and reforms through the establishment of new forms of community-based social contract.

Later versions of conflict theory reflect competition amongst capitalist factions and between various social, religious, and other groups, and have been used to explain a wide range of social phenomena. However, at its essence, the implications are that communities are inevitably prone to internal social disruption between different socio economic classes over the unequal division of resources. Consequently, the fear amongst the relatively wealthy of losing power and land is the main driver of social reform. This is manifest in the "enlightened self-interest" of the advantaged, seeking a social contract with the disadvantaged which includes the expansion of democracy and the introduction of civil rights designed to achieve the peaceful and acquiescent acceptance by the masses of their relative poverty. It's a compelling theory which still has traction!

In contrast, the *functionalist* school of thought takes a utilitarian approach, and has its origins in the work of the 19th century French sociologist Émile Durkheim who in a time of political turbulence sought to provide for peaceful ways of achieving a more stable society.[4] This theory suggests that society is an organism consisting of a number of social institutions that materialise to fulfil different and evolving needs. They depend for their existence on connection with each other, and stability and synergy are achieved through mutually beneficial co-operation. Durkheim also suggests that when one component becomes redundant, the others will adapt to fill the void. Key examples in a civil society are various versions of family including the clan system, elected governments, institutions providing for legal due process, industrial and commercial organisations established to facilitate various forms of economic activity, the media, educational establishments, and religious bodies. According to functionalism, institutions are prone to atrophy and when a new need arises, a new institution will emerge. The truth of this idea is certainly borne out by what happens to commercial organisations in a capitalist system.

In the functionalist view of the world, the operation of effective collective human activity depends on a considerable degree of trust and interdependence as well as acknowledged mutual benefit. To give an example, a society needs citizens that have the skills and competence to work in economic and other institutions that form part of the whole. To this end, there is a need for educational institutions which individuals alone do not have the economic means to finance. Accordingly, they are willing to pay taxes to political institutions that then use "public funds" to establish educational institutions that meet the wider community need. In the process, the children grow up to become law-abiding citizens (who accept the need to pay taxes for the education of *their* children), and the family supports the institutions that deliver this benefit. From the functionalist perspective, if all goes well, this delivers a society in which there is order, mutual support, and advancement.

In more recent times, the above and other theories have been the subject of critical assessment to the point that none is accepted as a sufficient explanation of how communities operate and change. This has led to the development of *Complexity Theory* which embraces the concepts of belonging and shared destiny. At the same time, the new imperative for a "sustainable existence" has emerged which requires collective action to drive the *transformation* of society for the public good. The success of these forces requires a recognition of the *connectedness* of everything, and a commitment to a social contract in which individuals trust the system to provide a timely and just transition from old to new industries with minimal pain. In developing this theory, proponents have been keen to emphasise that a *viable* community encompasses a range of concepts that recognise an almost organic sense of bonding based on actual and perceived realities. These ideas have given rise to a more nuanced definition of community with the following *inter-connected* characteristics:

a)   Identification with a geographical location.
b)   Living in a functional relationship with each other.
c)   Having opportunities for individual self-fulfilment.
d)   Sharing a sense of identity and/or unity of purpose.
e)   Commitment to a common destiny.

With this more up-to-date version of the definition of community in mind, we finally come to the question of what one might call *social engineering*. This concept is of particular relevance to this book given the recent legislation in Scotland designed to achieve land reform, community empowerment, and organisational development. Much of the research on this concept derives from models used by First World countries to assist native peoples taking control of their own destiny in the many new nations that have emerged following decolonisation in the 20th century. However, there is a parallel set of work which applies to regenerating neglected or declining parts of First World countries, including policies designed to address global warming through a just transition from carbon-based to renewable-energy economies.

Models for this kind of deterministic change often focus on identifying why some communities are relatively static, and even inclined to atrophy, whilst others develop and flourish. A dominant model is the *Basic Needs* theory which suggests that relatively underdeveloped communities are often caught in a self-limiting culture. This is characterised by people having a blinkered view of what constitutes a reasonable life, in which they accept certain external constraints and focus on the achievement of an agreed set of very basic needs. Although there may be a variety of causes for this phenomenon of "limited development", the failure to "develop" is often explained by a combination of ignorance, self-interest, or just an inherent lack of ambition. In any event, to break through these barriers to change, and achieve sustainable community development, it may be necessary for some external intervention which seeks to amplify the basic needs of a community, confront vested interests, and remove or alter the constraints. This is certainly how well-meaning developed countries intervene in the Third World, empowering primitive communities to aspire to a higher level of needs and an improved quality of life. Of course, the timing of external intervention is of the essence, and the need for preparing and empowering a community to take the self-improving steps is paramount. Many overseas development projects have failed through failing to recognise the timing factor.

Much of the above is highly relevant to communities such as the Highlands and Islands. This is not to suggest that these places are backwaters of the modern world! Far from it. Indeed, in many respects, the ancient and modern history of places like Mull reflects the operation of most of the elements of what constitutes a health community with many attributes that less successful communities in the modern world might like to consider and emulate. Having said that, until recently, the Hebrides were sadly trapped in a cycle of decline. While there are nearly 100 inhabited islands in Scotland, there are many more that only have the ruins of what were once thriving communities. They are beautiful places, often untouched by the excesses of modern development, but they have been the victims of challenging circumstances with significant depopulation. The exodus from the Highlands and Islands over the last 200 years was driven through destitution as much as public policy, and was the end product of a series of cultural and economic developments in which ordinary people were unable to sustain their families in their traditional lands. These included the following:

- The crown imposed a feudal system of land title that paid scant regard to the traditional clan-based ownership of land,
- Legislation sought to unravel the social contract between mutually supportive communities,
- Those on the right side of history often became absentee owners of land with scant regard for traditional loyalty to local people,
- Land became an economic commodity in which landowners were landlords rather than benign community leaders, and clansmen paid rent that they increasingly couldn't afford,
- Following the Jacobite rebellions, the government imposed a form of ethnic cleansing and community disempowerment,
- The British Empire provided opportunities which led people living in poverty to seek a better life in the lowlands, in military service and overseas,

- There was an agricultural revolution in which people employed in traditional labour intensive farming were replaced by sheep, and
- The country experienced the failure of crops through adverse climate and disease.

Furthermore, in the last 100 years, as power has been ever more strongly centred in the corridors of power, the Scottish islands have been the subject of serious public policy neglect. As stated in the Introduction to the National Islands Plan Implementation Route Map issued by the Scottish Parliament in 2018:

"What history tells us is that islands have often been on the periphery of public policy. Island communities have felt that decisions which would end up affecting them were taken by people who were not living on the islands and who were completely detached from the reality of life away from the mainland."

Thankfully, in the 21ˢᵗ century, the tide has turned and, with the devolution of power to a Scottish Parliament, and the enactment of significant legislation which is triggering community development and release of private land to community ownership, island communities are beginning to flourish. We will return to this theme in Chapter 17.

Finally, in preparation for what follows, I need to say something further about the meaning of belonging which is a vital element in feeling a sense of comfort with the community in which a person lives. After the wave of migration that has taken place across the world in recent times, this is a prescient subject, and it is of particular relevance for Mull because the modern community consists of many current inhabitants who have little or no specific connection to the traditional peoples of the island. This muddies the water where belonging is concerned, and I think it's important to understand that, for societies where there is population churn, the health of the community relies on the ability of new inhabitants to achieve a balance between two potentially countervailing forces – the culture that I join and the culture that I bring.

In talking about this, I can speak from personal experience. I have spent my life living in two countries, Britain and Australia. For the uninitiated, despite a shared language, these two nations are not just distinct in terms of landscape and climate. Their cultures share only superficial similarities. When I migrated from one to the other in mid-life, I convinced myself that in a new location it would be possible to establish a sense of belonging based on a revised version of myself. Accordingly, when I moved to Australia, I put behind me all those things that I associated with the UK, and embraced what I perceived to be the essence of the new place. As a migrant, there is a lot to be said for this approach. Attachment to your past can make one homesick, and constant references to your place of origin can be a source of great irritation to those already living in the adopted country.[5] However, in recent times, I have come to realise that this approach is partly flawed.

First of all, when first arriving in Australia, I lived in almost complete ignorance of the traditional owners who have occupied the land for 60,000 years. Without questioning, I adopted a relatively superficial view of my own existence based on the culture created by British people who invaded and settled the country over the last 250 years. However, as I became acquainted with the native peoples, I began to develop a sense of unease which undermined my sense of belonging. In recent times, I have come to realise that the source of this discomfort is the failure to adjust to the existence, experience, culture, and connection to land of Aboriginal peoples. Sadly, this understanding is not shared by many people in Australia, which is why the country recently voted NO in a referendum designed to recognise native people in the constitution. It also explains why many Australians are happy to have a foreign Head of State, and to maintain a flag that rejoices in a symbol of the colonising country!

A second flaw in my personal approach to developing a sense of belonging in an adopted land is the commitment to disowning my past. Whilst this is a wise approach when first arriving in a new community, it is foolish to persist in denying your ancestry. It is like trying to live without an arm or a leg, and it denies the adopted country of the benefit of external experience.

Finally, it almost goes without saying that a pre-condition for the development of a sense of belonging in a new community does require a degree of commonality and sympathy with the culture and values of one's origin and destination. In talking to the many people who have settled in Mull over recent decades, a key element in successful migration is that they sought to live in a community with values that they anticipated would be largely consistent with their own. That is a pre-condition of developing a sense of belonging.

This brings me back to what underpins the health of the current community on the island of Mull. Descendants of native residents are comfortable in their skins and are thriving in the renaissance of a community-based society that held sway in medieval times, even if that is a dim and distant memory. The secret of the success for the wider community is that, for the most part, those who have migrated to the island (and their descendants) whether inspired by landscape or a symbiosis with the community they have chosen to join, have embraced the local culture and developed a sense of belonging that is fortified by a consistency between their own values and those of local people. Natives and migrants with fresh perspectives working together make a powerful combination.

ENDNOTES

1   For certain parts of this section, I am indebted to a paper by Dr De Wet Schutte of the Cape Peninsula University of Technology, Cape Town, South Africa published in 2015.

2   Herbert Spencer published a variety of books on the subject culminating in The Synthetic Philosophy published in 1896.

3   This material is based on an article by John Offer of the School of Applied Social and Policy Sciences, Ulster University, Coleraine, UK in 2019.

4   This material is from an article on Thought Co by Ashley Crossman (2020).

5   This phenomenon gives rise to many English migrants to Australia being called "whinging poms". The word "pom" is perhaps a reference to the sun-burnt heads of the migrants which were likened to the pomegranate.

PART ONE

HEBRIDEAN LANDSCAPE

DÙTHCHAS
LANDSCAPE AND COMMUNITY IN MULL AND IONA

GEOLOGY AND GEOGRAPHY

Throughout my adult life, apart from the dark days of the Covid-19 pandemic, I have had the privilege of being able to travel to exotic places across the globe. In reflecting on many journeys, I am struck by the diversity of memories about a place visited. For some locations, it is the architecture both ancient and modern, and the history of existence that goes with those monuments of human endeavour. For others, I recall the life and energy of communities with which I engaged in social interaction. However, the thing that has reached deepest into my soul is the inspiration derived from the distinctive local manifestations of the natural environment. In my personal experience this has encompassed the towering cliffs of ragged coastlines, the richly coloured stretches of rhododendrons across the foothills of the Himalayas, snow-capped volcanos in South America, and the unexpected appearance of a noble beast in its natural habitat. As I have got older, and communed with family and friends in many different places and environments, I have come to realise that it is this environmental aspect of place that is at the core of my own sense of belonging.

The purpose of this Part of the book is to share with the reader the particular characteristics of the natural environment of Mull that underpins the identity of local residents, and relentlessly marks them in terms of their day to day experience of life. And we begin with a description of the geology and geography of Mull which, consisting of very considerable diversity, explains much about the rich character of both the island, the society and the individual people.

Geology

In the modern era, most people visiting Mull catch their first glimpse of the island from the east. As the ferry from Oban cuts across the Firth of Lorn, and enters the Sound of Mull heading for Craignure, the south eastern approaches which are dominated by Duart Castle give only a hint of the spectacular geology that lies beyond. As the notable geologist Dr David Stephenson has written:

> "Mull is a part of Scotland in which the underlying geology truly dominates the landscape".[1] Steep cliffs of lava, like those of Staffa, dominate northern Mull, while the high mountains of the midlands expose the roots of a huge volcano that erupted 60 million years ago. In marked contrast are the low-lying rounded knolls of pink granite, and the welcoming sandy beaches of the Ross of Mull in the south west of the island. And, just a short distance across the Sound (of Iona), some of the oldest rocks in Scotland form the low craggy hills of Iona. The mountains show the effects of glaciers that covered the area during the last Ice Age, and all around the coast are signs of changing sea levels that followed the melting of the ice in recent geological time."

Like many areas of the planet, the part of the Earth's crust on which Mull sits did not start its existence in its current geographical location. The oldest rocks on the island were formed in the southern hemisphere and, to explain the complex origins of the diverse geology of the island, it is necessary to understand the fundamentals of continental drift.

The idea that continents, sitting upon plates, travel across the surface of the planet was first propounded by the Belgian cartographer Abraham Ortelius in 1596. In subsequent centuries, as coast lines were more accurately mapped by explorers, it was noticed that the shapes of continents on opposite sides of the Atlantic Ocean seemed to fit together. And, in 1912, the German meteorologist and geophysicist Alfred Wegener began to lecture about the concept of continental drift. In 1915, he published a book which identified a super-continent that he subsequently named Pangaea.[23] Wegener's theories were not well received, because he didn't have a scientifically-founded model to explain how the continents moved apart and collided against each other. However, his ideas were later vindicated as scientists established the concept of continental plates floating on the Earth's lithosphere, and accumulated empirical evidence of ecosystems shared between current continents now far distant from each other.[4]

Modern theories of continental drift suggest that the areas of land on the planet have actually been through a number of cycles, involving agglomeration and segmentation. Thus, Pangaea is only the latest of at least five super-continents. And research suggests that this most recent manifestation of a super continent was formed around 335 million years ago and remained intact for about 160 million years. It was located on the equator and was surrounded by a super ocean, covering around 70% of the planet, named Panthalassa.[5] During this period, important development in life took place with evidence of coral, sharks, and boney fish in the sea. And on the land life was dominated by lycopsid forests inhabited by insects and other arthropods and the first tetrapods.[6] This time was also significantly impacted by several mass extinction events.

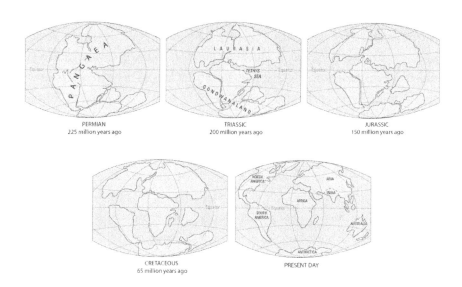

US Government Geological Survey – USGS Publications Repository

By the time Pangaea broke up, around 175 million years ago (in the Middle Jurassic Period), the seas were swarming with molluscs, ichthyosaurs (resembling modern day dolphins), sharks, rays, and the first ray-finned bony fishes. Life on land was dominated by forests of cycads (palm like plants) and conifers in which dinosaurs flourished, and the first true mammals made an appearance. The break-up of the continent went through several major phases as shown in the above maps.[7]

In the first phase, Pangaea split into Laurasia and Gondwanaland, with the North Atlantic Ocean opening up between the two continents. During this time, as the supercontinent rotated clockwise, the area including the Hebrides is thought to have moved from the southern hemisphere in a northerly direction.[8] In the process, this land mass passed through the equator and ended firmly in the northern hemisphere. In the second phase, Gondwanaland broke up into the modern-day continents of Africa, South America, Antarctica, and Australia, with India moving north to eventually lodge itself into what had become Eurasia. Finally, North America split away from Eurasia, opening up the Norwegian Sea between Scandinavia and Greenland, with the Hebrides lodged in between and moving east.

This drift of land masses over 175 million years resulted in an amazing transformation for the geology of the Hebrides. In particular, the rocks to be found in Mull preserve elements of all the climatic zones in which they have existed since the days of Pangaea including the geology of land that currently lies in the Southern Hemisphere. And evidence of Mull's time in the equatorial region of the planet are evident in soils on the island that are also found in the modern day Middle East. In Particular, the Triassic rocks in Mull reveal desert conditions, desiccated cracks found at Gribun on the north-west coast of Ardmeanach reflect massive flash floods, and conglomerates in the same area show desert wadi like conditions. In later times, when North America split from Eurasia, shared geology demonstrates that Mull was connected to the land mass which now forms Greenland. In the final stages of evolution prior to the modern age, the Hebrides, Northern Isles, and the northwest part of Scotland split away from Greenland and Iceland and drifted towards the western coast of Eurasia where they connected with what became the British Isles. Evidence of this most recent part of the geological journey is marked by Scotland's rift valley known as the Great Glen which runs for 100 km from Inverness to the Firth of Lorn and marks the meeting of two continental plates. Interestingly, the tail end of this fault runs through the south east corner of Mull. To the north and west of this physical feature (including the Hebrides) the geology has much in common with Greenland and Iceland. To the south and east, the geology is predominantly Eurasian.

Given this rich history of continental drift, the geology of Mull is hugely diverse, reflecting all its previous associations with other land masses and climates. In the somewhat poetic words of a local website:

> *"Mull is constructed rather like a multi-tiered wedding cake. Thick layers of basalt lava sit on top of a complicated basement of much older rocks which peep out around the edges rather like the silver base does on the lowest tier of a wedding cake. The oldest rocks on Iona are about 2,000 million years old, and this island has distinctive structures and rocks the study of which has contributed enormously to an understanding of igneous processes.*[9]

In more scientific terms, apart from the evidence in the soils of its southern and Middle Eastern origins, most of Mull is made of lava poured out of fissure volcanos when the North Atlantic was forming. And Mull's "stepped" tablelands were formed from the molten lava which started to erupt around 60 million years ago. Into these, at a later stage, intrusions of other "rocks formed by fire" took place, forming the mountains in the centre of the island. At that time, regular volcanic explosions and intense earthquakes shook Mull. One of the old fault lines arising from that activity, the Great Glen which divides the modern state of Scotland, is still occasionally active with tremors. The current periphery of Mull has largely been carved by huge glaciers which only melted away 10,000-15,000 years ago, leaving deep "U" shaped valleys between the mountains and long glaciated lochs which are both freshwater and marine. Mull doesn't have any precious gems on the surface, but geologists know that deep below the island, in the earth's mantle, there must be priceless specimens. For those of a scientific bent, the following is a summary of the current geology of Mull as available on Wikipedia.

> "The eastern part of the island of Mull is dominated by the circular Central Intrusive Complex, in which three caldera structures have been recognised. The coastal sections of the complex consist of lavas intruded by acid bodies and later basic dykes. Tertiary lavas cover most of the western and northern part of the island, though the Ross of Mull in the south-west is formed of a Caledonian biotite rich granite with a distinctive pink or red colour. The Lower Devonian lavas and Upper Cretaceous greensand at Loch Don, and the Rhaetic (Lower Jurassic) Beds in western Mull, give a glimpse of the complex geological history of the region, now extremely difficult to unravel because of the almost complete erosion of the units and the thick cover of Tertiary basalt. The Moine Thrust, a major structural feature of northwest Scotland, is thought to lie close to the west of Mull. The rocks to the west of this line are generally older than those to the east."

Geography

Mull is but one of an extensive and diverse set of islands off the west coast of mainland Scotland. There are two distinct groups, the Outer Hebrides of more than fifty islands includes Harris, Lewis, Barra, Benbecula, and North and South Uist. The Inner Hebrides consists of some 36 inhabited islands including Skye which is the largest, Mull, the adjacent Coll and Tiree, Islay, Jura, and Raasay.

Mull sits at 56.45N and 5.77W and covers an area of 875 sq km with a coastline of 480 km. As the crow flies, it stretches 40 km from north to south (80 km is the shortest distance by main road) and 45 km from east to west. The terrain is dominated by mountains and moorland, and the land is an average of 431 metres above sea level, with several significant peaks, the highest of which is Ben More which reaches 966 metres (3,169 ft) above current sea level. Radiating from the central core, there are three main peninsulas divided by Loch na Keal, and Loch Scridain.

North Mull includes the main town of Tobermory and other significant settlements at Salen, Dervaig and Calgary. Dominated by mountains, the central peninsula known as Ardmeanach (meaning middle point) is largely unpopulated. To the south west, lies the peninsula called the Ross of Mull which includes the villages of Bunessan, Pennyghael, Uisken and Fionnphort.[10] In the south east corner, there are three main population centres at Craignure, Lochbuie, and Lochdon.

Around the coast of Mull there are numerous islands. In the mouth of Tobermory Bay lies Calve Island. Off the western coast, the most notable and inhabited islands are Iona, the tidal island of Erraid, Inch Kenneth, Ulva and Gometra.[11] Smaller uninhabited islands include Eorsa in Loch na Keal, Little Colonsay, the Treshnish Isles including Lunga, Bac Mor (known as the Dutchman's Cap), and Staffa with its famous Fingal's Cave.[12]

Three kilometres off the south west coast of Mull, there is a substantial set of reefs, islets and skerries called the Torran Rocks. These extend over 39 sq km. Given the hazard to shipping, there are two rock-based lighthouses on the adjacent isles of Dubh Artach and Skerryvore. To the south west of Port Ohirnie, a small sheltered bay on the south coast adjacent to the Firth of Lorn, is Eilean Sraid Eun (Island of the Bird's Walk) also known as Frank Lockwood's Island.[13]

As with much of the rest of Scotland, the shelf on which Mull sits is still rising, at approximately 3 mm per annum. Thus, although global sea level is rising at approximately 1-2 mm per annum because of global warming, relative sea level is falling. The tidal range is significant and can reach as much as 3.5 – 4.0 metres off the west coast of Mull. The threat of flooding and erosion affects only a relatively small number of low-lying areas, because of the combined effects of land uplift, the rocky shorelines, and the absence of major areas of land claim.[14]

The coast of Mull is mainly rocky, with only small areas of inter-tidal sediment, usually at the heads of lochs. The most extensive areas of sediment are in Duart Bay and Loch Don in the east, and the sand flats sheltered by the island of Erraid in the south-west which at low tide is accessible by foot from the mainland of Mull. In some places there are high cliffs, especially on the south and west coasts.

Finally, it is worth noting Mull's nearest neighbours, which from time to time figure strongly in the island's history. To the west, lie the islands of Coll and Tiree which both have predominantly low, rocky coastlines with a large number of sandy bays suitable for beaching a boat and ranging up to about 3 km across. 25 km to the south of Lochbuie, there is the island of Colonsay.

ENDNOTES

1   This description is an adaptation of words in the book Mull and Iona, A Landscape Fashioned by Geology, by Dr David Stephenson, Scottish Natural Heritage, Perth 2011.

2   Pangea is a word based on the Greek words Pan (whole) and Gaia (earth).

3   Alfred Wegener's book published in 1915 was entitled The Origins and Continents and Oceans.

4   The lithosphere is the solid, outer part of the Earth, including the brittle upper portion of the mantle and the crust.

5   Panthalassa is a word based on the Greek words Pan (whole) and Thalassa (Sea). It is the direct antecedent of the modern Pacific Ocean.

6   Lycopsids are the oldest form of vascular plants. Arthropods are invertebrate and tetrapods are amphibians and reptiles.

7   These maps come from the US Government Geological Survey, USGS Publications Repository.

8   The Hebrides consist of the Inner Hebrides including Mull and the Outer Hebrides also sometimes known as the Western Isles. However, "Western Isles" is also sometimes used to describe all of the Hebrides. For this book, I have adopted the term Hebrides to describe all of the isles.

9   Much of this wording is a precis of material that is taken from the Web Site "isle-of-mull.net".

10 Fionnphort takes its name from the mythical character Fionn mac Cumhaill (or Finn MacCool) who was known for his exploits in slaying giants.

11 Inch Kenneth is named after St Kenneth, a follower of Saint Columba, who is said to have founded a monastery on the island and is commemorated at a mausoleum at Lochbuie. In 1773, Sir Allan Maclean was in residence and was visited Dr Johnson and Boswell. In the early 1930s the island was owned by Sir Harold Boulton who wrote the words to the Skye Boat Song, and in the late 1930s, it was owned by the Mitford Family who sold it to the current owners the Barlow family in the 1960s.

12 The name Treshnish reflects both Gaelic and Norse etymology, including the Norse words "ness" and "nish" that mean headland. Staffa is from the Norse for standing cliffs. Fingal comes from the Gaelic meaning "from Finland", but is also said to be the son of the above mentioned Fionn.

13 Frank Lockwood (1846-1897) was a Liberal MP for York. He was sometime UK Solicitor General, and famously led for the Crown in the trial of Oscar Wilde. He was married to the sister-in-law of Murdoch, the 23rd Chief of the Clan Maclaine, and he spent many holidays on the island.

14 The material in this paragraph is taken from the Parliamentary Report on Region 14.

CLIMATE

Climate is a significant driver in the character and temperament of peoples and, over the years, this will certainly have affected the residents of Mull, not least in terms of the type of shelter required and the ability to grow food. Over the last 800 years, Scotland has experienced two periods of colder weather, in the 12th/13th centuries, and between the mid-16th and early 18th centuries.[1] Although the variation may have been by only a degree or two, the impact was significant. In modern times, despite its reputation as being a little bleak, the weather in most parts of the island is mostly temperate with occasional bursts of warmer or colder days and sometimes four seasons in one day. Of greater significance is the fact that the island sits a long way north of the equator. This delivers long winter nights, and an extended period of twilight in summer when the sun barely dips beneath the horizon for six or seven hours.

Weather Systems

The climate on the western coast of Scotland is exposed to the North Atlantic Ocean. Although global warming is modifying the weather systems, there continue to be two dominant features that impact the island. The North Atlantic Oscillation controls the strength and direction of westerly winds and the location of storms tracking across the North Atlantic. The Gulf Stream (encompassing the North Atlantic Drift, and the Norway Current) brings warm water from the Gulf of Mexico to North Western Europe. As a result of these two systems, the climate in Mull is relatively mild, with an inclination to be wet and windy on many days. In the warmer months it is cloudy half the time, and in the colder months it is cloudy 75% of the time.

Mull does not have its own weather station, and records of temperature, rain, humidity, clouds, and sunshine are based on data recorded at three outlying weather stations, at Oban Airport (19 km to the east), Tiree Airport (68 km to the west), and Islay Airport (90 km to the south). The data recorded at these locations is adjusted for differences in elevation according to the International Standard Atmosphere, and using information from the MERRA-2 satellite.[23] Given the distance of these weather stations from Mull, the readings are calculated as a weighted average of the data from the three remote locations using the following formula: Oban (72%), Tiree (17%) and Islay (11%).

Rain

The rainfall in Mull is frequent and regular, but varies considerably around the island. Whilst the average annual precipitation for Tobermory is 1,576 mm, some parts of the island experience an average of over 2,000 mm. The wettest months are October through January, with inclement weather on 21 days per month and average monthly rainfall of around 180 mm. The driest months are April through August, with rain falling on 18 days per month and average monthly rainfall of around 90 mm.

From this data, it is evident that the island has a damp climate, without torrential rain and flooding. And, even in the summer months, at least 5mm will fall every one in three days. Like other parts of Scotland, the island is known for its "Scotch Mist" or mizzle which is somewhere between mist and drizzle. Given all of this, it is always wise to have a raincoat and umbrella to hand!

Temperature

In the course of an average year, the temperature ranges from a minimum overnight of 2°C to a maximum of around 17°C during the day. It is rarely below -2°C or above 20°C. The warm season lasts for 3-4 months, from early June to mid-September, with an average daily high temperature of 15-16°C. The cool season lasts for 4 months, from late November to late March, with an average daily high temperature of around 8°C. The coldest day of the year is usually in mid-February with an average high of 6°C.

Wind

The irregular form of the coastline and the mountainous nature of the interior cause great variation in the strength and direction of wind. It is rarely still, but storm force gales are not that common. During the winter months there are winds of more than 50 km per hour on an average of five days a month. During the summer, there are winds of more than 20 km an hour on about ten days.

Sea Level and Depth

To the west of Mull, reflecting the island's connection to the rest of the Hebrides, the sea floor is generally flat and lies at a depth of between 40 and 80 metres. To the north and east there are narrow and deeper channels which separate the island from the mainland and continue into adjoining lochs. The channel west of the island of Lismore at the entrance to Loch Linnhe is over 200 metres deep.

Global Warming

Global warming is recognised by the authorities as a real and present danger. Accordingly the Scottish government has prepared a plan to mitigate this phenomenon with the aim of achieving net-zero carbon emissions before 2045.

In general terms, the local impacts of warming on Scotland are as follows:

- warmer and wetter winters
- more frequent and longer periods of dry weather in the spring and summer
- more extreme single weather events
- higher maximum temperatures
- fewer days of snow and frost
- much more rain on the wettest days of the year

Specifically for the Hebrides, there is evidence that the strength of the Gulf Stream is diminishing because of a southerly flow of cold water into the North Atlantic arising from the melting of the Arctic Ice Cap. The long term impact on Mull's climate, following the disappearance of the Ice Cap remains to be seen. However, in a Scottish Natural Heritage Report (No 488), a variety of scenarios have been examined and there is already a good deal of anecdotal evidence for a significant change in the climate in the rest of the 21st century.[4] This information suggests the following:

- Coastal dunes and arable plains, that protect low-lying communities, are eroding because of rising sea levels and an increase in the number and severity of storms.

- Extreme winds and wetter winters are causing damage to native woodlands, with more frequent flooding, early leaf fall, and dying trees in poorly drained soils.

- The growing season for crops (April through November) may be shorter. This impacts sustainable agriculture.

- Low lying islands such as Gometra may be deluged either permanently or during extreme weather.

- The Scottish government continues to monitor all these potential impacts, and its mitigation plans are being regularly updated and implemented as a matter of urgency.

ENDNOTES

1   This comment on Scottish climate is based on research into temperatures over the last 800 years undertaken by a team led by Milos Rydal at St Andrews University and published in 2017.

2   International Standard Atmosphere (ISA) is a model used for the standardisation of aircraft instruments. It was established in 1975, with tables of values over a range of altitudes, to provide a common reference for temperature and pressure.

3   MERRA stands for Modern Era Retrospective analysis for Research and Applications, and the satellite was launched by NASA in 1980 as part of its programme to track global weather systems.

4   Scottish Natural Heritage is Scotland's agency for nature conservation, which commissions extensive research to provide evidence for the conservation of the country's nature and landscape. In 2020, it changed its name to NatureScot.

FLORA AND FAUNA

In keeping with the rich variety of soils on the land, and the diversity of waters within and around the island, Mull has an abundance of flora and fauna. There are many scholarly books on this subject, references for some of which are shown in the bibliography. The aim of this chapter is to provide an appreciation of the biodiversity which the people of the island enjoy as part of their natural heritage. In the Habitat section, an indication of flora and fauna is provided by habitat types. Further information on individual species is then provided in the separate sections on Flora and Fauna.

Human Impact

The presence of the human species has had a profound impact on Mull's ecosystem. After many centuries of human occupation, the environment has been modified to what Littlewood and Jones have called *"a fractured mosaic of adulterated habitats and biodiversity"*.[1] The exploitation of the environment has taken a heavy toll, not least in the clearance of forests to establish arable land and pasture and the introduction of a sequence of animals used for food and trade. In the Iron Age, with a population of distributed and largely self-sufficient communities, arable land was used to grow flax for clothing, and barley. And the economy was dominated by cattle, goats, sheep and pigs with peat burnt for heat. In the Middle Ages, subsistence farming continued to be the prevalent use of the land with minimal impact on the environment. However, by the 19th century, ownership of much of the land had fallen into the hands of a few absentee landlords whose imperatives were to maximise the return from grazing sheep, and to amuse themselves by stalking deer. This landed gentry also introduced stands of beech, sycamore and pine for aesthetic purposes which hugely impacted the native ecosystem.

Habitats

In the modern era, Mull provides a wide range of ecological habitats, with rugged shorelines some of which are exposed to the power of the North Atlantic Ocean, mountainous uplands, mid-level moors and woodland, arable plains, internal lochs, extensive sea lochs, and sounds.[23]

Shorelines

Mull is noted for its spectacular cliffs including some that are 80 metres in height to the south of the island. The largely inaccessible cliff habitats are the home of a wide range of sea birds that nest in the rocks, far away from predators including humans. These remote parts of the landscape are also home for scavenging wild goats.

Uplands

In the mountainous Uplands, the vegetation is largely dominated by sedges, mosses and lichens, alpine ladies mantle, yellow saxifrage, mountain everlasting, roseroot, and deer-grass. With three species of heather, the moorland blooms in the late summer with shades of purple and pink. This vegetation provides nesting habitat for curlews, waders, and divers. On the upper slopes of Ben More, ptarmigan and snow bunting have been sighted.

Arable Plains

Western Scotland is well known for its dune-based maritime grassland. This is known as *machair* which is a Gaelic word meaning "fertile plain".[4] The machairs of Mull probably go back to the earliest days of human habitation, when the settlers who arrived after the last Ice Age cleared woodland to grow crops and establish grazing for cattle and sheep. By nature, machairs are highly calcareous, and are often accompanied by marshland and lochs.[5] This type of habitat can be found in various parts of the island, most notably on the Ross of Mull in the south west, at Lochbuie in the south east, in the centre of the island on the southern banks of Loch na Keal, and in the Mornish district in the north-west.

As the early settlers in Mull would have discovered, machairs do not in fact provide the best earth for growing crops or feeding cattle and sheep. This type of sandy soil tends to be low in nutrients, with a low count of trace elements such as copper, cobalt and manganese. And in modern times, the soil has proven to be resistant to the application of artificial fertilisers. As a result, the types of crop that can be grown is confined to certain strains of barley, oats and rye. And, to maintain their health, it is necessary to feed grazing stock supplements and/or move them to pastures inland for certain parts of the year.

Given these reservations about the machair, local farmers have found that one of the best ways to improve the productivity of land is the use of seaweed. For many generations, the shorelines of Mull have been inundated with kelp which has served a variety of purposes. This plant softens the impact of waves which can erode the beaches, and provides a protective cover. As it rots, it adds nutrients to the soil and attracts sand flies that provide rich feeding for flocks of starlings and other passerine (perching) birds, wintering waders, and gulls. This process is compounded by grazing animals that trample the seaweed into the upper layer of soil creating sward.[6] In summer, these grasslands are dotted with a myriad of wildflowers, including bluebells, daisies, marsh grass, yellow rattle, cat's ear, field gentian, frog orchid, common stork's-bill and common centaury. This flora attracts rabbits and sand martins nesting along the banks of water courses flowing into lochs.

Lowland Moorland

Lowland Moorlands are extensive in the southern part of the island and widely grazed by sheep. On these moors, the dominant plant is purple moor-grass although, in many drier areas, invasive bracken has taken over. Where grazing is under control, a wide variety of plants thrive including heathers, the heath spotted orchid, northern marsh orchid, marsh lousewort, heath milkwort, tormentil, ladies bedstraw, bog asphodel, bog myrtle and cotton grass. This terrain also encourages the devil's-bit scabious, which is a significant source of food for the marsh fritillary butterfly. In wetter areas there are sphagnum mosses, with sundews and butterworts lining the peat along the edges of pools, especially where deer, cattle or sheep trample regular tracks.

The most common birdlife in this habitat is the meadow pipit. There are also considerable numbers of wheatear, stonechat, skylark, short-eared owl, merlin and kestrel. The heather attracts mountain hares and red grouse.

Lowland Woodland

Mull includes significant remnants of some ancient deciduous woodland which are a reminder of what early settlers would have experienced in abundance. According to Littlewood and Jones "Pollen analysis and radiocarbon dating has confirmed that birches were scattered in coastal and sheltered areas of Mull around 9,500 BCE, and hazels had become widely established as woodlands by 8,800 BCE". These temperate woods are collectively known as *Celtic or Caledonian Rainforest*, because of their dampness and clean air that sustains a rich diversity of mosses, liverworts, lichens, and fungi. They are dominated by gnarled and twisted sessile oak and ash trees with an under-storey mainly comprising oak, hazel, rowan, birch, and goat willow. There are fine examples of this vegetation in the Torloisk area, around Ardura, along the banks of Loch Ba, at Scarisdale by Loch na Keal, and on the road from Dervaig to Calgary. One of the finest examples can be found on the Tireragan estate near Knockvologan in the south-west corner of Mull south of Fionnphort.

The more extensive areas of mature deciduous forest provide nesting habitats for birds such as redstart, wood warbler and pied flycatcher, while the speckled wood butterfly is now quite numerous on the periphery. In steeper and rocky places that are inaccessible to grazing animals, there are also small pockets of juniper and aspen.

The island also has woodlands with several non-native species of trees, including sycamore and beech, mostly adjacent to the houses of the larger estates such as Aros Park. Sycamores support a particularly rich epiphytic flora of mosses, lichens and ferns on their trunks and branches.[7]

Forestry Plantations

Mull has significant plantations, some of which are now community owned and managed by NWMCWC, SWMID, and MICT.[8] Whilst many of these forests are dominated by Scots pine and non-native species, there are plans to reintroduce native trees which will support native wild life. However, the pine forests are home to a few invertebrate species, especially beetles with wood-boring larvae, which attract insectivorous birds such as treecreeper and goldcrest chaffinches. The non-native treescape also attracts siskin, robin, wren and common crossbills. The larger coniferous trees attract white-tailed eagles which nest in higher branches. The conifer forests also support large numbers of fungi in the autumn.

Flora

The various habitats on Mull support well over 5,000 species of flora, too numerous to list here. However, in addition to those already mentioned, the various open habitats are home to sea holly, wood bitter vetch, Scot's lovage, and numerous orchid species such as greater butterfly, northern marsh, heath spotted, twayblade, broad-leaved helleborine and bird's-nest. In late spring, the yellow flag iris blooms in profusion along the banks of watercourses, and white meadowsweet and purple loosestrife are to be found in many a damp ditch. Bluebells abound in many parts of the island, not least around Gruline and on the road to Grass Point.

Land Mammals

The most evident mammals living on modern Mull are various breeds of cattle and sheep. There are highland cattle all over the island, many of which stroll along the narrow roads with a statutory right of way and suitable disdain for human traffic. And there are significant herds of dairy cattle in fenced paddocks, most notably in the northwest and along the banks of Loch na Keal. There are several varieties of sheep, including a significant herd of the small Black Hebrideans on the Ardalanish property on the Ross of Mull.

The entire coastline of Mull is inhabited by Eurasian otters and signs of their territorial markings can be found all around the shoreline. They hunt in the sea, and raise their cubs on shore.

There is an abundance of red deer on the island, particularly since the wolves were hunted to extinction in the 18th century. In summer months, many feed on the higher reaches of moorland. But in winter they are more often sighted around the coast, moving along the shoreline, feeding on the fresh seaweed that has been washed onto the beaches and rocks. The breeding season reaches its peak in October when the roar of the stags can be heard echoing across the moorland. Mull also has small herds of fallow deer, most notably in the woodlands around Knock, Lochbuie and Gruline.

Mull has small herds of the horned wild goat which graze the more remote parts of the coastline such as Carsaig to the south of the Ross of Mull. They sustain flower-rich habitats in places inaccessible to other grazing animals. Mountain hares occur in small numbers in many areas, with numbers diminished through loss of heather (due to over-grazing by sheep and deer) that robs them of their natural cover and food. In the meantime, rabbits are omni-present.

The island sustains small numbers of stoats and weasels, and there a few native polecats and pine martens. Several hundred years ago, moles were introduced to the island, and there are also hedgehogs although currently not in sufficient numbers to be a problem to ground-nesting birds. In some years, the island supports a number of other smaller mammals such as the short-tailed field vole which become the staple diet of birds of prey such as the buzzard.

Despite this significant biodiversity, there are a number of mammals which are common on the mainland but have not found their way to Mull. For example, there are no badgers or squirrels. In earlier times, the island did have foxes and wild cats, but these were hunted to extinction in the 17th and 18th centuries.

Finally, Mull has at least one significant pest, the American mink which abounds along the coastal shoreline. They cause significant damage to the habitat of ground-nesting shorebirds including Arctic and Common terns and are the subject of a culling programme. There are also a few domestic cats that have run feral.

Sea Life

The Hebrides sit on a considerable length of continental shelf, with proportionally large amounts of run-off from land to sea, and complex patterns of water circulation. These factors have given the North Atlantic waters around Mull a significant proliferation of plant and animal species that is second only to that of the Pacific Ocean. A large variety of seaweeds inhabit the shallower continental margins and coastal areas, and algae of commercial value include kelp luminaria (a source of iodine, potassium, and algin), Irish Moss (from which the thickening agent carrageenan is derived), edible seaweed such as dulse, and porphyra.

As with many other islands, the sea around Mull is noted for its diversity and abundance of fish, crustaceans and other marine life. The Sound of Mull is one of several proposed Marine Protection Areas based mainly on its importance for the common skate. Throughout the year, there are harbour porpoise and bottlenose dolphins, and in summer months they are joined by other species of cetaceans including the common dolphin, white-sided dolphin, Risso's dolphin, minke whale and killer whale (orca). The latter species sometimes come close to the shore as they pursue harbour seals when pupping. In summer, the waters are visited by sharks who feed on large blooms of plankton which breed in the warming waters of the Gulf Stream.

Mull boasts both common harbour and grey seals. Harbour seals can regularly be seen in the main sea lochs or basking on offshore islands and rocks around the coast. Grey seals are usually found further out to sea, although they occasionally come closer to shore when they see an opportunity to feed as fishermen land their catch. Along the shore of Loch na Keal, there have also been sightings of the bearded seal which is a visitor from the Adriatic!

In most years, the waters around the island support healthy populations of pollack, conger eel, skate, rays, cod, whiting, spur-dogs, plaice, wrasse, and sand eel. Wrasse are important for use in salmon farms, and the eels are critical for the breeding success of the sea bird colonies. In recent times, an increasing number of 'exotic' species have turned up in Mull coastal waters. These include leatherback turtle, sperm whale and several species of fish more normally found in Mediterranean waters (a possible indication of climate change and warming sea temperatures).

The main species of fish to be found in local inland waters are salmon, trout, eel, stickleback, and flounder.

Amphibians and Reptiles

The freshwater habitats of the island support strong populations of frogs, toads and palmate newts which also spawn in brackish rock pools close to the sea shore. In the drier areas of moorland and grassland, there are adders and one of their main items of prey, the common lizard. Slow worms are evident, particularly around current and past human habitation. There are no grass snakes.

Invertebrates

Mull is home to a range of rare insects which include the northern colletes bee, the great yellow bumblebee and the moss carder bee. There are also many species of moths and butterflies, including some of the rarest species in Europe. There are records of the emperor moth, the narrow-bordered bee hawkmoth, the new forest burnet moth, and the slender scotch burnet moth which is unique to Mull. There are many species of butterfly including marsh fritillary, dark green fritillary, small pearl-bordered fritillary and grayling (not the fish!), speckled wood, peacock, scotch argus and common blue. Occasionally there are large migrations to the island of other butterflies and moths including the peacock butterfly, painted lady, silver Y moth and the hummingbird hawk moth.

In summer, dragonflies occur in profusion, including the gold-ringed and common hawker. The island also supports numerous other invertebrate species including beetles, hoverflies and cave spiders.

Birds

Mull is a haven for an enormous range of bird species, and many species of non-resident seabirds can be seen from boats and the shoreline. The island attracts many ornithologists, and there are frequent surveys and copious records maintained across a range of locations. The results are presented in numerous guide books.[9] Amongst the species worthy of mention are the following:

- *Raptors* including Golden Eagle, the reintroduced White-tailed Sea Eagle, Hen Harrier, Peregrine Falcon, Kestrel, Merlin, Sparrow Hawk and Buzzard.
- *Owls* including Barn Owl, Long-eared Owl and Tawny Owl. The Short-eared Owl visits to breed.
- *Ducks* including eider, mallard, teal and widgeon.
- Migrating *swans* and *geese*.
- *Shags* and *cormorants*.
- *Corvids* including Ravens and Hooded Crow.
- On the coastline, waders and birds of passage include Whooper Swan, Bar-tailed Godwit, Greenshank, Redshank, Snipe and Whimbrel.
- *Seabirds* including gannet, puffin (with a significant colony on the island of Lunga), Manx shearwater, guillemot, razorbill, black guillemot and various species of gull, tern and skua.

Biodiversity and Environmental Threats

In the modern era, like the rest of the planet, the Hebrides is subject to the threat posed by human-induced warming of the planet. In Mull, there are numerous projects to establish sources of renewable energy and to effect a transition to a low carbon economy. There are several other significant threats to the ecology of the island. Apart from the aforementioned minks, there is an overload of deer. And, some parts of the island's native ecosystem are being slowly choked by the rampant spread of rhododendrons. Another serious issue is posed by bracken which is a poor source of food for native species. It used to be kept in check by cattle which trampled it into the ground. But when sheep became the animal of choice, it spread freely across the landscape. Fortunately, in more recent times, the population of sheep has declined and a certain balance between herbivores has been established. And, despite the damage to soils and habitats such as machair arising from over-use of herbicides and fertilisers, Mull is blessed with mostly enlightened landowners who are mindful of the soil and are practising sustainable agriculture.

ENDNOTES

1 Some of the material in this chapter relies on the book entitled Wild Mull – A Natural History of the Island and its People by Stephen Littlewood and Martin Jones, published by Pelagic Publishing, Exeter 2021.

2 This material is based on data provided in a range of studies including the report on Region 14 by the Parliamentary Joint Nature Conservation Committee ("JNCC"), published in 2013.

3 The word sound is derived from the Norse word sund, and means a narrow body of water between the mainland and an island. Typically sounds are formed as an invasion of river valleys by the sea.

4 Machair is low-lying arable or grazing land, formed near the coast as sand and shell fragments are deposited by the wind. It is an essential feature of the island in terms of the food growing capability of the land.

5 Calcereous means "chalky", containing calcium carbonate.

6 Sward refers to an upper layer of soil which is usually covered by grass.

7 An epiphyte, also called an air plant, grows on another plant for physical support with no attachment to the ground.

8 The NWMCWC is the North West Mull Community Woodland Company. MICT is the Mull & Iona Community Trust, and SWMID is the South West Mull an Iona Development organisation. Detailed accounts of these organisations are provided in Part Six of this book.

9 The information herein is sourced from the Mullbirds Online Website, courtesy of Allan Spellman. The website includes much more detail relating to species identified in a range of specific locations including Loch Don, Loch na Keal, Loch Scridain, the Treshnish Isles, Ross of Mull, and Iona.

PART TWO

HEBRIDEAN COMMUNITY

DÙTHCHAS
LANDSCAPE AND COMMUNITY IN MULL AND IONA

MISTS OF TIME

I t is generally accepted that Homo sapiens became established as a species in East Africa some 200,000 to 300,000 years ago. For a time, they co-existed with earlier species such as Homo neanderthalinsis who had evolved in Europe and the Middle East around 500,000 years ago.[1] The first evidence of these direct ancestors of *modern man* spreading across Europe dates back to around 70,000 BCE, and it could be said that this marks the beginning of human history. The period is characterised by the emergence of fictive language amongst "hunter gatherers" and eventually the first *Agricultural Revolution*, with permanent settlements, the domestication of animals, and the growth of crops in warmer climes commencing as early as 12,000 BCE.

Scottish Pre-History

D uring the Ice Ages (the first of five such cooler periods began 2.4 million years ago and the last finished around 9,500 BCE), Scotland was almost permanently covered by ice, making it uninhabitable for humans. Whilst some more southerly parts of the country may have been visited by Stone Age hunter gatherers during warmer interludes, there is no direct evidence of a human presence until the Mesolithic period (c. 10,000 BCE – c. 4,000 BCE). The first signs of settlement in Scotland, found in Edinburgh, have been dated to around 8,500 BCE.[2] At this time, stone continued to be the main material for tools, and flints were set into wood for spears.

Farming (with domestic animals and crop growing) was introduced into Britain in the Neolithic (New Stone Age) period commencing around 4,000 BCE with pottery made for storing, cooking and eating food. In Scotland, we have evidence of these times from the Orkney Islands, where the village at Skara Brae was occupied from about 3,180 BCE to 2,500 BCE.[3]

Around 2,400 BCE saw the start of the Bronze Age, with bronze being forged from copper and tin for tools and household objects. During this time, there is evidence of the development of hierarchical social structures and armed conflict. By the year 800 BCE, iron was becoming the metal of choice for making tools, and there is evidence that humans began to form into tribes, living together in communities centred at one location. Towards the end of the Iron Age in the first century BCE, there was contact between inhabitants of the British Isles and the Roman Empire, and in CE 43 the Romans invaded southern England.[4]

Pre-History in Mull

In the Hebrides, there is material evidence that humans lived on Islay and Tiree during the Mesolithic period (prior to the Neolithic period commencing in c. 4,000 BCE). The discovery on the coastal fringes of Mull of flint chippings suggests that humans were at least visitors to the island around this time.[5]

Typical examples have been found along the shores of Ulva and near Dervaig on the shores of Loch a' Chumhainn (meaning "good inlet" in Old Norse). A fireplace at nearby Criet Dubh has been carbon dated back to more than 6,000 BCE. Other evidence from archaeological research suggests that in the later part of the Mesolithic period the landscape was highly forested with birch, oak and hazel trees.[6]

The nomadic people would have hunted deer and wild cattle as well as seals that were valued for their pelts.

There is no doubt that there were settlements in Mull during the Neolithic period (commencing in c. 4,000 BCE), with the Kildavie Project near Croig providing significant material evidence of human occupation.[7]

From the research at Kildavie and off-shore islands, it is reasonable to assume that there was farming activity. And on the island of Ulva there is evidence from that time of pottery called *"unstan ware"*.[8] To what extent the Ulva population were living in settled communities is unknown, but there is speculation that farming practices may have spread from the Orkneys or even northern France. At this time, it is probable that the population developed the ability to make axes, and around the year 3,850 BCE there is evidence of the felling of trees in the ancient woodlands to make room for arable land. The most important example of Neolithic farmers is the chambered cairn at Port Donain, on the coastline between Loch Spelve and Loch Don, where a burial chamber was found to contain remnants of pottery and stone tools from that time.[9]

There is substantial evidence in Mull of Bronze Age society (2,400 BCE to 800 BCE), with the spread of copper and bronze tools. Remnants of a dagger, a beaker, and a variety of tools have been found in stone chest burial chambers (known as cists) at Salen. And analysis of dental remains suggest that these people were migrants from continental Europe. Similar remains have been found at Glenforsa to the east of Salen. Dating from around 950 BCE, a bronze bracelet and amber beads have been found at Croig Cave next to Loch a' Chumhainn.

Mull is also the home of significant standing stones, examples of which may be found at Fionnphort, Dervaig, Ardnacross, Glengorm, and Lochbuie. In all, around the island there are 13 single stones, 14 combinations, and the circle which stands between Ben Buie and the sea. Dating from as early as 1,000 BCE, this monument is thought to have originally consisted of nine granite stones, and was first excavated by the archaeologist Edward Lhwyd who visited Mull on the way to Iona in 1699.[10]

Although there are relatively few directly relevant excavations in Mull, from all the current evidence it is considered that the Iron Age, and the beginning of tribal communities based on well-defined areas of land, began in the Hebrides around 700-800 BCE. During this period, the predominant architectural style was *the Atlantic roundhouse,* which in the Western Isles is known in Gaelic as a *dun.* A typical example, of which

A Crannog: Wikipedia

there are several on the island, is *Dun nan Gall* which may be found near Ballygown on Loch Tuach. This type of building comprised a circular single storey drystone wall with inner and outer facing stones, an entrance, and a thatched conical roof supported on upright timbers. The diameter of the inner circle was between 7 and 12 metres and had a wooden floor supported by stones jutting out from the walls. Around the shores of Loch Scridain in the south, there is a string of nine such constructions, each within signalling distance of the next. This suggests a co-operative population of loosely connected communities, each engaged in growing food, caring for herds of small highland cattle, and covering each other's back.

Mull also has a number of larger versions of the dun called the *broch*. Typically, these were built on the top of hills with defensive cavity walls, a diameter of at least 15 metres, and sometimes several storeys in height. They are mostly found on the coast line, and probably served both as defensive refuges and centres for community celebrations and storing grain. One of the most significant examples, *Dun an Fheurain*, is strategically placed at Ardalanish to command views to the north and south of the Ross of Mull. Other examples are *Dun Aisghain* at Burg on the shore of Loch Tuath and opposite Gometra, at Creag a Chasteil at Calgary, and at Dun Cul Bhuirg on Iona. There is also evidence from this period of *crannogs* which were houses built on artificial islands connected to the shore by a walkway and made up of brushwood, stone and peat.

What all of this demonstrates is that in this period of pre-history, Mull was a place of competing tribal groups where people that had settled on the island were living in sustainable communities with a need to defend themselves from their external threats, possibly including their neighbours.

Roman Scotland

There is little known about life in Mull during the Roman occupation of Britain between CE 43 and CE 411, but it is was probably a relatively independent entity. Although the Romans circumnavigated the northern coastline of the British Isles, Roman rule did not extend to the Hebrides or for that matter to Ireland. However, the island of Mull was certainly known to them, with the Greek astronomer, geographer and mathematician Ptolemy (CE 100-170) naming the island Malaois.[11] This is not to say that the Romans didn't try to take control of northern Britain. Indeed, according to written accounts of their campaigns, there is plenty of evidence that on arrival they intended to take the whole of the British Isles.

The most important documented event in Scotland during Roman times is the military action recorded by General Agricola when he defeated the Caledonians at the Battle of Mons Graupius in around CE 83/84.[12] According to mythology, after the battle and with heavy losses, the Caledonians characteristically disappeared into the woods and hills to fight another day. Later, beginning in CE 112, the Romans constructed a defensive position across Britain (Hadrian's Wall), stretching from Segedunum at Wallsend on the River Tyne in the east to the shores of the Solway Firth in the west. And, for a time in the first half of the 2nd century, the boundary of the empire was defined by the more northerly Antonine Wall. Constructed in CE 142, this ran between the Firth of Clyde and the Firth of Forth. Further north, there were outposts such as Inchtuthil (north of modern day Perth), and there is evidence of Roman camps as far north as the Moray Firth and Elgin. However, constantly harassed by the Caledonians, around CE 160 the Romans retreated back to Hadrian's Wall. So, despite a series of attempts to incorporate the highlands into the Roman Empire, including the deployment of up to 25,000 troops, the Romans never really established a firm hold far beyond the lowlands. At most, Roman military presence in Scotland lasted for no more than 80 years, and at no time was even half of Scotland's current land mass under Roman control. From archaeological work, while they made incursions and built forts to the north as far as Aberdeen, there were few if any expeditions to the north-west beyond the Great Glen, and certainly none to the Hebrides. Indeed, at times, the Romans found themselves defending territory to the south of Hadrian's Wall as the combined forces of the Picts and Scoti tribes launched several attacks including a significant assault in CE 297.

What can be said about this period is that, during the Roman occupation of Britain, the native tribes in Scotland had started to separate into three distinct groups. The central and northern parts of the country were dominated by the Caledonians who coalesced into a confederation that became the Pictish Nation. To the south, the lowlands were controlled by Brittonic tribes within the Roman Empire.[13] And to the west, the islands and adjacent mainland were controlled by intermittent Gaelic speaking invaders from Ireland. In particular, the area now known as Argyll was occupied by a people that the Romans called the Epidii from which the word Hebrides is thought to have derived, and Epidion was the Roman name for the island of Islay south of Mull. By the 5th century, their territory eventually became the heartland of the kingdom of Dál Riata about which there will be more in the next chapter.

Despite the arm's length nature of Roman influence, the legacy for Scotland should be recognised. During their time, the seeds were sown for what would eventually become the dominant religion of Christianity. And they left the British Isles with Latin, which was the main script for literature and would become the main medium for written communication in church and government affairs for many years. Their impact on the wider course of events across Caledonia is an open question.

ENDNOTES

1   The information in this paragraph is derived from the book Sapiens – A Brief History of Humankind by Yuval Noah Harari, Penguin Books, London, 2015. Neanderthals became extinct around 30,000 years ago.

2   The origins of the current settlement date to the early Middle Ages, and the name is thought to come from a leader named Eidyn and the word "burgh" meaning "fort".

3   Skara Brae is a Neolithic stone-built settlement located on the west coast of the main island of Orkney, with stone houses, stone furniture, and a primitive sewer system. It was "discovered" after the buildings were uncovered during a great storm that removed top soil in 1850.

4   The material in this section is based on a briefing about Prehistoric Britain presented by the British Museum.

5   This refers to the remains arising from turning flint pebbles which were mounted on the tips of spears and used for hunting or used as hand tools.

6   This is drawn from an article in the Proceedings of the Prehistoric Society, 84 pp.77-100 entitled "The interpretation of Mesolithic structures in Britain: new evidence from Criet Dubh, Isle of Mull, and alternative approaches to chronological analysis for inferring occupation tempos and settlement patterns" S Mithen & C Wicks 2018.

7   The Kildavie Project encompasses an ongoing archaeological programme in the North West of Mull which commenced in 2014.

8   This is according to David Caldwell in his book Mull and Iona. Unstan Ware refers to pottery from 4th and 3rd millennia BCE.

9   Some of the material in this chapter is sourced from a booklet published by Jean Whittaker entitled Mull: Monuments and History, Brown & Whittaker 2004.

10 Edward Lhwyd (1660-1709) was a widely travelled naturalist, geologist and botanist born in Shropshire who became a fellow of the Royal Society in 1708.

11 The Greeks called the main island of the British Isles Albion, and Ireland was known as Ierne. The Romans named their province covering England, Wales, and the Scottish borders, Britannia. The northern lands were known as Caledonia, with Ireland known as Hibernia.

12 The location of the Battle of Mons Graupius is uncertain, but was probably in modern-day Aberdeenshire.

13 The word Brittonic refers to the ancient Britons who had been assimilated into the Roman way of life. The word derives from the Welsh for the native peoples of the British Isles before the arrival of Gaelic and Anglo Saxon tribes.

DÙTHCHAS
LANDSCAPE AND COMMUNITY IN MULL AND IONA

IRISH AND NORSE
HERITAGE

With the Roman withdrawal from Britannia in CE 411, and the conclusion of what is known as pre-history, the early 5th century marked a significant change in the tide of events. At this time, Scotland was made up of four kingdoms, Pictland, Dál Riata, Strathclyde (a Brittonic kingdom with strong Roman influence in SW Scotland), and Bernicia (an Anglian kingdom in SE Scotland and NE England). Pictland covered eastern and northern Scotland with a heartland in modern Aberdeenshire, and was populated by the descendants of the people known to the Romans as Caledonians.[1]

For the next 1,000 years, Mull would be governed by a succession of Gaelic, Norse, and initially autonomous Scottish regimes that had dominion over the Hebrides. During this time, the island called Malaois in Roman times would become known as Muile (bald head) in Gaelic speaking Dál Riata, Myl during the Norse speaking Kingdom of the Isles, and eventually Mull within the Scottish Lordship of the Isles.[23]

Dál Riata

Tradition has it that in the second half of the 5th century, the kingdom of Dál Riata was established in the Hebrides by a diverse Gaelic speaking people called the *Scoti*. Giving their name to the modern state of Scotland,

Fig 1

they comprised a number of tribes which populated the south west of Scotland called *Cenels*.[4] Initially, they were itinerant travellers between Ireland and Scotland, and the most significant were the Cenel Loairn to which people in Mull belonged, the Cenel nOengusa (who settled on Islay), the Cenel nGabrain (in Kintyre), and the Cenel Comgail (in the Isle of Bute).

At its height in the 6th and 7th centuries, this kingdom extended from the north-east of Ireland to encompass much of the western seaboard of the Scottish mainland including modern day Argyll and Bute (see Fig 1), and western Inverness-shire. For several hundred years, the political capital of the kingdom was at Dunadd evidence of which are ruins of a hill fort (this is eight km north of modern day Lochgilphead which coincidentally is the administrative centre for the modern day Argyll and Bute Council).[5] And the spiritual centre was the monastery on Iona. A realm based on many islands, Dál Riata had a strong seafaring culture, with a large fleet that was periodically deployed to defend and expand the kingdom. After two centuries of trade, migration and settlement, by the end of the 7th century the dominant language of the people was Gaelic, while the rest of Scotland spoke either Pictish or, in the previously Roman controlled south, Welsh.[6]

The first recognised king of Dál Riata, who is credited by some as being a founder of Scotland, was Fergus the Great. Becoming king in 498, the historical record for the existence of this man is an entry in the *Annals of Tigernach*, for the year 501, which states in Latin that: "Feargus Mor mac Earca, cum gente Dál Riada, partem Britaniae tenuit, et ibi mortuus est". (*Fergus Mór mac Eirc, with the people of Dál Riata, held part of Britain, and he died there.*)7 Fergus is a man whose name would be remembered for many generations, and subsequent Scottish and British kings as well as many clans have sought to claim a direct lineage from him. He is also credited with bringing from Ireland to Iona the Stone of Destiny on which successive monarchs of Scotland and Britain have been seated during their coronation.[8]

Thereafter, although written records are sparse, we know that there was a succession of kings, stretching from 498 to 850, with domain over an increasing amount of territory. Indeed, at one stage, Áedán mac Gabráin (574–608) led naval expeditions to Orkney and the Isle of Man and is also known to have conducted assaults on Strathclyde and the Anglo-Saxon kingdom of Bernicia to the south. However, in 603 his ambitions were checked by the Bernician King Æthelfrith who defeated him in the Battle of Degsastan. Subsequently there was a significant schism. In the early 7th century a dispute developed between the King of Ireland Domnall II and his stepson Congal who was King of Ulster. The King of Dál Riata, Domnall Brecc sided with Congal and in 637 things came to a head with victory by King Domnall at the Battle of Moira. Thereafter, Dál Riata was a predominantly Scottish entity.

By the 730s, Dál Riata was under constant attack from the Pictish king Óengus I (who ruled Pictland from 732 to 761), and in the Annals of Ulster, it is recorded that in 736 *"Aengus son of Fergus, king of the Picts, laid waste to the territory of Dál Riata and seized Dún At, binding in chains the two sons of Selbach"* with their father fleeing to Ireland.9 Consequently, by 740, most of Dál Riata was subject to Pictish overlordship and, for the next century, there was a succession of kings with varying degrees of autonomous power.

The strongest evidence of Mull's association with the kingdom of Dál Riata is the activity of missionaries such as St Columba who settled on Iona in 563, the ruins of a settlement at Baliscate near Tobermory, and a grave on Iona of Loarn mac Eirc who may have been Fergus's brother. During this period, it is likely that the landscape in Mull was dotted with brochs, duns, and island-based crannogs. With the clearance of many of the ancient woodlands, farming communities were growing grain and raising cattle and sheep, with milk products and bread an essential part of their diet. Although the buildings associated with the original monastery at Iona are long gone, evidence of these times may be found in the carvings of crosses and other symbols in Nun's Cave at Carsaig on the south coast, and carvings at Scoor (near Bunessan on the Ross of Mull).

Norse Kingdom of the Isles

For more than two centuries, Mull was a place where the human condition was nourished by Christian traditions. However, commencing in the late 8th century, there were sporadic Viking raids along the western seaboard of Scotland and Ireland, and Iona was a favoured target.[10] The first recorded attack on this island was in 795, and there were other raids in 802 and 806. In 825, most of the community were murdered and the largely wooden Abbey burned to the ground. Those that escaped retreated to Ireland with their relics including bejewelled covers of illustrated religious manuscripts. However, the settlement did survive and intermittently flourished right through to the Reformation in the 16th century.

These Viking raids were mainly aimed at looting valuable objects such as gold crucifixes and silver chalices, but eventually some of the raiders settled in Ireland, on the Scottish mainland, and on the neighbouring islands, establishing autonomous settlements with a tenuous loyalty to the Norwegian crown. Following a major military defeat in 839 at the hands of the Vikings, in the late 9th century the Picts ceded Dál Riata to Norway, and Mull then became part of the Norwegian Kingdom of the Isles which covered the Northern and Western isles and adjacent coastal areas of the mainland. In the meantime, the rest of Pictland became known as the Kingdom of Alba which eventually transitioned to become Scotland.

For Mull, the influx of Norsemen had a significant impact over an extended period with new arrivals from Scandinavia slowly wresting control of some of the land. The areas of Scotland that were eventually subject to Norse rule, with varying degrees of autonomy, included what the Norse called the Northern Islands (Orkney and Shetland), the Southern Islands (Hebrides), islands in the Firth of Clyde, and adjacent parts of the mainland.[11] [12] There are various theories about the ebb and flow of Norse colonisation, although it is clear that the Northern Isles of Orkney and Shetland were the first parts of Scotland to be conquered and, in 1472, the last to be relinquished by the Norwegian crown.

The culmination of this influx of Norsemen was the establishment on the west coast of Scotland of the *Kingdom of the Isles* known by the Norse as the *Sudreys*. In the absence of clerical record keepers, the era is poorly documented, with origins of the kingdom sometime in the mid-9th century. In any event, commencing in 848, there are references in various Norse sagas to a succession of kings and lords of Scotland, the Hebrides, and the Orkneys. By the 11th century, the territory was ruled by the Norse King Godred Crovan with his capital in Dublin. Godred had ambitions to expand his realm not only through the Western Isles but also mainland Britain. Consequently, in 1066, as England was invaded by the Normans and Anglo-Saxon control of that country wavered, he launched an invasion of northern England and annexed the Isle of Man. This consolidation of Norse rule would last for two hundred years.

Despite the ambitions of people like King Godred, the geographical extent of the Kingdom of the Isles was always quite small and at most had a population of around 50,000. Despite military campaigns, the staple activity of the kingdom was farming, although it is thought that considerable income was earned from the provision of mercenary services to other territories. The people were also responsible for a certain amount of piracy, and one can only imagine the opportunities available to a sea-faring nation, with sophisticated longboats, dodging in and out of Hebridean sea lochs. As to the nature of the society, it is thought that the basic system of community established in Dál Riata persisted. It is acknowledged that, although tribal in nature, Nordic society in the Middle Ages did not involve a particularly strong connection to given areas of land. However, in provinces such as the Kingdom of the Isles which operated on an autonomous basis, the tribal system was almost always attached to well-defined areas of land which the tribe shared. The upshot was a society which probably shared many of the characteristics which would later epitomise the traditional Scottish clan.

Following Godred Crovan's death on Islay in 1095, there was something of a hiatus, leading to a direct intervention by his Norwegian overlords. In 1098, the Norwegian King Magnus III (known as Barelegs and arguably the last Viking king) conducted raids through the Orkneys, the Hebrides and the Isle of Man.[1314] This culminated in a treaty with the Scottish/Alban King Edgar that confirmed Norwegian control of lands including Mull.

Magnus built several forts on his new base at the Isle of Man, and then conquered Galloway and Anglesey (part of the Kingdom of Gwynedd).

After campaigns in Sweden, in 1102, Magnus embarked on a final campaign in Ireland, and had the misfortune to be killed in an ambush set by Ulaid (Ulster) tribesmen in 1103.[15] Thereafter, Norwegian overlordship of the Hebrides lapsed for 50 years until 1153 when King Godred's grandson (also called Godred) secured a treaty with the Norwegian King Ingi (1136-1161) in which he accepted a new overlordship with the payment of a feudal fee in return for protection from invasion by Scotland.

Written records of the subsequent history of the Kingdom of the Isles suggest that, through most of its existence, it was subject to considerable internecine warfare fought between King Godred's descendants. In 1104, he was succeeded by his son King Olaf, and in 1140 Olaf's daughter Raggnhild married a man who would become famous in Scottish annals, Somerled, who was leader of the Clann Somairle.[16] In 1153, King Olaf was murdered and succeeded by Somerled's brother-in-law Guðrøðr Óláfsson also known as King Godred II. Following another hiatus, in 1156 Somerled defeated King Godred II in a naval battle. Godred went into exile and, within two years, Somerled had taken control of the entire Kingdom of the Isles.

In 1164, Somerled began an extended war against the Scottish King Malcolm IV. In various early sources, he is recorded as having command over a massive invasion force of men raised from throughout the Kingdom of the Isles. He sailed up the Clyde, and made landfall near what is today Renfrew where he was defeated and killed in battle.

Following Somerled's death, his kingdom disintegrated. His brother-in-law Godred II returned, installing himself on the Isle of Man, and extending his domain to include Harris, Lewis, and Skye. Notably, Somerled's eldest son Dougall took Morvern, Ardnamurchan and Mull, while his second son Ranald (or Donald) took Kintyre, Islay and the smaller islands in the southern Hebrides. These are the roots of subsequent and long-lasting clans McDougall and Macdonald that held sway in the Inner Hebrides for many centuries. Godred's third son Aonghas had control of the remaining lands in the north of the kingdom including Skye. From the annals, it is known that from the start Ranald in particular had pretentions to be the head of the whole territory as he variously styled himself as "King of the Isles", "Lord of Argyll and Kintyre", and Lord of the Isles"; and there was no love lost with his brother Aonghas, with Ranald's sons eventually being responsible for Aonghas' death. Interestingly, for the mainland part of his territory he acknowledged allegiance to the King of the Scots. Dougall and his descendants would continue to hold sway over Mull until the Clan McDougall fell out of favour with King Robert I in the 14th century.

There are only sparse records for the history of the next 100 years. However, we know that the 1153 treaty with the Norwegians for protection from Scottish attack was triggered on two occasions. In 1230, the Norwegians were successful in deflecting the Scots, but this did not deter King Alexander II who had already taken control of most of the adjacent mainland. In 1249, he commenced another campaign to consolidate his position, but on his way he died of a fever, with his 8 year old young son becoming king. There followed a hiatus until King Alexander III reached an age to renew his father's mission. In 1263, troops led by Alexander Stewart (the 4th High Steward of Scotland) defeated the Norwegians at the Battle of Largs. Given the aftermath, this engagement is sometimes claimed as one of the greatest victories in Scottish history.[17] In fact, the battle was inconclusive but, afterwards an ailing Norwegian King Hakon IV retreated to the Orkneys where he died during the winter. Hakon's successor, King Magnus VI, sued for peace and negotiated the Treaty of Perth which was signed by Magnus and Alexander on 2 July 1266. Under this treaty, possession of the Hebrides and the Isle of Man were transferred to Scotland in return for an annuity and annual payment of 4,000 marks, whilst Scotland acknowledged continuing Norwegian sovereignty over the Orkneys and Shetlands. Subsequently, the Isle of Man was annexed as an autonomous territory by England.

Today, there is relatively little remaining evidence of the Viking occupation in Mull. The archaeological remains are confined to several brooches and a sherd from a small oval fort at Mingary in north-west Mull.[18] However, Norse roots are evident in names like Aros (river mouth), Scallastle (cattle milking place), Forsa (waterfall), Fishnish, Mishnish, Quinish, Treshnish, Dervaig, and Carsaig, and any settlement that contains the word "penny/pen", such as Pennyghael, Pennygown, Pennycross and Penmore.[19][20][21] And Gruline (the Norse for assembly place marked by stones) is still used as a central point on the island. More broadly, Scots English has many Norse roots (eg kilt comes from *kjalta* meaning tuck, hame comes from *Hjem* meaning home, bairn comes from *barn* meaning child, the suffices *ness* and *nish* mean headland, and *aig* means bay) and there are many place names that reflect the Norse influence.

Despite the inclination to adopt Norse names for various settlements, the evidence suggests that, although the leaders of the kingdom spoke Norse, most of the population continued to speak Gaelic. Accordingly, Gaelic culture is more self-evidently manifest throughout the island, not only in the names but in the customs, language and buildings including many castles constructed in medieval times.

ENDNOTES

1   The Angles invaded South-East Scotland from Schleswig-Holstein which is the most northern state of Germany next to Denmark.

2   Perhaps Bald Head refers to Ben More in the centre of the island.

3   Norse is a Germanic language spoken by the Vikings until around 1300.

4   The word Cenel is a source of the word clan which came into use in the 12th Century, meaning an extended network of families with loyalties to a particular chief. King Conall mac Gomail is said to have granted Iona to St Columba.

5   Dunadd Fort rises from Moine Mhor – the 'great moss' – an expanse of bog that carpets the southern end of Kilmartin Glen.

6   The Celtic languages consist of two major branches. P-Celtic (Brittonic) encompasses Welsh, Cornish, and Breton and was spoken by people in the south of Scotland. Q-Celtic (Goidelic/Gaelic) encompasses Irish and Scottish Gaelic and Manx. Pictish was a P-Celtic language that is thought to have strong Gaulish influences. It became extinct c. CE 1100.

7   The Annals of Tigernach are chronicles thought to have originated in Clonmacnoise, Ireland. A copy is held in the Bodleian Library, Oxford. They are written in a mixture of Latin and Gaelic and provide a record of events for the period 489–766, 973–1003 and 1018–1178. Coverage of the period 766 to 973 survives in abbreviated form in the Chronicon Scotorum which are held in the Archives of Trinity College Dublin.

8   The Stone of Destiny, is a block of red sandstone on which monarchs are seated as they are crowned. According to legend it may have been brought to Ireland from the Holy Land. It resided in Iona between 500 and 850, until it was removed to Scone by King Kenneth McAlpine. In 1296 the English King Edward 1 took it to Westminster Abbey where it stayed until it was returned to Scone in 1996. The authenticity of the current stone is in question.

9   The Annals of Ulster are written in Gaelic and Latin, covering the period 431 to 1540. Selbach was king of Dál Riata until his abdication in 723.

10   The era of the Vikings ended in the 11th century when Norwegian became the more common usage. Norse is the language spoken.

11   The Norse were a Germanic people who settled in Scandinavia between the 8th and 11th centuries. Many were farmers and traders. But some were warriors and colonisers known as Vikings. 'Viking' is derived from the word vík, meaning a bay. And Vikings were people that used boats to visit bays, fjords, and lochs.

12   The principal sources of information about these times are the Irish annals and the later Norse sagas.

13   Magnus acquired this name because he chose to wear the Scots Gaelic kilt.

14   Arguably, use of the term "Viking" ended in 1030 in a battle they fought with Christian forces led by King Olaf II Haraldsson (later known as Olav the Holy). Although the largely pagan Vikings won the battle, Christianity gradually became a dominant force and the term Norwegian increasingly came into use.

15   Ulaid is a territory which approximates to the Northern Irish part of the Kingdom of the Isles.

16   As leader of the Clann Somairle, Somerled styled himself as Lord of Argyll, Kintyre and Lorn. These titles have strong resonance with latter-day chiefs of the clans Macdonald, Campbell and Maclean.

17   The Battle of Largs took place on 2 October 1263. With the weather playing a significant role, the Scots achieved a tactical victory over larger enemy forces using a three-tiered strategy involving ships, cavalry and infantry.

18   The small oval fort, measuring 15 by 30 metres, is known as Dun Sgaillean and is located on a rocky knoll south east of the local farm.

19   Some material on the origin of Norse names is taken from the PhD thesis of Alasdair C Whyte (Glasgow 2017): Settlement-names and society: analysis of the medieval districts of Forsa and Moloros in the parish of Torosay, Mull.

20   The prefix Penny denotes that a given piece of land is a unit for assessment under the Norse taxation system.

21   Viking remains include brooches, which are worn in pairs on the front of a Viking woman's dress and were used to display a string of beads.

22   Some of the material in this chapter relies on the book entitled Wild Mull – A Natural History of the Island and its People by Stephen Littlewood and Martin Jones, published by Pelagic Publishing, Exeter 2021.

23   The information in this paragraph is derived from the book Sapiens – A Brief History of Humankind by Yuval Noah Harari, Penguin Books, London, 2015. Neanderthals became extinct around 30,000 years ago.

24   The origins of the current settlement date to the early Middle Ages, and the name is thought to come from a leader named Eidyn and the word "burgh" meaning "fort".

DÙTHCHAS
LANDSCAPE AND COMMUNITY IN MULL AND IONA

A LAW UNTO THEMSELVES

Following the annexation of the Hebrides in 1266, the region including Mull finally became a part of Scotland. However, for many years it would have a significant level of autonomy, with its own culture and system of governance. By the early 14th century, the dominant clan would style themselves as Lords of the Isles and this primacy would continue until 1493. Thereafter, the Lordship was abolished; but the independent nature of the society would persist for another century before, in the early 17th century, the government in Edinburgh finally managed to impose effective central control.

Lordship of the Isles

When the Hebrides became part of Scotland, the leading families in the southern Hebrides were the Clan Macdonald and the Clan MacDougall who were direct descendants of the Norse leader Somerled's sons, Ranald and Dougall.[1] By now, the clan system was firmly established.

The 13th century was a turbulent period, with the Macdonalds and MacDougalls vying for supremacy. The outcome of the mounting hostility between them, as they also participated in national affairs, would be seminal in determining the emergence of the Clan Maclean of Duart as the leading family in Mull, and the long term future of the island.

When Mull became part of Scotland it was controlled by the Clan

MacDougall who held sway in Argyll. They were based at Dunollie Castle (north of modern day Oban) and initially they had the edge over the Macdonalds based in Islay. In maintaining their position, they constructed a number of other fortifications including Aros Castle which was their headquarters on Mull, Duart Castle, and Cairn na burgh Castle on Treshnish.

At the same time, the Clan Macdonald was led by Angus Mor Macdonald. He was Lord of Islay and married to a member of the Clan Campbell. Although he had supported Norwegian resistance to the Scottish takeover at the Battle of Largs, he had actually been a somewhat grudging vassal of the king of Norway and he welcomed the relative independence that came with being part of Scotland. In the following years, he maintained civil relations with the Scottish crown and, on the death of King Alexander III in 1286, he and his son Alistair Og were party to organising the succession of Queen Margaret.

On the death of Angus Mor Macdonald in 1293, he was succeeded by his son. Alistair Og had a tough start in life. Born in 1255, he had been taken hostage by King Alexander III during the dispute between Norway and Scotland; but in his teens he was released and married Juliana MacDougall who came from Mull. This might suggest some rapprochement between the two clans. However, when Queen Margaret died, he and his wife's families eventually took opposite sides in the contest for succession to the Scottish crown between the Balliols and the Bruce family. Initially, following King Edward I's intercession, both clans supported the appointment of John Balliol. However, following the forced abdication of the new monarch in 1296, the Macdonalds switched sides. During the Interregnum which followed, things came to a head and in 1299 Alistair Og was killed by one of Juliana Macdougall's relatives. He was succeeded as Lord of Islay by his younger brother Angus Og.

Not surprisingly there was no love lost between Angus Og and the MacDougalls. Like his father, he supported the Bruce family in their claim for the throne. Following the accession of King Robert I in 1306, he was rewarded for his support by being granted control of MacDougall lands in Lochaber and Glencoe. Later, Angus Og would take part in the Battle of Bannockburn in 1314 which further strengthened the position of the Clan.

When Angus Og died in around 1330, his son and heir John was a ten year old boy and for a time the Clan Macdonald was led by other family members. However, in the late 1330s John would take control and prove himself to be an astute leader. In 1332, Edward Balliol briefly took the Scottish throne from King Robert's son David II. John supported Edward and the King gave him power over significant additional territory including parts of the mainland and a number of islands. For our story, it is most notable that these new Clan Macdonald lands included Mull, and Knapdale which was the home of the Clan Maclean led at the time by Lachlan Lubanach Maclean. In Mull, Aros Castle, known then as Dounarwyse Castle, would become a centre of Macdonald administration for the island and a periodic base for Lordship troops. When King David II resumed the throne, through some careful diplomacy, John managed to hold onto his new won territory.

In 1346 John married a distant cousin named Amie and took control of yet further territory including Ardnamurchan to the north of Mull. John and Amie had several children including Mary Macdonald. In 1350 he then allied himself closely with the eventual heir to the throne, Robert Stewart, (grandson of King Robert I) who persuaded him to divorce Amie and marry his daughter Margaret Stewart. John and Margaret would have one son, Donald. In the years that followed, John continued to work closely with Robert (who eventually succeeded to the throne as King Robert II in 1371), providing advice and military support.

Apart from his skills in diplomacy, John was also a patron of the arts and the church. Although the Bishopric of the Isles, based at Snizort on Skye, was outside his control and to some extent acted as a political rival, John controlled Iona which was the spiritual cradle of Scottish Christianity, and the monastic establishment was run with John's approval by members of the Clan MacKinnon (several of whose family were abbots). John also founded an Augustinian priory at Oronsay (an island between Mull and Islay). In maintaining his position, he availed himself of the services of the Clan Maclean based in Knapdale who were notable sailors and became influential in John's circle as leaders of the Lordship armed forces. As we will see in Chapter 8, in 1367 this led to the marriage of John's daughter Mary to Lachlan Lubanach Maclean, with a dowry that handed lands on Mull to Lachlan and his brother Hector.

With this much enhanced position, John eventually began to style himself as *Lord of the Isles*. However, although he held a position of considerable individual power, it appears that he chose to rule through a process of consultation, with advice from a Council, membership of which included the following:

- The four "great men of the royal blood of Clan Donald" (Macdonalds of Clanranald, Dunnyvaig, and Keppoch, and MacIain of Ardnamurchan),
- The four "greatest of the nobles or lords" (Maclean of Duart, Maclean of Lochbuie, MacLeod of Dunvegan (Skye) and MacLeod of Lewes),
- The four "thanes of less living and estate" (Mackinnon of Strath, MacNeil of Barra, MacNeill of Gigha and MacQuarrie of Ulva),
- Certain "Freeholders" representing various communities within his realm, and
- The Bishop of the Isles and the Abbott of Iona as ex-officio members.

In practice, the membership of this Council, probably varied with the times; but again, for our story, in later annals (prepared in 1545), it is reported that in the early 15th century membership specifically included the following known historical figures from Mull: *Hector Maclean of Duart, Murdoch Maclean of Lochbuy, Allan Maclean of Torloisk and John MacQuarrie of Ulva.*

In 1386, John died and was succeeded by his son Donald who was the brother-in law of Lachlan Lubanach Maclean. Donald's time as Lord was volatile as his authority was challenged by his brother John Mor. He was successful in countering this opposition, with John Mor exiled to Antrim, but his loyalty to the crown brought him into conflict with the Albany section of the Clan Stewart. He pursued a series of military campaigns on the mainland and, in 1411, he mustered an army including many members of the Clan Maclean led by Red Hector which fought on behalf of King James I with the Duke of Albany at the inconclusive Battle of Harlaw (near Inverurie in Aberdeenshire). In 1423, and nearly 70 years old, he died on Islay.

Donald was succeeded by his son Alexander whose time as Lord was tumultuous through tussles with the crown. In the early days, he continued his father's policy of supporting King James I against the growing power of the Albany Stewarts. In the process, he was granted the title Earl of Ross. However he then found himself at odds with the King. In 1428 he and his family were imprisoned and the King tried to replace him as Lord of the Isles with his brother Angus. When this move failed, Alexander was released and immediately took against the King besieging Inverness Castle and burning the town. The King brought an army against him and he initially fled to Islay but then handed himself in. With Alexander imprisoned in Tantallon Castle, the King set about dismantling the Lordship; but Alexander's supporters led by Donald Balloch fought back inflicting defeats on the King's forces at the Battles of Inverlochy and Drumnacoub in 1430. In 1431, the King then released Alexander who was eventually able to take control of Inverness and Dingwall and style himself as Earl of Ross. Following the murder of King James I in 1437 in what turned out to be a failed coup led by his uncle Walter Stewart, Alexander consolidated his position and in 1439 he was appointed as Chief Justiciar of Scotland. This was a high point in the Lordship of the Isles.

When Alexander died in 1449, he was succeeded by John II who was the last person to be fully acknowledged as Lord of the Isles until the title was revived in modern times. He was a pivotal figure. In 1462, he made a secret and fateful treaty with King Edward IV of England (the Treaty of Westminster-Ardtornish) the aim of which was to conquer and partition Scotland. This was eventually discovered by King James III who had succeeded his father King James II in 1460. The King stripped John of his position as Earl of Ross and his control of Skye, Knapdale and Kintyre was forfeit although he retained his position as Lord of the Isles including Mull.

In the aftermath, John's illegitimate son and heir Angus did not accept this settlement with the King and took up arms against his father to recover the full extent of the Lordship territory. With members of the Clan Maclean supporting John, in around 1480 the dispute came to a head at the naval Battle of Bloody Bay (3 km north of Tobermory). Angus emerged victorious and, after the battle, he seized power from his father. In the same year, he went on to defeat a royal army led by the Earl of Atholl at the Battle of Lagabraad and took control of Dingwall Castle and Easter Ross. However, these victories would prove pyrrhic. During the Battle of Bloody Bay, nearly half the clan's fleet had been sunk, and during the conflict with his father many clansmen had been killed. Consequently, the power of the Lords of the Isles was greatly diminished. In 1488 Angus did manage to recapture Inverness but, in 1490, he was murdered by his musician. In the aftermath, Angus's infant son Domhnall Dubh Macdonald ("Black Donald") was captured by the Royalist 1st Earl of Argyll Colin Campbell and imprisoned at Innischonnel Castle on Loch Awe.

In the meantime, elsewhere in the kingdom there was insurrection with rebel forces securing the King's fifteen years old son, the Duke of Rothesay, as their figurehead. Following the King's death after the Battle of Sauchieburn in 1488, the Duke became King James IV. Initially plagued with guilt over his father's death, he eventually settled into the role and determined to sort out the recalcitrant Western Isles once and for all. In 1493, he abolished the Lordship and demanded that local chiefs assemble at Dunstaffnage Castle near Oban, to pay homage. Nearly all of them attended, and the elderly John Macdonald handed himself in. He was brought back to court as a pensioner, spending his final days at Paisley Abbey where he died in 1503. Thereafter, the crown assumed responsibility for the granting of charters for ownership of land, although this had relatively little impact until well into the 16th century because of an inability to enforce the new rule of law.

Lingering On

Despite the formal abolition of the Lordship of the Isles, this was not quite the end of the region's autonomy. Over the next century, the local clan leaders would continue to exercise effective control. Following the surrender of John Macdonald, his grandson *Black Donald* was still at large, and John's nephew Alexander Macdonald of Lochalsh was also loath to accept the loss of the family heritage. In the mid 1490s, he attempted a rebellion and was eventually killed on the island of Oronsay (north of Islay). To quell the opposition, the Royal Council enacted legislation that made local chiefs responsible for rebellious acts, but this proved ineffectual. In 1498, King James IV then commanded the Chiefs to attend a meeting for a granting of charters at Kilkerran Castle near modern day Campbelltown. Few local clan chiefs turned up and the king gave orders to the Earl of Argyll to bring them to heel and hand over the young *Black Donald*. Argyll met with little success and a plan for the boy to be surrendered into royal custody in Inverness in 1501 failed when his guardian Torquil MacLeod of Lewis failed to show. After this defiance, King James transferred Torquil's lands to Alexander Gordon, the 3rd Earl of Huntly. Then, in 1504, a royal fleet sailed north from Ayr to attack the Castle of Cairn na Burgh, in the Treshnish Islands off Mull, where it was thought that Lachlan Maclean of Duart was harbouring the young Donald. In June the castle surrendered; but Donald remained at large. Finally, in September 1507, Torquil MacLeod was besieged at Stornoway Castle on Lewis and Donald was captured. To make sure that the Lordship never again emerged, he was imprisoned for 37 years, and eventually died in Ireland in 1545. This ended all attempts to revive the Lordship, although the position is still remembered as a title held by the Princes of Wales in the current era.

The end of the Lordship did not bring a sudden change in the clan based society in places like Mull. The 16th century in Scotland was a period of great turbulence when central government was weak and it proved difficult to integrate regions like the Hebrides into the system of central governance that applied in the rest of Scotland. There were several reasons for this. In 1513, Scotland was defeated by the English at the Battle of Flodden Field with King James IV being killed. His son was a babe in arms and the kingdom was ruled by regents. The 16th century would also see the Scottish Reformation during which there was a lengthy struggle for control of the government in Edinburgh. Finally, in the absence of a royal navy, logistics in the Highlands and Islands were challenging. For all these reasons, people in the Hebrides were largely left to their own devices until King James VI came to power at the end of the century.

ENDNOTES

1   The name Macdonald comes in three forms – Macdonald, MacDonald and McDonald. It is derived from the Gaelic MacDhòmhnaill meaning son (mac) of the world (domno) ruler (nal). In this book, the version Macdonald is used.

PART THREE

THE CLANS

DÙTHCHAS
LANDSCAPE AND COMMUNITY IN MULL AND IONA

THE NATURE OF CLANS

In modern times, the word "clan" has taken on a somewhat generic quality reflecting family connection. However, amongst people of Scottish heritage, including a significant diaspora, it has a more specific meaning in which people with a given surname share a sense of common identity and belonging. Where the leader's line is extant, clan loyalty also involves respect and even a form of fealty to a chief who provides a direct link with ancestors, traditional lands, and buildings such as castles dating from the Middle Ages.

Whilst this tribal phenomenon is an important aspect of Scottish culture, for most of the country its viability as a form of governance was relatively short-lived. From the 12th century, most of Scotland became increasingly subject to a feudal system in which those in positions of authority (both Royal and clerical) suppressed the inclination of people to have loyalties that were beyond their hierarchical reach. However, in the Highlands and Islands, the clan system of communal governance persisted through most of the Middle Ages, bringing mutual security, identity, and wellbeing to many communities living in remote and sometimes environmentally hostile places.[1]

Despite the dogged persistence of this form of social contract in the Highlands and Islands, its days were numbered. In the 150 years following the union of the Scottish and English crowns in 1603, a series of people and events would slowly erode the clan-based system. In particular, many of the clans found themselves on the wrong side of history, leaders of the clans were disconnected from ordinary clansmen, the traditional social contract in which land was occupied in return for military service was largely eliminated, land would take on an economic value that would drive new forms of management, and the ownership of property was transferred to absentee landlords. These changes culminated in the defeat of the Jacobites at Culloden in 1746 and subsequently native people were driven from their lands to accommodate the imperative of agricultural efficiency.

Despite this turn of events, although the structure and practices of the clan system were lost, the spirit of what clan life actually meant for many people in Scotland was never entirely extinguished. To some extent, the memory was retained and even romanticised through literary works. Perhaps more significantly, the imperative in remote places for a society based on mutual support is so deeply engraved in the psyche of ordinary people that it was never fully eliminated. Instead, the spirit of community lay dormant, ready to be unleashed like epicormic growth in the flowering of a renewed Scottish identity in the 21st century. This renaissance of community-based living in Mull will be described in Parts Five and Six of the book.

The Clan System

The concept of community-based living is obviously not unique to Scotland. It is manifest in most cultures, and is a central feature of what it means to be human, reflecting a bond between groups of people who identify with each other. The most common term used to describe this phenomenon is the Middle English "tribe". This word derives from the Latin *tribus* and the Romans used it to describe various communities within the empire, including the Germanic and Celtic peoples living in central, northern and western Europe. In Scotland, the prevalent version of this tribalism is reflected in the word "clan" and, in its fully developed form, it involved both kinship, mutual support in the event of external threat, and a shared entitlement for sustenance to a well-defined piece of land. To understand the true meaning of the word, we need to return to the early Middle Ages.

When the Romans left Britain in CE 411, they left behind a form of governance that was strongly influenced by Roman concepts of power and hierarchy. However, in Ireland, which had never been conquered by the Romans, there was a particularly resilient society based on the concept of "clann" which reflected a very different way of living with fellow human beings.[2] The Irish used the word in combination with the word "*mac*" meaning "*son of*", so "*Clann Macdonald*" meant the members of the family descended from Donald. This widely used system for describing identity included a well-defined model for determining the leadership and governance of the group. In the early days, the chief (usually a male) was elected by his kinsmen on the basis of his physical stature and leadership qualities. However, the clanns would eventually adopt "agnatic patrilineal descent", with leadership passing through the male members of the chief's direct family.[3]

As noted in Chapter 5, this form of social contract for organising community was brought to Scotland in the late 5th century when the Irish tribe called the Scoti settled in the Western Isles and Argyll, and was certainly a significant characteristic of the kingdom of Dál Riata that was established in the 6th century. It continued after the merger with the Pictish kingdom of Alba in 843, along with the use of the Gaelic language and, subsequently, the system would spread across most of the Scottish Highlands and Islands. Thereafter, during Norse rule between 850 and 1266, some form of clan system continued during the Kingdom of the Isles, and this concept of a community-based society persisted until the end of the Middle Ages.

Written evidence of a clan system in Scotland does not really emerge until Norman times, and this is the earliest date back to which most modern day clan chiefs can trace their origins. For the Island of Mull, most of the documented hereditary clan lines begin in the 13th century when, with the Treaty of Perth in 1266, the Western Isles were transferred from Norwegian rule to become an autonomous part of Scotland. Thereafter, society in the Highlands and Islands comprised well-defined family-based community networks which were characterised by the fact that members shared a surname, had loyalties to one of their number who was respected as the military leader and/or "chief", and had a territorial view of their existence in terms of occupying and sharing a given area of land for sustenance. However, membership of a given clan also often extended to dependent families known as *septs*, who might have a different surname but who looked to the chief of the dominant clan as their head and protector.

By the 13th century, the clan system already provided for a significant sense of land ownership by the leading family, although this had less weight than in later times because land was not seen as a resource with economic value and was not initially subject to enforceable legal title.[4] The Clan Chief held the land in trust, was responsible for leading his kin in battle, and wielded significant and sometimes arbitrary power in the administration of the community, including the resolution of disputes and the determination of contractual issues.

As the clan system evolved amongst a growing population, and the hereditary principle became an established practice for leadership, the leading family also developed a degree of hierarchy. Eventually, the leading group would encompass both the clan *chief* and his immediate family, and a group of *chieftains* who were heads of family branches (accordingly, in Mull, the Clan Maclean of Duart included several "cadet" branches such as Torloisk and Brolass).[5] There were also two complementary but distinct concepts of heritage. *Dùthchas* reflected a community approach to the occupation and defence of well-defined territory, with clan members recognising the personal authority of the chief to act as a leader and a trustee. Initially, the pre-eminence of leader and his family did not involve ownership of the land or an economic relationship with other members of the clan. However, eventually, leadership did encompass property rights. Under what was known as *oighreachd*, while occupation of land was shared by clansmen, it was recognised that the "crown" was entitled to grant a charter of land ownership to the chief and sometimes to other members of the gentry, with implied hereditary inheritance. This aspect of the feudal system soon became a significant element in clan-based society, and it was an arrangement keenly sought by clan leaders in return for loyalty to the monarch.

The elite group in this society were known as the *"fine"*, an Irish expression which originally inferred a commitment to look after each other's children, but later came to mean the extended family of the chief. Within the *fine*, the chief's heir was known as the *tainistear* and, in time, customs were developed to protect his land-owning heritage from dilution. In particular, land became the subject of what was called *entail* whereby territorial entitlement was passed to the senior member of the chief's descendants, and could not be split up between several family members. That wasn't how it always worked out, with the eldest son sometimes overlooked for a more politically astute or militarily accomplished member of the family. However, Parliament eventually passed the *Law of Entail* which prescribed the rights of the eldest male heir over any claim made by siblings. This specifically prevented estates from being broken up, or being passed to female heirs and potentially lost to another clan through marriage.[6]

In the latter part of the Middle Ages, other systems were established which facilitated the military action in which clans were often involved. Under the system of *Manrent*, smaller clans, or clans that had lost their chief through lack of an heir, could elect to be bonded to serve a larger clan in return for protection even if they did not live on territory owned by the main clan.[7] The subjects of this arrangement effectively became vassals which meant that, although they would always retain a first duty to their own immediate clan members, they were duty bound to follow the alliances of the dominant clan and participate in their conflicts. These protection bonds were often reinforced by periodic payments called *calps*, usually in the form of surrendering a beast.[8] The call for joint collective action was symbolised by a system in common use in the Middle Ages for communicating significant events. In the case of Highlanders and Islanders, this was epitomised by the *"lighting of the fiery cross"* which was seen as a summons for members of the clan to band together.[9][10] The Highland clansmen also had arms that distinguished them from their counterparts in the rest of Scottish society. The weapon of choice was the *claymore (claidheamh mor* meaning "big sword" in Gaelic) which originated in the 15th century and continued in use until the 18th century. This was a basket-hilted broadsword weighing two to three kilos which was either held in one hand for slashing and stabbing while a shield was held in the other hand, or was deployed with two hands for delivering fatal blows including beheading.

With the growing financial impositions by the King, including taxation to finance international wars and other national commitments, clan chiefs began to develop more formal economic relationships with other members of the clan to enable regular financial contributions towards meeting the clan's responsibilities and expenses. Over time, the implementation of *oighreachd* gradually changed the clan system from one of mutual and fraternal support to a structure more akin to landlord and tenant with clansmen paying some form of rent in return for access to not just the land where they lived and grew their food but also other jointly owned resources. Initially, a mutually co-operative approach was retained. However, as land began to take on an economic value, the essentially feudal basis of this arrangement would slowly transform the relationship between those holding land title and their tenants. Eventually, the gentry appointed people called *tacksmen* who operated as economic managers of the clan territory as well lieutenants in the militia. The tacksmen would allocate a strip of land with an identified rent called a *runrig*, supply seeds and tools for managing the land, and organise the droving of cattle to the lowlands for sale with a commission for services rendered. Tacksmen also had responsibility for mobilising the clan in response to military commitments, organising other collective activities such as weddings and funerals, and convening annual hunts in August which might include a variety of sporting activity.[11]

The *runrig* system of agriculture usually consisted of three types of land use, infield, outfield, and hill grazing. In the spirit of shared resources, access to the strips was allocated through drawing lots on an annual basis. Typically, depending on the topography, the strips of land closest to a village were called *"infield"* which were the subject of continuous cultivation and fertilisation. Everything possible was used for fertilisation, including cow dung provided through the process of "teathing, seaweed, and bracken.[12] The *"outfield"* involved a mix of cultivation and grazing by rotation and, in accord with the ancient custom of "souming", the number of animals was strictly controlled.[13] The third element in this system, *"hill grazing"*, involved animals left to roam freely on hill side pastures. Whilst their animals were grazing, clansmen would live in a settlement called a "shieling", occupying a hut called a *"bothy"* which was a small round or oval structure which might be six feet in diameter. Of particular note in all of this was the raising and sale of cattle which was central to the economy. The ordinary people would never have survived on just growing crops.

It should be stressed that the undermining of the *mutual obligation* nature of the clan system was not just a presumption of land ownership by the leading family. Following the end of the Lordship of the Isles in 1493, the king persisted with his right to issue charters, and successive kings sought to set aside traditional land ownership arrangements in favour of their supporters by issuing charters that did not recognise traditional boundaries. This "divide and rule" approach would exacerbate traditional rivalry between neighbouring clans, and potentially fracture the long held and territorially based loyalties between the clansmen and their chief. It also encouraged chiefs to think in terms of the economic value of title which might be realised in difficult financial times by sale to absentee landlords who had no loyalty to the traditional clansmen.

By the 18th century, in an effort to increase the income from their estates, clan chiefs started to restrict the ability of tacksmen to sublet. This meant that more of the rent paid by those who actually farmed the land went directly to the landowner. The result was the removal of this layer of clan society. In response, many of the tacksmen as well as the wealthier tenant farmers (who were tired of repeated rent increases) chose to abandon the traditional clan lands. The first major step in what was a long and sustained programme in Highland and Island districts, was the decision of the Dukes of Argyll to put tacks (or leases) of farms and townships up for auction. This began with Campbell property in Kintyre in the 1710s and spread after 1737 to most of their holdings including those in Mull. In the next 100 years, this would contribute to the slow decline within the clan-based society of the spirit and principle of the system of *dùthchas*.

Clan Life

Whilst the above account provides some historical context for the evolution of the clan system, there are few records that give a meaningful account of the life of ordinary people. However, several people have written about the subject including Martin Martin, Jackie Le May and Sarah McWhinney, and the following includes material based on their accounts.[14]

The first thing to say about clan life in the medieval period is that the mutually supportive basis for survival, in terms of securing food, shelter and safety in an unforgiving climate, provided a degree of comfort in a hostile world. The basic social contract for people in Mull was that they looked out for each other, and expected to share the good times and the bad. Of course, there would have been all the usual manifestations of human character with challenging inter-personal disagreements, criminal and dishonest behaviour, and the exercise of power by leaders that might be benign or punitive. There would also have been the sometimes all too frequent and disruptive call to arms. However, taking all things into account, it would probably be fair to say that compared with those living in a strictly feudal system where ordinary mortals were serfs, the clan community operated as a relatively "civil society", with accepted customs and processes that ensured co-operation, tolerance and fair play.

In the latter part of the Middle Ages, we do know a little more about ordinary day-to-day community life. In Mull, clansmen lived with their families in small villages called *bailes* which typically involved 10 to 20 families.[15] These were located on the coast or within protected areas of a glen. Their houses were mostly made of peat and wood with thatched roofs but, in some settlements, there would have been some larger stone buildings for wealthier people and for communal gatherings. The lives of ordinary clansmen involved growing food (mostly oats, and barley for ale and whisky) and other crops (such as flax for clothing), tending and trading their beasts (cattle, sheep, pigs and goats), and raising children.[16] The amount of arable land was limited, and the supply of food subject to the vagaries of the weather. The citizens of Mull made the most of a difficult terrain using a system called *"feannagan"* or *"lazy bed"*.[17] However, by the 17th century, cattle had become a staple part of existence with droving to the lowlands for sale in return for meal. Although coinage existed, people mostly traded through barter using livestock, grain, fish, poultry and cloth, and traversed the land on horse with the occasional two and four wheeled vehicle for transporting people and goods on very uneven tracks some of which still exist in the modern era if you know where to look.[18] More often than not, they would also take to boats, both to visit other parts of the island, and to access other islands and the mainland. Clansmen had a right to bear arms and, when the time came, they rallied to the collective cause bringing their own weapons to defend their lands from invaders or follow their leaders' inclinations to pursue feuds and acquire more territory. However, for most of the time, life was relatively peaceful. In the 12th/13th centuries, due to a cooling climate, there were periods of cold weather which would have made life very tough, but they took solace from the community to which they belonged.

This was a relatively civil society where "Folk Right" held sway. Under this form of community justice, there were rules regarding crimes such as murder and theft, rights to compensation and retribution for victims of misdeeds, and a clear understanding about inheritance through the male line. Justice was dispensed by Chiefs and the chieftains. While the church might act as moral arbiter, its principal role was to administer records, organise ceremonies for births, deaths and marriages, and dispense services to the sick, the destitute, and the elderly. The lawful age of marriage was fifteen for girls and eighteen for boys, and marriages often involved the provision of dowries known by the Gaelic word *tocher,* and taking the form of livestock, money and/or land. There is also evidence of some pre-nuptial trial cohabitation, and there was provision for fostering children without parents. Women could seek divorce/separation as easily as men and, when obtained on her behalf, the woman kept all the property to which she had acquired an entitlement during the marriage.

In these times, there was no formal system of education. With the population being largely illiterate, they would learn about history, myths and recent events through family word of mouth and the songs and stories of travelling bards who inspired loyalty to the clan and served to raise spirits when times were hard. Despite a tough day-to-day existence, there were periodic social gatherings, for special occasions, and more generally. These took the form of what was called a *ceildh* which was an occasion for making music and storytelling.[19] For music, several instruments were used including the Celtic harp and bag pipes. There is evidence of the wide use of the Celtic harp through stone carvings from as early as the 8th century.[20] There is some debate as to the origin of bag-pipes although it seems likely that they were brought from Ireland.[21] Artistic endeavour was mainly confined to making items of jewellery such as broches for female cloaks, and Celtic crosses for graves.

While the above account provides a picture of life on Mull during the Middle Ages, we also have written evidence of life during the final days of the clan system in the 17th and 18th centuries. An account of life on the island in the 17th century is provided in the book entitled A Description of the Western Islands of Scotland Circa 1695 by Martin Martin.[22] And there is similar material in the book by Jo Currie entitled "Mull, the Island and its People".

Regarding the climate and vegetation during that time, Martin noted that *"the air is temperately cold and moist, although the fresh breezes that blow from the mountains do in some measure qualify it."* Consequently, *"the island is lush with woods along the coast of birch, hazel, rowan and holly". "There is an abundance of native plants, including many that had medicinal purpose".* Martin also notes that *"the natives are accustomed to take a large dose of Aquavitae as a corrective"* and he also refers to the availability in the west of *"black and white Indian nuts which are a source of medicine to treat diarrhea"* and *"the heather which affords an abundance of peat for burning."*[23]

On the land native animals included red deer, wild fowl and foxes and, in the waters around the island, there were seals, snakes, and otters with plentiful food in the form of herring, cod, and ling, as well as mussels, oysters and clams. Inland, several rivers afforded salmon, and there were fresh water lakes with trout and eel. There were many springs and fountains and Martin makes special mention of Tonbir Moray, or Mary's Well (a reference to what would become Tobermory) which is a harbour and source of excellent water which was said to have medicinal qualities.

Regarding economic activity, Martin records that *"the natives grow barley and oats and the mountains and valleys provide good pasturage for cattle, sheep, goats and deer. The black cattle are small but their flesh is delicious."* Jo Currie indicates that people mostly got around by riding small horses or by boat. Martin makes reference to importance of various bays for anchorage, with the bay to the north of Duart being of special note. The harbour at Lochbuie was described as "indifferent". While anchorages at Tobermory Bay and Bunessan were useful.

Apparently the people were mostly tall with a fair complexion in keeping with their Irish/Norse heritage. The ordinary folk *"had great respect for their Chiefs and heads of tribe"*. The men wore kilts and plaids with distinctive patterns, and the more affluent wore a coat, waistcoat and breeches. The women wore blankets and necklaces. Most of the men wore bonnets, and shoes (brogues) made of un-tanned hide. Most of the people spoke Gaelic but those of higher rank spoke English. According to Martin, the inhabitants were all Protestant apart from a few Catholics.

Finally, in Martin's account there is reference to Duart Castle as the seat of Sir John Maclean which had recently been forfeit to the Earl of Argyll, Moy Castle which is the seat of the Maclean of Lochbuie, a ruined castle at Aros, a number of "duns" built by the Norse, and fortifications at Cairn na Burgh in the Treshnish Isles, which were almost impregnable because of the rocks and tides. Before the arrival of the Argylls, the great hall at Duart was known as a place where clan members met for celebrations.

Clans in Dispute

Inevitably with any system based on the occupation and/or ownership of land, there was the potential for friction between neighbouring clans. In the first half of the Middle Ages, there were never ending feuds regarding the control of territory and this was a particular feature of the Hebrides. In the late Middle Ages the traditional spread of clan lands was as shown in the accompanying map (See Fig 2). An account of feuds involving the clans occupying the island of Mull and its neighbours is given in Chapter 8.

Another source of friction between the clans was the time honoured pastime of rustling. With little means of identifying the ownership of stock, from the early days young men were inclined to steal cattle from the land of neighbouring clans in a practice known as *reiving* or *creach*. Increasingly, this would involve forays into the lowlands, with small bands of young highlanders rounding up livestock and holding them for ransom. Taking advantage of the practice, some

Scottish Clans: Wikipedia

clans on the borders of the Highlands even went so far as to offer lowlanders protection against such raids for a small fee in what was a classic sting.

Harmony between clans in the Hebrides was further disrupted with the decision of King James IV in 1493 to abolish the Lordship of the Isles. In particular, with the removal of the Clan Macdonald from their leading role, James deliberately pursued the process of issuing feudal charters which paid little respect to pre-existing traditional boundaries or the distribution of clansmen on long held lands. This opened up disputes between clans which were rife in the 16th century.

In the late 16th century, King James VI decided to put an end to internecine squabbles. In 1587, Parliament passed two acts. The first was designed to deal with rustling, and provided that a clan chief was accountable for the actions of his clansmen, even if they had acted independently. This would eventually be enshrined in the Statutes of Iona enacted in 1609. The second, called the *"Slaughter Under-Trust Act", provided that any action by* a Clan Chief to settle a dispute by murdering his opponent(s) would be considered as an act of treason. If proven, the sentence was death and the forfeit of all lands and rights for both the Clan Chief and his heirs. The first recorded use of this law was in 1588 when Sir Lachlan Maclean was prosecuted for the murder of 18 members of the Macdonald clan at the wedding of his mother to John MacKayne at Torloisk in Mull. The charges did not stick, but his stepfather was subsequently imprisoned for a time for his alleged involvement in "murderous acts".

Feuding between the clans continued through most of the 17th century, with numerous battles, skirmishes, and settling of old scores during the civil wars of the 1640s. Reportedly, the last of these conflicts took place in 1688 as a result of a long-running dispute about lands in Lochaber on the mainland to the north east of Mull. In the 15th century the chief of Clan Mackintosh had been granted a charter for the lands of Glenroy and Glen Spean which had previously been controlled by the Macdonalds of Keppoch. The Macdonalds had refused to acknowledge the transfer of title or pay rent for what they regarded as false possession, and the matter was eventually concluded at the Battle of Mulroy when, despite the fact that the Clan Mackintosh was supported by government troops, the Macdonalds won the day with a little help from their friends the Camerons. The chief of the Clan Mackintosh was then forced to renounce his claim.

However, probably the most famous example of a feud between clans took place in 1692. In 1691, the government was seeking to obtain from known Jacobite supporters declarations of loyalty to the new protestant monarchs William and Mary. The Macdonalds of Glencoe were deemed to be recalcitrant and, seeking to make an example of them, the government ordered a military intervention. On a cold and gloomy night on 13 February 1692, government forces consisting of the 10th Earl of Argyll's Regiment of Foot (members of the Clan Campbell) slaughtered an estimated 30 members and associates of the Clan Macdonald (including women and children) in the infamous Glencoe Massacre.[24] In the aftermath, there was a Commission about the brutality of this intervention with consequences under the *Slaughter Under Trust Act*. Although there was no holding to account, it passed into folk memory as a dastardly deed commemorated to this day.

Scotland's Wars

The inclination of clan members to engage in internecine conflict was nothing compared with their commitment to wars in which the Scottish state sought to expand and defend its territory. Commencing in the

11th century, as the Scottish crown began the long journey of consolidating its hold over the West and North of the country, the reliance on clan based forces slowly expanded. The consolidation of territory began with the subjugation of Moray (between 1078 and 1130). Subsequently, Caithness and Sutherland were slowly annexed between 1124 and 1202, the North Hebrides were subjugated in 1244, the Kingdom of the Isles including Mull was annexed from Norway in 1266, and Orkney and Shetland became part of Scotland in 1472.

Most of the peoples joining the Scottish population during this period consisted of Celtic or Gaelic clans and people of Viking descent with established military credentials. Indeed, many clan members were specialist warriors, with a long tradition of forming into elite mercenary troops to fight overseas wars. In the 13th century, the number of warriors also expanded through an influx of settlers with a similar clan tradition from other countries. Examples of such groups include the Camerons (from Denmark), the Frasers (from Anjou), the Menzies (from Rouen), the Chisholms (from Normandy) and the Grants (from Nottingham in England).

Eventually, the fighting qualities of these clansmen became essential to Scotland's prowess on the battlefield. And by the time of the Wars of Scottish Independence which began in 1296, the Highlands had become a rich source of military manpower. Many of the engagements involved the English, and in later years the clans were not always on the same side. In the early 14th century, King Robert I (The Bruce) sought to formalise the availability of this resource. He introduced feudal tenures, with the awarding of charters for land in return for a commitment to fighting the English.

In the next several hundred years, the power and influence of given clans would wax and wane according to the alliances that they espoused and the battles in which they engaged. It is a rich history which extends into the 18th century. And the fortunes of various clans of note for the history of Mull are noted in subsequent chapters. Sadly (for them), this amazing contribution to the establishment and consolidation of an independent Scottish nation would eventually come to a sticky end as traditional clans people were scattered to the wind.

ENDNOTES

1   Material in this chapter is drawn from a number of sources including "The Island of Mull, Its History, Scenes and Legends" by John MacCormick, published by Hannan in 1923.

2   Clann is believed to derive from the Latin planta meaning shoot or offspring.

3   Agnatic literally means kinship traceable through males. Succession through the female line is called enatic, while succession through either is called cognatic.

4   Successive monarchs did attempt to enforce legal title and this was largely ignored by local chiefs.

5   The lairds of Brolass initially spelt their name as Brolas.

6   This provision was enshrined by Act of Parliament in 1685. The provisions survived until most were abolished in 1914. However, vestiges of this feudal system survived until the Abolition of Feudal Tenure Scotland Act 2000.

7   Although Manrent usually involved one party providing protection to another, in some cases two clans would enter into a treaty of mutual support.

8   Calps was abolished by Parliament in 1617.

9   This custom was taken by Scots to North America, but is not linked to practices in modern times adopted by the Kl Klux Klan.

10   The lighting of fires was not always a call to arms, but was also a signal to commune for celebrations such as the birth of an heir.

11   These annual gatherings, probably originated in Ireland and were brought to Scotland by the Scoti. They were the forerunners of Highland Games.

12   Teathing involved the release of cattle onto the land which would drop their dung and trample the ground.

13   A soum is the area of pasturage which will support a cow or a sheep, or the number of such cattle or sheep that can be pastured on a given area of land.

14   The booklet "Ardmeanach – A Hidden Corner of Mull" was written by Jackie Le May and first published by Iona Press, Inverness in 1995. Ardmeanach is Gaelic for "middle promontory" which aptly describes the location on the western side of Mull. Mouth to Ear Memory by Sarah McWhinney was published in 1992.

15   Baile is a Gaelic word meaning place or piece of land and has been anglicised as a prefix into "Bally" as in Ballygown on Loch na Keal.

16   There is some evidence that monasteries were distilling of whisky in the early Middle Ages. The first record is in the Exchequer Rolls of 1494.

17   Feannagan involved the raising of layers of soil, with furrows in between, in which plants were grown. Seaweed and manure was used as fertiliser.

18   Coinage was in circulation in some parts of Scotland before the Norman era. However, the first Scottish king to mint his own coinage was David I (1084-1153) with his image shown in profile.

19   In modern times, the ceilidh is a gathering for musical entertainment and dancing. In medieval times, it referred to the custom of visiting ones neighbours for sharing stories and poems, and entertaining each other with songs. This was prevalent in the winter months and even as the participants were mending their nets, spinning, or making ropes.

20   Images of "harps" have been found on rocks dating from 15,000 BCE in France. The word comes from the Anglo-Saxon and Norse word for "pluck". By the 13th century it was mostly applied to the triangular form of the instrument. The Gaelic word for the instrument in the Middle Ages was cláirseach.

21   The bag-pipe is a wind instrument consisting of a bag, a pipe and a drone. The player blows into the airtight bag which is a reservoir that regulates a continuous flow of air through the pipe which is played using one or two hands. The "drone" is a mechanism for altering the pitch.

22   A Description of the Western Isles of Scotland Circa 1695 was written by Martin Martin and published by Andrew Bell in Cornhill in 1703.

23   "Acquavitae" is a reference to whisky.

24   The force was led by Robert Campbell of Glenlyon whose relatives included members of the Maclaine family in Mull.

DÙTHCHAS
LANDSCAPE AND COMMUNITY IN MULL AND IONA

CLANS OF MULL

The clan-based system of community was gradually established in Mull during the period of Scoti settlement in the early Middle Ages, and continued during the kingdom of Dál Riata, the Norse Kingdom of the Isles, the Lordship of the Isles, and well into the 16th century. Thereafter, a variety of people and circumstances brought about its slow demise. In providing a brief history of these clans, it should be noted that the story is told through the lives of chiefs, about whom there are written accounts as listed in the bibliography and in Wikipedia. Inevitably, in writing about people and events from long ago, some information provided is apocryphal.

Clan MacDougall

The Clan MacDougall takes its name from its ancestor Dougall MacSomairle, a son of the Norse King Somerled. The motto of the Clan, "conquer or die" perhaps provides some insight into their approach to life. After his father's death at the Battle of Renfrew in 1164, Dougall inherited control of most of the current day mainland district of Argyll including Mull, Jura, Tiree, and Coll, while his brother Ranald took Skye, Islay and other neighbouring islands. The descendants of Ranald would eventually become the dominant Clan Macdonald whose history is covered later in this chapter, and Dougall's descendants would become the Clan MacDougall of which he is acknowledged as the first chief.

The name Dougall (or Dugald) is derived from the Gaelic *dubh-gall*, which means *black stranger*. In Norse times, Dougall's royal descent was acknowledged by the King of Norway and he is reported to have styled himself as *'King of the South Isles and Lord of Lorn'*. In 1207, he was succeeded by his son Duncan whose hold on power was at times tenuous. He would lose some of his authority when Argyll was invaded by King Alexander II and he found himself beholden for that territory to Scotland. He was also temporarily relieved of responsibility for the Hebrides (including Mull) in favour of his brother Uspak.

In 1247, Duncan was succeeded by his son Ewan and King Hakon of Norway granted him the title of King of the Isles. During their time, Duncan and Ewan built many castles to defend their territory, including Aros and Duart in Mull, Dunstaffnage near Oban on the mainland, Cairn na Burgh on the Treshnish Isles, and Dunconnel on the Garvellach islands to the south of Mull. Their fortifications would figure strongly in the history of Mull in the centuries that followed and are monuments to their endeavours. In the 1260s, when Scottish ambitions to control the Western Isles led to hostilities with Norway, Ewan found himself between a rock and a hard place. Eventually, he sided with the Scottish King Alexander III and, when sovereignty for the Hebrides was transferred to Scotland following the Treaty of Perth in 1266, the MacDougall lordship over Argyll and the Hebrides was confirmed. Shortly thereafter, Ewan died.

By now the Clan MacDougall was the most powerful clan in the Western Highlands and Islands with many clan members living in Mull. In 1267, the 4th Chief of the Clan, Sir Alexander of Argyll (or Alisdair of Ergadia) married Julienne Comyn and became a close ally of the Comyn and Balliol families. This would prove to be a fateful union. In particular, Alexander was a staunch supporter of King John I (John Balliol) who had come to the Scottish throne in 1292, and in the Wars of Scottish Independence, the MacDougalls sided with King John and his allies, against the forces of the rival claimant to the throne Robert Bruce. After a series of battles, the MacDougalls ended up on the losing side and, as King Robert took power, he transferred their territory to his supporters. In particular, control of the Western Isles including Mull was transferred to the chief of the Clan Donald would go on to become Lord of the Isles, while the Clan Campbell took control of much of current day Argyll on the mainland.

In the centuries following their exclusion from Mull, the fortunes of the Clan MacDougall would wax and wane as they repeatedly found themselves on the wrong side of history. Although they never regained a foothold in Mull, their fortunes were somewhat restored in the time of the 6th Chief John Gallda MacDougall. In the mid-14th century, he married a niece of the reigning King David II, and regained the clan's ancestral lands on the mainland including Lorn. However, following a subsequent dispute with members of the Stewart dynasty in the late 14th century, parts of their Lorn homeland were passed to the Campbells.

In the 17th century during Wars of the Three Kingdoms including the English Civil War, the Clan would again figure on the losing side. They committed troops to the royalist cause, and for a time lost the remainder of their territory in Lorn. However, following the restoration in 1660, King Charles II rewarded them for their loyalty and restored some of their lands.

During the Jacobite rising of 1715 the Clan supported the Jacobite cause and, after the defeat at the Battle of Sheriffmuir, the 22nd Chief John Donollie MacDougall was forced into exile. He later returned to Scotland to live as a fugitive and was eventually pardoned in 1727. His successor as chief, his eldest son Alexander, did not take part in the Jacobite rising of 1745, although his brother Duncan and some 200 clansmen perished at the Battle of Culloden in 1746. Despite this divided loyalty, some of the MacDougall lands in the north of Lorn were eventually restored in the late 18th century, and the lands accommodating Dunstaffnage Castle and Dunollie Castle near modern day Oban continue to be their traditional home to this day.

A reminder of the clan's association with Mull can be seen on a promontory overlooking Oban. As you board the ferry to Mull, significant parts of the ruins of Dunollie Castle still stand adjacent to Dunollie House. The current and 31st Chief of the clan is Morag Morley, MacDougall of MacDougall and Dunollie.

The Clan(s) Maclean

The Clan Maclean comprises two families eventually emerging as the Clan Maclean of Duart and the Clan Maclaine of Lochbuie. The separation of their respective histories began in the late 14th century when the two brothers, Lachlan Lubanach and Hector were granted rights to land in different parts of Mull. The history of the Clan prior to that date is a shared heritage.

The Ancient and Shared Line

Maclean is an Anglicisation of the Scottish Gaelic MacGilleEathain which translates into the son of the "Servant of Saint John". Genealogical research suggests that the clan can be traced back to an Irish king Tuirmhih in 320 BCE, with the family migrating from Ireland to the Western Isles during the Early Middle Ages and members of the Clan related to several kings of Dál Riata. Whatever the veracity of this genealogy, it is probably safe to say that the Clan is of both Irish and Norse heritage and that the progenitor was a man named Old Dubhgall (Dugald) of Scone during Norse times. He was born in around 1050 in the ancient province of Lorn which approximates to modern day county of Argyll. The exact location is uncertain, but the descendants became a dominant family in the district of Knapdale which is in the Mull of Kintyre, and were known for their seamanship which would eventually earn them the right to live in the strategically positioned Tarbert Castle at the mouth of Loch Fyne.

The first person to be recognised as Chief of the Clan was a direct descendant of Dugald of Scone known as "Gillean of the Battle Axe". Gillean was born in Knapdale in 1210 and became the leader of the Clan in 1230 during the final days of the Norse Kingdom of the Isles. In 1240, he was succeeded by his son Malise mac Gillean (a name that foreshadows Maclean) who is said to have fought valiantly for the Scottish cause in the conflict with Norway for control of the Western Isles at the Battle of Largs in 1263. This inconclusive exchange led to the Treaty of Perth that provided for the establishment of the autonomous Lordship of the Isles with the

Hebrides becoming part of Scotland in 1266.

In the years that followed, the Clan Maclean would become significant players in the Wars of Scottish Independence. Their support for the Bruce family would eventually be pivotal in their gaining a significant foothold on the island of Mull, at the expense of the Clan MacDougalls who supported the Balliol family and lost control to the Clan Macdonald. In particular, King Robert the Bruce was in need of an effective maritime force and the Maclean family fitted the bill. Consequently, they were entrusted with control of strategic castles including Tarbert. The 3rd Chief of the Clan Malcolm mac Giliosa also consolidated the clan's position by marrying the daughter of the Earl of Carrick who was the mormaer of South West Scotland. Malcolm was a gallant warrior in the battles of Glen Trool (in Galloway) and Loudon Hill (in Ayrshire) in 1307, and at the Battle of Bannockburn in 1314.[1] In the century that followed, through the service they provided to the Clan Macdonald, the influence of the Macleans would slowly expand.

By the middle of the 14th century, the Clan was led by the redoubtable Lachlan Lùbanach Maclean (Lachlan the Wiley).[2] Born in Knapdale in around 1330, Lachlan was raised in relatively modest circumstances during a period when the victory at Bannockburn still resonated across the country. In his early life, Scotland was decimated by the arrival of the Black Death which is said to have killed as many as a third of Scotland's population including a fair number of the nobility.[3] However, the impact in dispersed rural communities was relatively benign and Lachlan survived in good health. With evident leadership skills and physical prowess, in his twenties he became a trusted ally of the Clan Donald and in 1365, he became the 5th Chief of the Clan. In May 1367, after a special dispensation from the Pope, he married the 17 year old Mary Macdonald, daughter of John Lord of the Isles.[4] Mary was a direct descendant of King Robert the Bruce and she came with a dowry which included much of the island of Mull including both Aros Castle and Duart Castle over which the Clan Macdonald had sovereignty following the transfer from the Clan MacDougall. This fortuitous combination of events would bring both Lachlan and his brother

Hector from Knapdale to Mull.

In the years following his accession, apart from consolidating his family, with his wife giving birth to five children, Lachlan was increasingly active in local politics. He not only consolidated his hold over most of Mull but was appointed as Lieutenant General of the Lord of the Isles military forces commencing a tradition that would follow for several generations. Mind you, his time was not all plain sailing. In 1386, Lachlan's brother-in-law Donald Macdonald succeeded his father as Lord of the Isles and fell out with his brother John Mor. Lachlan sided with John Mor who was eventually sent into exile. However, Lachlan was quickly forgiven and, in 1390, Donald granted him a written charter for not only Duart Castle but also property in Islay and Jura. For the next three hundred years, Duart Castle would be the home of Lachlan's descendants. And during that time, the Clan would at various times be granted control of the islands of Coll and Tiree, and territory on the mainland including Lochaber and Morvern. Lachlan died in 1405 at the age of 75.

In the account which follows, the subsequent history of the Clan is provided in two sections to reflect the fact that the descendants of Lachlan Lùbanach and his brother Hector went their separate ways. In summary, from the mid-14th century the Clan Maclean of Duart would become the dominant family on Mull. Aros Castle would become the administrative centre of the clan with Duart Castle operating as the family home, and the leadership role would prevail for more than 300 years until it was relinquished to the Earl of Argyll through financial difficulties. Thereafter, the Clan had little say in the affairs of Mull until they reclaimed Duart Castle in the 20th century. Their demise, and that of the community-based society over which they held domain, is reflected in the lives of a majority of the islands residents.

In the meantime, the descendants of Lachlan's brother Hector were granted control of Lochbuie and other lands in the south of the island. They would pursue their own path, including their loyalty to the Catholic faith, and would eventually differentiate themselves from their cousins by adopting the name Maclaine. Through marriage, they would also be allied with the lesser clans on the island, the Clan MacQuarrie and the Clan McKinnon.

While they were certainly drawn into military engagements during the tumultuous years of Civil War and the Jacobite rebellions, they kept a lower profile than their cousins and maintained control over their lands well into the 20th century before financial challenges eventually forced their exit.

The Clan Maclean of Duart

Returning to the history of the Clan Maclean of Duart, after nearly forty years as leader, Lachlan Lùbanach was succeeded as chief in 1405 by his son Hector.[5] A red-head, and perhaps with an aggressive temperament, he was known as *Red Hector of the Battles* and, on his succession, he had already taken over from his father as leader of the Lordship of the Isles armed forces. Hector married the daughter of the Earl of Douglas who was allied to the crown. However, despite representations from his father-in-law to change allegiances, Hector was committed to maintaining the autonomy of the Lordship of the Isles and led its army in a series battles with royalist barons from the north-east of Scotland representing the relatively ineffective King Robert III (who died in 1406). Continuing his loyalty to the Lord of the Isles, in July 1411 Hector eventually lost his life in arm-to-arm combat at the inconclusive Battle of Harlaw against the forces of King James I led by the Earl of Mar.

Following Hector's death, he was succeeded by his 12 years old son Lachlan Bronneach (the swag bellied). Lachlan was on the battlefield at Harlaw, and was taken prisoner by the Earl of Mar. Consequently, he would spend a good many years in captivity, but the Earl of Mar looked kindly on the boy and allowed him to be raised and educated within the confines of the Mar household although his upbringing did not include military training! In his youth, Lachlan became acquainted with the Earl's daughter Lady Margaret Stewart and, in due course, the Earl agreed to their marriage. The couple were then allowed to take up residence at Duart and, for a time, they lived a quiet life. However, Lachlan eventually became embroiled in the attempts by King James I to assert his authority over the Highland and Islands. In 1427, the king assembled the chiefs in Inverness demanding an oath of allegiance. Met with intransigence, he had some of the chiefs beheaded, and Lachlan was arrested along with Alexander Macdonald (who had succeeded his father Donald as Lord of the Isles in 1423).

Lachlan would remain in custody for two years. On his release in early 1429, Alexander Macdonald requested his support in wreaking vengeance on King James, and a significant force of men from the Clans Donald, Cameron, Mackintosh and Maclean then attacked Inverness which they burnt to the ground. In response, the king sent an army which caught the Lordship of the Isles forces unawares. In the Battle of Lochaber fought on a marsh near Fort William in June 1429, and during which the Clan Cameron changed sides, the King's army won a decisive victory. While the Lord of the Isles Alexander Macdonald escaped, both Lachlan and his father-in-law the Earl of Mar were captured and imprisoned at Tantallon Castle. Eventually released in 1431, Lachlan then made his peace with the king who in settlement granted him control of the island of Coll. However, Lachlan's troubles were not over by a long chalk. Although Alexander Macdonald eventually also made his peace with King James, he decided to take retribution against the Clan Cameron for their defection at the Battle of Lochaber. He transferred the lands around Fort William to the Macleans and, after a lull, in 1470 the Clan Cameron attempted to reassert their rights. At the Battle of Corpach, the Clan Maclean were routed, with Lachlan narrowly escaping from the battlefield. He died in 1472, of natural causes.

Lachlan was succeeded by the 8th Chief, Lachlan Og. He, and his son Hector Odha (the Swarthy) who succeeded him on his death in 1476, were the last Chiefs to lead the Clan Maclean before the abolition of the Lordship of the Isles. The events leading to this major change in the autonomous status of the Hebrides are outlined elsewhere in this book. However, in settling differences with the crown, John the Lord of the Isles fell foul of his illegitimate son Angus who did not agree to the terms. Internecine conflict ensued, with Lachlan supporting Angus, and in 1480 this culminated in the Battle of Bloody Bay fought in waters adjacent to modern day Tobermory, with the Clan Maclean suffering significant casualties. Whilst Angus was the victor, the battle left the fleets of the Lordship decimated. Subsequently, while Angus ruled as Lord of the Isles for ten years, in 1490 he was murdered in his sleep by his harpist. He left a young son, Donald, but his death would spell the end of the Lordship's rule.

In the final years of the Lordship of the Isles, there was one final conflict involving members of the Clan Maclean. In 1491, they supported a small force of the Clan Macdonald who fought with the Clan Mackenzie for rights over the province of Ross in the North-West of Scotland. In the Battle of the Park, the Clan Maclean would suffer heavy casualties through drowning. Finally, in 1493, King James IV abolished the Lordship of the Isles.

Despite the abolition of the Lordship of the Isles, local autonomy was maintained for some time. In the immediate aftermath, King James granted charter to the Clan Maclean for the lands in Mull and, during the 16th century, central government was relatively weak allowing the traditional customs of the clan-based society to linger on. At this point, the extent of Clan Maclean of Duart territory had reached its zenith, encompassing most of Mull (apart from Lochbuie, and lands held by the Clans McKinnon and Macquarie territory), Coll, Tiree, parts of Jura and Islay, and significant territory on the mainland including Morvern to the north east of Mull, Knapdale in Kintyre, and other territory on the mainland such as Ardour, Kingairloch, Dochgarroch and Dunconnel.

In 1496, Hector Odhar Maclean was succeeded by his son. Little is known about Lachlan the 10th Chief except that the Clan Maclean was involved in an ill-fated attack on Northumbria by King James IV and the pretender to the English throne Richard of York, which ended with a shattering defeat at the hands of King Henry VIII at the Battle of Flodden Field in 1513. During this battle, not only King James, but Lachlan and many other Macleans were killed.

Lachlan was succeeded by his son Lachlan Cattanach (the shaggy) who had a somewhat blemished beginning in life and came to a sticky end. From the outset, it was unclear as to whether he was the son of Lachlan or an illegitimate son of his grandfather Hector. In any event, during his ten years as Chief, there were tensions with both the royalist Clan Campbell and the independently minded Clan Macdonald. In the early years, he was an active party in resisting the attempts by King James IV to assert his power over the Hebrides, although he eventually towed the line and ingratiated himself with the royalist side by marrying Catherine Campbell the daughter of the 2nd Earl of Argyll. Sadly, this marriage was not a success and, childless, Lachlan suspected his wife of trying to poison him. Legend has it that in 1527, in a fit of vengeance, he attempted to murder Catherine by abandoning her on a rock in Mull Sound (the Lady's Rock, which is south west of the isle of Lismore). Anticipating the success of this venture, he then faked a funeral. Unfortunately for him, Catherine was rescued by her kinsmen. She returned to Inverary Castle, and the attempt on her life was then avenged by her brother Sir John Campbell of Cawdor. On 10 November 1523, he organised to have Lachlan murdered while asleep in bed during a visit to Edinburgh. Despite this unhappy history, the clan did thrive during Lachlan's time, extending its influence across the Hebridean islands and the mainland.

Lachlan was succeeded by his 26 year old son Hector Mor (Hector the Great, referring to his height). The 12th Chief led the clan for forty-five years during what was a very troubled period of Scottish history, including rule by regents and the reign of Queen Mary. During this time, Hebridean autonomy largely went unchallenged. Hector is said to have been a brave and accomplished leader who honoured the spirit of *dùthchas*. He was said to have been a fair administrator who engendered a sense of well-being and community. To encourage improvements in the estate he granted extended leases to many of the clan, and he expanded his home at Duart Castle by building the Great Tower which was thrown open for community gatherings. He also regularly attended the Parliament in Edinburgh, and his counsel is said to have been valued by King James V. Like many highland chiefs, he maintained a standing army, but there were few disputes and the clansmen were able to focus on the welfare of their property and families. Nevertheless, the second half of the 16th century was not without opportunities for those of a military bent, and several younger members of the Clan Maclean joined with others from the Clan Mackay and Clan MacLeod to become mercenaries. Called the Gallowglass, they travelled to Ireland to serve King Shane O'Neill in resisting English occupation.[6]

During Hector Mor's time, King James V confirmed the rights of the Clan Maclean over Duart and significant other territory in Mull. According to Joe Currie, at this point the main landowners on the island were:

CLAN	TERRITORY
Macleans of Duart (& Torloisk/Brolass branches)	60% of the island including the east, the midlands, central south, and parts of the north west
Macleans of Lochbuie	South East corner
Macleans of Coll	Parts of North West and Coll
MacQuarries	Ulva, Staffa and adjacent lands around Loch na Keal
MacKinnons	Mishnish in the West of Mull, and land in the North
Monks of Iona[7]	Ross of Mull and Iona

In 1568, Hector Mor died of natural causes, and his death coincided with a significant change in national affairs. In 1567, Queen Mary had been forced to abdicate and the accession of her young son King James VI would in time herald significant changes to the nature of Scottish society with the weakening of the traditions of highland life driven by successive legislation including the Statutes of Iona enacted in 1609. Hector Mor was succeeded by his son Hector Og who was in his late 20s and had astutely married Lady Janet Campbell the daughter of Archibald the influential 4th Earl of Argyll. Whilst Hector Og maintained a presence at court in Edinburgh, in less than a decade, he would undo much of his father's achievements. He was profligate, and accumulated rising debts. However, he did consolidate the scope of the Clan's hold on Mull, expelling most of the Clan McKinnon, and constructing a residence on Iona. He died in 1573.

Hector Og was succeeded by his son Lachlan Mor Maclean who is arguably the greatest ever leader of the Clan. In his case, it can be rightly said that the word "Mor" reflected not only his physical stature but also his worldly-wise intellect, chivalry and leadership skills. Indeed, the twenty five years of his tenure were the Mull community's *halcyon* days before the turmoil of the 17th centuries and 18th centuries changed the body politic and wrecked the wider clan-based community for ever.

Lachlan was born in 1558 and was just 15 years old when he became the 14th Chief. Well ahead of the stipulation in the Statutes of Iona, he had been raised and educated in Edinburgh. Apparently, he was a well-read and likeable fellow, and there was no doubt about his loyalty to the crown in a time when the Protestant faith was in the ascendancy. On becoming chief he returned to Mull to find a somewhat tumbledown Duart Castle. With youthful vigour he quickly engaged his fellow clansmen to implement a programme of repairs. From all the evidence, these were happy days, with the people of Mull still living under a community-based clan system as opposed to the more feudal system that applied in most other parts of Scotland. And, from all the evidence, in these early days he was much beloved by his clansmen on whom it is said that he bestowed many acts of kindness. As he reached the age of majority, he sought a wife and, in 1577, he married the 14 years old Margaret Cunningham who was the daughter of the 6th Earl of Glencairn. Lachlan and Margaret appear to have had a happy marriage with six children who between them would consolidate the family's position on Mull. Apart from his eldest son Hector Og who would succeed him, his son Lachlan Og would become the 1st Laird of Torloisk, and his daughter Bethan would marry Hector the 9th Chief of the Clan Maclean of Lochbuie.

Having established a happy family life in Duart, and still in his 20s, Lachlan turned his mind to what he would do with his inheritance. With the Hebrides still enjoying considerable autonomy, he quickly recognised the opportunity to extend his power and influence. This led him to pursue certain territorial objectives. In particular, over the next decade, he proceeded to engage in a series of disputes with the once powerful Clan Macdonald while maintaining a somewhat brittle peace with his mother's family (the Argylls) with whom he shared the Protestant faith as well as a dislike of the Macdonalds. His disputes with various members of the Clan Macdonald would be one of the last internecine feuds amongst Highland clans before King James VI legislated an end to the fighting on pain of death.

With existing territory on Islay, in the early years, Lachlan was determined to take control of the peninsula called the Rhinns. He began his campaign in 1578, by laying siege to Loch Gorm Castle in northern Islay, but was eventually repelled by the members of the Clan Macdonald. Suitably

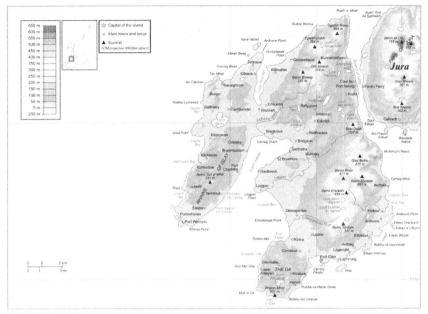

Island of Islay: Pinterest

chastened, he returned to tending his estate. Then, in 1585, he commenced what is known as the "Battle of the Western Isles". This involved a series of engagements over several years involving Mull, Jura, Islay, and Tiree, and the Maclean traditional family homeland on the mainland.

The new round of hostilities began innocently enough, when Donald Gorm Mor Macdonald of Sleat set off to visit his kinsman on Islay. His boat was caught in a storm and he ended up in Maclean territory on Jura. A disaffected member of his party took advantage of the situation and stole some sheep. News filtered through to Lachlan who, requiring little pretext, set sail for Jura with a significant force. He took the Macdonalds by surprise, killing most of the party. Donald Gorm Mor escaped and returned to Skye where he rallied support to seek redress. He then sailed up Loch na Keal, taking Lachlan by surprise. Lachlan took refuge at a defensible position on Ben More but, when Donald then retreated, Lachlan followed in hot pursuit inflicting serious casualties.

Skirmishes of this kind continued throughout 1585, with significant losses amongst the male population of Mull that seriously disrupted life and weakened the community. One can only imagine what life in Mull would have been like, wondering who might turn up next to inflict retribution. Eventually, the young King James VI attempted to intervene in the continuing hostilities, and engaged Norman the Chief of the Clan McLeod in Skye to persuade the Macdonalds to desist. Norman was happy to oblige as the Clan McLeod were also periodically at war with the Macdonalds and Donald was persuaded to back off. In the spring of 1586, Lachlan Maclean's brother-in-law Angus Macdonald from Islay then sought to negotiate a peace, meeting with Donald on Skye and with Lachlan at Duart Castle.[8] This turned out to be a foolhardy expedition. Not to be denied his interest in the Rhinns of Islay, or his hostility towards the Macdonalds, Lachlan threw Angus and his party into the dungeons demanding that the Macdonalds cede ownership of the Rhinns. Pending an outcome, while Angus was released his two sons James and Ranald (his nephews) were held as hostage.

Not surprisingly, when Angus returned to Islay he was in a very black mood and set on revenge. In the meantime, Lachlan sought to use the leverage provided by the hostages to further his designs on the Rhinns. In July 1586 he travelled to Islay with a group of 80 men and Angus' son James, while leaving his brother Ranald under armed guard back at Duart Castle. In preparation for a full-bloodied attack, he occupied Loch Gorm Castle, but then made a strategic blunder. Accompanied by a small group of his supporters, he reluctantly agreed to meet with Angus for dinner at Mulindry House. During the meal, it appeared that an agreement had been reached for the release of James in return for control of the Rhinns and Lachlan re-joined his supporters in outbuildings and retired for the night.

Later that night, Angus surrounded the Maclean party with a force of several hundred armed men. The deal was off, with the Macleans allowed to leave in peace if James was released. Given the odds, Lachlan accepted the deal, leaving just two of his men in the outbuildings. Having recovered his son, Angus then set fire to the building. The occupants were burnt to death and, over the next few days, he then killed the remaining members of Lachlan's men leaving only Lachlan himself alive. Safe only because he still had custody of Angus' other son Ranald, Lachlan returned to Duart Castle in high dudgeon.

News of these events eventually came to the attention of King James who again attempted mediation, through a leading member of the Clan Campbell.

Both parties agreed to a settlement with hostages taken by each side as an insurance and Angus then left for Ireland where he had some urgent family business. In his absence, Lachlan reneged on the fragile truce and again attempted to take the Rhinns peninsula by force. In the process he laid waste to Macdonald lands across the whole of Islay *"with fire and sword"*. Not surprisingly, when Angus returned from Ireland, he was incensed and mustered a large force. He invaded both Mull and Tiree, burning homes and killing many Maclean clansmen. In the meantime, having secured the Rhinns peninsular, Lachlan moved over to the mainland where he laid waste to Macdonald lands in Kintyre.

At this point King James stepped in with more decisive action to bring an end to hostilities. He issued a proclamation ordering that all the hostages should be delivered into the hands of the mediating Clan Campbell and held in safe keeping until the Macdonalds and Macleans resolved their territorial differences peacefully. To this end, Angus and Lachlan were commanded to attend Edinburgh Castle where they remained in custody until they had made a binding agreement to keep the peace. As surety of their good faith, each had to surrender their eldest son to remain in custody for a period. This settlement brought an end to the feud.

Despite this outcome, this was not the end of Lachlan's territorial ambitions. In the years that followed, he engaged in a variety of conflicts on both his own account and on behalf of the crown. In 1588, he attacked Mingary Castle, a Clan Macdonald fortress in Ardnamurchan to the north of Mull. This year is notable for the unsuccessful invasion of England by the Spanish Armada, and it is said that in besieging the castle Lachlan made use of troops from one of the Spanish galleons which had taken shelter in Tobermory Bay.

This continued inclination to pursue territorial ambitions brought Lachlan to a low point. In 1594, the Privy Council declared him to be an outlaw with forfeit of his lands. However, before this could be implemented, he redeemed himself by supporting the king in repelling a plot by Catholic forces to depose him. In September 1594, he committed members of the Clan Maclean to join an inexperienced royalist army of questionable loyalty led by the 19 year old Archibald the 7th Earl of Argyll to deflect a rebellion by Catholic sympathisers. The plan was to join forces with a royalist army sent from the east. However, things quickly went awry with Argyll's army caught unawares and defeated at the Battle of Glenlivet. A few days later, the royalist reinforcement finally arrived and the Catholic forces were dispersed, with their leaders fleeing to the continent. However, in the process, many Macleans lost their lives.[9]

After this disaster, Lachlan returned to Duart Castle to rest and recuperate. However, he was still a young man and continued to have designs on Islay. In 1598, he again took up arms against the Macdonalds and in August he landed a significant force on the island at Loch Ghruinneart which is north of the Rhinns peninsula. The Macdonald forces were led by no less than his nephew the same James Macdonald (now Sir James Macdonald) that Lachlan had previously taken hostage as a boy. Clearly, there was no love lost between them, and their forces engaged in the Battle of Traigh Ghruinneart. The Macdonalds were victorious through a superior positioning with their backs to the sun and, after the battle, many of the Macleans fled to their boats while others perished as they sheltered in a chapel which the Macdonalds burnt to the ground. Lachlan himself was killed after the battle by a dwarf hiding in a tree and James Macdonald was seriously injured although he later recovered. Interestingly, after the battle, King James decided to award the Macdonald lands on Islay to the Campbells, although this did not take effect until 1612 when Angus Macdonald sold his title to Sir John Campbell of Cawdor.

Following his death, Lachlan Maclean was succeeded by his 20 year old son Hector Og (the 15th Chief) who immediately saw it as his duty to avenge his father. He mustered a fresh force which included men from the Clans McKinnon, MacLeod of Dunvegan and Macneil of Barra. He landed on Islay where he caught up with Sir James Macdonald who was supported by members of the Clan Maclean of Lochbuie. At the Battle of Benvigory, Hector Og scored a decisive victory, with the Macdonalds fleeing to Kintyre and James Macdonald fleeing to Spain.[10] Afterwards the Macleans laid much of Islay to waste, and Hector of Lochbuie was for a time held prisoner. This would be the last of the engagements between the Macleans and Macdonalds.

In response to the long-running internecine warfare across the Hebrides, in 1598 King James VI passed legislation to impose levies on Clan Chiefs who did not maintain the peace. Inter-clan warfare became an act of treason punishable by death and this brought an effective end to the bloodshed. However, the King was clearly concerned about the aggressive character of the Clan Maclean and, in 1602, he arrested Hector Og who was imprisoned in Edinburgh. He was eventually released and returned to Duart Castle, but in the meantime, the King doubled down on his strategy to weaken clan-based society with the passage in 1609 of the Statutes of Iona. Subsequently, Hector maintained a low profile and was eventually successful in receiving royal charters for Iona, Tiree, parts of Islay, and various land in Mull. However, through failing to turn up at an important convention he forfeited certain Maclean lands in Lochaber. He died peacefully at Duart Castle in 1623.

Hector Og was succeeded by his eldest son Hector Mor who died three years later of natural causes. Dying without issue, he was succeeded by his brother Lachlan who became the 17th Chief in 1626. He would live through a period of national turbulence, with the Maclean family and the people of Mull playing a significant part. Things began well enough. Lachlan was a loyal supporter of King Charles I who had come to the throne in 1625 and, in reward for his loyalty, in 1632 he was appointed as Baron of Morvern, and Baron of Nova Scotia.[11] Sadly, this attachment to the crown would not serve him or the Clan Maclean well. In the 1630s, there was mounting tension between King Charles and the Covenanter Parliament in Scotland which led to the Wars of the Three Kingdoms. In the 1640s, Sir Lachlan was approached by the Earl of Argyll to join the Covenanter forces, but he declined and instead made a commitment to the crown. He would subsequently lead 750 members of the Clan Maclean, alongside members of the Clan Macdonald led by the famed MacColla (Sir Alistair Macdonald), in the armies led by the 1st Marquess of Montrose (Jamie Graham).[12] In 1645, Montrose's royalist army defeated the Covenanter government forces led by the Earl of Argyll at the Battles of Inverlochy, Auldern and Kilsyth. Afterwards, many members of the victorious Maclean forces dispersed giving members of the Clan Campbell "a bloody nose" on their way back to Mull. This event would not be forgotten by the Earls of Argyll and, unfortunately, the battles were pyrrhic victories because, in June 1645, King Charles was defeated at the Battle of Naseby in England. In September, a depleted Montrose army largely consisting of Irish mercenaries was defeated by a Covenanter Army led by Sir David Leslie at the Battle of Philiphaugh (on the borders near modern-day Selkirk). After resorting to guerrilla warfare, with the Clan Maclean ready again to join the fray, Montrose received orders from King Charles to lay down his arms and Sir Lachlan's fighting days were over. However, there would be one last military encounter. In 1647, a force comprising members of the Clan Campbell landed in Mull and confronted Sir Lachlan at Duart Castle. The attack failed. In April 1649 Sir Lachlan died of natural causes and was succeeded by his son Sir Hector. Thereafter, there would be a long running feud in which the Campbells continued to have designs on both Duart Castle and other Maclean territory in Mull, and the Macleans would intermittently take their revenge through attacks on the mainland.

Following his trial, in January 1649 King Charles I was executed for treason and Oliver Cromwell established the Commonwealth. In 1650, Montrose followed the King to the scaffold, but in Scotland the Covenanter Government recognised King Charles II as the new king of Scots. Not surprisingly, this was not well received in London and in 1650 Cromwell sent an army led by John Lambert to invade Scotland and impose English rule. For a while, the Scottish forces led by David Leslie evaded a battle. However, they were eventually defeated at the Battle of Dunbar after which the English occupied Edinburgh. The Royalist forces then rallied at Stirling and negotiated the support of highland forces led by Sir Hector Maclean. Things came to a head on 20 July 1651 at the Battle of Inverkeithing. The English army prevailed with more than 1,000 clansmen slaughtered including Sir Hector, 700-750 members of the Clan Maclean, and 100 men of the Clan Macquarrie. The battle is renowned for the selfless sacrifice of many individual clansmen who stepped up to defend their Chief with the battle cry "Another for Hector!" It is said that only 35 of the Clan Maclean troops would make it back to Mull.

The untimely death of Sir Hector and his loyal clansmen was something of a disaster for the Clan Maclean's position in Mull and elsewhere. Their support for the Royalist cause would lead to a mounting series of setbacks which would ultimately see them ousted from both Duart Castle and much of Mull. For the rest of the 17th century, the Clan was hugely depleted with not enough men to tend the fields, feed the population, or pay the rent for the maintenance of the estates; and the Clan was bereft of leadership. Sir Hector had been killed without an heir and was succeeded by his six years old brother Sir Allan Maclean. Given Sir Allan's age, for the next ten years the leadership of the clan fell to his guardians, Donald Maclean (Laird of Brolass) and Hector Maclean (of Lochbuie), and Macleans were marked men with little recourse to defend their position within the new Commonwealth led by Cromwell. In September 1653 Duart Castle was attacked by a Cromwellian fleet and, in haste, leading members of the Maclean family took refuge on the island of Tiree. However, the assault was unsuccessful because much of the fleet was wrecked by a freak storm. In the immediate aftermath, Duart Castle remained in Maclean hands, but the family's support for the royalist cause had left them with mounting debts and a range of creditors not to mention a small Cromwellian garrison on Mull installed to maintain the peace.

Meanwhile, across the Sound of Mull, the 8th Earl of Argyll (known as Archibald the Grim because he was cross-eyed) was lurking. Over the previous few years, the Earl had gradually acquired what were the mounting and unpaid debts of the Maclean family accumulated in part through their failed support for the Royalist cause. And, in 1659, he obtained a court order which vested in him the ownership of Clan Maclean lands. However, he was initially deflected from pursuing this claim by the untimely death of Cromwell and, following a brief period of rule by Richard Cromwell, and in 1660 the monarchy was restored. Archibald Campbell was arrested and executed for supporting Cromwell, with his demise no doubt a cause for celebration in Mull. However, the new 9th Earl of Argyll (also named Archibald) was a royalist supporter and subsequently King Charles II confirmed the Argyll claim over the Clan Maclean lands in Mull.

In 1674, the 29 years old Sir Allan died of natural causes and was succeeded by Sir John Maclean when he was only four years old. Effective leadership of the Clan was again in the hands of guardians, Lachlan the 2nd Laird of Brolass and Lachlan the 3rd Laird of Torloisk. The two Lachlans did their best to keep the family estates intact, but there were considerable debts estimated to be in the order of £200,000. Taking advantage of the situation, the Earl of Argyll obtained a ruling from the Privy Council which granted entitlement to Clan Maclean lands, and in 1678 he invaded Mull. For a time he took control of Duart Castle with the eight years old Sir John Maclean taking refuge at Cairn na Burgh Castle in the Treshnish Isles. As the Earl of Argyll consolidated his position on the east coast of Mull, many of the Clan Maclean tenants were driven from their traditional lands, with some fleeing to the hills to conduct guerrilla warfare over an extended period. This might have been the end for the Macleans; but then there was another twist. In 1681, Parliament enacted the Test Act requiring affirmation of the Protestant faith. The 9th Earl of Argyll was slow to sign up and then did so grudgingly. He was accused of treason, fled to the continent, his lands were forfeit, and he was eventually arrested and executed. This gave the Maclean family some respite, and the 11 years old Sir John was able to resume life at Duart Castle. Subsequently, he was invited to be educated at court, and records show that he grew into a witty, and good natured man who was well read, and fluent in several languages.[13]

Just as things were looking up for the Clan Maclean, political events would turn again. In 1685, King Charles II died to be succeeded by his brother King James VII. Soon thereafter, the 10th Earl of Argyll was fully restored to his estates. Within a short period, King James then found himself at odds with Parliament and in 1688 he was forced to abdicate in favour of the Protestant monarchs William and Mary. Unfortunately, the Clan Maclean were caught wrong-footed and, even though they were Protestant, they joined the Jacobite cause in support of the deposed king while the Argylls sided with the new joint monarchs. This would be the death knell for the Maclean position in Mull. Initially, on 27 July 1689 Viscount Dundee supported by a major force of over 400 members of the Clan Maclean led by the nineteen years old Sir John defeated the government forces at the Battles of Knockbreck and Killiekrankie. However, on 21 August, the Jacobites were defeated at the Battle of Dunkeld, and a further defeat at the Battle of Cromdale on 1 May 1690 brought an end to the rebellion.

These events left the Maclean forces and finances even more depleted, and the new Archibald 10th Earl of Argyll (who for services to the new monarchs would become the 1st Duke of Argyll in 1701) now took his opportunity to complete annexation of Clan Maclean lands in Mull. In 1690, he went to court and formally called in the Maclean debts, and in early 1692 Sir John Maclean had no choice but to surrender Duart Castle. The Campbells then demolished some of the building and scattered the stones around the estate.[14] Ownership of the Duart estate would not return to the Maclean family for more than 200 years.

With his heritage destroyed, and his kinsmen fleeing to the four corners of the Hebrides, Sir John Maclean was now destitute and initially retired to Cairn na Burgh Castle on Treshnish. Later in the year, he made his peace with King William III and then went into exile in France. During this period he married Mary the daughter of Sir Aeneas Macpherson of Invershiel and they had two children – Sir Hector Maclean who was born in 1700 and Katherine. Following the Act of Indemnity, in 1703 he returned to Scotland and established reasonable relations with Queen Mary. However, there was no prospect of reclaiming his heritage and, following the Act for the Division of Commonties, the Duke of Argyll began to dismantle the traditional attachment between members of the Clan Maclean and their lands.

In the years that followed, Sir John continued to harbour support for the deposed King James and the Jacobite cause. In 1715, Sir John mustered his clansmen to join the Jacobite army led by John Erskine, the 6th Earl of Mar while John Campbell the 2nd Duke of Argyll was appointed to lead government forces. The Clan Maclean troops were present at the Battle of Sheriffmuir when the Jacobites were outwitted by government troops leading to an inconclusive outcome. Afterwards, Sir John retired to Gordon Castle where he died in March 1716 and, in November, at the Battle of Preston, the Jacobites were defeated.

On the death of his father in 1716, the new and 21st Chief of the clan, Sir Hector Maclean, affirmed his support for the Jacobite cause and was rewarded with a Jacobite peerage.[15] At this point, apart from the estates held by the Torloisk and Brolass branches of the family, Maclean lands were confined to the islands of Coll, Tiree, Muck and Eigg. With the loss of Duart Castle, Sir Hector was continually on the move and, with the Jacobite cause still rumbling on, there were rumours that he was a French spy. In 1744, he was responsible for raising a petition calling on Charles Edward Stuart to reclaim the throne and, when the last Jacobite rebellion broke out in 1745, he was arrested in Edinburgh and sent to the Tower of London. In the meantime, the Clan Maclean led by John Maclean of Drimmin (Morvern) and supported by the Clan Maclean of Torloisk joined the Jacobite forces that took part in the Battle of Culloden in 1746. Most of the Clan Maclean forces were slaughtered, and afterwards Duart Castle would slowly fall into ruins like the Jacobite cause. Sir Hector, was released from prison in a general indemnity in 1747. Although he had married, in 1751 he died without issue in Paris.

Sir Hector was succeeded by his closest living relative, his third cousin Sir Allan Maclean.[16] Sir Allan was born in Torloisk in 1710 and educated in Edinburgh. Without significant estates, he pursued a career in the army and, after service in the Netherlands, he fought with distinction in Canada under the command of General Wolf. Following an injury, he returned to Britain to recuperate and lived for a time on the island of Inch Kenneth where he was visited by Dr Samuel Johnson and James Boswell in October 1773. An account of this visit is given in Chapter 16. In 1775, he returned to North America to take part in the American War of Independence, and he was instrumental in resisting an attempt by Benedict Arnold to capture Quebec. On returning to Britain he was made a Brigadier General and he died at home in Mull in 1783.

With no children, Sir Allan Maclean was succeeded by his fourth cousin Sir Hector Maclean of Morvern. In his early years, Sir Hector also served in the army, but took early retirement and lived peacefully at a residence in Yorkshire. He died in 1818 without an heir, and was succeeded as 24th Chief by his half-brother Sir Fitzroy Maclean. Born in 1770, Sir Fitzroy joined the army when he was 17 years old. By 1803 he had reached the rank of Colonel and was commanding officer of the Batavian Regiment in the Dutch West Indies. After capturing the Danish islands of St Thomas and St John, he was appointed as Governor from 1808 until 1815 when he returned to England

and took up residence in London. By now he was a Lieutenant General. Sir Fitzroy was married in the West Indies and had several children. He died in 1847. During Sir Fitzroy' time, the Duke of Argyll sold the remains of Duart Castle and associated grounds to the Clan Macquarrie.

Sir Fitzroy's son Sir Charles was born in the West Indies in 1798. He was educated at Eton College and in 1816 joined the Scots Guards eventually commanding the 81st Regiment. He also served as military secretary in Gibraltar, and he retired in 1846 as Colonel of the 13th Light Dragoons. Following his marriage, he settled in Kent and had several children. He succeeded as the 25th Chief in 1847. During his time, ownership of the Duart estate changed hands twice. In the 1830s, the Macquarie family sold the property to the Carter-Campbell of Possil family who kept it as a ruin in the grounds of a mansion they constructed in 1858 called Torosay Castle. In 1865, they then sold the property to Arbuthnot Guthrie. Sir Charles died at home in 1883.

Sir Charles's son Sir Fitzroy Maclean was born in Kent in 1835 and became the 26th Chief of the Clan at the age of 48. Like his father he joined the army as a 17 year old and, by 1861, he had been promoted to Lt Colonel of the 13th Light Dragoons. He had a distinguished career in the British Army serving in Bulgaria and the Crimean War. For his outstanding service, in 1897 he was invested as a Companion of the Order of the Bath and, in 1904, he was knighted. In December 1910, he was appointed a deputy lieutenant of Kent. Sir Fitzroy had an abiding interest in the history of the Clan and took it upon himself to restore the family to some vestige of its former position in Mull by reclaiming Duart Castle. After lengthy negotiations, in September 1911 he purchased the property and began the long process of restoration, which included both structural works to re-establish the building as it exists today and the installation of modern services. Having re-established the Clan Maclean presence on Mull he sought reconciliation with previous foes. In 1932 there was a special gathering with members of the Clan Campbell to "bury the hatchet" between the two clans. And on his 100th birthday in 1935 he planted a rowan tree in the castle grounds to ward off evil spirits. Sit Fitzroy married Constance Ackers, and they had five children. He died on 22 November 1936 aged 101.

On the death of Sir Fitzroy, the title of Chief passed to his grandson. Sir Charles Maclean was born in 1916 and saw active service in World War II while serving in the 3rd Battalion Scots Guards. After the war, he became a farmer in Scotland. From 1954 to 1975, he served as Lord Lieutenant of Argyllshire and, in 1959, he was appointed as Chief Scout of the United Kingdom and the Commonwealth. In 1971, he was created as a Life Peer, as Baron Maclean of Duart and Morvern and was subsequently appointed as Lord Chamberlain and Lord High Commissioner. Sir Charles married Elizabeth Mann and they had two children, Sir Lachlan Maclean and his sister Hon Janet Maclean. He died in 1990.

Lord Maclean was succeeded by his son Sir Lachlan who became the 12th Baronet and 28th Chief in 1990. Born in 1942, Sir Lachlan was educated at Eton College and then served in the army. In 1966, he married Mary Gordon, who died in 2007. His eldest son and heir is Malcolm Maclean, who was born in 1972. Sir Lachlan was appointed as Deputy Lieutenant of Argyll and Bute in 1993 with responsibility for the Isle of Mull. Until 2009 he was adjutant of the Royal Company of Archers, the Queen's Bodyguard of Scotland, for which he was made a Commander of the Royal Victorian Order in 1999. In 2010, Sir Lachlan married Rosemary Mayfield. He now lives at Duart Castle, and a brief account of his stewardship of the castle and his leadership of the Clan is provided in Chapter 25. Meanwhile, members of the Clan Maclean still look to Mull as their ancestral home.

The Clan Maclaine of Lochbuie

The name of the Clan Maclaine of Lochbuie is translated in Gaelic as *Mac'ill-Eathain Locchabuide*.[17] While sharing a common heritage with the Clan Maclean of Duart, the clan also claims descent from Maurice Fitzgerald, an Anglo-Norman who moved from Ireland to settle in Scotland to found both the Clan Maclean and the Clan Mackenzie. The Clan then traces an identical lineage to the Macleans of Duart from Gillean-na-Taughe (Gillean of the Battle-Axe) through to the 4th Chief of the Clan Maclean John Dubh who had five sons including Lachlan who would marry the daughter of John the Lord of the Isles and his brother Hector. At this point the two brothers were granted lands in Mull and Hector received domain over the Lochbuie lands in the south of Mull.

Hector Maclean (known as "the Astute") took up his entitlement in about 1370, and in around 1400 set about the construction of Moy Castle, a tower house at the head of Loch Buie, which would remain as the family home until the 18th century. Further information on this monument is provided in Chapter 25. In the years that followed, the Clan held lands on the islands of Scarba, Jura, and Tiree. They also held territory on the mainland in Morvern, and Locheil. Although of lesser status and power than his brother at Duart, Hector was a well-respected Chief who sat on the Council of the Isles as did subsequent chiefs of Lochbuie until the Lordship was abolished in 1493.

On Hector's death, he was succeeded by his son Murdoch, and we have little information about him or his successors the 3rd (John) and 4th (Hector) Chiefs. However, Iain Og the 5th Chief who was born in 1470 figures in various national annals and was a friend of King James IV. This led to his involvement in various battles. He is also noted for his dispute with one of his younger sons, Ewan. In the late 1530s, Ewan was living on a crannog in Loch Sgubhain which is about six kilometres north of Lochbuie, and his wife was constantly pressing her husband to obtain more land from his father. This led to a dispute which ended in a pitched battle at Glenn Cannir with Ewan supported by Hector Maclean of Duart. Sadly, Ewan was decapitated, but his horse with the headless body continued galloping to the dismay of all those present. The horse was eventually stopped and Ewan's body was buried on the island of Iona, but the episode haunts the more delicate minded to this day.

Iain Og Maclean died in 1537, and the succession was disputed. Initially, in 1539 Iain's brother Murdoch of Scallastle claimed the title of chief and Iain's son (also called Murdoch) fled to Ireland. However, in 1540 the son returned to successfully reclaim his inheritance and in 1542 the lands were consolidated into the Barony of Moy. In the latter part of the 16th century, Murdoch would support the Clan Macdonald in their continuing resistance to the King's attempt to enforce control over the Hebrides.

Little is known about the 7th and 8th Chiefs (Iain Mor and Hector although the latter is reputed to be the first to use the spelling Maclaine). The 9th Chief, Hector Odhar received a royal charter for Lochbuie from King James VI in 1612. Avowed Catholics, the Clan was on the same side as their cousins the Macleans of Duart in the Wars of the Three Kingdoms, supporting the royalist cause of King Charles I, and Murdoch Mor, the 10th Chief, fought in the army led by the Marquess of Montrose in 1645. Following the defeat, his lands were temporarily forfeited although they were reinstated in 1661 following the restoration. On his death in 1662, he was succeeded by his brother Lachlan who supported the Macleans of Duart in their attempt to hold onto their estates. The 12th chief, Hector, was the victor at the first battle of the Jacobite campaign of 1689, and also took part in the successful Battle of Killiecrankie. However, when the rebellion failed in 1690, Hector was forced to surrender Moy Castle to the Earl of Argyll. He reclaimed it in 1697 even as the Macleans of Duart were being evicted from their lands.

In the next half century, the Clan largely avoided national affairs and, in 1745, they determined not to join the Jacobite forces. This spared them the aftermath of Culloden. Later, many members of the clan became Presbyterians. In 1752, John the 17th Chief built Moy House where he was visited by Dr Johnson and James Boswell in 1773. (This is not to be confused with the later Georgian style Lochbuie House completed in 1790). Later in the 18th century, many Maclaines participated in the American War of Independence with many members of the Clan settling in North Carolina.

In the 19th century, a number of the Chiefs served as officers in various regiments of the army. Murdoch the 23rd Chief was a noted war correspondent for the Times newspaper during the Franco-Prussian War and was awarded the Iron Cross! Sadly, in 1920 the 24th Chief Kenneth Maclaine got into financial difficulties and lost ownership of the estate. A subsequent account of the ownership of the estate is provided in Chapter 25.

The current and 26th Chief of the Clan Maclaine and Baron of Moy is Lord Gillean Maclaine who currently lives in KwaZulu-Natal, South Africa.

Clan MacQuarrie

The Clan MacQuarrie is one of the oldest clans of the Scottish Highlands and Islands.[18] Its ancestry has been traced back to the 9th century and King Kenneth MacAlpine, the first King of Scots in CE 843, with the clan being one of the seven Alpin families descended from the kings of Dál Riata.[19] A surviving 15th century manuscript (MS1467) describes the descent of the clan from *Fingon* and *Anrias* (also an ancestor of the Clan Gregor). This document provides a listing of antecedents going back to Ferch Fota in the 9th century, together with a reasonably reliable succession of chiefs for the period from the mid 12th to the late 14th century.[20] The earliest chief for which there is a record is Aibertach who died in 1164 and had an association with the Somerled family. His grandson *Guaire*, who lived in the early 13th century is accepted as the progenitor and first in a line of 16 chiefs. Confirming the emerging status of the clan, early sources indicate that in those times the chief was entitled to be buried in the Reilig Odhrain (St Ronan's cemetery) on Iona. This was attested in the 1690s by the author Martin Martin who actually found a tombstone in the cemetery with the MacQuarrie name (since eroded away).

Whatever the roots, the Clan MacQuarrie is strongly associated with the island of Ulva which sits in the mouth of Loch na Keal. It is difficult to say when exactly the clan became the dominant family, although the early 13th century seems to the most likely date. In any event, right through to the 18th century the clan not only owned Ulva but also, at various times, one or more of the neighbouring islands of Gometra, Staffa, Little Colonsay, and Inch Kenneth, together with adjacent territory on the mainland of Mull. A history of Ulva through to modern times is provided in Chapter 19.

There are relatively few records of the early chiefs of the clan, although it is likely that the 3rd Chief Turcall participated in the Battle of Largs during the hostilities between Scotland and Norway in the 13th century. It is also known that, following the Scottish annexation of the Norse Kingdom of the Isles in 1266, the Clan MacQuarrie were strong supporters of the Lords of the Isles. During the Wars of Scottish Independence in the 14th century, they were recognised as fierce fighters and, although they may have initially supported the Balliol cause through their association with the Clan MacDougall, they were certainly fighting with King Robert the Bruce at the Battle of Bannockburn in 1314. Thereafter, the Clan consistently supported the Clan Macdonald and are noted for their contribution to the Lordship's victory against the royal house of Stewart at the Battle of Harlaw in 1411. As respected members of the Lordship's community, the chief became a member of the Lordship of the Isles Council alongside the chiefs of other clans from Mull.

In the second half of the 15th century, when the Lord of the Isles was under considerable pressure from King James III, the leader of the Clan MacQuarrie was John and he was a stalwart supporter of the Macdonald cause. When he died in 1473, he was succeeded by his son Dunslaff the 8th Chief. Dunslaff will almost certainly have played a part in the Battle of Bloody Bay in the 1480s and was the chief of the clan when the position of the Lord of the Isles was abolished in 1493. With the fall of the Macdonalds, the MacQuarries gained a certain degree of independence, but increasingly sided with their powerful neighbours the Clan Maclean of Duart. However, through marriage, they also maintained cordial relations with the Macleans of Lochbuie. In the 16th century, their association with the Macleans of Duart led them to be intermittently involved in disputes with their previous liege lords the Macdonalds, and 10th Chief Hector was bound over to keep the peace by King James VI. In the Wars of the Three Kingdoms, the clan joined the Macleans in support of King Charles I and remained loyalists throughout the difficult times of the Civil War and the Commonwealth. Following the abortive arrival of King Charles II, many MacQuarrie clansmen including the 13th Chief Alan MacQuarrie were slaughtered at the Battle of Inverkeithing in 1651 when Cromwell's army destroyed royalist forces. With Ulva being in a relatively remote area of the Highlands, the clan did not suffer retribution, but in the years that followed the clan went into a slow decline as they saw their allies in Duart Castle being evicted by the Earl of Argyll. While some of his cousins from Ormaig in the south of Ulva were participants in the 1715 rebellion, he did not get involved. However, he was suspected of being a Jacobite sympathiser. On his death, he was succeeded by his son John of whom little is known. He in turn was succeeded by his son Lachlan who would be the last of the line.

Lachlan the 16th Chief was born in 1715 and grew up in troubled times. As a young adult, he married Alice Maclean who was the daughter of Donald the 5th Laird of Torloisk. They had eight children but none left a male issue. Famously, it was he who was in residence when James Boswell and Dr Samuel Johnston visited Ulva in 1773 by which time Lachlan was in his late 50s. Boswell described the MacQuarrie residence as "mean", but also recorded that Lachlan was intelligent, polite, and very much a man of the world, whilst also being heavily in debt which meant that his property would need to be sold.

As noted by Boswell, in 1777 Lachlan did indeed sell his estates and, to eke out a living, in his sixties he joined the army. On his retirement in 1785, he took up residence on Little Colonsay, and subsequently lived at Gribun and finally Ballygown. He died in 1818 at the age of 103 and the long line of chiefs died with him. However, this was by no means the end of the clan. Lachlan had eight children, including four sons. Three died without issue, but his third son Donald had a daughter called Agnes who was married in 1816 at Holy Trinity Church, Liverpool, to Captain William Danson. In the 1820s, Danson took commission as Master of the *Thisbe of Liverpool* and in 1824 this ship set sail for Quebec. Sadly it was wrecked and all the family perished except a daughter named Thisbe. While the title of chief has laid dormant since 1818, her descendants who live in North America would have a claim.

Finally, there is one last member of the clan who arguably outshone all who went before him, Lachlan Macquarie. His father Lachlan was a distant cousin of the 16th Chief and his mother Margaret was the sister of Murdoch Maclaine the 19th Chieftain of Lochbuie. Lachlan was born on 31 January in 1762 in the Ormaig district of Ulva. He was brought up on the family farm at a time when the island was a relatively prosperous place. In his early teens, the family moved to Oskamull on the mainland of Mull where the family were tenants of the Macleans of Torloisk.

While the place of Lachlan's education is uncertain, like many young men of his time, in 1777 he volunteered to join the army and became an ensign in the 84th Royal Highland Emigrants, a corps that was raised by Lt Colonel Allan Maclean, the brother of the laird of Torloisk. This was one of several regiments formed after the Jacobite rebellions that sought to utilise the fighting qualities of highlanders in building the British Empire. His membership of this regiment took him to North America and, although he saw action at sea, he did not take part in any significant land battles. In 1781 he was commissioned as a First Lieutenant in the 1st Battalion 71st Regiment of Fraser's Highlanders and then, after a stint in Jamaica, in 1784 he returned to Scotland with his regiment disbanding.

For a while, Lachlan took up a job as factor on the Lochbuie estates of his mother's family but three years later, and somewhat in debt, he joined the 77th Regiment of Foot (the East Middlesex) for service in India, with the patronage of his mentor the now General Allan Maclean. In 1788, he was posted to Bombay in India and was promoted several times as he became active in wars with the locals. In the process he saved £1,000 which was more than enough to pay off his accumulated debts. His new found solvency enabled him to get married and, in 1793, he wed Jane Jarvis who was a daughter of Thomas Jarvis the former Chief Justice of Antigua.

Continuing to live in India, Macquarie was active in several campaigns against the Dutch, but then his life was hit by tragedy. While he was in what is now Sri Lanka, his wife contracted consumption. He returned to Bombay and, in the hope of achieving a recovery, in 1796 they took a boat trip to China. However, within 14 days Jane died in Macao and he returned to India to bury her remains in Bombay.

Shortly after his wife's death, Lachlan was promoted to brevet-major and in 1800 he was appointed as Military Adviser to the Governor of Bombay, Jonathan Duncan. Then, in 1801, he joined General Baird in a force despatched to Egypt to oust the Napoleonic French. After a successful campaign he remained in Egypt for a while as commanding officer of the residual forces before again returning to India.

Despite his exploits in Egypt, in the immediate aftermath of his wife's death, Lachlan was disconsolate and countenanced a slow decline into obscurity. However, in times that were increasingly tough for ordinary clansmen, he decided to commit himself to helping members of his kin and was eventually responsible for recruiting into the army a large number of young men of the Clans MacQuarrie and Maclean. Having inherited a significant sum from his wife (£6,000), he also turned his mind to restoring the fortunes of his clan. At the time, his brother Charles was also in India on military duty and in 1801 they established a plan to acquire land in Mull. Shortly afterwards, Charles was wounded in battle and returned to Mull. On arrival, he discovered that land in the Lochbuie district owned by his uncle and mentor Murdoch Maclaine was up for sale. Given his now substantial wealth, Lachlan gave instructions to Charles to acquire 10,000 acres on their joint behalf. The property ran from the shores of Loch na Keal across to the Glenforsa River and down to Loch Spelve on the edge of Glen More. Lachlan took the larger portion with a property that stretched from Gruline and Killiechronan on the shores of Loch na Keal, across to Salen. Charles took a smaller estate called Glenforsa which ran from Pennygown down to Loch Spelve.

In early 1804 Lachlan returned to London where he was appointed as Assistant Adjutant General of the London district and a lieutenant-colonel. Shortly afterwards, having been absent from Britain since 1787, he was given two months leave and in June he travelled back to Mull to take possession of his part of the new estate. Sadly, on arriving at his uncle's home he found that Murdoch Maclaine was seriously ill. Following Murdoch's death, on 16 July he and his brother formally took possession of their new family estate and at a subsequent dinner he announced that he had decided to name his property *Jarvisfield* after his deceased wife. His brother named his estate Glenforsa.[21] In the aftermath of Murdoch's death, the younger sister of his wife Jane, Elizabeth Campbell of Airds, visited to help with looking after the Maclaine family children. She and Lachlan began what would turn into a serious relationship.

In 1805, Macquarie returned to India for a brief tour of duty as an officer in the 73rd Highland Regiment of Foot, before leaving the sub-continent for the last time. He travelled back to Britain overland, delivering various despatches along the way, and visiting both the Middle East and St Petersburg in Russia. Arriving back in Britain in 1807, he rendezvoused with his now betrothed Elizabeth Campbell and they were married in Devon. They then travelled north where he re-joined his regiment in Perth.

At this point in his life, events would take a momentous turn. In 1808, trouble was brewing in the new colony of New South Wales in Australia. Lachlan's commanding officer George Harris was selected to replace the deposed Governor William Bligh with Macquarie as Lieutenant Governor. Then, when Harris got cold feet about being sent to Australia, he volunteered for the position of Governor. Interestingly, in support of his application, he wrote a number of letters to prominent people including Sir Joseph Banks who had stayed with his family on a visit to Mull in 1772 when Lachlan was 10 years old. In 1809, Macquarie was appointed as Governor of New South Wales, and thus began his last great adventure.

In May 1809, Macquarie, his new wife and his regiment set sail for Australia, on a voyage that took seven months travelling via Rio de Janeiro and Cape Town. They arrived in late December and, on 1 January 1810, he was sworn in for an initial period of eight years. As he had done earlier in his career, he was accompanied by several relatives from Mull who would serve in a number of roles. In March 1814, he also added to the population with his wife giving birth to their son Lachlan!

Macquarie served as Governor of NSW with distinction and would eventually be appointed as a General. During his time, he would implement many reforms, including the introduction of local currency (Spanish dollars were converted into two coins by punching out the central section to form what was called *the holey dollar* and *the dump)*, establishment of a local bank, introduction of a new tax system, and significant other changes to administration of the colony.[22] He also set about implementing an ambitious programme of public works, including the construction of a new army barracks, a hospital, a road to Parramatta, and over 200 other projects. In the meantime, he endeavoured to improve the productivity of the agricultural sector, although his efforts were undermined by intermittent drought. He also travelled widely, encouraged exploration of the hinterland, and named many new settlements, one of which took his own name - Port Macquarie.[23]

Under instructions from the British government, one of Macquarie's main jobs in NSW was to address what was considered in London to be the low level of public morality. To this end, he recruited new policemen and instituted a range of regulations including a ban on co-habiting, a requirement to observe the Sabbath, and rules for the operation of public houses. He established a number of schools, enabled time-served convicts to become full citizens, and attempted to soften policy on dealing with aboriginal people. Also, on 12 December 1817, after receiving copies of maps prepared by the explorer Matthew Flinders in 1804, he recommended to the Colonial Office that Australia should be adopted as the name for the continent and this was eventually confirmed in 1824.

Macquarie's time in Australia was not all plain sailing. His enlightened view on convicts, and inclination to appoint judges with similar views, stirred up considerable opposition from non-convict settlers, which eventually found its way back to London. This led to the establishment of an investigation into what was alleged to be his lax regime, the Bigge's Inquiry. With the outcome of the Inquiry pending, in 1818 Macquarie tendered his resignation, but this went unacknowledged. In the next three years, he continued to serve and made two further attempts to resign. Finally, in late 1821, the resignation was accepted, and Thomas Brisbane was appointed to take over as Governor. At the same time, London decided to significantly change the governance system.[24]

In February 1822 Macquarie left NSW and began the long journey back to Britain. In the meantime, his opponents in Parliament were attempting to sanction him for his alleged maladministration and deprive him of his pension. On arrival back in London, the Bigge's Inquiry was still under way and he returned to Scotland. In the early part of 1823, he then took leave and the family undertook a grand tour of Europe during which he began to prepare a full record of his time as NSW Governor. In July 1823, he attempted to publish this document but this was blocked by his opponents.

Fortunately, he had some powerful allies in the government and, in 1824, attempts to sanction him were abandoned and he was awarded a pension of £1,000 with a letter of commendation for his Australian service.

Sadly, now aged 62 years, Macquarie did not get to enjoy his retirement. In June, whilst still in London, he fell ill and he died there on 1 July 1824. His funeral, with a parade down Regent Street, was attended by the Duke of Wellington, the Duke of Argyll, and many other notable people from Mull and Scotland. Afterwards, his body was taken by boat to Mull, and he was buried in the Mausoleum that stands in a small enclosure near his home in Gruline. His property was inherited by his son who died childless and ownership passed out of the family.

Finally, before he died, Lachlan did harbour thoughts of further acquisition of lands in Mull, including the re-possession of Ulva which had been sold by his kinsman and the last Chief of the Clan in 1777. He did not live to realise that dream, but his brother Charles did acquire Ulva and other traditional lands next to Loch na Keal in 1825. Sadly for the MacQuarrie kin, faced with significant financial pressures, this ownership only extended for ten years with the property sold after his death in 1835. The subsequent history of Ulva is provided in Chapter 19.

Clan McKinnon

The MacKinnons claim their descent from the royal family of Kenneth McAlpine.[25] The clan rallying cry of "Cumnich Bas Alpin" or "Remember the death of Alpin" refers to the great-grandson of Kenneth, who was slain by Bruch, King of the Picts, in 837. His son and the 4th Chief Fingon is hailed as the progenitor of the clan. The name is an Anglicisation of the Gaelic Mac Fhionghuin which means "fair born".

Reference to the Clan in written records emerges in the 14th century during the Scottish Wars of Independence, and the McKinnons are noted for having given King Robert I refuge after his defeat at the Battle of Carrick. After the victory at the Battle of Bannockburn in 1314 they were rewarded with land on the Isle of Skye. The Mackinnon chiefs then lived at Dunringall Castle and were styled "of Strathardale" and also owned a broch at Dunakin which commanded the narrow sound between Skye and the mainland. Even in the early days they were an enterprising family and, according to folk law, from Dunakin they ran a heavy chain across the sound and levied a charge on all passing ships!

It is not known when the McKinnons gained control of the territory that they held in Mull but, at various times, they held the Ardmeanach peninsula between Loch Scridain and Loch na Keal, and the land referred to as Mishnish in the north west of the island. They also had a close connection with the religious community on Iona and this is reflected in their Coat of Arms which bears the hand of St Columba holding the Cross. Several "MacKinnons" were Benedictine Abbots of Iona. However, their hold in competition with the Macleans was at times tenuous and, in what was one of their final skirmishes, in 1400 the two clans met in the Battle of Doire Shuaig which is near Gribun in Ardmeanach. After losing the battle, members of the clan sheltered in a cave now named after them, but the Macleans smoked them out.26 Some members of the McKinnon party then fled by boat to Staffa and the clan surrendered significant lands. Eventually during the 16th century, with Iona Abbey abandoned during the Reformation, the Mcleans drove them out of Mull completely.

Despite their demise in Mull, the Clan McKinnon was long known for its loyalty to the Stuart dynasty. During the Wars of the Three Kingdoms, the McKinnons followed the Marquess of Montrose, and took part in the Battle of Inverlochy on 2 February 1645. The chief of the clan, Lachlan MacKinnon, also raised a regiment in aid of King Charles II and took part in the ill-fated Battle of Worcester in 1651 and was knighted for his services. Subsequently, they joined the Jacobite rebellions. In 1715, 150 McKinnons fought with the Macdonalds of Sleat at the Battle of Sherrifmuir and afterwards McKinnon lands in Skye were forfeit. Lachlan McKinnon was pardoned in 1727, but then again answered the call in 1745, when he and 200 McKinnon clansmen was present at the Battle of Culloden. Afterwards, tradition has it that the MacKinnons assisted Charles Edward Stuart in his escape by concealing him in a cave somewhere in the Hebrides before he eventually escaped to France. Lachlan Mackinnon was later captured by Government troops and spent a year in confinement before being put on trial with his wife in London. He was eventually pardoned because of his advanced age, and it is said that, upon leaving the courtroom, the Attorney General asked him *"If King George were in your power, as you have been in his, what would you do?"* Lachlan is reported to have replied *"I would do to him, as he has this day done to me; I would send him back to his own country"*. Because of the chief's support of the Jacobite rebellion the lands controlled by the clan were eventually confined to property on Skye.

The last chief in direct line of succession died unmarried in 1808, and was succeeded by a cousin William Alexander Mackinnon (1784–1870), who became thirty-third chief. A later attempt by the McKinnons of Corriechatachan (a cadet branch) to claim the chiefship generated a great deal of controversy and a certain amount of local support in Skye. Subsequently, Francis Alexander Mackinnon was recognised as the legitimate and 35th chief. Francis was a sportsman and for many years was the longest lived first-class cricketer.[27]

The current chief of the clan is Madam Anne Gunhild Mackinnon of Mackinnon, 38th Chief and the clan continues to have a presence in south eastern Skye.

Clan Campbell (The Argylls)

Unlike many of the other clans featured in this book, the origins of the clan appear to lie in the Brittonic tribes of Strathclyde who were left after the departure of the Romans. The earliest chief is Arthur who lived in the 6th century and over the next 500 years there are 17 successors in line including the first to be named Archibald who lived between 1041 and 1091. In the early part of their existence they seem to have been based in the eastern part of Scotland with ancestors who were Knights of Menstrie which is to the north-east of Stirling.

However, in the 13th century, Sir Colin Campbell (who is recognised as the 4th Chief of the Clan Campbell) married an heiress whose dowry included the Lordship of Lochow (Loch Awe) located in the province of Lorn. Taking up residence in Innis Chonnell Castle, Sir Colin would be the first of six Lords of

Lochow and is known as Colin the Great (in Gaelic, Cailean Mor). Initially, he was a lesser player to the dominant Clan MacDougall who were Lords of Lorn. However, during the dispute between the Balliol and Bruce families this was an uneasy relationship. At the time, Sir Alexander MacDougall had allied himself with King John Balliol and in 1293 he was appointed as Sheriff of Argyll. In enforcing this position, he found himself in dispute with both the Clan Macdonald who had recently assumed the Lordship of the Isles, and the Campbells who supported the Bruce family. As a consequence, in the Battle of Red Ford in 1295, Sir Colin Campbell was killed.

After this setback, and with the fall of the Balliols, the Campbells found themselves on the right side of history. They supported the Bruce family and, through prudent marriages, they proceeded to acquire lands, titles and growing power. In 1285, Sir Colin's son Sir Neil Campbell married King Robert I's sister and, after the Battle of Bannockburn in 1314, he was granted lands forfeited by the MacDougalls including the Lordship of Lorn within the Lordship of the Isles.

In the next two hundred years the Campbells would emerge as one of the most powerful families in Scotland, dominant in Argyll and capable of wielding a wider influence across Scotland and throughout the Western Isles. During this period, Campbells persistently supported the crown, and the family's royal links were consolidated with the marriage in around 1425-1430 of the 9th Chief Sir Duncan Campbell to Lady Marjorie Stewart who was the daughter of King Robert II's son, Robert Stewart, 1st Duke of Albany. In the early 1430s, the Chief's family built a castle at Inverary on the shores of Loch Fyne, and in 1445 Sir Duncan was created as Lord Campbell.28 Following his death in 1453, in 1457 his son Lord Colin Campbell was created the 1st Earl of Argyll. In 1493 after the abolition of the Lordship of the Isles, the Campbell lords became natural successors to the Clan Macdonald as leaders in the Hebrides and bastions of Gaelic culture. This change in the power structure also became a driver for the traditional enmity between Campbells and Macdonalds.

In the troubled 16th century, the Campbells had their ups and downs. In 1513, the 2nd Earl Archibald Campbell was killed at the disastrous Battle of Flodden Field and, following the abdication of Queen Mary in 1567, in

1568 the 5th Earl commanded her forces at the Battle of Langside. He was soundly defeated by the forces representing the Queen's young son James VI. For a time, support for the Queen set the Campbells on the back foot, but the family then switched allegiances and embraced the Protestant cause. As a result, the 7th Earl Archibald was appointed at the young age of 18 to command royal forces to counter a Catholic rebellion. As we have seen earlier, in 1594 his army was defeated by a Catholic army led by the Clan Gordon. However, Archibald survived and the success of the Catholics was short-lived as a larger royal army later dispersed their forces.

In the 17th century, for a time, Campbell support for the Stuart dynasty brought them significant rewards. In 1607, the 7th Earl was granted the former Macdonald lands of Kintyre. And in 1615 Archibald the 8th Earl was allowed to purchase parts of the Isle of Islay which had previously belonged to the Macleans of Duart. In the Civil War that eventually engulfed Scotland, Archibald backed the Scottish government forces of the Covenanters and in 1641 the 8th Earl was granted the title of Marquess. In 1645, at the Battle of Inverlochy, he led the government forces against a royalist army led by the Marquess of Montrose which mainly comprised members of the Clan Macdonald, Clan Maclean, and some Irish mercenaries. The royalists won and, after the battle, Montrose and the Macleans burnt Castle Campbell (near Dollar in Clackmannanshire) although it remained in Campbell hands. In the wake of the battle others raided Campbell territory and, in return, the Campbells attacked Mull and for a time held Duart Castle. Eventually, King Charles I was defeated and executed and, for a time, the Campbells were at peace. However, with the restoration of the monarchy in 1660, the chickens would come home to roost. Archibald the 8th Earl was tried for high treason, and in 1661 he was beheaded. Subsequently, in 1663, his son Archibald the 9th Earl was reinstated and he resumed the family's vengeance on the Clan Maclean, invading Mull and taking Duart Castle. However, in 1681 the 9th Earl then made a fatal miscalculation by supporting the Protestant Monmouth rebellion against King James VII. He was captured and tried for high treason with all lands forfeit. Like his father, he too was beheaded.

The downfall of the Argylls did not last long. In 1685, King James VII was forced to abdicate and the Protestant Argylls came back into favour. In 1685, Archibald the 10th Earl was reinstated and by stealth he sought to finally get the family's revenge on the Clan Maclean. He carefully bought up the mounting debts of the Maclean Chief and in 1692 he evicted him from Duart Castle. The Macleans were despatched for more than 200 years and, for much of that period, the Argylls would hold sway in most parts of Mull. As his crowning glory, for services rendered in 1701 Archibald the 10th Earl was created the 1st Duke of Argyll.

From 1701, and for the next two hundred years, the Dukes of Argyll were frequently involved in the government of what became Great Britain including the defeat of the Jacobite rebellions of 1715 and 1745. On 23 October 1715, John Campbell, the 2nd Duke routed a detachment of rebels in what was known as the Skirmish of Dunfermline. A month later the British Government forces, including men from the Clan Campbell, fought and defeated the Jacobites at the Battle of Sheriffmuir. In 1725, as Jacobite sentiment continued to simmer, members of the Clan Campbell joined a militia of Highlanders loyal to the crown colloquially called the *Black Watch*.29 During the Jacobite rising of 1745, the Clan Campbell continued their support for the British Government. At the Battle of Falkirk Government forces were defeated, but shortly afterwards the Campbells played a leading role in successfully withstanding the Siege of Fort William. They then played a major part at the Battle of Culloden in 1746 when the Jacobites were finally defeated. Government forces included four companies from the Campbell of Argyll Militia, three companies from Loudon's Highlanders who were under the command of Lieutenant Colonel John Campbell, and one company from the 43rd Highlanders who were under the command of Captain Dugald Campbell of Auchrossan.

In the years that followed, the clan went from strength to strength and served with distinction as significant leaders in the building of the British Empire. Two Dukes were Field Marshals and one was a Four-Star General. In the middle of the 18th century, the family built the current Inverary Castle, and in the 19th century, George Campbell the 8th Duke would become a peer of the United Kingdom and a Cabinet Minister in the British government. In the second half of the century, his son Lord Lorn married Queen Victoria's daughter and was eventually appointed Governor General of Canada.

Despite their long connection with Mull, in recent times the family has gradually disposed of many of their local property, with residual holdings on the Ross of Mull, on the north of Loch na Keal, and at Calgary. The current and 13th Duke of Argyll, Torquhil Campbell, was born in 1968 and lives intermittently in Inverary Castle. His son and heir, the Marquess of Lorn, Archie Campbell, was born in 2004 and was a sometime page to Queen Elizabeth II.

The Beaton Family

Although not a clan in the traditional sense, there is one more family that are worthy of mention as residents of Mull.30 The Beatons originated in Béthune in France.[31] In the early Middle Ages, they settled in Ireland where they became a family of hereditary physicians. In Ireland, they were known as the Clan Macbeth and during the 14th century several of them migrated to Scotland. By the 16th century, most of them had adopted the name Beaton and, through four centuries, there are known to have been at least 70 physicians with the name in Scotland.

Although the earliest record of the family in Scotland is a branch living in Dumfries, it is known that they mostly settled in the Highlands and Islands. In particular, in the early 14th century Agnes the daughter of the head of the Irish Clan O'Cathan married Angus Og Macdonald, and one or more Beatons accompanied her as part of her retinue.32 Thereafter, various family members took on the role of community physician, not only to several clans in the Highlands and Islands including the Clan Maclean in Mull, but also to a succession of Scottish monarchs from King Robert I in the early 14th century to King Charles I in the 17th century.[33] The last of the family died in 1714.

There are manifest stories about the medical feats of the Beaton family. They were noted for maintaining records about their sources of ancient medical knowledge, and their treatments (essentially "case notes"), which were supplemented through regular contact with the medical profession on the continent, They carried Gaelic translations of their papers with them as an attachment to their clothing to facilitate easy reference. Some twenty-five Beaton manuscripts have survived, including Lilium Medicinae from 16th century, and are kept at the National Library of Scotland (formerly known as The Advocates Library).[34]

Members of the family eventually settled in Mull and, after proving themselves worthy physicians, in the 1570s the chief of the Clan Maclean Lachlan Mor awarded Andrew Beaton rights to lands at Pennycross to be available as long as the family continued to provide a service to the clan. The property is located to the west of Pennyghael. This presence began a dynasty of physicians through several generations with the members of the family travelling to the continent for education and training, and establishing a local physic garden with all manner of herbs.

The role of physician did not necessarily fall to the eldest son, but to the brightest and most suitable member of the family in each generation. The last of the official physicians to the Clan Maclean was Dr John Beaton who in the late 17th century served the 20th Chief Sir John. When the Earl of Argyll evicted Sir John, the family retained control of the land at Pennycross, and succeeding family members continued to provide medical advice to the local community although not all were trained physicians. Eventually the Maclean family re-asserted their title to Pennycross turning the Beatons into tenants, and in 1761 Neal Beaton took the matter to court and won the case for possession. He then sold it to another doctor, Dr Alex Maclean, the same man who is mentioned in Boswell's account of his visit to Mull in 1773!

Evidence of the role of the Beatons endures to this day. The Beaton house has not survived, but the location of the property and its Physic Garden on the southern banks of Loch Scridain is known with a small safe mooring place (Port na Birlinne) where patients used to gain access to the physician's home. In the days of the medical practice, the mooring was marked by an ancient cross sitting on a headland. Recently, thanks to a project conducted through the "Adopt a Monument" programme with funding from the RCAHMS, this cross (known to local people as the Beaton Cross or the Physicians' Cross) can be found in a small commemorative plot not far from Pennyghael.[35]

ENDNOTES

1   In Gaelic, Malcolm means son of Columba.

2   A fictionalised account of Lachlan's life is presented in the book The Isles of the Sea by Sir Fitzroy Maclean (not a Chief), published by Collins in 1986.

3   Arriving in 1348, in the next three hundred years, the Black Death would return to Scotland on several occasions. The final outbreak was in the 1640s.

4   Lachlan and Mary were just within the four degrees of consanguinity that constituted a barrier to marriage under canon law. With the loss of population because of the plague, the rules of consanguinity were relaxed because there were too few members of the nobility to ensure continuity of the line. Mary's father John Macdonald had also received the same dispensation in 1350.

5   The Clan Maclean of Duart motto is Virtue Mine Honour.

6   The word Gallowglass comes from the Irish Gaelic gallóglaigh and means foreign warriors.

7   After the Reformation, the monks left Iona with the Abbey falling into ruins. The Macleans of Duart then held Iona until evicted by the Argylls in 1648.

8   Angus Macdonald was married to Lachlan's sister, Mary.

9   Typical of the time, this was a battle royale in terms of clan enmities, with the largely Protestant clans of the Campbells, Macleans, Mackintosh, Murray, Stewart, Forbes, McIlvray, Grant and Macneil, pitched against the Catholic clans of Gordon, Cameron, Hay and Comyn.

10   Eventually James would return to London where he lived on a royal pension until his death in 1626.

11   Rights to land in Canada, which for many years were held by France, were granted by King James VI to the Scottish explorer Sir William Alexander in 1621. He named the territory Nova Scotia, and control of this land changed hands several times before becoming part of the British Dominion of Canada. The title of Baron of Nova Scotia is extant.

12   Montrose is a town in eastern Scotland, and the home of the Clan Graham. Patrick Graham became the first Lord in 1445 during the time of King James II, and William Graham was created an Earl in 1503. In 1644, Jamie Graham was created the 1st Marquess of Montrose by King Charles I in recognition of his role in leading Royalist armies in the Civil War. James Graham, the 4th Marquess was created a Duke in 1707 as a reward for supporting the Act of Union. Ironically, in the 20th century, James the 6th Duke was the leader of the Home Rule Scottish Party founded in 1932 which was one of the main groups that formed the Scottish National Party.

13   This view of Sir John is recorded in a memoir by Ewen Cameron of Lochiel who was the Chief of the Clan Cameron and a Stuart loyalist. According to Joe Currie, Ewen was known as the "Ulysses of the Highlands" and killed the last wolf to be recorded in the British Isles in 1680.

14   It is said that some stones were taken to Torloisk by Donald the Laird.

15   Jacobite peerages are not recognised by either the English or Scottish systems.

16   Sir Allan Maclean was the son of Donald Maclean the 4th Laird of Brolass.

17   Like the Clan MacDougall, the Motto is Vincere Vel Mori (Conquer or Die).

18   It should be noted that the accepted spelling for the name of the clan is MacQuarrie. However, in modern history, there are other spellings including Macquarie such as in the famed Major General Lachlan Macquarie.

19   The Clan Motto is Turris fortis mihi Deus (God is to me a tower of strength).

20   Some of this material is drawn from the book entitled Clan MacQuarrie: a History by R W Munro and Alan MacQuarrie the 2nd Edition of which was published by NWMCWC in 2023.

21   Charles Macquarie's land approximates to the north western section of the current much larger Glenforsa estate.

22   Eventually, in 1825, the British government mandated that the British Pound would be the only legal tender in Australia.

23   Several places were also named after his wife, including Mrs Macquarie's Chair (a sandstone outcrop on a peninsula in Sydney Harbour, carved into the shape of a bench by convicts in 1810) and Elizabeth Street in Hobart.

24   The 1823 New South Wales Act provided for the crown to appoint a Legislative Council of local residents to advise future governors, and the establishment of a new court system which shifted

legal deliberations towards compliance with statute law rather than relying on common law. The Legislative Council had its first meeting in 1824.

25   The clan motto is Audentes Fortuna Duvat (Fortune favours the brave).

26   McKinnon's Cave is the second longest sea cave on the west coast of Scotland.

27   This record was beaten by New Zealand cricketer Eric Tindill who died in 2010 aged 99.

28   There are no remains of the original castle, with the current Inverary Castle constructed in the 18th century following the creation of the dukedom.

29   The Black Watch probably got its name from the colour of their uniforms. Other clans involved were the Clans Fraser of Lovat, Munro and Grant.

30   In the section which follows, I am indebted to both John Clare and Christine Leach for alerting me to the contribution of this family.

31   The family should not be confused with and had no connection to the religious scholars who were prominent members of the Catholic clergy during the 16th century as mentioned in other chapters of this book.

32   Angus Og later became the Chief of the Clan Macdonald who were eventually Lords of the Isles.

33   A Beaton family member is recorded as physician to the Lord of the Isles (the Macdonalds on Islay), the Macleans of Duart, the MacLeods of Skye, the Frasers of Lovat (Inverness), and the Monroes of Foulis (Ross).

34   This is available through the Library's ISOS (Irish Scripts on Screen) system.

35   RCAHMS is the Royal Commission on the Ancient and Historical Monuments of Scotland.

DEMISE OF THE CLANS

Much has been written about the causes for the decline of the clan-based society. Some historians have sought to focus on the defeat of Jacobite forces at the Battle of Culloden in 1746, with the subsequent legislation to outlaw many aspects of clan life including the use of the Gaelic language. However, as Professor Sir Thomas Devine has noted, Culloden was but the culmination of a long process over several centuries rather than a determining event.[1] The reality, particularly for a place like Mull, is far more complex.

There are a range of factors that drove the evolution of Highlands and Islands society from the time that the clan became the basic unit of communal organisation in the Middle Ages. For the Hebrides, with its long period of autonomy beyond the reach of central power, the clan and customs of *dùthchas* survived as the dominant basis for the day-to-day existence of the average person for a good deal longer than in most other parts of Scotland. For Mull, the main historical events that contributed to the slow unravelling of clan society, can be traced in chronological order as follows.

Resistance to Feudalism

The clan system was brought to the British Isles from Ireland in the Early Middle Ages, and it became widely embedded in the kingdom of Dál Riata and the Norse Kingdom of the Isles. In 1066, the Norman invasion of the British Isles saw the arrival of a feudal based society, in which the crown asserted ownership of land and a right to grant title in return for homage and rent. In the meantime, Mull was part of the Kingdom of the Isles which functioned as an autonomous province of Norway. In this realm, although the leaders of clans held a form of land ownership, the clan system based on a communal society of mutual support was still the basis of governance.

Annexation of the Kingdom of the Isles

Following the Scottish annexation of the Kingdom of the Isles in 1266, King Alexander III sought to enforce a feudal right over the Hebridean islands but, for more than 200 years, the central government had little success. As an autonomous region, the Lordship of the Isles largely maintained the pre-existing social structure with the Clan Donald acting as a benign overlord. In the middle of the 14th century, the Clan Maclean became the leading family in Mull in a realm where there continued to be a mutual support system in the spirit of *dùthchas*.

Abolition of the Lordship of the Isles

After a number of attempts to assert central authority, and with continuing internecine conflict, in 1493 King James IV abolished the Lordship of the Isles. In theory, the aim was to bring an end to the systems and customs of the autonomous region, and impose a feudal system with land title rights granted by the crown. Ironically, given a growing disdain for the clan system amongst the Scottish ruling elite, James was the last king to speak Gaelic and his rule was actually marked by an approach that was sensitive to local customs. In any event, the end of the Lordship did not bring an end to the clan system. This was because, after the good King James IV died in 1513, Scotland entered a period in its history when central authority was weak. For most of the 16th century, there was a succession of monarchs who were babes in arms, and the authority of central government was disrupted by the Reformation. Access to the Highlands and Islands was also difficult with few roads and the crown did not at this stage have a credible naval presence to enforce its will. Consequently, several attempts to integrate the recalcitrant citizens of the Hebrides proved to be unsuccessful. In the meantime, and, at some cost to clansmen, internecine feuds within the Western Isles continued, with clan chiefs intermittently buying into turmoil at the national level.

King James VI

In 1567 King James VI came to the throne as a one year old child. For fifteen years, the country was governed by regents and a Protestant government that was preoccupied with stabilising its hold on power in the face of sustained Catholic resistance. However, by the 1580s, King James began to rule in his own right and, with the central government achieving a degree of stability, he was able to turn his attention to dealing with what he regarded as the recalcitrant Highlands and Islands. The new King was a very different man from his predecessors. He had been educated in English, and it is said that he despised those of his countrymen who spoke in Gaelic. Indeed, he considered the people of the Highlands and Islands to be backward and unruly, with unpredictable loyalties and questionable faith. In initial moves to assert his authority, the King reinforced his right to grant land title and, in 1598 he issued an order that all landowners must produce title documents to demonstrate ownership. This was largely ignored by the chiefs of Mull, with the Macleans of Duart considering themselves to have security of tenure from a royal charter granted in 1495.

In 1603, James acceded to English throne and, apart from one fleeting visit to Edinburgh, he disappeared to London for the rest of his reign. Anxious to overcome initial perceptions of his somewhat rustic persona in the English court, and determined to bring the Highlands and Islands to heel, in 1609 he instituted the Statues of Iona, the details of which are provided in Chapter 13. This legislation sought to undermine many of the communal customs associated with *dùthchas*, and encouraged a growing division between landowner and tenant according to a feudal hierarchy. The consequent gentrification of the chiefs brought them significant financial burden, and many began to focus on the commercial exploitation of their lands, rather than managing them as part of a social system. James also availed himself of the naval resources available from England to enforce his power.

A few years later King James doubled down on his attempt to require clan chiefs to prove ownership of land. In 1617 he promulgated *The Registration Act* which established a system for recording deeds of ownership in what was called the Register of Sasines.[2] Again, the chiefs in Mull were slow to comply, with Murdoch Maclaine of Lochbuie not submitting appropriate paperwork until 1643 and Hector Maclean of Torloisk waiting until 1658. Notably, and still relying on their 1495 charter, the Macleans of Duart did not comply at all.

The consequences of all these measures to eliminate local customs and to enforce land title were the slow erosion of the clan-based society. And the financial impact of compliance on clan leaders was significant with many divesting their land ownership to a small number of powerful dukes and earls who became absentee landlords with neither family ties nor any sense of loyalty to their tenants.

17th Century Conflicts

The 17th century was a tumultuous in Scotland in terms internal and external conflict. In the first half of the century, clansmen were drawn into a succession of wars including the Wars of the Three Kingdoms, the Bishops Wars, and the English Civil War. The impact of these conflicts was significant, both in draining the finances of Clan Chiefs, weakening the strength of communities through loss of men, and exacerbating divisions between and within clans. Later in the century, the clans were again in the fray as they were drawn into opposing sides in the Glorious Revolution of 1688.

These events left many clan chiefs with chronic indebtedness. In particular, the Clan Maclean were repeatedly on the wrong side of history. In the early part of the century they had backed the royalist cause. And in 1689, even though they were Protestant, they had supported the first Jacobite Rebellion after the forced abdication of King James VII. In the meantime, while the Argylls had had mixed fortunes in terms of political allegiances, they had acquired the Clan Maclean of Duart debts. In 1692, this enabled the Earl of Argyll to oust the Chief from Duart Castle. Apart from removing the leadership of the Clan this brought a heavy burden on his clansmen, with an absentee landlord demanding increases in rents without any regard to loyalty and mutual support. Indeed, achieved by stealth and evil intent, it was a death-knell for the clan system on Mull.

Union and the Jacobite Denouement

The 18th century would bring yet more strain to the clan based society. With the absorption of Scotland into the new nation of Great Britain in 1707, the Highlands and Islands were firmly on the periphery and, after the failure of the Jacobite rebellion in 1715, the defeat at the Battle of Culloden in 1746 resulted in measures that consolidated what had already occurred in Mull. The aftermath saw the passage of a range of legislation which was designed to remove the basis and customs of the clan system once and for all, extinguishing the right of chiefs to hold courts and transferring this role to a crown appointed judiciary, forbidding the Gaelic language, and even banning the wearing of traditional clothes. In the meantime, there were savage punitive expeditions against clans that had supported the Jacobites.

With the loss of the Clan leader, the outcome of the Jacobite rebellions must have seemed like the end of the world for many people living in Mull. With the newly ennobled Dukes of Argyll owning their land, people would have been living in fear of their lives, not to mention an inability to house and feed their families.

Agricultural Reform and the Clearances

Despite the dramatic impact of Culloden, the successive Jacobite rebellions in the late 17th century and first half of the 18th century were not the main reason for the continuing decline in the clan. Indeed, it could be argued that the rebellions were a mitigating factor, in that the war-like character of clansmen endeared them to central governments who saw the potential of their military prowess in pursuing the interests of the nascent British Empire. As we will see in Chapter 14, there were other trends in Scottish society which would undermine the clan-based society. By the mid-18th century, the country was in the grip of a major agricultural revolution which delivered an ever greater concentration of land ownership into an increasingly small and powerful set of landlords and the implementation of a significant change in land use in which many people were replaced by sheep.

Amongst others, we can thank Adam Smith for providing an intellectual basis for this change in society mores, with his concept that "the public good is best served by the pursuit of individual interests"[3] The philosophy he propounded in his book *The Wealth of Nations* would encourage Scottish landlords to see the people who tilled the land as a resource rather than a community, with the focus for landowners on optimising these use of these resources. This would give the landowners a social licence to remove clansmen from their traditional land and, in the initial phase of what are now called the Clearances, many clansmen were evicted and resettled into newly created townships, usually in coastal areas. For many, life in these communities was not sustainable, and many people in Mull abandoned clan territory completely, to become seasonal or permanent migrants.

In the 1840s, a second wave of the Clearances was triggered by the failure of the potato crop. As a consequence, already overpopulated crofting communities were no longer able to support themselves and "assisted passages" were provided to destitute tenants by landlords who found this cheaper than continued cycles of famine relief to those in substantial rent arrears.

The impact of these two phases of the agricultural reform was that, in the 18th and 19th centuries, the vast majority of clan members in Mull were without a resident chief and completely separated from their traditional lands.

The Romanticisation of Clan Life

By the 19th century one might have expected that the traditional customs of clan community would be gone for ever. However, this was not entirely the case. The peoples who left the Highlands and Islands carried with them a deeply ingrained commitment to a community view of their existence. And, even though many Highlanders may have been viewed by the ruling elite as savages, in the 19th and 20th centuries their fighting qualities were acknowledged and admired with Highland regiments becoming the backbone of British armies in the building of the British Empire.

In Victorian times there was also a revival of interest in traditional Scottish culture with a number of writers, such as Sir Walter Scott, seeking to remind the Scottish people of their Highland and Islands heritage with stories that presented a romanticised view of the noble "savage", living in a bucolic society. This fantasy, which even extended to Queen Victoria and her circle, put fresh energy into long-lost causes. For the most part, the revival did not embrace the reality of the community-based society, and it is not until recent times that the true nature of "clan life" has been recognised through the scholarship of some notable historians, and the presentation of well researched TV series.

In the meantime, for Mull, the 20th century would bring both good news and a sad departure. In 1911, the 26th Chief of the Clan Maclean of Duart, Sir Fitzroy Maclean purchased and refurbished Duart Castle to re-establish a presence on the island. However, a few years later, the long stewardship of the other main clan on Mull was terminated. In 1922, the 24th Chief of the Clan Maclaine relinquished his hold on Lochbuie.

Renaissance

Finally, as Scotland resumed self-government in 1999, it is no accident of history that the need to redress the slow demise of community-based living has emerged as a significant agenda for the Scottish Parliament. As we will see in Chapter 17, some of the very first Acts of the new Scottish government involved Land Reform and Community Empowerment. Also, in the 21st century, many Scottish people retain a connection with a geographical area through their ancestry. Research into family history has become the subject of serious scholarship, and clan societies are flourishing as a means for people to celebrate and connect with the people and buildings that define their identity.

ENDNOTES

1   An exposition on this subject is contained in the book by Professor Sir Tom Devine entitled "The Scottish Clearances – A History of the Dispossessed", Penguin Books, 2019.

2   In Scots law, a Sasine (pronounced 'say-zin') is a document that records the transfer of the ownership of property. It usually provides the names of the new and previous owners and a basic description of the property transferred. In traditional ceremonies of 'giving sasine', the signing of a deed was accompanied by the transfer of symbols of the land such as earth and stone.

3   Adam Smith was born in 1723 and died in 1790. His seminal work, The Wealth of Nations was published in 1776.

DÙTHCHAS
LANDSCAPE AND COMMUNITY IN MULL AND IONA

PART FOUR

CREATION OF A NATION

DÙTHCHAS
LANDSCAPE AND COMMUNITY IN MULL AND IONA

SCOTLAND THE BRAVE

Through much of the Middle Ages, the Hebrides existed as a separate. However, as noted in Part Two, in 1266 Norway ceded the Western Isles to Scotland. Initially, the region would operate as an autonomous territory named the Lordship of the Isles before these lands became an integrated part of modern Scotland. In Part Four of this book, for those readers who are interested in the wider context, we trace the back-history of how the rest of Scotland evolved during that time.

Pictland

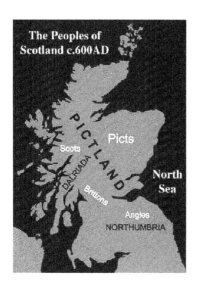

Following the departure of the Romans in the 5th century, Pictland was the biggest of several kingdoms in the north of the British Isles. Although there had been incursions, their territory had never been conquered by the Romans. Tall, red-headed, and wearing woad, they were a proud people speaking Pictish. They held sway over most of the Scottish mainland to the north and east of the Clyde and Forth estuaries, and co-existed with the Scots in Dál Riata to the west, the Brittons in Strathclyde to the south west, and the Anglians in Northumbria to the south east.

In the early part of the Middle Ages, there was no leader with dominion over the whole of Pictland. The first and very important step towards integration occurred in the 9th century with the establishment of what would initially be called the kingdom of Alba.

Alba

It is generally accepted that the Kingdom of Alba came into existence in 843 even as the Hebrides were becoming part of the Norse Kingdom of the Isles. The first king, who also used the title "King of the Picts", was Kenneth I (Kenneth MacAlpin).[1] Apart from the northern and western isles and adjacent parts of the mainland, it was one of the few areas of the British Isles to withstand the full force of Viking invasion.

On his death, in 858 Kenneth was succeeded by his brother Donald I who, in relatively quick succession, was succeeded by Kenneth's sons Constantine I and Aed, and Kenneth's grandson Eochaid. The next king was Constantine's son Donald II who took the crown in 889. He was the first man to be styled as *King of the Scots*, and he spent most of his reign fighting the Vikings. These wars were financed by frequent levying of taxes on a long suffering people which did not make him the most popular of rulers. His nickname was *dásachtach*, which is Gaelic for "madman".

On his death in 900, Donald II's successor was Constantine II. The son of Aed, he reigned for nearly half a century, and initially he spent most of his time in fighting the Vikings. However, alliances then changed. He fell foul of a treaty with England and the English King Æthelstan invaded Scotland. Constantine joined forces with the Viking King Olaf of Dublin and the Brittonic King Owain of Strathclyde. Things came to a head at the Battle of

Brunanburh in 937, in which King Æthelstan was victorious.[2] Subsequently, Constantine was forced to pay tribute to the English king and lost favour at home. In 943, he retired to become a Culdee monk at St Andrews monastery. Despite this denouement, he is credited as the man who, with Bishop Ceallach of St Andrews, brought the Catholic Church in Scotland into conformity with the rest of the Gaelic world. And it was during his reign that the English began to call the people of the northern kingdom, with its mix of Picts and descendants of the Scoti, *Scottish* rather than *Pictish*.[3]

Following Constantine II's abdication, he was succeeded by his cousin Malcom I (son of Donald II) during whose reign Alba began a slow and lengthy period of expansion. In 945, King Edmund of England invaded the kingdom of Strathclyde and transferred it to Alba on condition of a permanent peace. Whilst fine in theory, this transaction was easier said than done, and Alba would not fully assume control of the territory until the next century. In the meantime, Malcolm had eyes on Moray to the north although he failed to consolidate control.

In 954, Malcolm I was succeeded by his son Indulf, who is credited with capturing the Anglo-Saxon fortress called *Oppidum Eden* (the site of modern day Edinburgh). However, he died an early death in 962 in renewed hostilities with the Vikings and, over the next 50 years, he was succeeded by a series of kings with relatively short reigns (Dub, Cuilen, Amlaib, Kenneth II, Kenneth III and Constantine III). During this period, there was a series of campaigns to take over the central region of Scotland, Lothian. In 1005, Malcolm II (son of Kenneth II) became king and his reign over the next 30 years would see the completion of the conquest of the lowlands and border areas (Lothian and Strathclyde). In 1018, Malcolm and King Owain Foel (Owen the Bald) of Strathclyde combined in a war against Uhtred of Northumbria with a decisive victory at the Battle of Carham. With King Owen relinquishing any interest in Northumbria shortly before his death, for a time this settled the border with England at the River Tweed. A meeting and negotiations with the immensely powerful English King Canute in 1031 seems to have further secured these southern parts of the kingdom, although the consolidation of Scottish rule over Lothian and the Scottish Borders to the east was not fully realised until the conquest and annexation of that province during the Scottish Wars of Independence in the late 13th and early 14th centuries.

Following Malcolm II's death in 1034, he was succeeded by his grandson King Duncan I who continued his father's work of nation-building. In 1039, he led an unsuccessful attempt to extend Scotland's position in Northumbria, and in 1040 he led an army into the northern territory of Moray ruled by Lord Macbeth who was another grandson of Malcolm II.[4] At the Battle of Pitgavenny, Duncan was killed and Macbeth took the crown.[5] Subsequently, King Duncan's wife and her two young sons, the future kings Malcolm III and Donald III, took refuge in England. Despite the reputation promulgated in Shakespeare's play, for about fifteen years King Macbeth had a relatively uneventful reign. However, he did come to a sticky end. In 1057, the future Malcolm III brought an army from England and defeated Macbeth in the Battle of Lumphanan. Macbeth was beheaded, and he was briefly succeeded by his stepson, Lulach who reigned until March 1058 when he was assassinated by Malcolm's supporters.

Malcolm III and the Advent of the Normans

Taking the crown in 1058, Malcolm III is known as "Canmore" or "the Great Chief".[6] He was born in 1031, and his reign of 35 years would see the beginning of a 150 year period when the *mainland* of Scotland was consolidated into a country with borders that broadly resemble the modern nation. Increasingly under the influence of the Normans after their invasion of England in 1066, he would have two wives, both of strategic importance. Initially, he was married to Ingibjorg the daughter of a Norwegian nobleman (Finn Arnesson) with whom he had sons Duncan and Donald. Following Ingibjorg's death in 1069, in 1070 he married the Anglo-Saxon Margaret of Wessex, a member of the English royal family who was eventually canonised for her piety and charity. Malcolm and Margaret had five sons, including Edgar, Alexander, and David, and two daughters including Matilda.

In the early part of his reign, Malcolm III consolidated his control over the mainland. Although, following the Norman invasion of England in 1066, it eventually became apparent that King William had ambitions to extend his rule to the whole of the British Isles, there was no immediate threat.

Consequently, with England in disarray, when news of the Norman invasion first reached Scotland Malcolm took the opportunity to raid Northumbria. With his wife being the sister of Edgar Ætheling who had been elected as King of England after the death of King Harold, Malcolm initially lent support to English nobles resisting the Norman occupation. However, once King William had consolidated his hold in England, in 1072 he sent a force north to confront the Scots. With weaker forces, Malcolm retreated and then sued for peace. He eventually met William in Perthshire and, in the Treaty of Abernethy, he agreed to accept William's overlordship for lands he held in England, and negotiated a peace between William and Edgar who was granted lands in Cumbria. He also handed over his 12 years old son Duncan as a hostage to fortune. Duncan was whisked away to Normandy where it is said that he was raised in a kindly manner in William's court and trained as a knight. The boy also became good friends with King William's son Rufus and, when King William died in 1087, the now 27 years old Duncan joined the court of King William II almost as part of the family.

Despite the Scots' apparent accommodation with the Normans, in the early 1090s hostilities with England resumed. In 1091, the English invaded Cumbria and Edgar Ætheling fled to Scotland. In response, Malcolm attacked Newcastle, and an all-out war was only narrowly averted by Edgar's mediation. However, after a hiatus, Malcolm resumed hostilities and in 1093, on his way to battle with the Duke of Northumberland, he was ambushed and killed.

Malcolm III's natural successor was his exiled son Duncan.[7] However, with Duncan still in the English court, Malcolm's brother Donald seized the throne to become Donald III. Suitably outraged, and now in his early 30s, Duncan raised an army to claim his birthright. With the King William II's help he invaded Scotland and, faced with overwhelming odds, Donald retreated north. In 1094 Duncan II was crowned at Scone, but this would prove to be a pyrrhic victory.[8] Given his upbringing, Duncan was understandably perceived by some of the Scottish lords as a creature of the Normans and, in response to criticism that his crown depended on the power of "occupying" foreign troops, he sent the English knights who had formed the backbone of his invading force back to England. In the meantime, Donald had been raising an army of supporters drawn from the highlands. With Duncan's position weakened, Donald launched an attack in which Duncan was killed, with his body eventually buried on Iona.

With Duncan gone after just seven months, Donald now resumed his position as king. However, with other sons of Malcolm III in the wings, he did not last long. While Malcolm's second son Edmund supported Donald, in 1095 his brother Edgar claimed the throne supported by his other brothers, Alexander and David. Initially, the rebellious trio fled to France. However, with support from the English, in 1097 Edgar took the throne with Donald sent to prison where he died in 1099. Edgar went on to rule for ten years, before dying in suspicious circumstances in 1107. In the meantime, in 1100 his sister Matilda had married King William II's son Henry.

With no heir, Edgar was succeeded by his brother Alexander, who was crowned under an arrangement established by Edgar that his younger brother David would have sovereignty over Cumbria as a form of principality. With the crowns of Scotland and England now connected by both upbringing and marriage, his reign was a period of co-operation between the two countries, with Alexander even sending troops to support William II in his campaigns against an independent Wales.

Scotland and the Davidian Revolution

In 1124, Alexander I died of natural causes and was succeeded by his younger brother who became David I. Now 40 years old, David was the sixth and youngest son of Malcolm III and Margaret of Wessex and arguably the best of the bunch. Although raised in Scotland, before taking the throne David had spent some time in the English court and was married to an English Countess. From his time in living with the Normans, he had acquired a range of ideas about the role of kings and the governance of a nation, and his accession would herald an era of 30 years when Scotland (not including the Hebrides and the northern territories ruled by Norway) would become a modern medieval state. According to records, it was also the period in history when references to Alba would be replaced by Scotland.

The *Davidian Revolution*, which is also characterised as the "Normanisation" of Scottish governance, encompasses a very wide range of reforms including the establishment of the office of High Steward for the conduct of domestic affairs (a hereditary position which would one day lead to the Stewart dynasty). At the core was a radical change to the ownership of land, with implications for all parts of Scotland including the Hebrides. Hitherto, property had been the subject of customary entitlement with a strong sense of family ownership extending to the wider community. This was replaced by the European feudal system of *enfeoffment*.9 With an influx of French and Anglo-French knights, the King granted them rights over land in return for their service, and these individuals began to construct fortified homes (castles and mottes) from which they governed their territory, demanding the homage and fealty of the local population. This was in stark contrast to the mutual support family system that had previously characterised Scottish society and still held sway in the Highlands and Islands. The government also began to appoint royal agents who were responsible for law enforcement and collection of taxes, and a number of existing communities were established as burghs, at Berwick-upon-Tweed, Dunfermline, Edinburgh, Roxburgh, Scone, Stirling, and Perth.10 In these towns, dignitaries were appointed with powers for administration delegated from and directly accountable to the crown. For the most part, these communities were located in the parts of Scotland which would eventually be called "the lowlands"; and they were populated by people who spoke a Scots version of English and adopted a feudal English culture that was at considerable variance with the traditional Gaelic ways of those living in the north and west of the country.

Apart from this radical social engineering in the central and southern parts of the country, David also invested considerable energy into spiritual matters. During his reign he established a number of monasteries, became a patron of others, and defended their independence from the Archbishops of Canterbury and York.

Finally, David did not neglect longstanding Scottish territorial claims. He consolidated Scottish control over Moray and, on the death of English King Henry I, he supported Henry's daughter Margaret against King Stephen, which enabled him to take control of parts of northern England.

He also extended Scottish control over the far north of the mainland, through strategic marriages and alliances involving local mormaers who were the mainland equivalents to the Clan Chiefs in the western and northern isles. However, his attempt to wrest control of the Orkneys from the Norwegians through the marriage of the son of the Mormaer of Atholl and the daughter of the Norse Earl of Orkney Haakon was unsuccessful.11

Despite his efforts to modernise Scotland's governance, in 1152 David was hit by tragedy. His son and only heir died from natural causes. Now nearly 70 years old, he quickly made arrangements for the succession by nominating his 11 year old grandson Malcolm as the next king and his younger grandson William as Earl of Northumberland. He also appointed the senior Mormaer of Scotland, Donnchad of Fife as regent. In 1153, David died in Carlisle and his strong connection to Cumbria (which would eventually revert to English control) is reflected in the reference to him in the *Annals of Tigernach* as *"David, son of Malcolm and King of Scotland and England."*

Following David I's death, as planned, he *was* succeeded by his grandson Malcolm. Unfortunately, for much of his reign, Malcolm IV was ill, although in 1164 he did withstand an attack led by the King of the Isles with Somerled killed at the Battle of Renfrew.

The Lion and English Overlordship

Following Malcom's death in 1165, he was succeeded by his younger brother William who was 24 years old. With a mop of red hair, William was a powerfully built and spirited young man known as "the Lion". This nickname reflected his adoption of a standard consisting of a Red Lion Rampant with a forked tail on a yellow background.12 William had been brought up in the English court of King Henry II. However, in 1173, he took part in a revolt against Henry, and subsequently formed an alliance with France which was the first of its kind. This did not end well. In 1174, in the Battle of Alnwick, he was captured and despatched in chains to Normandy, while Scotland was occupied. Held for twelve months, William was eventually released under the Treaty of Falaise in which he agreed to swear feudal loyalty to King Henry II at a ceremony in York Castle, pay some hefty taxes, and acknowledge the sovereignty of the English over the

Scottish church. In the scheme of things, these concessions did not augur well for future Scottish independence, sowing the seeds of the Wars of Scottish Independence which took place 100 years later.

During the rest of William's reign, conflict between Scotland and England continued, he put down several local rebellions, and deflected attempts by the Orcadians to infiltrate the mainland from the north. However, William's reign showed some significant achievements. He founded new burghs, updated and clarified the criminal law, promoted trade, and accommodated further French settlements. However, there was no love lost with many of his subjects who did not accept his English ways, especially the Gaelic speaking Highlanders.

Alexander II and the English Border

When King William I died in 1214, he was succeeded by his 16 years old son Alexander II who like his father had spent part of his life in England. In the early days, after quelling a revolt, Alexander joined forces with English barons in their struggle against the much reviled English King John. King John retaliated by sacking Berwick on Tweed. However, an army led by Alexander made it to the south of England and, in Dover, he paid homage to the King Louis VIII of France (a pretender to the English throne) for his English territories. In 1216, King John died and was succeeded by his nine year old son King Henry III. Reconciliation was cemented in 1221 when the now 23 year old Alexander married Henry's sister Joan. Notably, around this time, Alexander was active in subjugating the parts of Argyll that were not part of the Kingdom of the Isles. In response, in 1230 the Kingdom of the Isles signed a treaty with Norway to come to their defence in the event of further Scottish incursions. This bought the Kingdom of the Isles some time from a looming loss of sovereignty. However, when the treaty was triggered later in the century, it did not save the Hebrides from annexation by Scotland.

After further disputation with the English, in which King Henry III demanded homage and Alexander asserted his claim over northern England, the two countries came to a significant accommodation. In 1237, they signed the Treaty of York which defined the English/Scottish border as it exists today, confirming that Northumbria, Cumbria and Durham were part of England. In 1249, Alexander then set out to wrest control of the Kingdom of the Isles from the Norwegians. To this end, he curried favour with local chiefs including the Mormaer of Lennox, Sir Gillespie Campbell, and Allan Lord Galloway who had a substantial fleet. However, this gambit failed. He then launched his own fleet, but this was in vain as he died on the way to a battle that did not take place.

Apart from his very active foreign policy, the reign of Alexander II is notable for the emergence of a Parliament which worked together with the King and his Council of advisers. The first known reference to this body is in annals dated 1235. Initially, it was an institution consisting of representatives of the *Three Estates* - the clergy, the nobility, and the "burghers" who represented the middle class and lesser mortals appointed through their local communities.

Alexander III and the Lordship of the Isles

In 1249, Alexander II was succeeded by his seven year old son who became Alexander III. Continuing the close links with the English crown, when he was 10 years old he was married to an 11 years old Margaret who was the daughter of King Henry III. In the process, Henry tried to get Alexander to swear fealty, but he refused. When he reached the age of majority, Alexander re-engaged with his father's mission in the west. He attempted to get the Norwegian King Haakon IV to accept Scotland's dominion over the Western Isles and Haakon responded in 1263 by sending a fleet to defend the territory. As noted in an earlier chapter, Haakon's mission failed, and in 1266 his son King Magnus VI ceded the Hebrides to Scotland in the Treaty of Perth. At this point, the Island of Mull and its people became part of the mainstream history of Scotland.

Subsequently, Alexander made further attempts to bring more of the Mormaers and chieftains of the Highlands into active support of the Scottish state. Consequently, with a slow but steady consolidation of Scottish power in the west, the number and proportion of Gaelic speakers under the rule of the Scottish king practically doubled. This would be of great strategic significance in the years ahead, as it was the Gaelic speaking warriors of the western territories that eventually enabled King Robert I (a

Scoto-Norman) to emerge victorious during the Wars of Independence.13

Despite his momentous life, Alexander III was beset with tragedy. Through his marriage to Margaret, he had three children, Margaret, Alexander, and David. In 1275 his wife died, and then in the early 1280s the children all pre-deceased him. Only his daughter Margaret, who had married King Eric II of Norway, left a successor. Born and living in Oslo, she too was named Margaret. Concerned about succession, in 1285 Alexander obtained the agreement of Parliament that, in the absence of any other heir, the young Margaret would become queen. In the meantime he selected a new wife, the Countess Yolande de Dreux, with whom he hoped to produce some new heirs.14 However, on the night of his betrothal in 1286, he met an untimely death of his own making in a riding accident. Thus ended the 250 years of what was known as the *Dunkeld* dynasty with a lineage strongly connected to the kings of Dál Riata.15

The Wars of Independence

Events would now conspire to bring a period of significant vulnerability and instability, with mounting pressure from the English King Edward I to accept some form of overlordship. On the death of Alexander III, the government sent an urgent message to Oslo for the transfer to Scotland of the three year old *Maid of Norway* as she was called.16 Pending her arrival by boat, she was crowned as queen, with effective control passing to a group of regents called the *Guardians* during what was called *The Interregnum*. Unfortunately, on arrival in the Orkneys in September 1290, Margaret had an accident and died.

With no obvious heir, the Guardians invited claims to the throne.17 Several people declared an interest, with John Balliol and Robert Bruce having the strongest claims. Fearing civil war between the Bruce and Balliol families and their supporters, the Guardians invited the King Edward to arbitrate. Sensing the vulnerability of the Scots, Edward saw an opportunity to assert his sovereignty over Scotland. He agreed to meet the Guardians and, at the meeting at Norham in 1291, he laid down certain self-serving conditions for his involvement.18 Before proceeding to arbitration, he insisted that the claimants to the Scottish throne should recognise him as "Lord Paramount" of Scotland. Initially they refused, and he then issued an ultimatum suggesting that if they didn't agree to his terms he might need to pursue other means of enforcing his sovereignty. He gave them three weeks to think about it, during which time he gave orders for his armies to advance to the Scottish border. With a lot to lose in terms of property held by both families in England, the Balliol and Bruce families eventually agreed to Edward's terms.

In the weeks that followed, Edward ruthlessly enforced his claim of sovereignty. Apart from the troop movements, he demanded that all Scottish royal castles be placed under his control, and that every Scottish official should resign their office and be re-appointed by him. In response, the Guardians convened and decided to accept Edward's terms. Consequently, on 13 June 1291, they and several other Scottish nobles assembled in Upsettlington to swear their allegiance to the English king. Absentees were given until 27 July to come to heel.19 In the meantime, taking up residence in Berwick, Edward commenced the process of assessing the competing claims to the Scottish throne, receiving submissions from all the interested parties which required proof of a connection to the Scottish Royal line through descent from King David I. Eventually Edward shortlisted John Balliol and Robert Bruce. These two then made further submissions, with Balliol emerging with the strongest case as David I's great-great-great grandson. The matter was then decided by the vote of a panel of 104 men, 40 from each of the contenders and 24 chosen by Edward. At a meeting on 17 November 1292, this panel elected John Balliol to be known as King John of the Scots.

After his coronation, King John swore homage to Edward and Edward then began to treat Scotland as a vassal state. In particular, he had plans to attack France and in 1295 demanded the support of a Scottish army. John took this proposal to his Council who rejected the idea. In keeping with previous strong associations with the French, Parliament then sent emissaries to King Philip IV warning him of Edward's intentions. They also negotiated a mutual defence pact called the Treaty of Paris (signed in October 1295 and to be the foundation document of the *Auld Alliance* which was frequently renewed well into the 16th century). The Council also concluded a treaty with the late Queen Margaret's father King Eric II of Norway to secure his support in the event of English hostilities.

Eventually King Edward learnt of the Scottish agreement with the French and, given his hostile intentions towards France, he began to prepare his defences against what he feared would be an attack by Scotland. He strengthened his hold of royal castles on the border, and he obtained the support of the Bruce family by appointing Robert Bruce as governor of Carlisle Castle. In response, King John issued a call to arms amongst the Scottish nobles, not all of whom responded.

This sequence of events began a series of wars which would continue for several decades during which King Edward I would acquire the title *The Hammer of the Scots*. Hostilities commenced in 1296, with Edward's army sacking Berwick and defeating the Scots at the Battle of Dunbar. As King John appeared to falter, in July 1296 the Guardians forced him to abdicate and assumed control of Scotland's defences in what was called the *Second Interregnum*. Fleeing to England, John quickly found himself imprisoned in the Tower of London and was eventually despatched to his estates in France where he died in obscurity in 1314.

By August 1296, the English had subdued most of Scotland and, to prove a point, King Edward removed the sacred Stone of Destiny from Scone Abbey and transported it to Westminster Abbey.20 He then convened a parliament at Berwick, where the Scottish nobles were required to pay homage to him. If he thought that this was an end to it, he had another thing coming. Within a short space of time revolts sprung up across the country, with William Wallace and Andrew de Moray leading the fray supported by a number of clans including the Lord of the Isles Alistair Macdonald. After a capitulation at the Battle of Irvine, in 1297 the Scots secured their first victory at the Battle of Stirling Bridge. While de Moray was killed in the fighting, Wallace, who had used innovative military tactics to counter the usual dominance of the English cavalry, was rewarded for his success. Hailed as a hero, in March 1298, he was appointed Guardian of Scotland.

Despite this setback, King Edward was not easily repelled. In mid-1298 he again invaded Scotland and in July he defeated the Scots at the Battle of Falkirk. However, he did not consolidate his victory, and Wallace was able to flee to France where he stayed until he returned to Scotland five years later. In the meantime, the Scottish Parliament appointed a new set of Guardians, the previous claimant to the throne Robert Bruce, John Comyn (a Balliol supporter), and William de Lamberton the Bishop of St Andrews.

In the next two years, Edward consolidated his position. In 1301 and 1302 he made fresh attacks on Scotland, there was a truce, and then there was another campaign in 1303/04 when he managed to secure Stirling Castle despite Wallace's return. At this point, most of the Scottish nobles agreed to pay homage to Edward and, to cap it off, in 1305 William Wallace was captured through the treachery of a fellow Scot and ignominiously executed. It seemed that all was lost.

With Scotland in disarray, in early 1306 the two Guardians Robert Bruce and John Comyn had a serious falling out. Bruce wanted the Scots to rebel and Comyn did not. After weeks of tension, on 10 February the two men met in Greyfriars Church in Dumfries. Bruce accused Comyn of treachery and then struck him with his sword. His supporters finished off the job. Bruce then began to instigate rebellion, quickly rallying most of the Scottish nobles and bishops to the cause, as well as the Lord of the Isles. Within six weeks, on 26 March 1306, Robert was crowned king and he then began a new military campaign to free Scotland from the English yolk. This would be a long journey.

At the outset of the *First War of Independence*, support was far from universal. After killing John Comyn, Robert had some serious enemies and the Comyn family controlled significant lands in the north. In June 1306, Edward marched north and defeated Robert at the Battle of Methven west of Perth. Afterwards, Robert fled to the highlands and was declared an outlaw. Edward went in pursuit and caught up with some of his relatives who were either executed or imprisoned. It is not certain, but it is thought that Robert eventually escaped to the Hebrides where he was able to shelter over the winter. In February 1307 he returned to the mainland with two sets of supporters. Together with his brother Edward, he successfully conducted guerrilla warfare in south west Scotland; but the other group led by his brothers Thomas and Alexander were captured and executed. Robert was then successful in a sequence of skirmishes against the English, including a victory at the Battle of Loudon Hill in Ayrshire, and the capture of several English-held castles further north.

At this point, time would catch up with King Edward I. In July 1307, he died and the English cause was taken up by his son King Edward II. The new king did not have the military flare or killer instinct of his father and, emboldened by Edward I's death, many recruits rallied to Robert's cause. However, in late 1307 King Edward II led successful campaigns in the north winning several skirmishes and taking several castles. In May 1308, he won the Battle of Inverurie and proceeded to lay waste to much of the Comyn territory in Moray, Aberdeen, and Buchan. In the meantime, Robert had turned his attention to the MacDougalls in Argyll. They had supported Wallace against the English, but were connected through marriage with the Comyns who as supporters of the Balliol family were enemies of the Bruce family. His conflict with them ended with a victory at the Battle of Pass of Brander in around 1307. As we have seen earlier in this book, this would have a profound impact in Mull where MacDougall lands were forfeit and eventually transferred to the Clan Macdonald. Afterwards, Robert secured Dunstaffnage Castle north of Oban.

In March 1309, Robert summoned his first Parliament at St Andrews, and by August he controlled most of the country. In 1310, the Bishops in Council resolved to re-affirm him as king, and he unsuccessfully attempted to secure a peace with the English. With no joy, he continued his war of attrition, taking one castle after another to the north, laying siege to Stirling Castle, securing Edinburgh and reaching down into England. In June 1314, he began negotiations for an orderly takeover of Stirling Castle and this spurred King Edward II into action. He mustered a huge force and travelled north. On 23 June, English troops attempted to cross a burn surrounded by marsh land and quickly found themselves confronted by significant Scottish forces who outmanoeuvred and overwhelmed them in a crushing defeat at the Battle of Bannockburn. Edward fled for his life and, shortly after, Stirling Castle fell. Robert's total victory was secured and is remembered to this day in the Scottish national hymn *Flower of Scotland.*

Despite Bannockburn and the capture of the final English stronghold at Berwick in 1318, Edward II refused to renounce his claim to the overlordship of Scotland. As a consequence, in 1320 the Scottish nobility submitted the seminal Declaration of Arbroath to Pope John XXII, declaring King Robert as their rightful monarch and asserting Scotland's status as an independent kingdom. In 1324, the Pope recognised Robert as king of an independent Scotland, and in 1326, the Franco-Scottish alliance was renewed in the Treaty of Corbeil.

By now recognised as a failure, at war and through his wayward conduct in his own court, in 1327 the English King Edward II was forced to abdicate in favour of his 15 year old son Edward III. Later that year, he met his death at Berkeley Castle and, in the following year, Robert drove home his advantage by invading the north of England and defeating the English again at the Battle of Stanhope Park. In the aftermath, the young English king narrowly escaped and eventually agreed to make peace, signing the Treaty of Edinburgh–Northampton on 1 May 1328. This formally recognised the independence of Scotland and Robert as King. To further seal the peace, Robert's son and heir David married Edward's sister Joan.

The Second War of Independence

This might well have been the end of Scotland's fight for independence. And the Treaty of Edinburgh-Northampton is the definitive statement of Scotland's separation from England until it relinquished its independence in the Act of Union in 1707. However, with the death of King Robert I in 1329, the scheming and fighting would continue for another 30 years in what is called the Second War of Independence.

On Robert's death, his son and successor David II was only five years old. Accordingly, Parliament appointed Robert's nephew and friend Thomas Earl of Moray as Guardian. Despite the Treaty of Edinburgh-Northampton, King Edward III struggled to accept that Scotland was an independent nation and, sensing a period of vulnerability, he sought support in Scotland to undermine the new king. He found willing allies in Edward Balliol (the son of the deposed King John) and Henry Beaumont, both of whom had forfeited lands after supporting the English at the Battle of Bannockburn. Without giving them overt support, King Edward III encouraged a rebellion, and in August 1332 Edward Balliol launched an expeditionary force that landed at Fife. These troops engaged the Scots army and defeated them at the Battle of Dupplin Moor. Following this victory, Edward Balliol then had himself crowned as King Edward of Scotland. Back in the Scottish court, a newly appointed Guardian Sir Archibald Douglas sued for peace, suggesting that the right to kingship should be determined by the Scottish Parliament. Emboldened, Edward Balliol retreated to Annan just north of the English border to await the outcome of the Parliament's deliberations. Foolishly, he let many of his supporters disperse and chose this moment to declare his fealty to the English King as well as promising the return of Berwick to the English crown. Taking advantage of Edward's weak defences, Sir Archibald Douglas despatched troops and routed Edward Balliol who fled to Carlisle.

Despite his ignominious flight, this was not the end of Edward Balliol's attempts to be king. In April 1333, he and his English supporters laid siege to Berwick. In an attempt to raise the siege, Sir Archibald Douglas was defeated at the Battle of Hallidon Hill and killed. Meanwhile, the nine year old King David and his child wife Joan were moved for safety to Dumbarton Castle. With the situation in Scotland highly unstable, in early 1334 the French offered David asylum and he set up a court-in-exile at Château Gaillard in Normandy.

In David's absence, a series of Guardians continued to maintain his rule as the rightful king of an independent Scotland. In November 1334, the English King Edward III launched another army northwards, but he accomplished very little because he couldn't bring the Scots to battle. In February 1335 he retreated, only to return in July with Edward Balliol and an army of 13,000. This time, he advanced through Scotland, creating mayhem in Glasgow and Perth. However, he was again unable to engage the Scottish army in pitched battle. Finally, in November 1335, the English met the Scottish army at the Battle of Culblean in Aberdeenshire. With many Scottish leaders having defected to David's cause, this proved to be a decisive victory for the Scots.

In 1341, and now 17 years old, King David II decided that it was time to return to Scotland from his court in France and claim his rightful inheritance. On arrival, he found a country ravished by endless war, with many of its nobles killed and the economy in ruins. Mindful of his father's inheritance, he rejected any subservience to England and honoured a now strong connection with the French King Philip VI by supporting France in what became the One Hundred Years War with England. This led him to launch a series of diversionary attacks on England which assisted the French by forcing the English to commit troops in defence of their northern border. In 1346, matters escalated, with King Philip appealing for a full-blooded invasion of England in order to draw English troops away from their defence of Calais. David accommodated Philip and personally led a Scots army southwards with the intention of capturing Durham. In reply, an English army moved northwards from Yorkshire and, on 14 October at the Battle of Neville's Cross, the Scots were defeated. David was injured and captured and, after a period of convalescence, he was imprisoned in the Tower of London. He remained there for eleven years, during which time Scotland was ruled by his nephew, Robert Stewart, 7th High Steward. This would be a telling inter-regnum for the future history of Scotland.

Following David's incarceration, Edward Balliol who was now in his 60s returned to Scotland with a small force, in a final attempt (with English support) to seize the throne. He only succeeded in gaining control of part of Galloway. There he languished until, in January 1356, he finally relinquished his claim. In the meantime, in the *Treaty of Berwick* in 1357, the Scottish Parliament negotiated David's release from the Tower of London under terms that involved a very significant ransom that would dog David for the rest of his life. This Treaty effectively brought an end to the Second War of Scottish Independence with Scottish sovereignty intact.

End of the Dynasty

On his return to Scotland in 1357, King David II was confronted with a country that was still being ravaged by the Black Death which had arrived in 1348 after skirmishes with the English, and burdened with a very heavy public debt. In an attempt to cover payment of his ransom, he initiated a programme of taxes. Struggling to make ends meet, in 1363 he travelled to London in an attempt to renegotiate the terms of his release from prison. During the talks he even suggested that, in the event that he died childless, he would be succeeded by the English King Edward III's son Edward the Black Prince.21 Needless to say, the Scottish Parliament rejected *this* proposal and later secured another treaty in which the ransom was reduced. In the meantime, David became unpopular and, in 1371, he died a broken man.

With David leaving no direct heir, the throne passed to his cousin who became King Robert II. The son of Marjorie Bruce the daughter of Robert I, and Walter Stewart the 6th High Steward of Scotland, this would be the beginning of the House of Stewart which would continue until the death of Queen Anne in 1707, coincidentally the same year as the Act of Union with England.

ENDNOTES

1   There is conjecture that, before becoming King of Alba, Kenneth was the king of Dál Riata.

2   This battle at a site somewhere in Northern England is celebrated by the English for its contribution to consolidating England as a united Kingdom.

3   The first reference to the people as Scottish is recorded in CE 920.

4   These are the historical figures portrayed in Shakespeare's play Macbeth.

5   King Duncan I is buried in the cemetery on Iona.

6   Canmore is the name used for the on-line database of over 300,000 archaeological sites, monuments, and buildings in Scotland which, since 2015 has been managed by Historic Environment Scotland.

7   This was the start in Scotland of the French system of primogeniture (the right of succession belonging to the first-born male child).

8   In medieval times, Scone in Perthshire was the nearest thing that Scotland had to a capital city of territory and is the location of the Stone of Destiny and the traditional place for the crowning of Scottish monarchs.

9   Enfeoffment is an Anglo-French word referring to the granting of a deed in exchange for a pledge of service.

10   The word burgh is translated to borough in English. The earliest burghs, Roxburgh and Berwick were founded in 1124. The others listed were established over the next six years. They were centres of population and trade with military defences enabling control over significant territory.

11   Mormaer is the Gaelic word for ruler, coming from the Gaelic Mor (great) and maer (steward) and equivalent to clan chief in other parts of Scotland.

12   This eventually became the royal banner of Scotland and is still used today, quartered in the British flag with those of England and of Ireland.

13   The term Scoto-Norman refers to people, particularly in southern Scotland, who have a mixed Scottish and Anglo-Norman heritage, including families such as the Clans Bruce, Comyn, Fraser, Grant, Murray and Stewart.

14   The Countess was related to the French royal family.

15   The Dunkeld dynasty is genealogically based on Duncan I.

16   As daughter of King Eric II of Norway, Margaret was a member of the House of Sverre named after King Sverre Siggurdson. The dynasty provided rulers of Norway between 1184 and 1319.

17   The Guardians were James Stewart High Steward of Scotland, William Fraser Bishop of St Andrews, Robert Wishart Bishop of Glasgow, Alexander Comyn, John Comyn of Badenoch, the Earl of Buchan, and Donnchadh the Earl of Fife.

18   Norham is a village 7 miles south of Berwick on Tweed.

19   Upsettlington Castle sits midway between Berwick on Tweed and Coldstream in the Scottish borders.

20   As previously noted, this stone was brought from Ireland to Iona and the first King of Alba, Kenneth I, transferred it to Scone in 834.

21   The Black Prince died of dysentery in 1376. As a consequence, on his death in 1377, Edward III was succeeded by his grandson Richard II.

INDEPENDENT NATION

In 1371, Robert Stewart, came to the throne as King Robert II. He was 55 years old and his succession was far from straightforward. His parents were Marjorie, King Robert I's only child by his first wife Isabella of Mar, and Walter Stewart the 6th hereditary High Steward. Following Isabella's death in 1296, in 1302 King Robert I married his second wife Elizabeth de Burgh. He was hopeful of an heir, but initially none was born. In the meantime, in 1316 Marjorie gave birth to Robert Stewart. Given the troubles arising from the Second Interregnum, in 1318 Parliament resolved that in the event that the Queen did not conceive a male heir, Robert Stewart would succeed his grandfather. However, in 1324, the Queen gave birth to a son named David and Robert Stewart's claim lapsed.

Notwithstanding this turn of events, Parliament continued to have concerns about the succession. So, in 1326 it decided to reaffirm Robert Stewart's entitlement in the event that the new babe in arms David did not grow up to have male heirs. At the time, Parliament also endowed the now ten years old Robert Stewart with substantial lands including parts of Argyll. As things worked out, when Robert I did die in 1329, he was succeeded by his five the five years old David. However, despite his eventual marriage, David did not have a male heir, and when he died prematurely in 1371, Parliament's edict regarding Robert Stewart came into effect.

Robert Stewart was brought up as a Gaelic noble on the Isle of Bute under the guardianship of Sir James Stewart. His accession would be the start of the *House of Stewart*, and also the beginning of 330 years of Scotland as an independent nation in which the character and destiny of the country would be radically changed.

It is interesting to note the origins of the name Stewart. In the 12th century, as part of his institutional reforms, King David I created the position of *High Steward* with responsibility for managing domestic affairs. In 1150, the first person to be appointed was Walter Fitzalan, a nobleman from Brittany. Over the next 200 years this office evolved into a position with great influence and, as happened with many roles in medieval times, it become hereditary. To consolidate their position, in the 13th century, the Fitzalans adopted the name Steward, to emphasise their connection with the position, and this name became Stewart (and then Stuart).[1] It continued to be a key role in the royal household, although the king ruled with a Council of advisers and a Parliament.[2]

By the time he took the throne, King Robert II had been married twice and had had 14 legitimate children (10 with Elizabeth Mure and, following her death in 1355, four with Euphemia de Ross). This large family brought considerable wealth and power. Apart from his six sons, he had eight daughters including Isabella who married into the influential Douglas family, Margaret who married the Lord of the Isles, Katherine who was wed to the Lord High Admiral, and Elizabeth who married the Lord High Constable. For people in Mull, Margaret's marriage was of considerable note because in 1367 her daughter Mary would marry Lachlan Lubanach Maclean. This would establish a direct line of descent from the royal family to the Macleans of Duart.

With such a supporting cast, King Robert II chose to rule by delegating responsibilities to four of his sons and a group of supporting Earls. The dominant sons were John who was heir presumptive, Robert, Alexander, and David. Leaving the government in what he saw as these capable hands, he made it his business to connect with the people, and in the early days of his reign he began to tour the country. After the failings of his predecessor, this earned him a certain popularity and facilitated the further consolidation of Scottish lands in the south of the country. Through his family's tradition as High Steward, he also had a sound grasp of business and stabilised the country's finances built on the back of a healthy wool trade. However, as he grew older, his largesse towards his head-strong sons and their families would bring him some grief.

By the early 1380s, with Robert approaching 70 years of age, his Council became increasingly concerned about his son Alexander's independent and autocratic style of administration in his designated spheres of influence, which comprised Buchan (part of modern-day Aberdeenshire) and Ross (a district to the north and west of Inverness). Frustrated with the King's apparent unwillingness to pull the wilful Alexander into line, in 1384 the Council appointed his eldest son John as Guardian of Scotland and effective ruler. This elevation would trigger a burgeoning rivalry between all of his sons which would dog the country for some considerable time.

In 1388, John the Guardian joined up with his younger brother Robert to fight with the English on the borders, and their brother-in-law James Earl of Douglas secured a famous victory at the Battle of Otterburn. On their triumphant return, Robert outmanoeuvred John with promises to the Council that he would pull his brother Alexander into line. In response, the Council appointed Robert as Lieutenant of Scotland with significant military responsibilities rivalling John's administrative role.

Despite these sibling rivalries, when King Robert II died at Dundonald Castle in 1390 there was an orderly succession, with eldest son and Guardian John taking the title of King Robert III. However, the new king struggled to take the reins. Having been injured by a horse kick, he intermittently ceded effective control to his brother Robert and elevated his son David. In 1398, he designated David as Duke of Rothesay and, in 1399, he appointed him to replace his uncle Robert as Lord Lieutenant. Robert, now styled the Duke of Albany, took on a role as mentor to the 21 years old and future king.[3]

Unfortunately, the relationship between David and his uncle Robert was not entirely harmonious, and in 1401 it was alleged that David had been unfaithful to his wife who was the sister of Archibald the Earl of Douglas (married to his Aunt Isabella). Robert and Archibald arrested David and imprisoned him in Robert's home at Falkland Palace in Fife. Within the year David was dead, reportedly from starvation, and his younger brother James became the heir apparent. Initially, James was under the protective custody of the Bishop of St Andrews, and then he tried to escape by boat to France. However, he was captured by English pirates and handed over to the English King Henry IV.

Shortly afterwards, in 1406, King Robert III died and King James I came to the throne languishing in the hands of the English king, and there he would remain for 18 years! In these extraordinary circumstances, the Scottish government was in the hands of his uncle Robert Duke of Albany who was appointed as regent with the title of Governor. He held control until he died in 1420 when he was succeeded as regent by his son Murdoch.

A prisoner in England, King James I was raised in the English court alongside the heir to the English throne, the future King Henry V who was ten years his senior. James was given a sound education and developed a close affinity with the much lauded Henry for whom he had great respect. His association with the English court also enabled him to learn about kingship and good governance, and slowly his position changed from being a captive to being an honoured guest. In 1413, King Henry IV died, and Henry V was soon engaged in wars against the French. In 1420/21, and now in his twenties, James joined the new English king in France and actually found himself fighting Scottish troops who were supporting the French.

In 1422 Henry V died from dysentery at the early age of 36 and, with his son only one year old, he was succeeded by regents. In good faith, they were keen to release James, but this was not welcomed by the Albany regime in Edinburgh who had ambitions to usurp the throne. Nevertheless, with the help of the Earl of Douglas, a ransom of £40,000 was agreed, and in 1424, shortly after marrying Joan Beaufort a niece of Henry IV, the 29 years old James was released.

Given his willingness to fight with Henry V against Scottish forces, when James returned to Scotland he was not immediately popular. To secure his position, and assert his authority over lands that had been acquired by various nobles during his captivity in England, he launched a series of pre-emptive strikes against usurpers. Not sparing his kinsmen, in 1425 he attacked and killed several members of the Albany Stewart family including his cousin Murdoch who was executed for treason. Then, in 1428, while attending a meeting of Parliament in Inverness, he detained Alexander Lord of the Isles. In 1431, he arrested Archibald Earl of Douglas, and in 1434 he detained George the Earl of March. He then turned his attentions to the lowlands. In August 1436 he failed in a siege of the English-held Roxburgh Castle and deflected an attempt by Sir Robert Graham to arrest him at a general council meeting. The following year, and still in his 40s, he was assassinated in Perth in a failed coup by his uncle, Walter Stewart, Earl of Atholl. James' wife, Queen Joan, was wounded during this assault; but she managed to escape and fled to Edinburgh Castle where she secured the safety of her six year old son, now King James II.

James II was one of twin brothers, with his elder brother Alexander dying at the age of one. He was nicknamed *Fiery Face*, because of a red facial birthmark, and was crowned in 1437. Initially he lived with his mother and five sisters while his cousin Archibald 5th Earl of Douglas was lieutenant general and de facto leader of the country.[4] The year 1437 is also of note in that, while Scone remained the place for coronations, Edinburgh became the effective capital of Scotland.

After Archibald's death in 1439, the eight year old James fell into the custody of the Livingstone family who are said to have orchestrated the assassination of Archibald's sons after a dinner at Edinburgh Castle in November 1440 (the so-called *Black Dinner*), with the young James pleading for their lives. In the years that followed, James was virtually a captive within the Livingstone household although, on 3 July 1449, the 18 year old was permitted to marry the fifteen-year-old Mary of Guelders. Shortly after, with the help of the Douglas family he escaped the clutches of the Livingstones, but then in 1452 he had a major argument with William the 8th Earl of Douglas who was attempting to forge an agreement with John Macdonald over the future status of the Lordship of the Isles. James met with William at Stirling Castle and, true to his reputation, he brutally murdered William in a frenzied knife attack. This triggered a brief period of inconclusive civil war led by William's son named James. As James Douglas was trying to rally support from England, this conflict ended on 1 May 1455 with King James having a decisive victory over the Douglas family at the Battle of Arkinholm. Afterwards, Parliament declared the extensive lands of the Clan Douglas forfeit and annexed them to the crown. James Douglas commenced a long English exile, while the king finally cemented both his own position and that of his successors.

During the next five years James ruled in relative peace. Indeed, although his reputation is blemished by the murder of William Douglas, he is acknowledged as a politically astute and accomplished king. Apart from some family disputes, during his reign he courted and was popular with commoners and enacted popular legislation. He facilitated the foundation of the Glasgow University, and he actively pursued the annexation of the Orkney and Shetland Islands. With an innovative approach to warfare, he also had a passion for the development and use of artillery. Sadly, this would be his downfall. In 1460, he successfully besieged Roxburgh Castle, which was one of the last Scottish castles still held by the English after the Wars of Independence (Consequently, Roxburgh is a part of Scotland to this day). For this campaign, he took a large number of cannons and he was killed as one of them unexpectedly exploded in his proximity. His grieving widow ordered the destruction of the castle!

With the untimely death of his father, his son became King James III at the age of nine. Like his father he would turn out to be a king that was constantly at war with those around him including his own family. Initially, Parliament appointed his Dutch mother as regent, followed by James Kennedy Bishop of St Andrews, Gilbert Lord Kennedy, and then Robert Lord Boyd. The Boyd family proved to be ambitious with Lord Boyd's son Thomas marrying the king's 13 year old sister Mary. Then in 1469, Lord Boyd successfully negotiated the king's marriage to Margaret of Denmark. As part of the marriage agreement, the annual fee paid to Norway for the Western Isles (as agreed in the Treaty of Perth of 1266) was discontinued, with Scotland also taking control of the Orkney and Shetland islands which completed the modern reach of the Scottish State.

In the early 1470s, now in his early 20s, James III began to consolidate his position. He fell out with his brothers, one of whom (John the Earl of Mar) died in suspicious circumstances while the other (Alexander the Duke of Albany) went into exile in France. Sick of the power of the Boyds, and having already executed several members of that family, in 1473 he annulled Thomas's marriage to his sister. He then turned his attention to the autonomous Western Isles. In 1475, he censured the John of Islay and Lord of the Isles for the attempted pact with the English in 1462, and required that John's son Angus submit himself for trial in Edinburgh for the "illegal" besieging of Rothesay Castle on the Isle of Bute. When Angus failed to appear, "the Isles" were deemed forfeit, but in 1476 the Earl came to Edinburgh and negotiated the recovery of some of the territory although he lost his title as Earl of Ross. As we have seen this agreement led to a dispute between John and Angus.

While all of this was going on, James was active in attempting to forge his own alliance with England. In 1474, he agreed with King Edward IV that his son should marry Edward's daughter Cecily of York. This was not popular with Scottish nobles, who still harboured memories of the Wars of Independence. In early 1482, the English invaded Scotland with a force including James's brother Alexander the Duke of Albany (who styled himself as Alexander IV) led by the Duke of Gloucester (the future English King Richard III). In July, while attempting to organise his defence, James was arrested by a group of disaffected nobles and imprisoned in Edinburgh Castle, with Alexander appointed "lieutenant-general". In the meantime, the English army ran out of money and returned to England, taking Berwick on Tweed along the way (This is the last time it changed hands and it remains part of England to this day).

In 1483, James was released from prison and gradually reasserted his authority and, with the death of King Edward IV later in the year, the dye was cast for his brother Alexander. Following the Battle of Lochmaben Fair in 1484, Alexander fled to England and was condemned to perpetual exile. Any hope of his resurrecting his claim to the throne was lost in 1485 when his last remaining supporter Richard III was killed at the Battle of Bosworth, the concluding event in the English War of the Roses.

In the final years of his life, having lost the trust of his nobles and attempted an alliance with England, James III survived several attempts on his life. He also fell out with his immediate family, being estranged from his wife and attempting to disinherit his eldest son the 15 years old James who in February 1488 was arrested and almost immediately became the figurehead of an opposition party in Parliament. Matters came to a head on 11 June, when the king faced the army raised by the disaffected nobles including the Duke of Argyll. At the Battle of Sauchieburn, the king was defeated and killed.

From all accounts, and despite being relatively blameless, the new King James IV bore the guilt for the death of his father for the rest of his life. Nevertheless, he would go on to be one of the more successful Scottish monarchs during a period that saw the beginning of the Scottish Renaissance. Still a teenager, in 1489 he faced his first challenge, with an attempted rebellion which was quickly squashed. In 1490, he then turned his attention to the Western Isles where, although he had been stripped of much of his lands, John of Islay was still the Lord of the Isles. Following a prolonged dispute between John and his illegitimate son Angus, the ability of this autonomous region to resist pressure from the crown to relinquish its independence was much diminished. The King sailed to the Hebrides and commanded all the local chieftains to attend him at Dunstaffnage Castle near Oban and swear loyalty. In 1493, Parliament then abolished the Lordship of the Isles and John of Islay was pensioned off. Despite this firm action, there was continued resistance to the authority of central government for many years to come.

In the early part of his reign, James IV was no friend of England and in 1496 he supported the attempt by the younger son of English King Edward IV, Richard Duke of York, to reclaim the English throne from King Henry VII.[5] However, at the Treaty of Ayton, he then made peace with the English and, in 1502, he signed the Treaty of Perpetual Peace part of which involved his fateful marriage to Henry's daughter Margaret Tudor. This convenient and politic marriage in 1503 would set in train the events 100 years later that resulted in the union of the Scottish and English crowns in 1603 as King James VI succeeded the Queen Elizabeth.

In 1507, with plans to launch a crusade against the Ottoman Empire, James was honoured by the Pope with the title Defender of the Faith. The crusade never happened because of conflicts among the European powers and, in the meantime, relations with England deteriorated. In 1509, Henry VII died and his son Henry VIII almost immediately declared war on France. For some time, James had been friendly with the French King Louis XII and he declared war on England. The Pope tried to intervene, ex-communicating James for *breaking treatie*. However, James established a naval force to join the French fleet and, taking advantage of Henry VIII's absence in France, he invaded Northumberland. This would bring his downfall. On 9 September 1513, he was killed at the disastrous Battle of Flodden Field. This was one of the country's worst military defeats, with the loss of not only a popular and capable king, but also a large portion of Scotland's elite. James son and heir, James V, was only one year old, and his minority was to be fraught with political upheaval and weak central government even as the Scottish Reformation was about to gather steam.

Despite this unhappy ending to his reign, James IV is remembered as a cultured and successful king. Reported by the Spanish envoy as "a good looking fellow of noble stature", he was multi-lingual in Latin, French, German, Flemish, Italian, and Spanish. *Notably, he was the last Scottish king known to have spoken Gaelic.* His court welcomed people from far afield including a number of Africans. He was a patron of the arts and supported the foundation of several academic institutions including King's College Aberdeen and St Leonard's College St Andrews. In 1496, he passed what has been described as Scotland's first Education Act which required that all barons and freeholders of substance had to send their eldest sons to school (which is probably why Lachlan Mor Maclean received a sound education). James was also interested in medicine and, in 1506, he granted a charter to the Incorporation of Surgeons and Barbers of Edinburgh. In 1507 he welcomed the establishment of Scotland's first printing press, Chepman and Myllar Press, and he built the Great Halls at Edinburgh and Stirling castles.

Following the disaster at Flodden Field, Scotland entered a period of significant instability. With a child as king, the country was ruled by a succession of regents who each sought to use their position to wield significant power. Initially, Parliament appointed his mother Margaret Tudor in this role, but she fell out of favour, and was succeeded by a series of nobles. Then, in the autumn of 1524, his mother proclaimed James as an "adult" ruler. In response, in 1525 Archibald Douglas, 6th Earl of Angus and the young king's stepfather, took custody of James for three years, exercising power in his name. Several attempts were made to free the young king before, at the age of 16 in 1528 he finally escaped.

Still a very young man, James V had the good sense to surround himself with wise counsel including a team of lawyers. He also appointed the Duke of Albany to act on his behalf in diplomacy with France and Rome. One of his first independent acts was to force the Douglas family into exile. He then subdued rebels in the south and in the west.

As James' reign unfolded, the Reformation began to sweep through Europe and this would have an immense impact on Scotland. His initial response in the 1520s was to maintain the Catholic faith and persecute a number of newly emerging Protestants. In 1529, he began to look for a bride and, given his alliances with the French and the Pope, he looked to the French court. Unfortunately, the daughters of the French king were betrothed and, in March 1536, a contract was made for him to marry Mary of Bourbon. In preparation, he travelled to France to meet his potential wife. However, in 1537 on a subsequent visit he ditched the Bourbon contract, renewed the Auld Alliance, and despite *her* pre-existing betrothal to a noble, married the French king's daughter named Madeleine. Sadly, this marriage did not work out because Madeleine did not enjoy good health and died soon after her arrival in Scotland in July. Determined to succeed in securing a French wife, in 1538 James then proceeded to marry Mary of Guise, who was the widow of the Duke of Longueville. He did this by proxy and, in the same year, he asserted his power over the church by appointing the Archbishop of St Andrew, David Beaton, as a Cardinal.

According to legend, James V was nicknamed "King of the Commons" as he would sometimes travel around Scotland disguised as a common man. At court, he maintained a band of Italian musicians who adopted the name Drummond and he himself played the lute. He was a patron of poets and authors, wrote poetry, and employed many foreign artisans and craftsmen in order to enhance the prestige of his renaissance court.

In 1541, James found himself at loggerheads with England. He failed to turn up to a meeting with the Henry VIII in York and he did not help Anglo-Scottish relations by declaring himself Lord of Ireland. The death of his English mother Margaret Tudor removed any incentive for peace with England, and war broke out. Initially, in August 1542, the Scots won a victory at the Battle of Haddon Rig; but in the following month his army suffered a serious defeat at the Battle of Solway Moss. Shortly after, James became ill with a fever. As he was lying on his death bed in December 1542, his only surviving child, Mary was born. There is an apocryphal story that, when he heard the news, he spoke the words *"it cam wi a lass, and it'll gang wi a lass"*. Purportedly, this was both a reference to the start of the Stewart dynasty when Marjorie Bruce (daughter of Robert the Bruce) married Walter Stewart in 1314, and a prediction that his daughter would be the last of the line. In fact, the last Stewart monarch in Britain was a female – Anne, Queen of Great Britain. But she didn't die until 1714!

When she came to the throne, the new Queen Mary was just six days old and, for the next twenty years, Scotland would enter yet another period of unstable regency. With the Reformation in full flow, the country became deeply divided between the mainly Protestant Pro-English and the mainly Catholic Pro-French Factions. In 1543 the Protestant Faction who controlled Parliament forged an agreement with the English called the Treaty of Greenwich. This provided for Queen Mary to marry King Henry VIII's son Edward, and for a union of the two countries. Under the treaty, Mary was to be delivered to England when she reached the age of ten. There was also an understanding that James Hamilton, the son of one of the Scottish negotiating team William Hamilton, would marry the future Elizabeth the daughter of Anne Boleyn and future Queen of England!

This attempt to consolidate the Protestant faith through closer ties with England produced a backlash from the Catholic faction, and there was a coup led by Cardinal Beaton who rejected the Treaty of Greenwich and became Lord Chancellor. This angered Henry VIII who declared war on Scotland and triggered what was known as the *"rough wooing"* in which the English attempted to enforce the Treaty. In 1544 an English army led by the Earl of Hertford laid waste to large parts of southern Scotland, and hostilities continued in 1545 until a Scottish army finally repelled the English at the Battle of Ancrum Moor. Subsequently, Cardinal Beaton pursued several people preaching the Protestant faith and in 1546 he was then murdered at St Andrews Castle.

In January 1547, King Henry VIII died and, with the young King Edward VI now on the throne, the new Protector of England, the Earl of Hertford, renewed the attempt to secure the alliance with Scotland. In the face of Scottish resistance, in September the Duke of Somerset led an army into Scotland and defeated the Scottish at the Battle of Pinkie, occupying much of the lowlands and territory as far north as Dundee.[6] To counter these advances, the Catholic Faction government sought the military support of the French, in return for the betrothal between Mary and the Dauphin (the future King Francis II). In 1548, Mary was then she was sent to France where she was subsequently raised and educated.

In 1553 the King Edward VI died and was succeeded by Mary Tudor who was married to the King of Spain. This finally put an end to the Treaty of Greenwich and, with a Catholic on the English throne, during the next few years the Catholic Faction held sway in the Scottish Parliament. However, with the mounting persecution of Protestant clerics, support in Scotland for the Protestant Faction began to grow and, in 1557, a group of lairds formed themselves into a group called the *Lords of the Congregation* with the specific intention of achieving a Protestant government. Following religious riots in Perth, this group organised military support for the Protestant cause.

1558 would prove to be a pivotal year. In April the sixteen year old Queen Mary married the Dauphin in Paris, and in November the Catholic English Queen Mary died. With the accession of the Protestant Queen

Elizabeth, the Lords of the Congregation renewed their campaign to ally with England, and in July 1559, they took control of Edinburgh. There were negotiations with the government in which the Catholic Earl of Arran noticeably changed sides. Eventually, the Protestant forces prevailed and, with the death of regent Mary of Guise in 1560, they took control of the Parliament. In the Treaty of Edinburgh, it was then agreed that all foreign troops would withdraw from Scotland, leaving the Scots to settle their own affairs. In no time, the Lords of the Congregation proceeded to enact widespread reform of the Scottish church which were designed to institute the Protestant faith. Still in France, Mary refused to sign a number these Acts, putting the legislation into limbo.

In December 1560, Queen Mary's husband the Dauphin died and, still only 19 years old, in 1561 she returned to Scotland to take up the throne. Given her Catholic education and faith, not to mention her recent marriage, she soon found herself at odds with the new Protestant government. However, they respected her claim to the throne and did allow her to practice her faith provided that she did not attempt to re-impose Catholicism on her subjects. This did not endear her to the Catholic nobles, and the next few years would see a series of internal crises.

For a time, Queen Mary lived as a widow while some of those around her sought to find her a husband. Amongst her potential suitors was her highly credentialed cousin Henry Stewart, Lord Darnley.[7] Darnley was the oldest surviving son of Matthew Stewart the Earl of Lennox (third in line to the Scottish throne) and Margaret Douglas who was a niece of Henry VIII. Active in affairs of State, in 1545 Matthew had been found guilty of treason by the Pro-Catholic Faction for changing sides over the implementation of the Treaty of Greenwich and he had taken up exile in England where Henry had been born in 1546. In 1563 Matthew was pardoned, and in February 1565 he and his son Henry made an appearance at the Scottish court. Henry was a handsome and athletic young man, with a passion for hunting. However, he was said to be hot-headed and irresponsible. In any event, on meeting Henry, the 23 year old Mary was smitten and, within six months, they were married. Mary soon became pregnant.

On marrying Mary, Henry was designated as a Consort but took the view that he should become a co-monarch. Mary would have none of that and, despite the affection between them, she afforded him very little involvement in affairs of state. This was not just because of his age. It didn't take her long to discover that he was inclined to be arrogant, wilful and unreliable, and subsequently there was anecdotal evidence that he was complicit in the murder of her powerful Secretary David Rizzio. In any event, on 19 June 1566 Mary gave birth to a son, and the arrival of James brought much celebration. Judiciously, while he was baptised into the Catholic faith, he had both the Protestant Queen Elizabeth and the Catholic King Charles IX of France as god-parents.

Despite this happy event, within six months tragedy struck. For some time, the 4th Earl of Bothwell, James Hepburn, had had designs on Mary. On the night of 9/10 February 1567, Henry's residence in Edinburgh was destroyed by an explosion, and he and some of his men were found murdered in the garden. There were strong suspicions that Bothwell, who had been a supporter of Queen Mary's mother, was responsible and he was arrested. However, at a trial in April 1567, he was acquitted and, a week later, he connived with a group of lords and bishops to sign what was known as the Ainslie Tavern Bond in which they agreed to support his marriage to Mary. On 24 April, he then kidnapped Mary on her way back from visiting her infant son in Stirling Castle and on 15 May they were married, Bothwell having divorced his existing wife just ten days previously!

These extraordinary events did not go down well amongst many nobles and in July 1567 there was an uprising against the newly married couple. Mary was imprisoned in Loch Leven Castle and forced to abdicate in favour of her one-year-old son, with the Earl of Moray appointed as regent. In the meantime, Bothwell was arrested for plotting through the use of witchcraft. However, he escaped and fled to Denmark, only to be captured off the coast of Norway.[8] In 1568, Mary escaped from her prison and, for several months, she was on the run around Scotland. Eventually, at the Battle of Langside, her supporters were defeated and she fled to England. Travelling to London, Mary naively expected a friendly reception from Queen Elizabeth. However, she failed to appreciate that there were fears in England about her potential claim to the English throne under the Treaty of Greenwich. With rumours of plots to remove Queen Elizabeth, for the next 18 years Mary was confined in a succession of castles and manor houses. Eventually, an English court found Mary guilty of plotting to assassinate Elizabeth and, in 1587, Mary was beheaded at Fotheringhay Castle. By now, her estranged 21 years old son James VI was well established on the Scottish throne.

ENDNOTES

1   The name Stewart evolved to Stuart in the 16th century through French influence because their alphabet did not have the letter "w".

2   At this point, the Council consisted of magnates appointed by both the king and Parliament and had both legislative and judicial powers. At meetings, they were often represented by university educated career administrators and lawyers. Increasingly, the Council had the right to grant titles to land and had significant powers in limiting the power of a regent.

3   The title Duke of Rothesay would be a title that heirs apparent to the Scottish throne would hold for ever thereafter. Rothesay is the principal town on the Isle of Bute, with a 13th century castle which had been occupied by the English during the Wars of Scottish Independence and it was a favourite residence of both Robert II and Robert III. In 1462, it was attacked by the defiant Lord of the Isles, it was frequently used by Kings James IV and James V, and it was occupied by Cromwell's army in the 1650s who partly demolished it on their departure. It was burnt to a ruin by Archibald 9th Earl of Argyll during the 1689 Jacobite rebellion. The current Duke of Rothesay is Prince William.

4   His sister Margaret married the Dauphin who later became King Louis XI.

5   Richard is named by the Tudor dynasty as Perkin Warbeck. He came to a sticky end at the hands of Henry VII.

6   This was the last pitched battle fought between Scottish and English armies.

7   Mary and Henry Stewart were both great grandchildren of English King Henry VII, and Henry was a great-great-great-grandson of King James II. Henry was raised as a Catholic but had Protestant leanings.

8   Bothwell was imprisoned in Bergen and died in prison in Sweden in 1578.

REFORMATION

The Christian faith came to Scotland through the settlement in Iona of St Columba in CE 593, at a time when the dominant Picts were adherents to various forms of Celtic religion. Following a period of evangelisation, Christianity became established across the whole country, with monasteries, nunneries, and parish-based communities. From the early days, the church maintained a relatively independent status within the global Catholic Church, and this was confirmed by Papal Bull in 1192 when the Scottish bishoprics were recognised as entities separate from the English sees of Canterbury and York. At that time, the Bishop of St Andrews became the most important ecclesiastical position in Scotland. In the next century, the church consolidated its position in Scotland. However, as in other parts of Europe, in the 14th century there were a range of factors at play which lead to what became the Reformation.

From the early days, the church in Scotland was administered by local monastic institutions which were financed through a process known as *appropriation*. This provided that most of the revenue generated at a parish level was passed to the church hierarchy. Eventually, this led to a concentration of wealth in the upper echelons of the church including the two powerful archbishoprics of St Andrews and Glasgow and concerns about the opportunity for corruption.[1] As a consequence, although the church did provide access to education, and relief for the sick and the poor, most Scottish parishes like those in Mull were relatively impoverished.

In the meantime, at an international level, there had been a major schism in the church. In 1309, with an increasingly fractious environment in Rome, Pope Clement V had moved the papacy to Avignon. In the next sixty years, a succession of Popes were French and many feared that the church had become captive of the French king. In 1377, Pope Gregory XI returned to live in Rome and, after his death in 1378, the hierarchies in Avignon and Rome each elected their own Pope, with Scotland and France supporting Avignon while England stayed loyal to Rome. This division continued until 1414, and seriously weakened the authority and cohesion of the church. One outcome was that in 1487 King James III felt free to wrest from the Pope the right to appoint Scottish bishops.

In addition to these financial and structural issues, in the 15th century there was a growing interest in humanist ideas and a desire to reinvent the Christian faith. These sentiments had reached Scotland through contacts with scholars such as the Dutchman Erasmus, who campaigned for reforms designed to eliminate corruption and encourage tolerance of divergent views.[2] At the same time, by the late 15th century, the wider manifestations of the Renaissance were sweeping through Scotland, with the development of an open royal court welcoming people from many backgrounds, a commitment to the arts, and an interest in the richness of antiquity.

First Martyr

Unlike some parts of Europe, the move away from the Catholic faith in Scotland would be achieved with relatively little bloodshed, and just a few martyrs. By the reign of King James V in the 1520s, the teachings of Martin Luther were being widely promulgated in Scotland by several clerics, including Patrick Hamilton.[3] The religious and royal hierarchy were not impressed, and his ideas were seen by some as revolutionary. As a result, in 1525, Parliament banned the circulation of what were seen as subversive books and papers. Undeterred, Hamilton continued to preach, and his activities came to the attention of David Beaton the Archbishop of St Andrews. Beaton indicated his displeasure and, in fear of his life, Hamilton fled the country. However, with the publication in 1526 of William Tyndale's translation of the New Testament into English, Hamilton returned to continue his mission. It didn't take long for Beaton to decide that he had heard enough and, in 1528, Hamilton was arrested and put on trial for heresy. He was found guilty and burnt at the stake. The treatment of this first martyr lit a flame of dissent that was never extinguished.

In the meantime, King James V extended his power to appoint clerics and control the church. At the time, there were tensions between the archbishoprics of St Andrews and Glasgow, and in 1538 he appointed Beaton as a Cardinal.[4] He also levied heavy taxes on the church, further impoverishing local parishes and their ability to support local communities. Despite growing discontent amongst many local clerics and gentry across the country, and a growing Protestant Faction, in 1541 Parliament reaffirmed its commitment to the Catholic faith including the authority of the Pope, the sanctity of the Mass, and other tenets of the traditional faith.

Growing Dissent

Following the death of James V in 1542, and the establishment of a regency led by the new Queen Mary's Catholic mother Mary of Guise, the Protestant Faction gained control of Parliament. They favoured religious reform and, amongst other things, they legislated the publication of bibles written in the vernacular. In 1543, they then concluded the Treaty of Greenwich which provided for young Queen Mary to marry the son of the Protestant English King Henry VIII in an attempt to weaken the Scottish link with Catholic France. This triggered a coup by Cardinal Beaton who both rejected the proposed betrothal to Edward, and reversed attempts to reform the church.[5] The English then declared war.

In the meantime an academic named George Wishart, who had been studying on the continent, returned to Scotland and began to preach the works of Calvin. His sermons included condemnation of the Catholic Church's corruption, and Cardinal Beaton had him arrested and brought to trial. Wishart was found guilty of heresy, and in March 1546 he was hanged and burnt at the stake.[6] Far from quelling attacks on the Catholic Church, his death triggered an ever growing interest in his ideas and burgeoning dissent. In May 1546 Cardinal Beaton was murdered by Wishart's supporters who went on to occupy St Andrew's Castle for 12 months until they were ejected by the government with the help of French troops. The survivors, including John Knox, were condemned to serve as galley slaves and this only served to inspire additional supporters for the Protestant cause. The authorities would rue the day they attempted to silence John Knox but let him live!

In 1547, King Henry VIII died. Determined to enforce the Treaty of Greenwich, the English Regent of the ten years old King Edward VI, the Duke of Somerset, invaded Scotland. As they advanced through the country, they distributed bibles and other religious texts, and this served to encourage local Protestants. In fear of a Protestant coup, in 1548 the government despatched the now five years old Queen Mary to the French court where she was subsequently raised and prepared for a betrothal to the son of the French King, the Dauphin.

The Reformation Parliament

During the next decade there was mounting conflict between the Catholic faction, led by Mary of Guise, and a Protestant faction named the Lords of the Congregation who acknowledged John Knox as their religious leader. This group was formed in 1557 by a group of lairds (including the Duke of Argyll) with the aim of establishing a Protestant Parliament, forging an alliance with Protestant England, and opposing the proposed marriage of Mary to the Dauphin.

Following riots in Perth, there were military skirmishes between representatives of the two factions. To stymie the Protestant cause, in 1558 Queen Mary was married to the Dauphin. However, the Lords of the Congregation were unruffled and, with the accession of the Protestant Queen Elizabeth to the English throne in the same year, they persisted in their military campaign. In July 1559 they occupied Edinburgh and, following negotiations with the government, during which the Catholic Earl of Arran noticeably changed sides, and subsequent military skirmishes, they prevailed. With the death of Mary of Guise in June 1560, they took control of the Parliament, and this sealed the future of Scotland's faith.

The "Reformation Parliament" as it was called approved the *Reformed Confession of Faith*, passed Acts that abolished papal jurisdiction over Scotland, banned the conduct of the Mass, and confirmed that there should be only two sacraments – baptism and the communion.[7]

In the meantime, Queen Mary had been hit by the first of several tragedies in her life. In 1559 the French King Henry II had died and she and her husband had become King and Queen of France. However, in December 1560 Francis died of an ear infection and, still only 18 years of age, she returned to Scotland. In one of her first acts, Mary refused to approve the Reformation Acts. Despite this, Parliament went on to publish the *Scots Confession* which became the church's creed for the next century. At the same time most of the trappings of the medieval church including the appointment of bishops, and the monasteries, were abolished. In their place, John Knox and others implemented a Calvinist system of church governance based on Presbyterianism.[8] This established the parish church as the main focus of religious activity, with Parliament financing the construction of community-based buildings with central pulpits to facilitate preaching.[9] These structural changes were accompanied by major changes in religious practice. Sunday became the single focus of religious observance, Latin was abandoned in favour of the vernacular, and an emphasis was put on the word of the Bible and interpretation of scripture through sermons. In 1562, a General Assembly of the Church adopted the Book of Common Order, a Gaelic version of which was produced in 1563.

To consolidate the reforms, the leaders of the Kirk determined to establish a school in every parish and institute major reforms in the university system.[10] However, not all their initiatives were consistent with the spirit of the renaissance. For example, they discouraged the performing of plays and poetry that were not devotional in nature, and terminated support for artists in providing church paintings. They also closed choral schools, disbanded church choirs, destroyed music books, and removed organs from churches to be replaced by the congregation's singing of psalms. On the other hand, women were admitted to more active roles although they were still subject to prosecutions for scolding, prostitution, and witchcraft! Above all, the focus was on *"the word of the Lord"* as evident in the Bible, and gradually the Kirk became the subject of considerable national pride.

With Queen Mary's continued obduracy towards the reform legislation and the many other issues that beset her in the 1560s, in 1567 Parliament forced her abdication. Under the now firmly entrenched Protestant government, although he had been baptised as a Catholic, her son James was raised in the new faith. And Parliament enacted laws that made support for Calvinism a prerequisite for appointment to public office. They also provided for the training of the clergy, and purged recalcitrant teachers in the universities and schools. In December 1567, a further parliament was called to ratify the earlier Acts. In the years that followed, the church in Scotland would go through many more changes as it moved to becoming one of the main institutions of the state.

As a footnote, at this stage, the majority of the population in Mull was probably still Catholic, with most people following the chief of clan, and the Kirk would find it particularly difficult to penetrate the Highlands and Islands. Interestingly, while the Macleans of Duart were early adopters of Protestant ideas, the Maclaines of Lochbuie would remain as Catholics. However the church committed to a gradual process of conversion that, compared with elsewhere, was conducted with prolonged patience and relatively little persecution.

ENDNOTES

1   St Andrews was established as an archbishipric in 1472, followed by Glasgow in 1492.
2   Erasmus lived from 1466 to 1536. As well as being an academic and philosopher, he was a Catholic priest.
3   Patrick Hamilton was born in Linlithgow in 1504 and educated at St Andrews University and the University of Paris. He travelled widely in Europe where he met several reform thinkers.
4   David Beaton lived from 1494 to 1546 and would be the last Scottish cardinal before the Reformation.
5   Henry VIII had established the Protestant Church of England in 1534.
6   George Wishart was born in 1513 and educated at Aberdeen University. In 1539/40 he lived in Switzerland, studying the teachings of Calvin. In 1543, he returned to Scotland and travelled the country teaching the Protestant faith. A constant companion was John Knox.
7   This legislation was written by John Knox and included what was called The Scots Confession.
8   The word Presbyterianism comes from the word Presbyter. Presbyters were people elected by the ministers and elders to govern the church in place of royal appointed bishops.
9   There were several churches erected in Mull but none survive.
10 The word kirk was in use in Scotland to describe the church since the 13th century and came into increasingly common use during the Reformation. It derived from the Norse kirkja which means church.

PART FIVE

UNION AND REBIRTH

DÙTHCHAS
LANDSCAPE AND COMMUNITY IN MULL AND IONA

BIRTH OF BRITAIN

The ascendancy of the Protestant religion, and assumption of effective control by King James VI as an adult king in the last decade of the 16th century, would see the start of a new era for Scotland. It would also spell significant changes for society in the Highlands and the Islands. In the next 150 years their separate identity defined by the community-based clan system would slowly be eroded as they became an integral part of the Scottish nation.

King James VI was born in June 1566 and baptised at Stirling Castle. He was the only son of Queen Mary and Henry Stewart and, following his father's murder and his mother's abdication in 1567, he came to the throne when he was only 13 months old. With his mother taking refuge in England, incarcerated and eventually executed for treason by Queen Elizabeth, James would never see her again.

As a baby, James was put under the care of the Earl and Countess of Mar, and anointed as a Protestant king in a ceremony in 1567 at which John Knox gave a sermon. James's education was entrusted to several tutors, including George Buchanan who instilled in him a love of literature and learning. Buchanan also sought to foster an acceptance of the limitations of monarchy, as outlined in his treatise *De Jure Regni apud Scotos*.[1]

During James's minority, Scotland had four regents. Given the outrage of his deposed mother's supporters, it was a position that came with significant risk. In 1567, the first person to be appointed to this role by the Privy Council was Queen Mary's illegitimate half-brother James Stewart Earl of Moray. During his time, he helped to hound his sister out of Scotland, and in 1570 he was assassinated by one of her supporters James Hamilton. His successor was his grandfather Matthew Stewart, 4th Earl of Lennox. Lennox did not last long, being fatally wounded in 1571 during a skirmish with Mary's supporters. At this point, the Privy Council turned to James's guardian, the Earl of Mar. However in 1572 he took ill at a banquet given by James Douglas, 4th Earl of Morton. Shortly afterwards he died, apparently of natural causes. Thereafter, Morton was appointed regent and would prove to be competent in the role for several years until October 1579 when the thirteen years old James was proclaimed as an adult ruler. Despite his honourable service, like his predecessors, Morton would come to a sticky end. In the execution of his duties, he made several enemies including Esmé Stewart who was a cousin and confidant of James.[2] In 1581, Morton was charged and found guilty of being complicit in the murder of James's father and was executed. Shortly afterwards, James made Esmé the 1st Duke of Lennox; but Esmé's elevated position was short-lived. Senior members of the court, including supporters of Morton, suspected him of having sexual designs on the king and hatched a plot to have him banished. In August 1582, the Earls of Gowrie and Angus lured James into Ruthven Castle where they held him captive for ten months until he agreed that Lennox should be exiled. After being suitably chastened by a sermon from the Royal Chaplain, James was then released and Lennox was despatched back to France where he died in 1583.

Following his release from captivity, James gradually took control of the government. After a more than adequate education, it is said that he quickly proved to be an astute king. Apparently a colourful character, with a wispy beard and of slight build, he appointed some able courtiers, and demonstrated considerable skill in mediating between warring factions. However, in the flush of youth, and with a firmly held belief in the divine right of kings, one of the first things he did was to try and assert his rights over the church, to which the crown had lost significant power during the period of regency. In 1584, he promoted what were called the Black Acts, which sought to re-assert royal authority, and denounced the writings of his former tutor Buchanan. The legislation had little impact, with Parliament continuing with its own legislation to further entrench the Presbyterian Church.

Of greater significance, in 1586 James negotiated a treaty with the English Queen Elizabeth. At its core, *The Treaty of Berwick* was a mutual defence pact, aimed at two potential Catholic adversaries, France and Spain. Under its terms, England made a commitment to pay an annual grant to Scotland of £4,000 in return for Scottish support. In signing the treaty, there is conjecture that Elizabeth also hoped to soften the blow of her plans for prosecuting James's mother for treason. Whether or not this is true, it is certainly the case that, when Elizabeth proceeded with Mary's execution in 1587, James made only the mildest of protests. For James, it would seem that the treaty had the potential to strengthen his ambition to succeed Elizabeth as King of England in the event that she remained without husband or heir. In any event, the first test of the treaty occurred in 1588, with the arrival of the Spanish Armada. Before this abortive invasion, there is evidence that the Spanish sought James's support which he refused. As we have seen in Chapter 8 with the military escapades of Lachlan Mor Maclean, afterwards some Scottish clans took advantage of wayward Spanish to pursue feuds with their erstwhile enemies.

As a young man, James showed little interest in women, and there is conjecture that he was homosexual. In any event, he was also keenly aware of his royal duties to provide an heir and, in 1589, the Privy Council arranged his betrothal to the 14 years old Anne of Denmark.[3] With some concern regarding her safety, the twenty-three year old James sailed to Norway and they were married in Oslo. They returned to Scotland in May 1590 and eventually had several children, with Charles the only surviving boy.

Despite a busy life, during this early period, James found the time to write several books and papers. In 1597, he published *The True Law of Free Monarchies* in which he set out the concept of the divine right of kings with a monarch having the prerogative to impose laws that "pay heed to God and tradition". In 1598 he then published *Basilikon Doron (Royal Gift)*, in which he argued a theological basis for monarchy as well as opining on what constituted good governance and a civil society. There is little doubt that these books were compulsory reading for his son Charles who subsequently practiced what his father preached. James was also paranoid about the influence of witches, with several burnt at the stake, and he published a book on demonology.

In the early years of James's reign, the far-flung Western Isles were very much back on Edinburgh's agenda. Apparently, those at court had a low opinion of people living on the periphery of the country, and there are contemporary written accounts which suggest that Highlanders were *"void of the knawledge and feir of God"* and prone to *"all kynd of barbarous and bestile cruelties"*.[4] It is also known that James disparaged the Gaelic language which had been spoken so fluently by his grandfather. At court, it was known as "Erse" or Irish, implying that it was foreign in nature and, seen as a source of backward culture, it was abolished as an official language.

It was against this background that in 1597 that the chief of the Clan McLeod in Lewis was served with a writ stating that his lack of legal paperwork exposed his estates to claims from the Crown. This stemmed from an Act of Parliament requiring the chiefs of all Highland clans to prove title for their property. Then in 1598 James signed an order that authorised 11 Scottish nobles called the *"Gentleman Adventurers of Fife"* to civilise the *"most barbarous Isle of Lewis"*. In this document, James wrote that the *colonists* were to act "not by agreement" with the local inhabitants, but "by extirpation".[5] The "colonists" made a landing at Stornoway but were driven out by the local clansmen. They would try again in 1605 with the same result, although a third attempt in 1607 was more successful. It was the beginning of much worse for inhabitants of the Hebrides.

Union of the Crowns

On her deathbed in 1603, the childless Queen Elizabeth nominated James to be her successor and, at the age of 37, he became King James I of England. His accession was no great surprise and something of an irony, given that Elizabeth had had his mother executed in 1587 because of the perceived threat that *she* posed to the legitimacy of the English crown. Almost immediately, James moved to London, promising to return to Scotland every three years.[6] On arrival at the English court, he was not universally welcomed. He was considered by many of the English aristocracy as a crude and unkempt Scot, and became the subject of a back-handed epithet *"the wisest fool in Christendom".*[7] In any event, in a few short years he would declare himself the first King of Great Britain and Ireland, foreshadowing the eventual Act of Union between Scotland and England in 1707. He was also responsible for delivering the Statutes of Iona which would have a particular significance for a place like Mull. The Statutes were an attempt to consolidate James's earlier attempts to change the autonomous nature of Highlands and Islands culture and drive them towards customs more akin to the rest of Scotland. The main provisions were as follows:

- All gentlemen with more than 60 cattle must send their eldest son to the lowlands for education.
- The households of chiefs were to be reduced, with less accommodation for extended families.
- Chiefs were to provide for the establishment of a network of community based kirks, with the appointment of a local minister for each parish.
- Chiefs were responsible for the actions of their clansmen, and required to prosecute anyone contravening the Statutes. There were severe punishments for failing to stop internecine conflict.
- Begging and protection of fugitives were outlawed.
- Roving bards were banned from sustaining traditional culture through performance of songs and story-telling characterised as "false myths".
- Inns were to be established, with the aim of discouraging the traditional custom of clansmen in accommodating visitors in their homes.
- Import of wine was to be restricted, with islanders permitted to distil whisky for their own use only.
- Firearms were banned, even for hunting.

As can be seen, these measures were far reaching, and very much a precursor of the punitive attempts to stamp out clan life adopted 150 years later after the Battle of Culloden. While they took a good many years to be fully implemented, particularly in Mull where the Clan Maclean of Duart felt no compulsion to dismantle the traditional society, and the Clan Maclaine of Lochbuie maintained their Catholic religion and customs, they became a vehicle for relentless change.

If this was not enough, a few years later King James doubled down on his earlier attempt to require clan chiefs to prove ownership of land. In 1617 he promulgated *The Registration Act*. This established the Register of Sasines which was constituted as a continuing record of deeds of ownership including transfers.[8] As a consequence, with many clan chiefs struggling to comply with the regulations, the power of the clan-based society in the Highlands would be gradually eroded by the consolidation of land ownership into the hands of a small number of powerful dukes and earls who were major players on the national political scene and largely absent from the estates over which they slowly acquired control. For the most part, the new land owners had neither family ties nor any sense of loyalty to the people who had now become their tenants. This would be a powerful force for driving the successful implementation of most of the Statutes of Iona.

Although the English Parliament succeeded in crippling his finances, and there were several attempts on his life such as the Gunpowder Plot of 1605 (after which Catholics were excluded from high office), James left quite a legacy. His achievements include:

- The creation of the first version of the Union Jack in 1606,[9]
- Early colonisation of America, with Jamestown established in the colony of Virginia in 1607,
- The introduction of what became the lucrative tobacco trade, with Glasgow a major port for the whole of Britain,
- The Statutes of Iona in 1609, designed to civilise the Highlands and Islands, and
- The publication of the world's first "Authorised" version of the Bible printed in English in 1611.

King Charles I

On his death in 1625, King James VI was succeeded by his son Charles. Born in 1600, the new king had spent most of his childhood in England with an English nanny. However, his father appointed a Presbyterian Scot Thomas Murray as his tutor. On his accession, marriage became an imperative and, after a failed attempt to marry the Spanish Infanta, he married the fifteen year old Catholic daughter of the French King Henry IV, Henrietta Maria.

King Charles emulated his father's belief in the divine right of kings and, in the early years of his reign, he lent support to several Catholic causes on the continent where the Thirty Years War between Catholic and Protestant forces was intermittently raging. As a result of this, and his wife's commitment to the Catholic faith, the Protestant Parliaments in Scotland and England became increasingly suspicious of his Catholic leanings. There ensued an almost continuous struggle between Charles and the respective Parliaments over a range of issues, including his attempt to unify the Scottish and English churches, the machinations of his adviser the Duke of Buckingham who was assassinated in 1628, and his attempt to unilaterally raise taxes. In 1629 things came to a head. When the English Parliament passed several Acts to Charles's disliking, he arrested several MPs and dissolved the English Parliament. This would be the beginning of eleven years of personal rule.

With a free hand, in the 1630s, Charles attempted to impose his views about the role and structure of the church. In 1633, he appointed William Laud as Archbishop of Canterbury with a remit to implement a programme in England that would roll back the appointment of non-conformist preachers, insist on use of the Church of England Book of Common Prayer, and mandate a range of other Protestant practices implemented during the Reformation. In 1637, when he attempted to pursue the same policies in Scotland without consulting the Scottish Parliament or the Kirk, he met serious opposition with riots breaking out. In November 1638 the General Assembly of the Church of Scotland resolved to adopt the National Covenant which rejected Charles's reforms including the use of the English Book of Common Prayer. Subsequently, at a meeting in Glasgow, the

General Assembly voted to abolish bishops appointed by the monarch in favour of presbyters elected by the ministers and elders of the church.

In the next 15 years, there were a number of military conflicts in England, Scotland and Ireland sometimes known as the *Wars of the Three Kingdoms*. Hostilities began with what have been called the *Bishops Wars*. In 1639, and without recourse to either Parliament, the King marshalled three forces to bring Scotland to heel. These comprised:

- An Irish army led by the Earl of Antrim to invade western Scotland from Carrickfergus where he would join forces with the Macdonalds and other Royalist clans including the Macleans of Mull,
- An amphibious force of 5,000 under the Marquis of Hamilton to land at Aberdeen in the east and link up with Royalist troops led by the Marquess of Huntly, and
- An army of 20,000 of mostly English troops to advance on Edinburgh from the south.

In response to the threat posed by the Irish army, the Scottish government appointed the 8th Earl of Argyll to lead a force which quickly occupied Dumbarton to block any landing. Then the Marquess of Montrose, James Graham, stymied Hamilton's attack on Aberdeen. Finally, on the southern front, Montrose's army defeated the English army at the Battle of Brig of Dee.

Subsequently, the Scottish Parliament confirmed proposals from the General Assembly designed to consolidate a range of religious reforms and institute tri-annual Parliaments. In response, and desperately in need of funds to raise an army to impose his rule in Scotland, King Charles recalled the English Parliament. They made the supply of funds dependent on the resolution of other long standing issues which the King refused to address and he dissolved the Parliament. Meanwhile, in Scotland Covenanter government forces occupied Aberdeen.

In 1640, there was a second round of hostilities. In June, the Scottish Parliament gave the Earl of Argyll a commission to put down all rebellion in the west. Argyll proceeded to seize the lands of Royalist supporters including those of the Macdonalds in Lochaber and Fort William, and to occupy

Dumbarton Castle. Meanwhile, a Scottish government army took control of Edinburgh Castle and occupied Newcastle. King Charles then sued for peace and, under the Treaty of Ripon in 1640, the English agreed to pay the Scots £850 per day, with the Scots occupying Northumberland and County Durham pending final resolution of terms. Subsequently, under the Treaty of London, in August 1641 the Scots evacuated English territory.

No sooner had these hostilities been resolved, than a rebellion broke out in Ireland. With tensions between King Charles and the English Parliament about how to quell the uprising, in 1642 this led to the outbreak of the English Civil War into which Scotland was eventually drawn. Between 1644 and 1645, there were hostilities between Royalist supporters (led by the Marquess of Montrose who had changed sides) and the Scottish government who supported the English Parliament. Initially, with the help of Irish troops, the Royalists gained the upper hand in what was called *The Year of Victories*. Afterwards, Montrose had high hopes of establishing a pro-Royalist government in Scotland that would roll back some of the religious reforms. However, his efforts were to no avail, as supporters drifted away and he was eventually defeated by the Scottish government forces at the Battle of Philiphaugh. Montrose then fled to France.

In the meantime, there was full bodied war in England between Charles's forces and the English Parliament's New Model Army led by Oliver Cromwell. After early victories, the tide turned against Charles and, with his defeat at the Battle of Naseby in 1645, and the siege of Oxford in 1646, he ended up fleeing into the hands of Scottish forces in Newark. The Scots removed him to Newcastle and in 1647 they handed him over to the English for the princely sum of £100,000. Charles was incarcerated, and eventually brought to trial. He was executed in January 1649 with Cromwell declared Lord Protector.

King Charles II

The death of King Charles I posed a problem for the Scottish government most of whom had little sympathy for republicanism. At a meeting after Charles' execution, the Parliament resolved to acknowledge Charles's son as

King Charles II. This encouraged the exiled James Graham the Marquess of Montrose to organise a force supporting the new king which landed in the Orkneys in March 1650. He was not well received and, when he crossed to the mainland, he was hunted down and defeated at the Battle of Carbisdale in Ross-Shire. After being on the run for a time, he eventually surrendered and was put on trial in Edinburgh. Despite protesting his devotion to the Covenant, he was found guilty of treason and hanged on 21 May 1650.

Meanwhile, the Scottish Parliament's endorsement of King Charles II brought a direct confrontation between Scottish and English armies. In July 1650, Cromwell invaded Scotland, and in July 1651 he confronted the Scots at the Battle of Inverkeithing in which there were heavy Scottish casualties including many Macleans. In September, Cromwell decisively defeated an army led by King Charles II at the Battle of Worcester, and, for a time Scotland found itself part of the Commonwealth.

In 1660, following the death of Cromwell and the failure of his son to show any ability in succeeding him, the English Parliament resolved to abolish the Commonwealth and invite King Charles II to take up the English crown. Already accepted as monarch in Scotland, in 1661 the King sponsored the *Rescissory Act* which sought to restore bishops to the Church of Scotland. With significant opposition, Charles subsequently used Highland levies, known as the "Highland Host", to terrorise Protestants into compliance. Following a series of armed rebellions, in 1681 the resistance got the upper hand and the Scottish Parliament passed the Test Act. This confirmed the supremacy of the Protestant faith and excluded from public office those not swearing an oath of allegiance to the Kirk.[10]

King James VII and the Glorious Revolution

In 1685, Charles II died without heir and was succeeded by his younger brother James VII (James II of England). With his Protestant first wife Anne Hyde he had had two daughters, Mary and Anne and this had appeared to augur well for a Protestant succession. However, in 1671 the Queen had died. In 1673, James had then married the Catholic Mary of Modena and there were soon rumours that he had converted to Catholicism. Nevertheless, when his daughter Mary had married the Protestant William of Orange in 1677, there was a collective sigh of relief that Protestantism would prevail.

When James came to the throne, he was initially on good terms with his parliaments. However, when they refused to exempt Catholics from some provisions of the Test Act, he suspended and ruled by decree. His approach led to mounting dissent and, in 1688, things came to a head in what was known as the Glorious Revolution. In June, not long after James Catholic wife Mary had given birth to a son named James Edward Stuart, there were anti-Catholic riots. With mounting unrest, a group of English politicians (the Immortal Seven) wrote to James' son-in-law William of Orange inviting him to intervene on behalf of his wife Mary. There was talk of James' wife having actually had a still birth with the new male baby being an imposter.[11] Although this was not true, William did not need any encouragement and, in November 1688, he landed with a force at Torbay in Devon. He quickly found the English army deserting to his cause and in December King James fled to the continent.[12] Shortly after, the English Parliament resolved that James had abandoned the throne.

As these events were unfolding, there were similar concerns about a Catholic revival in Scotland and, on 7 January 1689 the Scottish Privy Council liaised with William about his intentions. A Convention of Presbyterian and Episcopalian representatives was then convened to agree the basis for the future governance of Scotland. In a desperate attempt to regain his Scottish throne, on 12 March James landed with supporters in Ireland and despatched a letter to the Convention demanding obedience to the crown and threatening reprisals for those who disobeyed. It was read out aloud with a mixed reception. Some participants were outraged, and the Episcopalian supporters of James withdrew. With tempers running high, supporters of the King sought to protect his position, with the Duke of Gordon taking control of Edinburgh Castle and Viscount Dundee recruiting Highland levies including supporters from Mull. Then, in an attempt to preserve Episcopalianism, the Scottish Bishops proposed Union with England but this was rejected by the English Parliament.

In the weeks that followed, the dye would be cast. The English Parliament formally invited William and Mary to be joint monarchs of England and Ireland, and on 11 April 1689, a newly elected Scottish Convention formally ended the reign of King James VII. They adopted the Articles of Grievances and the Claim of Right that made the Scottish Parliament the primary legislative power in Scotland. On 11 May 1689, William and Mary accepted an invitation to become joint monarchs of Scotland, and on 5 June the Convention assumed the role of Parliament.

In December 1689, the English Parliament passed the historic Bill of Rights. This is a seminal law in British history, identifying limits on the powers of the monarch, setting out the rights of Parliament, and proclaiming the rights of individual citizens including *"the right to bear arms"* in defence of the Protestant religion.[13] In 1690, the Scottish Parliament passed the Act of Settlement confirming that the Kirk was the official Church of Scotland, and in 1701 the English Parliament confirmed the supremacy of the Protestant faith in England with its Act of Settlement which excluded Catholics from becoming the monarch.

Union with England

In the immediate aftermath of the Glorious Revolution, the Protestant succession appeared to be secure and, although there were vestiges of the old religion in places like Mull, the Kirk was firmly back in control. However, in the final years of the 17th century, Scotland was troubled by a range of economic and political issues. In the 1690s, there were successive harvest failures, there were mounting tensions in trade with England, and Scotland suffered a serious setback in attempts to establish an overseas empire at Darien in Panama.[14] Also, following the death of Queen Mary in 1694, King William was drawn into mounting tension with France in what would become the War of the Spanish Succession.[15] These factors would lead to mounting instability in the Scottish body politic.[16]

In 1702, King William died and was succeeded by his sister-in-law Anne. In Scotland, there was an orderly transition. However, even as the War with

France was in full flow, there were tensions over the Protestant Succession. Without consulting the Scottish Parliament, the English Parliament nominated the grand-daughter of James I, Sophia the Electress of Hanover.[17] In response, in 1704 the Scottish Parliament passed the Act of Security which provided that, if Queen Anne died without a successor, Scotland would appoint a Protestant successor of their own choosing from descendants of Scottish kings. In retaliation, in February 1705 the English Parliament enacted *The Alien Act,* which provided that Scots living in England would be treated as aliens, their English properties would be at risk, and there would be an embargo on the import of Scottish goods including cattle and coal. This was met with outrage and riots in Scotland, and in November the Act was repealed. In the meantime, moves were afoot to pursue a far more radical resolution to tensions between the two countries. In the spring of 1706, representatives from the Scottish and English Parliaments formed a committee to draft legislation that would provide for union of the two countries. It concluded its deliberations in July, with some 25 Articles that included a commitment to the Hanoverian Succession, significant concessions for Scottish trade, and a range of protections for Scotland's church and legal system. The legislation was also accompanied by a number of financial inducements, including compensation to the investors in the failed Darien project.

English support was secured without much debate, and in October 1706 the Scottish Parliament was convened. At this time, Scotland had a unicameral system with a Parliament of 227 MPs comprising Officers of State, nobles, and representatives of the burghs and shires. There were two main parties. The Court Party, which was in government and aligned with the monarch had around 100 MPs, and was led by the Duke of Queensberry with support by the 3rd Duke of Argyll. The Country Party, with a similar number of MPs was led by the Duke of Hamilton. There was also a small off-shoot of the Country Party, established in 1704, called the *Squadron Volante.*

Following the initial debate on Union, and the evident opposition of many ordinary citizens, the Parliament adjourned. In early 1707 it then reconvened and on 16 January the Bill for a Union was put to a vote. The outcome was far from unanimous, with 40 MPs either absent or abstaining.

However, the opposition was poorly led and compromised by offers of patronage to supporters of the Bill. In the event, the Act of Union, which established the United Kingdom of Great Britain and abolished the Scottish Parliament, was adopted by a vote of 110 to 67. Thus was sealed the fate of Scottish independence.

While this major constitutional change would bring huge and long lasting changes to every corner of Scotland, the commitment to the Hanoverian succession was far from guaranteed. As it became increasingly clear that Queen Anne would be childless, this gave fresh heart to James VII's son by his second wife, James Edward Stuart, to assert a claim to the throne.[18] In 1708, he attempted to land with a small force in the Firth of Forth. He was deflected by the newly constituted British Royal Navy, but this initiative was enough to raise his profile and engender some support for his right of succession particularly if he was prepared to renounce the Catholic religion.

Further Jacobite Rebellions

In 1714, Queen Anne died, and the commitment under the Act of Union to the installation of a Hanoverian monarch came into play. With the aforementioned Sophia having died two months before Queen Anne, the first in line as successor was her 54 year old German speaking son George. He didn't take much convincing and was crowned as George I in October. James Edward Stuart and his supporters were enraged, and they fostered riots in the streets of Edinburgh. Encouraged by this popular support, in 1715 Jacobites in Scotland and Cornwall took up arms, with support from the Clan Maclean while the government was supported by the newly ennobled Duke of Argyll. Despite the inconclusive Battles of Sherrifmuir and Preston, in December the self-proclaimed James III arrived by ship at Peterhead.[19] He briefly set up court in Scone but, in the face of advancing government forces, he then took flight. Now disavowed by the French who had recently formed an alliance with Britain, he was exiled in Rome. However, this did not stop him from rewarding his supporters, with Sir Hector Maclean of Duart receiving a Jacobite peerage when he succeeded his father as Clan Chief in 1716.[20]

Despite the failure of the 1715 rebellion, James Edward Stuart did not give up, forming an alliance with Spain who were now in conflict with England.[21] In late March 1719, Jacobite exiles supported by a small force of Spanish marines landed in Stornoway. However, any hopes of success were soon dashed, with a larger Spanish invasion fleet severely damaged by storms. In June the rising ended with defeat at the Battle of Glen Shiel in which 50 men of Mull's McKinnon clan were engaged. In 1722, supporters of the "Old Pretender" made a further failed attempt. Afterwards, James Edward Stuart lived out the rest of his life in Rome.[22]

Following the failure of these attempts at overturning the Hanoverian succession, the Jacobite cause was not finished. In 1719 James Edward Stuart had married Maria Clementine Sobieska (grand-daughter of King John III of Poland) and, living in Rome, in 1720 they had a son Charles Edward Stuart ("Bonnie Prince Charlie"). As he grew up, Charles developed a passion for the restoration of his father and, in 1743, he saw an opportunity to advance the cause. In October, France and Spain signed one of a series of Pacts that included a commitment to the restoration of the Stuarts to the British throne, and in January 1744, with British troops fighting the French in Flanders, France launched an attack on the south of Britain. This assault was stymied by bad weather and a determined defence by the Royal Navy. However, with talk of support from Highland clans, Charles travelled to Paris to brief the Scottish Jacobite envoy Sir John Murray with a view to obtaining French support for a landing in Scotland.[23] After his talks with the French, Sir John returned to Scotland to meet with local supporters and it soon became apparent that rebellion was contingent on a commitment from France to provide material support. Despite this contingency, Charles was determined to proceed with a landing anyway, arguing that once he had established his presence, the French would come to the party.

In the first few months of 1745, and encouraged by a petition of support sent to him by Sir Hector Maclean, Charles purchased significant weaponry, and commissioned two ships (the Du Teillay and the Elizabeth) to carry arms and troops to Scotland. This small fleet set sail from St Nazaire (near Nantes) but encountered the battleship HMS Lion and were forced to return to port. Undeterred, Charles tried again and arrived at Eriskay on the isle of Uist on 23 July. From there, he transferred to the mainland where, given the apparent lack of French support, he had a luke-warm reception. Nevertheless, on 19 August at Glenfillan, he launched the rebellion, with the raising of the Royal Standard that was witnessed by a force of 500-1,000 supporters from local clans.[24] He then marched on Edinburgh, recruiting as he advanced, with Lord George Murray joining the army in Perth and appointed as Commander. They entered the city on 17 September and, at the Battle of Prestonpans, routed a depleted force of government troops led by General Cope. The news of these events soon arrived in London and the government immediately ordered troops under the command of Prince William the Duke of Cumberland to return from Flanders where he was engaged in the War of the Austrian Succession.[2526]

To consolidate his position in Scotland, in early October Charles published two "Declarations". The first dissolved the "pretended Union (of 1707)," and the second rejected the Act of Settlement which barred Catholic monarchs. He also instructed the *Caledonian Mercury* to publish minutes of the 1695 Parliamentary enquiry into the Glencoe Massacre, often used as an example of post-1688 religious oppression. In mid-October, Jacobite morale was further boosted when the French landed supplies of money and weapons, together with an envoy, the Marquis d'Éguilles, which finally seemed to validate Charles' claims of French backing.

Despite these encouraging signs, all was not well in the Jacobite camp. Charles had somewhat antiquated views about the divine right of kings which led him to adopt an autocratic style of military leadership. At times he did not take kindly to the collegiate approach of the "Prince's Council" which met daily to manage his campaign, preferring to take advice from others including his Irish followers. In late October, there were significant discussions about whether to consolidate their position in Scotland or take the fight to England. Charles argued that an invasion of England was critical for attracting French support, and he was supported by his Irish supporters for whom a Stuart on the British throne was seen as a means of securing Irish independence. Charles also claimed he was in contact with

English supporters who were simply waiting for their arrival, while the French envoy d'Éguilles assured the Prince's Council that a French landing in England was imminent.

Despite the doubts of some members of the Prince's Council, in late October it was decided to invade England, on the presumption that English and French support would materialise. General Murray selected a route via Carlisle to pass through north-west England where there had been strong support for the 1715 rebellion. Advancing south, Murray divided the army into two columns to conceal their destination from General Wade, the British government commander in Newcastle. With little opposition, they reached Carlisle on 10 November, and Manchester on the 28th. Here they received the first notable intake of English recruits, who were formed into the Manchester Regiment under Colonel Francis Towneley, a Lancashire Catholic who had previously served as an officer in the French Army.

At this point, a number of the leaders felt that they had already gone far enough into English territory. However, the eternal optimist, and set on a triumphant arrival in London, Charles assured them that they would be joined by reinforcements in Derby. When they arrived there on 4 December, the additional support was not forthcoming. The following day, the Prince's Council convened to review their options. Given the lack of reinforcements, and with General Murray warning of the risk of being caught in a pincer movement by government armies advancing from the north (General Wade) and the south (General Cumberland), it was decided to retreat pending French intervention.

In the weeks running up to Christmas 1745, the Jacobites made good progress on their journey north and returned to Scotland on 22 December narrowly missing Cumberland's army. Now embedded on safer ground, the Prince's Council met to consider the next move. Charles continued to be at odds with General Murray over strategy. Murray took the view that the best course of action was a war of attrition in Scotland that would eventually bring the government to the negotiating table, because they had unfinished military commitments on the continent. In contrast, Charles was impatient to seize the day. Despite the fact that promises of a French invasion from

Dunkirk had proved to be illusory, when significant reinforcements from Aberdeen and Banff swelled the numbers of the army to 8,000, Charles initiated an attack on Stirling Castle. This proved unsuccessful and, now in the grip of winter, many supporters returned to their families, and a diminished army retreated to Inverness to await warmer weather.

By the spring of 1746, Charles was short of both food and money to sustain the army. In the meantime, the Duke of Cumberland had secured his position in Aberdeen with supplies arriving by sea. On 8 April, he headed south, and in a fateful decision the Prince's Council agreed that their best option was to join battle. The Battle of Culloden on 16 April lasted less than an hour and ended in a decisive Government victory. Government casualties were estimated at 50 killed and 259 wounded while the Jacobite army (which included many members of the Clan Maclean) is reported to have lost up to 1,500 dead, with many slaughtered after the battle was over, and 500 taken prisoner. Afterwards, an estimated 1,500 Jacobite survivors assembled at Ruthven Barracks (60 km south of Inverness) where they were ordered by Charles to disperse. In the meantime, he and his personal retinue fled to the hills. After five months on the run which took him to Uist, Skye, and Raasay, on 20 September he was eventually rescued by a French ship *L'Heureux*. His flight, assisted by the legendary Flora Macdonald, is remembered in the *Skye Boat Song*.

At odds with his Scottish supporters and unable to summon French support, Charles never returned to Scotland. After Culloden, Government forces spent several weeks searching for rebels, confiscating cattle and burning the homes of Catholics and Episcopalians who were suspected of being Jacobites. For several years thereafter, this took its toll across the Highlands and Islands including Mull. One can only imagine the treatment handed out to members of the Clan Maclean of Duart by the Clan Campbell following the eviction of their chief fifty years earlier, although there is no direct evidence of brutality. The rationale for punitive measures was a widespread perception on both sides that a French landing was imminent. Eventually, 3,500 Jacobite supporters were indicted for treason, of whom 120 were executed, 650 died awaiting trial, 900 were pardoned, and the rest were transported. In April 1747, some Jacobite Lords were beheaded. However, with public opinion against further trials, the remaining prisoners were pardoned in the 1747 Act of Indemnity. In the aftermath, the government then proceeded to confiscate a number of Jacobite properties, and strengthened their hold on the Highlands through construction of new castles and improvements to the road system to facilitate troop movements.

In the aftermath of Culloden, the government enacted legislation that would further weaken the traditional clan system. The most significant statute was the *Heritable Jurisdictions (Scotland) Act 1746*, which ended the mutual support structure of the clan system, established the crown's ownership of many properties previously controlled by clan chiefs, and removed many rights which came with such ownership such as the appointment of judicial officers. The *Dress Act 1746* outlawed Highland dress except as part of a military uniform. The *Act of Proscription* provided for wholesale disarming of clan members who previously maintained arms so they could respond to a call from the Clan Chief.

After 1746, the Jacobite cause did not entirely disappear, but disputes between its supporters ended its ability to pose a serious threat. Many Scots were disillusioned by Charles' leadership, and the same was true of Jacobite supporters in England. In 1748, Charles was expelled from France. Subsequently, his attempts to reignite the cause, including a secret visit to London in 1750 and a meeting in 1759 with French Chief Minister Choiseul to discuss another invasion, were to no avail. After James Edward Stuart's death in 1766, the Pope refused to recognise Charles as legitimate king, and he died of a stroke in Rome in January 1788, a disappointed and embittered man.

As a final reflection, in the 21st century, the Jacobite cause and the adventures of Bonnie Prince Charlie supported by Scottish Highlanders still engender a somewhat romantic view of the times, some of which are fanciful. It is a myth that the Jacobite forces were largely composed of Highlanders. In reality, the army included many units from the Lowlands, a number of English supporters gathered during the invasion of England in 1745, and several hundred French and Irish mercenaries. It is also interesting to note that, within a generation of the defeat at Culloden, there was an inclination amongst writers of the late 18th century to romanticise Highlanders as being some kind of noble warrior race. The fact was that, for a century before Culloden, rural poverty had driven increasing numbers of people from the Highlands and Islands to enlist in foreign armies. After 1745, it became illegal to join a foreign army, and the inclination to become a mercenary was replaced by a policy encouraging recruitment of the "warlike" Highlanders into the British army. Finally, it is a fact that many of those who participated in the Jacobite rebellions did so because they opposed the Union between England and Scotland, rather than because they opposed the Hanoverian succession in favour of the Stuart dynasty.

Conclusion

The aim of this relatively long account of events over 150 years from the accession of James VI is to provide some insight into the huge change in the nature of Scottish society which redefined community in every corner of the nation including Mull. In summary, key elements in this transformation included the following:

- With the accession of King James VI to the English throne in 1603, the centre of power moved to London with the Highlands and Islands were viewed as a far flung backward part of the country.
- The Statutes of Iona and related legislation provided a legal framework to consolidate the Scottish state at the expense of regional autonomy, and the unravel most of the traditional systems of for mutual support between members of a clan.
- Although Scotland retained separate legal and educational systems, the decision to embrace the Act of Union in 1707 consolidated the shift of power to the British Parliament.
- The legislation after Culloden further weakened the clan system, with the removal of the right of a clan chief to appoint members of the judiciary, and the active prohibition on any manifestation of clan membership and loyalty.

- The power of the Kirk established during the Reformation was strongly reinforced, with elected presbyters the arbiter of local morals, local laws and the provider of education.

Apart from these structural changes, there were other more subtle outcomes. The political union with a more populous neighbour would result in a more inwardly focussed narrative in which the distinctive character of what it was to be Scottish was subsumed by an attempt to establish a British narrative based on a "shared" *Unionist* cultural identity. Prior to this period, Scottish literature and learning fitted comfortably within a wider European culture. Scotland had strong, long-standing and independent links with neighbours across the North Sea, the English Channel, and the Irish Sea, not to mention the Pope in Rome. The formation of the union transformed the country to be more inwardly focused.

Despite this shift, the memory of the previous Scottish culture did not die. In the late 18th and early 19th century, a whole genre of writers and poets emerged who sought to sustain some form of collective memory of what Scotland used to be, using a uniquely Scottish vernacular. Writing in the Scots language, Robert Burns' poetry provided a rich source of inspiration for progressive thinkers.[27] In contrast, Sir Walter Scott's novels presented a highly romanticised take of history which sought to reassure the reader that all was well in the flow of events that led to Hanoverian rule.[28] In the meantime, others seeking to maintain a sense of being Scottish focussed on research into the earlier Gaelic history of the country or sought to echo a complex historical past with simplified but shared cultural traditions. This led to the Victorian inventions of Burns Suppers, Highland Games, a renewed interest in tartans, and the romanticisation of Mary "Queen of Scots" and "Bonnie Prince Charlie" which bore a sometimes tenuous connection with reality. This inheritance continues to shape modern perspectives.

ENDNOTES

1   George Buchanan (1506-1582) was a leading man of letters during the Reformation who was a strident critic of corruption in state and church. After the murder of James' father Henry Stewart, he became a bitter enemy of Queen Mary and provided evidence of her treachery to Queen Elizabeth.

2   Born in France in 1542, Esmé Stewart was a cousin of James's father Henry Stewart.

3   Anne was the daughter of King Frederick II of Denmark and Norway who had just died in 1588 to be succeeded by Anne's brother King Christian IV. She died in 1619.

4   This quote is taken from notes on a lecture to the Molesey History Society on 15 February 2011 by Alistair Grant.

5   The word "extirpation" came into usage in the 16th century. From the Latin, it meant to pull out by the roots.

6   In the next 20 years, he only returned to visit Scotland only once, in 1617.

7   The origin of this phrase is unclear, but some attribute it to the father-in-law of his son Charles who married the daughter of the French King Henry IV.

8   In Scots law, a Sasine (pronounced 'say-zin') is a document that records the transfer of the ownership of property. It usually provides the names of the new and previous owners and a basic description of the property transferred. In traditional ceremonies of 'giving sasine', the signing of a deed was accompanied by the transfer of symbols of the land such as earth and stone.

9   The first Union Jack consisted of St George's red-cross on a white background superimposed on St Andrew's white saltire on a blue background.

10 This Act was rescinded in 1690, but a similar Act which had currency in Scotland remained in place in England until it was repealed in 1828. All such declarations of faith were finally abolished in 1889.

11 William was the only child of the Prince of Orange who had married Mary the eldest daughter of King Charles I. When he married King James' daughter, this hugely advanced his claim to the British throne.

12 After being deposed King James II and his family lived in France under the patronage of Louis XIV who recognised him as the rightful King of Scots, and King of England and Ireland. He eventually died in 1701.

13 This has later echoes in the Second Amendment to the American Constitution passed in 1791 which provides for the right of the people to keep and bear arms as part of the Bill of Rights.

14 In the late 17th century, Scotland established the colony of New Caledonia at Darien in Panama, strategically located at the junction of the Atlantic and Pacific Oceans. Through failed crops, disease, a Spanish blockade, and withdrawal of English support, in 1700 the colony failed, leading to the ruin of many investors.

15 This War between 1701 and 1714 pitched a very powerful France against a range of Protestant countries including England and Scotland. For some in Scotland, remembering the Auld Alliance with France, this left them conflicted.

16 Some material in this section is drawn from the book The Scottish Nation – A Modern History by Professor Sir Tom Devine, Penguin London 2000.

17 Sophia was the daughter of Elizabeth Stuart, a daughter of James I, and Frederick V the Elector of Palatine, a state within the Holy Roman Empire.

18 Married to Prince George of Denmark, Anne had 17 failed pregnancies.

19 Jacobite takes its name from Jacobus the Latin for James. It applies to the supporters of the "senior" (male) line of the descendants of Charles I.

20 Sir Hector later proved his loyalty by lending support to the 1745 rebellion.

21 At the time, Spain and Britain were engaged in the War of the Quadruple Alliance in which Spain was trying to recover territories lost in the 1713 Treaty of Utrecht including Gibraltar.

22 James Edward Stuart died in Rome in 1766.

23 Sir John Murray was the son of Sir David Murray who had supported the rebellion in 1715. In 1741 he became the principal Jacobite agent in Scotland, reporting to the Duke of Hamilton.

24 Glenfillan is at the head of Loch Shiel, 25 km to the west of Fort William.

25 The Duke of Cumberland was the youngest son of George II who had succeeded his father George I in 1727.

26   The War of the Austrian Succession took place between 1740 and 1748, with Great Britain
      supporting Prussia, as a prelude to the Seven Years War (1754-1763) in which Great Britain vied with
      France and Spain for control of colonies in North America and the West Indies.

27   A national hero, Robert Burns was born in Alloway Ayrshire in 1759. His poem Auld Lang Syne still
      which rings out loud around the world on New Year's Eve, and his Scots Wha Hae served for a long
      time as Scotland's unofficial national anthem. He died of a rheumatic heart condition aged 37.

28   Sir Walter Scott was born in Edinburgh in 1771. A practising lawyer, he was an historical novelist,
      poet, and playwright. Although less lauded in modern times, in his day he was hugely influential in
      Europe and the USA.

CLEARANCES AND MIGRATION

Travelling across the landscape of Mull, particularly in the south-west part of the island, you can't fail to notice the vestiges of long-gone human habitation. The ruins of mostly 19th century cottages are legion, with the remains of a hamlet and lazy-bed furrows on the Ardalanish peninsula typical. It was a different picture 250 years ago. Research into what brought about a radical change in both the landscape and the community of rural Scotland in the 18th and 19th centuries reveals a sad piece of history for a people whose existence depended on their connection to their community and the land. The explanation for what has been called "The Clearances" is a complex story of rural depopulation, much of it on a voluntary basis, culminating in the imperative of largely absentee land-owners to improve agricultural productivity through the removal of sometimes recalcitrant tenants. The bitter memories of eviction live on in the minds of long-established families in Mull, and are poignantly reflected in the poetry of Sorley Maclean.[1]

Medieval Social Contract

In telling this story, we need to revisit the evolution of the clan system as presented earlier in this book. In medieval times, a central feature of the society in the Highlands and Islands established by the Scoti tribe was a social contract between clan members to share the use of well-defined territory. The system of living together, with loyalty to a chief and his family, and a commitment to mutual support for the benefit of all, generated a deep sense of community and connection to the land. For several hundred years, this form of society existed in Mull within the kingdom of Dál Riata and these arrangements continued within the Norse Kingdom of the Isles until Scotland annexed the territory in 1266. Thereafter, for another 250 years, the Hebrides was governed as a series of clan-based communities within the autonomous region called the Lordship of the Isles.

When the Hebrides including Mull became part of Scotland, the Crown presumed ownership of the land, with title granted to the hereditary chief. This entitlement was held by clan leaders in good faith without any intrinsic financial value, and there continued to be a tacit agreement that, in sharing the use of the land for food and shelter, the chief would provide leadership and due process in the administration of the community while, in return, appropriately aged males would respond to a call to arms for the defence of territory and the pursuit expansionary ambitions.

After a long struggle to impose royal sovereignty, in 1493 King James IV abolished the Lordship of the Isles. His aim was to limit local autonomy and impose a more centralised system of feudal-based governance under the Scottish crown. This might have spelt the end of the clan system, the legal status of which was never recognised in Scottish law. However, in the 16th century, the central government of Scotland was weak due to a succession of child monarchs and the Reformation, and enforcement though military action was challenging in the rough terrain. Accordingly, for the next century local clan chiefs continued to maintain a degree of independence that largely denied the royal prerogative, and the clan-based society persisted albeit with ownership of the land clearly in the hands of the Chief's immediate family. This is not of course to suggest that the Highlands and Islands were immune to the Reformation. Indeed, in the 16th century the Presbyterian system would percolate into every part of Scottish society and begin to promote a very different view about the role of citizens in a god-fearing community.

Crown Land

By the start of the 17th century the crown, in the person of King James VI, had successfully imposed a system of documented land title that consolidated the power of chiefs as landowners and threatened to fracture the social contract with their clansmen who "shared" the use of the land. Often, the new or re-issued royal charters bore little relationship to traditional ownership and territorial boundaries and, increasingly, land title was held by absentee landlords who had no residual commitment to local clansmen.

The union of the Scottish and English crowns in 1603 would also herald a further threat to the traditional society of the Highlands and Islands. Even before King James moved to London, he had a disdain for clan-based communities and, once established in the English court, this prejudice was reinforced. Consequently, at his behest, in 1609 the Scottish Parliament enacted the Statutes of Iona which sought to dismantle the community-based customs and "civilise" the wayward fringe dwellers. The imperative of complying with these and other measures not only undermined the traditional social contract between chiefs and their clansmen, but also imposed significant costs. Chiefs were required to spend extended periods away from their estates to attend meetings in Edinburgh and had to lodge surety bonds which guaranteed the good behaviour of their kinsmen. For many, these imposts led to mounting financial debts.

The upshot of these changes was that many highland chiefs began to see their title to land and their commitment to the community in a very different way, with land becoming a chargeable asset. The concept of shared occupation of land and mutual support was slowly replaced by a system of landlord and tenant in which rent was paid in return for access and use. In due course this would lead to an entirely new structure for the management of land in which the chief, as proprietor, would employ a trusted member of his clan to act as a *tacksman*, who both managed leases and acted as a lieutenant of the clan's military forces. This, and the other provisions of the Statutes of Iona, served to further distance the chief and his family from ordinary clansmen.

Wars and Rebellions

As the social contract for clan-based communities like Mull was evolving, the 17th and 18th centuries would also see a series of struggles, with civil unrest and war, which touched every corner of the Scottish state. In the course of these events, clan chiefs were under constant pressure to pick sides in conflicts not of their making and, in financing their involvement in military campaigns, many accumulated significant debts. Many also lost control of their traditional lands through picking the wrong side. This factor has particular relevance for Mull. In the late 17th century, financial issues led to the absentee Dukes of Argyll supplanting the dominant Clan Maclean of Duart. In the next fifty years, the impact of this change in land ownership was compounded by the defeat of the Jacobite cause at Culloden which was supported by Maclean clansmen. Thereafter, the new proprietors were openly hostile to their tenants, and this local circumstance was complemented by onerous if short-lived legislation designed to stamp out the last vestiges of clan culture.

Demography and Agriculture

Finally, despite all the deaths in battle, the 17th century actually saw a significant growth in population. This was because of improved and more secure food supplies and reduced infant mortality. In Mull, records show that between the early 17th century and the late 18th century the population actually doubled.[2] This would seriously test the capacity to grow enough food on relatively infertile land. Consequently, driven by starvation and destitution, many clansmen would migrate to the lowlands for work, returning what they could to support their impoverished families. Some did not return, and others would migrate to the booming colonies in North America.

For those who owned the land, the 18th century would also see the emergence of a new imperative which would radically change the social contract. With mounting financial burdens, land owners not only increased rents to cover their debts but also sought to improve productivity through significant changes in land-management practices. This process of "improvement" as it was euphemistically called involved a transformation in the use of pastoral land with people on small holdings replaced by sheep.

The Clearances

The impact of all these changes in Scottish society was both the voluntary exit of many people from the Highlands and Islands and, in some places, the forced expulsion of crofters and cottars in a process which is commonly referred to as "The Clearances".[345] The account which follows is focussed on Mull, and took over 100 years to unfold, but a similar story would apply to most of the Highlands and Islands.

The initial phase of this rural transformation actually began in the Lowlands in the early 18th century but, by the middle of the century, and perhaps helped by the significant improvement in communications, it had also taken hold in the Highlands and Islands.[6] By this time, many of the factors described in the early part of this chapter were already in full flow, and the legislation implemented after Culloden in 1746 which was directed at dismantling the vestiges of the previous social structure were but a final act in an already irreversible process. The way in which these changes unfolded was by no means uniform. For some landowners, particularly those who were traditional leaders of their local clan, they retained a commitment to the traditional social contract that connected people and land and this led them to adopt a humane approach to implementing new land-management practices with decisions sometimes compromising financial prudence. For others, they viewed Highlanders and Islanders as primitive people who spoke a backward tongue and had minimal rights as citizens. For these largely absentee landlords, with no residual loyalty to kinsmen, it was a relatively small step to adopt an increasingly strident approach to removing people who were incapable of paying the rent, and whose occupation of land impeded the adoption of new agricultural practices. In some cases tenancies were put up for tender and increasingly this eliminated the role of tacksmen. The response of tenants took many forms. Some, particularly those with some education, sought to take advantage of opportunities emerging in other parts of Scotland and beyond (including army service). Others stood their ground, and were subjected to varying degrees of persuasion and coercion to move.

Commencing in the mid-18th century, the first phase of transition in Mull involved the replacement of small holdings with large scale pastoral farms stocked with sheep. The principal agent of these changes was the newly installed land owner, the Duke of Argyll. The raising of rents and the removal of people brought much opprobrium to the Duke's factors (John Campbell in the south west and Hugh MacAskill in the north-west), and there was significant local resistance. However, the Duke persisted and gradually replaced Macleans with his own clansmen. By the 1740s, 15 of the 18 tacksmen responsible for Argyll lands in Mull and over half of the 152 tenants were Campbells.[7] Community relations were not helped by the fact that, whilst they had adopted the Protestant faith, the Macleans were loyal to the House of Stuart. In contrast, the Campbells had been staunch supporters of both the Glorious Revolution in 1688 and the Hanoverian succession in 1714. Consequently, the Macleans and Campbells continued to be bitter enemies through the years of the Jacobite Rebellions and, after the Battle of Culloden in 1746, the Dukes of Argyll would be party to the relentless implementation of legislation designed to eliminate the clan system that had been operated by the Macleans.

With some crofters already leaving the island on their own account, the crofters who wished to stay on the island were re-allocated to what were called "crofting communities" on coastal fringes. In Mull, the consequent social engineering was the wholesale removal of crofters into crofting settlements including the newly created township of Tobermory.[8] Tobermory was established in 1788 by the British Fisheries Association, specifically to accommodate people who had previously lived off the land as tenants, and the displaced crofters and cottars found themselves redeployed into an urban existence totally foreign to them which quickly became a slum. Initially the most significant forms of local employment in this new community were fishing and a variety of trades. However, many of the new townspeople could not afford to acquire a boat or learn a trade and/or were not inclined to do so. Consequently, they left the island completely, or supported their families by obtaining work in the lowlands. Others pursued opportunities in the burgeoning British Army, or acting as mercenaries, with Highlanders regarded as having suitable qualities for the pursuit of Britain's imperial ventures. This included the Napoleonic Wars in the late 18th and early 19th centuries and colonisation of territories in the Far East and Africa. Yet other displaced clansmen moved to the farming of kelp which for a time was a raw material used for processing into fertiliser, soap and glass. At this stage, most of those who remained in Mull still had a piece of land from which they obtained some sustenance, but it was no longer sufficient for survival.

Notwithstanding this somewhat bleak picture, some parts of Mull were relatively untouched. The lands south of Dervaig owned by the Macleans of Torloisk, and the properties held by the Brolass branch of the clan in central Mull, continued to be owned by local families. The same was true of the Lochbuie Estate of the Clan Maclaine, the autonomy of which was maintained not least through the fortune acquired in the Far East by the 21st Chief of the clan which would sustain their position until the early 20th century

The second phase of clearances involved the thinning out of what had become overcrowded and impoverished crofting communities. Following the end of the Napoleonic War in 1815 through to the middle of the 19th century, many of the crofters lost the means to support themselves, through famine and/or collapse of industries such as the relatively short-lived kelp trade.[9] In response, some landlords sought to encourage their tenants to migrate with "assisted passages". Provided with the fare of passage, tenants who were selected for this option had little choice. As a consequence, by the 1820s, while retaining some fishing activity, places like Tobermory ceased to be a repository for the dispossessed and by the 1820s this town was beginning to establish itself as a tourist centre.

By the 1840s, across Scotland, 75% of the land owned by traditional Chiefs and lairds had passed into the hands of merchants, bankers, lawyers and financiers. This was certainly the situation in Mull, and a grim account of the steps taken by the Dukes of Argyll to implement an increasingly hard line in implementing evictions is provided in the aforementioned book by Professor

Sir Tom Devine. At this time, the 7th Duke of Argyll, John Campbell became determined to clear his estates on the Ross of Mull, replacing the crofters and cottars who lingered on their small plots of land with extensive sheep runs. According to the 1841 census, at the time there were some 2,500 people living on the Ross of Mull peninsula, with some ten settlements on the more fertile land to the south where there were 167 households and 928 people. By 1861, the number of households had been reduced to 97, with a population of 391. The method of removing people from communities that had been in continuous existence since medieval times was sometimes brutal. As Professor Sir Tom Devine notes, *"Several evictions were enforced by draconian means with little concern for humanity or the welfare of the people. Racialist assumptions (*about the inadequacy of Gaelic speaking peasants) *undeniably helped to fashion the plans of those responsible for the strategy of dispossession."* The account of what happened to the 100 members of the crofting community at one such settlement, Shiaba in the Ross of Mull makes a chilling read. This was one of the more sustainable communities in the district with relatively fertile land that provided food and a subsistence level of living in which the people were relatively content with their lot using lazy-bed farming. Notice of eviction was first served by the 7th Duke's factor in 1845, without enforcement. Then, following the death of the 7th Duke in 1847, the factor served a further eviction notice. In response, a petition signed by 7 tenants requesting cancellation of the evictions was sent to the new and profligate 8th Duke. Their submission was either overlooked or ignored, and subsequently some tenants were physically escorted to the neighbouring beach and despatched by ship to Canada! Others were forcibly moved to poorer land on the north of the Ross of Mull, and yet others transferred from the island to the lowlands. In their place, a cattle dealer from Skye was installed as the sole tenant. By the time of the 1871 census there was only one shepherd and his family managing 92 hectares of land. And in 1937, following severe damage by storm, this dwelling too was vacated. Shiaba is now a derelict village to the south of Scoor Forest.

As if these trials and tribulations were not enough, in the middle of the 19th century the Highlands sustained two major hits to their food supply which would drive depopulation. Since around 1775, the staple diet for the remnants of the farming communities like those in Mull was the potato. Although less nourishing than oats, this had proven to be a highly resilient crop in the wet and cold environment. Due to inclement weather, in 1836/37 there was a serious harvest failure. Then, in 1846, this crop was destroyed through a water-borne virus called *phytophthora infestans*. This led to chronic food shortages and the establishment in 1847 of the Central Board of Management for Highland Relief to provide emergency food supplies. In Mull, grain boats were moored in Tobermory harbour, and food was distributed through Sir Charles Trevelyan's Highland Club. In 1848, conditions were made even worse with Scotland experiencing a significant recession and a cholera outbreak in the Lowlands. Eventually, there was donor fatigue and, with continuing food shortages, this provided a fresh impetus to migration.

In light of this disastrous situation in places like Mull, the government commissioned an inquiry undertaken by Sir John McNeill.[10] He investigated conditions in the western Scottish Highlands and Western Isles, and during his work he personally inspected twenty-seven of the most distressed parishes. The report on his review led to the passing of the 1851 *Emigration Advances Act* and he was a co-founder of the Highlands and Islands Emigration Society. Between 1841 and 1861, 10,000 went to Canada and 5,000 to Australia.

In many ways, this brings us to the conclusion of a sad chapter in the history of Mull and other parts of the Highlands and Islands. By the 1880s, there were relatively few crofters and no sub-letting cottars left in Mull. However, life on the island in the final years of the 19th century and early 20th century slowly recovered from the ravages of famine and de-population and, in the final decades of the 19th century, the crofting communities began to stick up for themselves. On the Island of Skye there was a rent strike which in 1882 led to the so-called *Battle of the Braes* in which troops were sent to quell unrest. The resulting publicity led to the formation of the Highlands Land Law Reform Association advocating crofters' rights. In 1883, in response to increasing civil disobedience among crofters because of excessive rents, loss of access to grazing land, and lack of security of land tenure, the Gladstone government then established a *Royal Commission of Inquiry into the Condition of Crofters and Cottars in the Highlands and Islands.*

The Inquiry was chaired by Lord Francis Napier, a distinguished civil servant and amateur historian. This led to the *Crofters Holding Act of 1886* that created legal definitions of a crofter and a crofting settlement, granted them security of land tenure and the ability to bequeath the entitlement, and established the first Crofters Commission which adjudicated on disputes between landlords and crofters on rent and other matters.[11] In the meantime, several Highland Land Reform Associations were formed which eventually coalesced in the Highland Land League with the aim of advancing the crofters' cause.

Despite these developments, enforcement of new laws were largely ineffective in countering the concentration of land holding, and were established well after the rural depopulation horse had bolted. Estimates of the impact of the Clearances suggest that some 70,000 left the Highlands and Islands and, by the year 2000, two-thirds of Scotland's land area was owned by only 1,252 landowners in a population of 5 million. The tide would not begin to turn until the re-establishment of a Scottish Parliament in 1999.

ENDNOTES

1   There is an account of the life of Sorley Maclean, whose poetry includes a reflection on the Clearances, in Chapter 16.

2   According to the book, Mull and Iona, by David Caldwell, Birlinn Ltd, Edinburgh 2018, the population of Mull in 1600 was around 5,000 and by 1821 it had reached 10,000.

3   A croft is a unit of arable land, typically of between 10 and 50 acres, rented from the landowner by a tenant undertaking a range of activities

4   The principal source of information for this section is the book by Professor Sir Tom Devine, The Scottish Clearances – A History of The Dispossessed published by Penguin Random House, London, 2019.

5   At the time, the term "Clearance" was not in use and did not have the emotive force associated with the word as we use it today. Perhaps the government of the day referred to "the urgent need for land reform".

6   After the 1715 Jacobite rebellion, the government commissioned General Wade to improve logistical infrastructure to facilitate the future movement of troops. Between 1725 and 1740, he built 400 km of new roads in the Highlands and Islands which greatly improved the movement of population and trade.

7   Mull & Iona Historical Guide, David Caldwell, Birlinn, Edinburgh, 2018.

8   Tobermory derives from the Gaelic Tobar Mhoire, the well of Mary.

9   From the later part of the 17th Century seaweed was found to have several industrial uses. Kelp ash contains soda and potash used for glass-making and soap. By 1800, Scotland was processing 20,000 tonnes per annum and, at its peak, as many as 40,000 people may have depended on kelp harvesting.

10   Sir John McNeill was born on the isle of Oronsay, which lies between Mull and Islay, and had considerable knowledge of and empathy for those affected.

11   The Act specified eight counties including Argyll where such crofting towns could be recognised and established rights where tenants had access to grazing during the 80 years since 1806.

AND BE THE NATION AGAIN

O ne of the things that has inspired me to write this book is the renaissance in recent years of what it means to be Scottish. This appreciation is not something that comes readily to someone brought up as being British in an English public school, even though in recent years I have uncovered my Scottish heritage on my mother's side. My enlightenment has been achieved by a diligent study of history from the perspective of someone living north of the border.

Over the last century, there are many factors that have driven the Scottish "re-awakening". These include the decline and fall of the British empire, with the loss of its economic advantages, the associated loss of opportunity for imperial and overseas service, development of a political movement that more adequately represents the community-based values of Scottish people as opposed to the conservative character of the English part of Britain, and most recently a commitment to sustain traditional connections between Scotland and the rest of the European family of nations through membership of the EU. A pivotal moment came with the re-establishment of a Scottish Parliament in 1999. However, before examining the impact of that organisation, it is worth tracing the journey that saw the Scottish people resume significant control over their own destiny.

Decline and Fall of Great Britain

In the second half of the 18th century and during the 19th century, Scottish identity was seriously eroded, with the Scots becoming an almost invisible people more evident in the diaspora than in the heartland. There were many dimensions to this. The traditional structures of community and partnership that had characterised local society had been devalued or even eliminated. The rural population had been decimated through the clearances and the concentration of land ownership into the hands of a few. Finally, the nation-defining Church of Scotland had fractured into several less effective parts.1 However, it was not all doom and gloom. By the start of the 20th century, for many, the idea of being British had become a meaningful substitute for loss of a distinctive sense of being Scottish and, many Scots shared in the wealth generated by the industrial revolution and the spread of empire. In particular, while it was relatively tough to live in the Highlands and Islands, in the major cities and the lowlands there was considerable prosperity based on flourishing trade and industry, and there were significant opportunities for advancement for all citizens of the country at home and overseas.

However, in the years following the end of the Second World War, change was in the air. The last Empress of India was Scotland's own Queen Elizabeth the Queen Mother, and post-war Britain was a country facing a post-imperial malaise, an inclination to inward reflection, and a need to re-invent itself.[2] At the same time, Scotland, which had been an engine for British Imperial prosperity, was beginning to languish and, as colonies were given independence, opportunities for colonial service overseas in which many Scots had participated with distinction was rapidly diminishing.

For Scotland, it was always the case that the motivation for union with England was primarily economic. In 1707, the country's finances were in a parlous state due to failed overseas ventures and English economic sanctions, and there was a clear prospect of synergy from the creation of Great Britain. However, economic imperatives and integrated governance were never the only basis for defining identity and, even after nearly 250 years of union, in the mid-20th century many of the characteristics of a separate country and culture remained, if latent. Scotland still had its own legal institutions, a separate system for compulsory and higher education, and three Scottish banks still printing their own bank notes. Also, against all the odds, written and spoken Gaelic had survived at the periphery, and Scottish English had developed a distinct vernacular and its own vocabulary. This is not to mention the many customs that constitute a national culture, including quite significant diversity between the industrial heartland of Scotland, the rural lowlands and border country, and the Highlands and the Islands.

The Scottish National Party

There are many books which describe the slow Scottish "reawakening" and, in our time, the most important development has been the re-establishment of the Scottish Parliament in 1999. In many ways, the journey to the achievement of this significant initiative, and the wider history of renaissance, are best told through the development of the Scottish National Party ("SNP").

The SNP was founded on 7 April 1934 by the amalgamation of the National Party of Scotland ("NPS") formed in 1928, and the Scottish Party ("SP") formed in 1932. The leaders of those two political organisations (respectively Robert Bontine Cunninghame Graham, and James Graham the 6th Duke of Montrose - no relation) became the first joint presidents and Sir Alexander MacEwen becoming the first Chairman of the party.[34] From the early days, there was tension between those who wanted "home rule" within the United Kingdom, akin to the recently established Northern Ireland (with its own assembly established in 1921), and those who wanted independence in the form of dominion status within the British Empire as achieved by Southern Ireland.[5]

The SNP had its first electoral success in the Motherwell by-election which was held in April 1945 following the death of the sitting Labour

MP. However, Robert McIntyre's victory was short-lived as the seat in the Westminster Parliament was lost in the General Election that followed in July. There was little progress in the 1950s. However, in the 1960s, the Party started to poll credible numbers in a number of constituencies, culminating in the famous 1967 by-election victory by Winifred Ewing in the seat of Hamilton.[6] This established the SNP as a credible political force. As a consequence, with the Welsh Nationalist leader Gwynfor Evans also having won a 1966 by-election in 1966 (Carmarthen), Prime Minister Harold Wilson decided to establish a Royal Commission on the Constitution. By now, the SNP was led by the redoubtable Billy Wolfe and, reflecting the progressive inclinations of a majority of the population, it had become a distinctly social democratic party.[7]

The remit of the Royal Commission was to examine the structures of the constitution of the United Kingdom and the government of its constituent countries, and to consider whether any changes should be made to those arrangements. A lengthy exercise, it was started in 1969 with Lord Crowther as the Chair, and completed by Lord Kilbrandon in 1972. The Kilbrandon Commission as it became known considered various models of devolution, federalism, and con-federalism, as well as the prospect of dividing the UK into separate sovereign states. The final report was delivered in October 1973, by which time the avowedly unionist Conservative Party had come to power led by Prime Minister Edward Heath. Amongst a range of conclusions, the Commission's report rejected the options of independence or federalism and recommended devolved, directly elected, Scottish and Welsh assemblies.

Following the publication of the Kilbrandon Report, in 1974 the SNP reached a pinnacle of electoral success. In the February General Election for the Westminster Parliament, it achieved 22% of the vote in Scotland and won 7 of the 71 Scottish seats. In the subsequent October General Election it won 33% of the votes and won 11 seats.[8] Success at local government level would follow. In the meantime, an incoming Labour administration at Westminster published a white paper entitled *Democracy and Devolution: Proposals for Scotland and Wales*. This led to the Scotland and Wales Bill. At the first attempt in February 1977, after the government tried to guillotine discussion, this Bill failed to pass Parliament. However, in the following year, two separate pieces of legislation providing for devolution were enacted: *The Scotland Act 1978* and *The Wales Act 1978*. Provisions in the Acts determined that the establishment of assemblies required approval by a majority of voters in local referendums.

The devolution referendums were held on 1 March 1979 with outcomes which were highly frustrating for those in Scotland supporting change.[9] 51.6% of the Scottish electorate voted for devolution, but there was a snag. In the course of debating *The Scotland Bill*, a Labour MP opposed to devolution, George Cunningham, had successfully inserted a clause that said the referendum would not pass unless it received the support of 40% of the whole Scottish electorate.[10] With a turnout of only 64%, only 32.9% of those on the electoral register had voted for devolution. So, the referendum was lost.

The results of the referendums led to the repeal of the respective devolution Acts in March 1979, and then the minority Labour government lost power, with the Scottish National Party joining the Conservatives, Liberals and Ulster Unionist Party in supporting a vote of no confidence. This led to the general election of 1979 and the beginning of 18 years of Conservative rule in which hopes for any form of Scottish self-government were forlorn. The decision to support the vote of no confidence in the Labour government would prove costly for the SNP. In the 1979 election the Party was reduced to just two MPs at Westminster.

In the 1980s the SNP entered a period of significant internal strife, between a nationalist left-wing faction and the more moderate social democratic majority of the organisation. However, under the leadership of Gordon Wilson, a Glaswegian who represented the constituency of Dundee East, it is notable that for the first time they embraced membership of the European Communities as the EU was then called.[1112] In the meantime, supporters of devolution regrouped to establish the Campaign for a Scottish Assembly ("CSA"). The objective of the CSA was to recommence the debate about Scotland's constitutional future, and they developed a formal statement to reflect their intentions. In so doing, they cast their minds back to the Declaration of Arbroath which, in a message to Pope John XXII on 6 April 1320, had asserted that the Scottish people had a right to live an independent existence and determine their own form of government.[13] Based on this ancient declaration, in 1989 the CSA published *A Claim of Right for Scotland* in which it was stated that:[14]

"We do hereby acknowledge the sovereign right of the Scottish people to determine the form of Government best suited to their needs, and do hereby declare and pledge that in all our actions and deliberations their interests shall be paramount. We further declare and pledge that our actions and deliberations shall be directed to the following ends:

- *To agree a scheme for an Assembly or Parliament for Scotland; and*
- *To mobilise Scottish opinion and ensure the approval of the Scottish people for that scheme; and*
- *To assert the right of the Scottish people to secure implementation of that scheme."*

On 30 March 1989, this Claim was signed by 58 of Scotland's 72 MPs, 7 of Scotland's 8 MEPs (Members of the European Parliament), representatives of the majority of local councils, and leaders of a range of other Scottish organisations including the churches and the trade unions. The signatories then formed the Scottish Constitutional Convention.[15] This group worked assiduously for several years, and on 30 November 1995 (St Andrew's Day) it published its blueprint for devolution, *Scotland's Parliament, Scotland's Right*, which provided the basis for a future Scottish Parliament.

In the meantime, in 1990 the SNP had elected Alex Salmond as leader.[16] Initially, Salmond had struggled to turn the tide with only three MPs elected in the 1992 General Election for the Westminster Parliament. However, in the 1997 General Election, when a Labour government was elected with a commitment to holding a referendum on devolution, the SNP doubled their representation.[17] Following that election, the new Labour Prime Minister Tony Blair was quick to honour his pledge, and in 1997 he introduced *The Devolution (Scotland and Wales) Bill* which included a commitment to hold a referendum. The Bill was passed, and the parties who belonged to the Scottish Constitutional Convention then joined forces with the SNP to campaign for a *Yes* vote. In the referendum, the Scottish electorate were asked to vote on two questions:

- "Do you agree that there should be a Scottish Parliament?"
- "Do you agree that a Scottish Parliament should have tax-varying powers?"

The rules for the referendum provided that a *Yes* vote would only succeed with the support of 50% of those voting and 40% of all registered voters. In the vote on 11 September 1997 which registered a 60% turnout, 74.3% voted *Yes* to the first proposition. This represented 44.4% of all registered voters and so the proposal was passed. The vote on the second question also received majority support although it failed to pass the "40% of registered voters" threshold.[18]

Scottish Parliament

The 1997 referendum on devolution was a pivotal moment in Scottish history. In response to the majority voting "Yes" to both referendum proposals, in 1998 the UK Parliament passed *The Scotland Act 1998*. This established a Scottish Parliament for the first time since 1707, with a Scottish Executive which would become the Scottish government.19 In the 1999 election for the 129 seat Scottish Parliament, using an electoral system called Additional Member Voting, the Labour Party led by Donald Dewar won 56 seats, and the SNP led by Alex Salmond won 35. The other seats were Conservative: 18, Liberal Democrats: 17, the Greens: 1, and two other minor parties one each.20 Given the recent election of a Labour government in the UK, the overall result raised few eyebrows. Short of a majority, Labour went into coalition with the Liberal Democrats. The Parliament initially met in the General Assembly Hall of the Church of Scotland in Edinburgh's Royal Mile on 12 May, and the devolution powers came into effect on 1 July 1999.

Following that first election, and continuing to campaign in favour of dissolving the 1707 Act of Union, over a period of years the SNP gradually gained the ascendancy. However, with the departure of their leader Alex Salmond to sit in the UK Parliament in 2001, in the next election for the Scottish Parliament in 2003 they actually fell back, and the Labour and Liberal Democrat coalition government was re-elected. Labour won 50 seats, the SNP 27, the Conservatives 18, the Liberal Democrats 17, the Greens 7, and the separatist Scottish Socialists 6. With unionist parties winning 85 of the 129 seats, this outcome was seen by some as an end to the independence movement, but that proved to be a false call.

In 2004, the Scottish Parliament moved into a purpose built Parliamentary complex in Holyrood, taking its place in the collection of buildings representing the historical centres of power in Scotland - Edinburgh Castle, Holyrood Palace, and the General Assembly Hall of the Church of Scotland. In the next Scottish Parliament election in 2007, and with Alex Salmond switching to the Scottish Assembly, the SNP came back with a vengeance. They won 47 seats to Labour's 46. The other seats were Conservatives: 17, Liberal Democrats: 16, Greens: 2 and Independent: 1. Initially, the SNP attempted to form government with support from the Liberal Democrats and the Greens. However, the unionist Liberal Democrats were not forthcoming. This heralded a difficult period of minority government, when it was challenging to get Parliamentary approval for any policy without considerable amendments. However, it gave the party significant credibility as being capable of government, and seriously undermined the other left-of-centre parties - Labour and the Liberal Democrats.

Despite its now leading role, the SNP did not always have things their own way. In late 2007, the Labour Government determined that it was time to review the effectiveness of the new Parliament. In December, it established the Calman Commission with a remit which included a final clause to which the SNP was opposed:

"To review the provisions of the Scotland Act 1998 in the light of experience, and to recommend any changes to the present constitutional arrangements that would enable the Scottish Parliament to serve the people of Scotland better, improve the financial accountability of the Scottish Parliament and continue to secure the position of Scotland within the United Kingdom."

The Commission deliberated for 18 months and delivered a report in June 2009 indicating that devolution had been a success, and recommending that the Westminster Parliament should transfer significant powers to enable the Scottish Parliament to raise taxes, and otherwise manage its own financial affairs.21

In the meantime, the SNP had been considering how best to advance the case for Scottish independence. In 2010, they tabled a Bill in the Scottish Parliament proposing that three options should be put to a popular vote, ranging from full independence to a modest further devolution of powers. In a vote of the Parliament, the legislation was lost, with 50 votes for the referendum (47 SNP, 2 Greens and Independent ex-SNP member Margot Macdonald) and 79 against. Whilst this loss was predictable, it served to strengthen the SNP's resolve on the independence issue. Consequently, in the 2011 election for the Scottish Parliament, the party gained a further 23 seats and an absolute majority. They now held 69 seats to Labour: 37, Conservative: 15, Liberal Democrat: 5, Green: 2, and Independent: 1. For the first time, the Party found itself able to pursue the wide-ranging progressive agenda that it had developed over the previous 75 years without the need for support from reluctant unionist parties. And a central plank of their manifesto was the holding of a referendum on independence.

2014 Independence Referendum

While the SNP was busy establishing a mandate for its vision of an independent Scotland, in 2010 there had been an election for the Westminster Parliament in which there had been a change of government.22 This had brought to power an administration involving a Coalition between the Conservatives and the Liberal Democrats led by Prime Minister David Cameron. One of the first things this new government did was to honour a commitment to implement the recommendations of the Calman Commission. In due course, amongst other things, *The Scotland Act 2012* provided for the Scottish Parliament to levy income tax. In the meantime, following the SNP's success in the 2011 election for the Scottish Parliament, Cameron offered to facilitate a referendum on further constitutional reform with legislation to be introduced into the Westminster Parliament. In response, Salmond indicated that he preferred a referendum legislated by the Scottish Parliament over which he would have control. After lengthy discussions, in 2012 the two Parliaments concluded the *Edinburgh Agreement* for a referendum to be conducted on terms that included the following:

- Provisions for the referendum would be legislated by the Scottish Parliament,
- The referendum would seek to deliver a decisive expression of the Scottish people that all would respect,
- The matter would be determined by a simple majority,
- The outcome would be legally binding, notwithstanding provisions in the 1707 Act of Union,
- The vote would be conducted with rules that commanded the confidence of parliaments, government, and people.

Subsequently, in 2013 the Scottish Parliament approved two Acts. The *Scottish Independence Referendum Act* provided for the Scottish people to vote Yes or No in response to a simple question,

"Should Scotland be an independent country?"

The Scottish Independence (Franchise) Act defined who would be allowed to vote. This enfranchised 4.3 million people, including all those normally registered to vote in Scotland (adults of 18 and over), people aged 16 and over, and Scottish people living in the EU.

In the run-up to the referendum, the Yes and No supporters fought a lengthy and sometimes passionate campaign. Those opposed to independence cast doubts on the ability of Scotland to stand alone as a separate country. They questioned which currency the country would use, the ability to maintain public expenditure in support of services, the acceptability of Scotland as a separate country within the EU, and the future of North Sea oil. The Yes campaigners dismissed concerns about economic viability as scare mongering, referred to the tide of history, and appealed to the need for Scottish people to reassert their identity within the European community of nations.

With many people holding their breath, not least in Holyrood House, the result on 14 September 2014 was a disappointment for those wanting independence. On a turnout of 84.6%, 55.3% voted No. An Exit Poll revealed that a deciding factor for No voters was concern about the future of the currency, while disaffection with "Westminster politics" was a major factor for those who voted Yes.23. Interestingly, the young (up to 24 years of age) and older demographic (people over 40) swung the day for the No vote, with those in their later twenties and 30s voting Yes.

The outcome of the referendum was a bitter blow for Alex Salmond. In November 2014 he resigned as leader of the SNP and the Unionists were quick to suggest that this was the end of the matter for a generation at least. The Party elected Salmond's Deputy Nicola Sturgeon as the new leader.24

Perfidious England

On becoming SNP leader of the SNP and First Minister of Scotland, Nicola Sturgeon was quick to take up the reins of the Party and its historic mission to achieve independence. Within six months, it was time for another British General Election which was held on 7 May 2015. On the back of the referendum, and with the benefit of Sturgeon's excellent communication skills, the SNP had its most successful ever election for the Westminster Parliament, winning 56 of the 59 Scottish seats with the Conservatives, Labour, and Liberal Democrat parties reduced to one seat each. At a UK national level, the Conservatives were elected to form government in their own right.25 In the next election for the Scottish Parliament on 5 May 2016, the SNP did even better than in 2011, winning 63 of the 129 seats.26

At this point, events outside Scotland would hold centre stage. Ever since the UK had joined the European Community in 1975, there were people in Britain who were opposed to such links with other European nations. This was manifested in the establishment of the United Kingdom Independence Party ("UKIP") led by Nigel Farage which advocated the reclaiming of British "sovereignty". The formation of UKIP threatened to split the Conservative Party and, in the 2015 British General Election campaign, the drive to leave the EU became a central issue. In response, to stave off a loss of votes and seats, Prime Minister David Cameron made a commitment to hold a non-binding referendum on membership of the EU. Consequently, within a few weeks of winning the election, he tabled a Bill to hold this referendum with the outcome to be determined by a simple majority of those bothering to vote, and notably without any reference to turnout. This meant that, if only 60% of people bothered to vote, a simple majority for leaving the EU might only require the support of just over 30% of the registered voters. This ill-conceived initiative was also concocted without any regard for the fact that the UK was a country formed by the union of several distinct entities (England, Scotland, Wales, and Northern Ireland). The Bill was duly enacted with royal assent on 17 December 2015, with only the SNP voting against it. The options to be presented on the ballot paper were:

Remain a member of the European Union
Leave the European Union

The campaign was fought with zeal, with Labour, the Liberal Democrats, and the SNP all supporting the case for Remain. The Conservative Party sat on the fence but, while David Cameron supported continued EU membership, many in his party joined with UKIP in campaigning to leave. Those wanting to remain stressed the economic, defence, and cultural benefits of EU membership. Those who wanted to leave focused on the re-establishment of British sovereignty, the threat of uncontrolled immigration, and the alleged heavy financial burden of EU membership.

The referendum was held on 23 June 2016, with an inconclusive result. In a 72% turnout, 51.9% voted to leave the EU which represented just 37% of registered voters. Notably, a significant majority of people in Scotland (62%) and Northern Ireland (56%) voted to remain in the EU, along with a majority of the multi-cultural citizens of Greater London (60%). The simple majority support for leaving the EU was largely a creature of relatively older and less well-educated people living in non-metropolitan parts of England and Wales.

This unexpected outcome to the referendum would lead to a period of great instability in British politics. Given what he regarded as a disastrous outcome, on 24 June 2016 David Cameron resigned. In the meantime, Nicola Sturgeon made it clear that Scotland had "spoken decisively" with a "strong and unequivocal" vote to remain in the European Union. She immediately announced that her government would commence planning for a second referendum on independence while communicating to the EU that an independent Scotland would wish to retain its membership of that body.

In July 2016, David Cameron was succeeded as British Prime Minister by Theresa May who, despite protests from many people that there was no mandate for change, in due course determined to implement Article 50 of the EU Treaty requesting departure. The negotiations proved to be tortuous, but eventually she emerged with a plan and decided to put it to the people in an early General Election. This was held in June 2017. She was a poor campaigner and, despite the fact that the Labour Party was led by the Socialist Jeremy Corbyn who was equivocal about EU membership, the Conservatives lost their majority.27 In Scotland, the SNP won 35 seats, Conservatives 13, Labour 7, and Liberal Democrats 4. This marked a downturn in support for the SNP which left the party with some concerns about its strategy. For the Conservatives, despite their relative revival in Scotland, the loss of the majority at a national level was a serious setback and, after two unsuccessful votes of No Confidence in Parliament, in May 2019 Theresa May resigned as Prime Minister. She was replaced by Boris Johnson, who renegotiated terms for exit from the EU and then went to the country in December 2019 when he won with a significant majority.28 This time, the SNP regained some ground on the back of Scottish support for remaining in the EU. Johnson subsequently concluded the UK departure from the EU. He also refused SNP requests for the conduct of another independence referendum.

An Uncertain Future

In the next election for the Scottish Parliament in 2021, the SNP won 64 seats and negotiated an agreement with the 8 members of the Green Party to continue the pursuit of a progressive legislative agenda including another referendum on independence before the next Scottish Parliamentary election scheduled for 2026. With the British Prime Minister rejecting this proposal, in 2022 the Scottish government took the matter to the Supreme Court which ruled that this was a matter for the Westminster Parliament to determine. In response, Sturgeon made it clear that in Scotland the next British General Election would be a vote on the holding of such a referendum.

In the meantime, the political situation in both Britain and Scotland entered a further period of considerable turbulence. For a variety of reasons, in 2022 the British Prime Minister Boris Johnson found himself under mounting pressure to resign, and was succeeded by first Liz Truss and then Rishi Sunak. Neither was inclined to give any ground on the aspirations of the Scottish Government for an independence referendum. Then it was Scotland's turn for political upheaval. In a shock announcement in February 2023, Nicola Sturgeon resigned as First Minister of Scotland, to be replaced in March 2023 by Humza Yousaf and then John Swinney in May 2024. This was followed by the Labour Party taking an SNP seat in the Westminster Parliament in a by-election. The year 2024 presents some interesting prospects with the Labour Party likely to win an imminent British General Election, helped by a decline in support for the SNP. This may well test the resolve of the SNP in pressing for a further referendum on independence any time soon.

Achievements of the Scottish Parliament

At this point clouds may hang over the SNP, but there is little doubt about the character of Scottish politics which has emerged over the last 25 years. It is avowedly social democratic in nature. Apart from the legislation relating to independence, the Scottish Parliament has pursued an agenda that has sought to address a wide range of issues that have gradually accumulated over many years of rule from Westminster. Mostly led by the SNP, the Parliament has sought to establish an active role for the State in securing social justice, a more enlightened education system, sustainable communities, and a healthy environment. In the remainder of this chapter we will briefly note the work of the Scottish Parliament over its first twenty five years. A more detailed account of the Parliament's attempts to re-engineer Scottish society through land reform is provided in Chapter 17.

Education and Children

Since the Middle Ages, Scotland has been at the forefront of education in the Western world. Although its universities were founded after Oxford (1096) and Cambridge (1209), they have been dominant centres of learning for more than six centuries providing the country with scholarship and learning that has delivered a nation of scientists, engineers, inventors, poets and authors that rival most countries in Europe. Until the 19th century, the centres of learning were at St Andrews (founded 1413), Glasgow (1451), Aberdeen (1495), and Edinburgh (1583). In the 21st century, Scotland now has 15 universities, is a party to the British Open University, and has three other institutions of further education.

Until recent times the main vehicle for educating children in Scotland was religious institutions. In the early days, the principal bodies were church choir schools and, by the end of the 15th century, the work of these establishments had been extended to include girls. A significant milestone was the 1496 Education Act which made it compulsory for the sons of the gentry to attend what were called grammar schools and, following the Reformation, the Church of Scotland had a central role in establishing schools at a parish level in every corner of the kingdom.

Following the Act of Union in 1707, the structure and funding of education in Scotland became increasingly influenced by British education policy designed to make attendance compulsory with a standard curriculum. In the 19th century, the number of schools was significantly expanded, with the establishment of a national system of free schooling and exams.

In more recent times, whilst secondary and primary education continues to be free, in 1998 Scotland adopted the system of tuition fees for higher education legislated by the Westminster Parliament. However, following the election of the Scottish Parliament in 1999, in 2007 university tuition fees were abolished for students under 25 years of age and this was later extended to students from the EU but not the rest of the UK. There has been a range of other legislation relevant to Education as follows.

The Standards in Scotland's Schools Act 2000 ordained that every child has a right to education, and specified the responsibilities of education authorities to ensure that a child's education is directed to the development of their personality, talents, and abilities to their fullest potential. The Act also states that authorities and schools must have due regard to children's views in decisions that significantly affect them, and established a new system for inspection of schools. The Act abolished corporal punishment, revised the system of governance for School Boards, strengthened standards that apply to independent schools, established rules for "home learning", and introduced the policy of 'presumption of mainstreaming', which means that unless special circumstances apply all children should attend mainstream schools.

The Children and Young People's Act 2014 aims to make Scotland the best place in the world for children to grow up. It facilitates a shift towards the early years of a child's life, including early intervention and adoption of preventative measures where a child's development is potentially compromised by personal circumstances.

The Education (Scotland) Act 2016 aims to accomplish the following:

- Institute measures designed to address inequality of access for children attending Primary and Secondary schools according to provisions in a National Improvement Framework,
- Provide for parents to opt for their children to be taught in Gaelic with English as a second language particularly at the Primary School level,
- Address inequality through such measures as the provision of free school meals and clothing grants,
- Mandate Head Teacher qualifications, and
- Give children a voice in matters that affect them, including input for those over 16 in determining support needs.

Environment

In the years just before establishment of the new Scottish Parliament, the UK Parliament established the Scottish Environment Protection Agency ("SEPA") which now reports to the Scottish Government. This body is responsible for implementation of policy on air quality, climate change, flooding, land quality, planning, management of radio-active substances, waste management, and water quality.

Of significance for Mull, following devolution the Scottish government established the Forestry Commission now known as Forestry Scotland. This body has responsibility for the sustainable management and expansion of forests and woodlands, providing expert advice to Ministers on forestry policy, and supporting landowners, forestry professionals, communities and a wide range of other stakeholders interested in forestry.

With these and several other agencies already in place, the Scottish Parliament has been at the forefront of legislation to protect the environment and address global warming. In the early years there was a focus on managing pollution but, subsequently, the Parliament has adopted an ambitious target for eliminating 45% of greenhouse gases by 2030.

In 2018, the Scottish government adopted the UK Withdrawal from the European Union (Continuity) (Scotland) Act. This includes significant environmental measures to protect Scotland as follows:

- The Scottish government is enabled to keep Scots law in alignment with EU Environmental law in so far as this is consistent with its devolved powers.
- A new body named Environmental Standards Scotland has been established with responsibility for monitoring, and securing compliance by public authorities with environmental law.
- The following four guiding principles of EU law have been enshrined in Scots law.
- *Precautionary Principle* (providing for power to use cost effective measures to deal with *a real or perceived threat* to the environment).

- *Prevention Principle* (providing power to prevent actual damage to the environment).
- *Rectification at Source Principle* (providing that damage should be rectified at source rather than by trying to mitigate effects).
- *Pays Principle* (providing that the person responsible for damage must pay for controlling it and remediating the damage.)

Land Reform

Following the establishment of the Scottish Parliament in 1999, for the first time in nearly 300 years a body representing the Scottish people set its mind to enacting laws and regulations to reverse the long history in which the ownership of land had been concentrated in ever fewer hands. There is a detailed account of the following legislation in Chapter 17 as context for the subsequent Chapters on current community activity in Mull.29

- Abolition of Feudal Tenure Act etc (Scotland) (2000)
- Scottish Land Fund (2000)
- Land Reform (Scotland) Act (2003)
- Community Empowerment (Scotland) Act (2015)
- Land Reform (Scotland) Act (2016)

Economic and Social Development

Membership of the European Union brought considerable benefits to the Highlands and Islands. This was manifest in a range of Rural Development policies designed to improve the competitiveness of agriculture, achieve sustainable management of natural resources, take action on climate change, and ensure balanced territorial development of rural areas. Implementation was financed through the European Regional Development Fund, the European Social Fund, and the European Agricultural Fund for Rural Development. The departure of the UK from the EU, against the wishes of the Scottish people, seriously compromised the achievement of a healthy and sustainable region. In 2018, the Scottish Parliament enacted The National Islands Plan, designed to foster viability and sustainability for relatively remote communities like Mull. The Plan has 13 Objectives designed to improve the quality of life for island communities over the next decade. It aims to:

- Address population decline and ensure a healthy, balanced population profile
- Improve and promote sustainable economic development
- Improve transport services
- Improve housing
- Reduce levels of fuel poverty
- Improve digital connectivity
- Improve and promote health, social care and wellbeing
- Improve and promote environmental wellbeing and biosecurity
- Contribute to climate change mitigation and promote clean, affordable and secure energy
- Empower diverse communities and places
- Support arts, culture and language
- Promote and improve education for all throughout life
- Support effective implementation of the National Islands Plan.

Conclusion

The parliamentary agenda identified above is but part of a much wider scope of legislation that has been adopted by the Scottish Parliament with the aim of transforming Scottish society to meet local needs as opposed to those of an increasingly meaningless union with other parts of the United Kingdom. To some considerable extent the scope of this legislation has been constrained by limits on tax raising powers. There is also a serious concern that the Parliament in Westminster is seeking to cancel the applicability of a whole range of EU related legislation which would undermine any future Scottish membership of that body. In the meantime, the Scottish Parliament has made significant strides in establishing a framework for Scottish culture and society which meets the largely progressive and community-minded aspirations of Scottish people. And, regardless of the party in power in Scotland, this will continue.

ENDNOTES

1   This view and some wording in this Chapter derive from the book The Scottish Nation, a Modern History by Professor Sir Tom Devine, Penguin, London (2012).

2   The late Queen Elizabeth the Queen Mother was the daughter of the 14th Earl of Strathmore and Kingholme, a title going back to the days of King James VI. The Earl is chief of the Clan Lyon, and descended from a French family de Léon who joined the Scottish court in Norman times. The title Empress of India terminated when India became an independent country in 1947.

3   The 6th Duke of Montrose was the direct descendant of his namesake the 1st Duke who voted for the union between Scotland and England in 1707!

4   The NPS was a left-of-centre party, and the SP a right-of-centre party. Both advocated Scottish Home Rule.

5   The United Kingdom of Great Britain (England/Wales and Scotland) and Ireland was established in 1801. Following rebellion, in 1921 Ireland was divided into two territories. Southern Ireland negotiated independence as a self-governing dominion called the Irish Free State. Northern Ireland, which had been colonised by the British in the 17th century, remained within the UK with its own parliament. The new political entity was the United Kingdom of Great Britain and Northern Ireland. The Irish Free State eventually became the fully independent Republic of Ireland in 1937.

6   The early SNP successes were in Glasgow Bridgeton in 1961 (18.7%), West Lothian in 1962 (23.3%) and Glasgow Pollok in 1967 (28.2%). The Hamilton By-election was called on the resignation of the Labour MP. Subsequently, Winnie Ewing was President of the SNP from 1987 to 2005.

7   William Wolfe was SNP national convenor from 1969 to 1979. Amongst other things, it was his idea to fuse the St Andrew's Cross with a thistle that led to the creation of the modern SNP logo.

8   This disproportionately low number of seats given the level of support reflected the inadequacies of the antiquated "First-Past-The-Post" British electoral system, totally unsuited for elections with more than two candidates.

9   A majority of the Welsh people voted against devolution for Wales.

10   George Cunningham was a Scot who represented a London constituency, and his independent-minded approach to politics scuppered not only this attempt at Scottish devolution but also the whole Labour government, heralding the Thatcher years.

11   Following Britain's entry into the Common Market under a Conservative government in 1972, in 1975 the Labour government held a referendum on whether to remain or leave the European Communities. 67.3% voted to remain on a turnout of 65%, including majorities in all parts of the UK.

12   The position of the SNP had been bolstered by the defection in 1976 of Labour MP Jim Sillars who, with fellow travellers, joined the SNP in 1982. Sillars won the seat of Glasgow Govan for the SNP in a 1988 by-election.

13   The Declaration of Arbroath asserted Scotland's history as an independent Christian kingdom, referred to the mythical origins of the Scots, and stated that they had lived in freedom and peace until King Edward I had invaded Scotland. The Declaration noted that the Scots had been saved by their present King Robert Bruce, and asked the Pope to persuade King Edward II to leave the Scots in peace. Although at first equivocal, in 1329 the Pope provided that the Bishop of St Andrews should anoint the King of Scots as the Pope's representative in an independent country.

14   This title is an oblique reference to the Claim of Right Act 1689, enacted by the then Scottish Parliament, which limited the power of the Scottish monarch.

15   The SNP initially participated but withdrew when the Convention refused to consider independence as an option.

16   Alex Salmond was elected as the MP for Banff and Buchan in the 1987 General Election.

17   In the 1997 UK election, 56 of the 80 Scottish seats were won by the Labour Party, 11 by the Conservatives, 10 by the Liberals and 6 by the SNP.

18   The vote for the establishment of a Welsh assembly was also successful.

19   Commencing in 1999, it was mandated that there would be an election every four years. In 2016, this was changed to every five years.

20   The Additional Member Voting system combines the First Past the Post system and a proportional representation system. Electors have two votes, one to elect a local constituency MP using the First Past the Post system (73 MPs in all), and one to elect regional representatives (there are seven MPs for each of eight regions) using proportional representation.

21   The Convenor of the Commission was the Chancellor of the University of Glasgow, Sir Kenneth Calman, a physician, notable academic, and some time Chief Medical Officer of Scotland.

22   The result of the UK election in 2010 was Conservative 306, Labour 258, Liberal Democrat 57, SNP 6, Green 1, Irish Parties 17, and others 4.

23   This assessment is based on a survey undertaken by Lord Ashcroft Polls – How Scotland Voted and Why – published in 2014.

24   The 44 year old Nicola Sturgeon had been elected to the Scottish Parliament in 2011. By 2014, she was a seasoned campaigner dedicated to the independence cause.

25   The 2015 British General Election resulted in an outright win for the Conservatives with the following seats: Conservatives 330, Labour 232, SNP 56, Liberal Democrats 8, and Others 24.

26   The election for the Scottish Parliament scheduled for 2015 was delayed because of a clash with the British General Election. In February 2016, the Scottish Parliament extended its term from four years to five years to avoid such clashes in the future.

27   The result was Conservatives 314, Labour 266, SNP 35, Liberal Democrats 14 and others 22.

28   In the 2019 election, the Conservatives won 365 seats, with Labour: 202, SNP: 48, Liberal Democrats: 11 and others: 24.

29   The total land area of Scotland is 19.252 million acres.

THEY PASSED CLOSE BY

In undertaking research for this book, a number of notable visitors to Mull have emerged. In modern times, this has included members of the royal family, with the then Prince Charles visiting the Ardnalanish estate to see the results of organic farming practices. However, if we turn the clock back 250 years there are several other visitors of note including the following.

Sir Joseph Banks

The outstanding natural environment in the Highlands and Islands of Scotland has attracted visits from many naturalists. Probably the most famous is Sir Joseph Banks, who has a strong association with the Antipodes.

Banks was born in Argyll Street in London on 23 February 1743, the son of a squire from Horncastle Lincolnshire. He was educated at both Harrow School and Eton College, and then studied Natural History at Christchurch College Oxford. However, with his father dying in 1761, he left university without taking a degree to assume responsibility for the family estate at Revesby Abbey in Lincolnshire. From then on, he divided his time between London and his estate.

In London, Banks mixed in scientific circles and met Carl Linnaeus with whom he corresponded.[1] As his influence increased, Banks was appointed as an advisor to King George III on the management of Kew Gardens and advocated royal support for voyages of discovery. In 1766, and still only 23, he was elected to be a member of the Royal Society. In 1766, Banks joined a school friend Constantine Phipps on an epic voyage to Newfoundland and Labrador, and made his name as a serious scientist by publishing the first Linnaean descriptions of the plants and animals of those territories. He also documented 34 species of birds, including the great auk which became extinct in 1844.

In 1768, Banks was appointed to join a Royal Navy/Royal Society expedition to the South Pacific on the *Endeavour*. This was the first of James Cook's voyages of discovery in that region, and Banks funded eight other scientists to join the voyage. The ship sailed via South Africa, Brazil, Tahiti, and New Zealand to arrive at the east coast of Australia. In Australia the ship was damaged on the Great Barrier Reef and, while it was being repaired, Banks and colleagues explored the hinterland and assembled the first major collection of Australian flora, describing many species new to science. As recorded in his diary on 12 July 1770, Banks also encountered an animal he called a "kanguru"!

When Banks arrived back in England a year later he immediately became famous. He intended to go with Cook on his second voyage, but the Admiralty would not finance his scientific plans. So instead he arranged an alternative expedition. In July 1772, he set sail with his friend Daniel Solander on the *Sir Lawrence,* to visit the Isle of Wight, the Hebrides, Iceland, and the Orkney Islands. During this voyage he undertook the first ever scientific visit to the island of Staffa including Fingal's Cave. The cave was already known to the local fishermen, but he was the first person to write about it and perhaps this led to the composer Felix Mendelssohn subsequently making his visit to the island in 1829. During his time in Mull in 1772, Banks stayed with the Macquarie family.

As Banks continued his research, in 1778 he was elected as President of the Royal Society a position he would hold with distinction for 41 years. In March 1779, he married Dorothea Hugessen and settled in a large house at 32 Soho Square. This continued to be his London residence for the remainder of his life. In 1781 he was knighted and in the years that followed he was also elected to many other national scientific bodies. In 1794 he became High Sheriff of Lincolnshire, and in 1795 he was invested as a Knight of the Order of the Bath. He died in 1820 without issue.

James Boswell and Samuel Johnson

In the 18th century, arguably the most famous visitor to Mull was Dr Samuel Johnson who was persuaded by his Scottish friend James Boswell into undertaking a *Tour of the Western Isles* as Boswell called it.

Dr Johnson was born in Lichfield, Staffordshire in 1709 shortly after the establishment of Great Britain. A student at Oxford, insufficient finances stopped him from completing a degree and he worked as a teacher before moving to London to become a writer and critic for *The Gentleman's Magazine*. He also began to write essays, biographies, poetry and plays while working as an editor and lexicographer. His most famous work, which took him nine years to complete was *A Dictionary of the English Language*. This appeared in 1755 with far-reaching effects on the vocabulary and use of modern English which would be the benchmark for more than 150 years. He is arguably the most distinguished man of letters in the English language and died in 1784.

James Boswell was the 9th Laird of Auchinleck, a town in Ayrshire. He was born in Edinburgh in 1740, and was the eldest son of a judge. Because of poor health, he was mostly educated by private tutors and enrolled into Edinburgh University at the age of 13. He would study there from 1753 to 1758, and then continued his studies at Glasgow University where he attended lectures given by Adam Smith. He then decided to become a monk but, with opposition from his family including a threat of disinheritance, he abandoned this idea and studied law. Living off a parental allowance, in 1762 he moved to London which was a base for extensive travel about which he would write at length. During this period, he met Dr Johnson who became a father figure and friend.

In 1766 Boswell returned to Edinburgh and completed his law degree to become an advocate which he practised for a number of years whilst still writing. His most famous work is his *Life of Samuel Johnson* which was published in 1791. It immediately became a celebrated book, not least because it included the record of many of his conversations with notable people. Boswell was married and had several children. He died in 1795.

The visit of Johnson and Boswell to Mull and other parts of the Hebrides took place in 1773. Boswell had been nagging Johnson to visit Scotland for some time, and Johnson (now in his sixties) eventually grudgingly agreed to make the journey north. The trip took place from August through to November, and details provided in Boswell's *The Journal of a Tour to the Hebrides with Samuel Johnson* provide remarkable insight into life in Mull and neighbouring islands in the 18th century. The journal was first published in 1785.[2]

Johnson and Boswell set out from Edinburgh in August 1773. As was his custom, Boswell kept a detailed diary including a record of conversations he had with Johnson and others. They took a circuitous route, travelling up to Aberdeen before crossing to Inverness and then venturing to the islands, commencing with a lengthy visit to Skye. On that island they mixed with Macdonalds and McLeods, most of whom spoke Gaelic which Boswell called Erse. The local chiefs lamented the disintegration of clan life through the departure of many of the locals, and provided detailed accounts of the period immediately after the Battle of Culloden, with the escape of Prince Charles Edward Stuart assisted by Flora Macdonald.

In early October, the pair left Skye and transferred to Mull via the island of Coll, travelling on several boats. It was not an easy trip, as they encountered a storm and rough seas for several days. Eventually, on 14 October 1773, *The Campbeltown,* arrived at Tobermory which Boswell describes as a busy harbour capable of handling 70 ships. The couple spent the first night in "a tolerable inn" and visited Dr Alexander Maclean who lived just outside the town and was noted for his history of the Clan Maclean. After being laid up due to bad weather, two days later they travelled overland to Loch na Keal with the aim of visiting the island of Inch Kenneth to stay at what was at that time the home of the chief of the Clan Maclean, Sir Allan Maclean.[3] In his journal, Boswell writes of this journey as follows *"we set out mounted on little Mull horses. Mull corresponded exactly with the idea which I had always had of it; a hilly country, diversified with heath and grass, and many rivulets.*

Dr Johnson was not in very good humour. He said it was a dreary country, much worse than Skye." In fact, for some of the journey (which presumably took them across to Dervaig and over the hill to Torloisk on what is now a narrow sealed road) they had to walk, as the weather turned nasty and water across the tracks was too deep for their horses to carry them safely. Eventually, they arrived at the crossing to Ulva and made the short trip across the Sound to stay at the home of Lachlan Macquarie the 16th Chief of the Clan. In his log, Boswell provides an enlightening picture of Macquarie and his home – *"M'Quarrie's house was mean; but we were agreeably surprised with the appearance of the master, whom we found to be intelligent, polite, and much a man of the world. He told us that his family had possessed Ulva for nine hundred years; but I was distressed to hear that it was soon to be sold for the payment of his debts."*

In their conversations, Boswell records a very interesting custom, vestiges of which remained on Ulva. *"M'Quarrie insisted that the "mercheta mulierum", mentioned in our old charters, did really mean the privilege in which a lord of a manor had the first night of all his vassals' wives. Dr Johnson commented that such a custom was thought to also exist in England, where there is a tenure called Borough-English, by which the eldest child does not inherit, from a doubt of his being the son of the tenant. M'Quarrie told us that still, on the marriage of each of his tenants, a sheep is due to him for which the composition is fixed at five shillings. I suppose, Ulva is the only place where this custom remains."*

The next day, Boswell and Johnson proceeded by a short boat trip to the island of Inch Kenneth and were cheered to find a decent track up to the house from the shore. With the loss of Duart Castle, Sir Allan Maclean had taken out a lease on the island and lived in a relatively well appointed single story house. He was already known to Boswell because their fathers were acquainted, and the visitors stayed for the whole day, exploring the island. The following day, Sir Allan took the pair by boat to Iona, passing the massive cliffs of Gribun with McKinnon's Cave, the island of Staffa, and Nun's Island which had extensive woodland. They continued into the evening, *"sailing by moonlight, in a rough sea, and often between black and gloomy rocks, with Dr Johnson saying that if this be not roving among the Hebrides, nothing is."*

On arriving at Iona in the late evening, Boswell shares with the reader his veneration of what is regarded as holy land. He writes *"We are now treading that illustrious island, which was once the luminary of the Caledonian regions, whence savage clans and roving barbarians derived the benefits of knowledge, and the blessings of religion."* Boswell also adds a footnote - *[Had our tour produced nothing else but this sublime passage, the world must have acknowledged that it was not made in vain. The present respectable President of the Royal Society was so much struck on reading my words that he clasped his hands together, and remained for some time in an attitude of silent admiration.]*

Boswell then provides a telling remark about local loyalties. He writes *"Upon hearing that Sir Allan Maclean had arrived, the local inhabitants, who still consider themselves as the people of Maclean, to whom the island formerly belonged, though the Duke of Argyle has at present possession of it, ran eagerly to him."* Later, Sir Allan is heard referring to a local with whom he has differences *"I believe you are a Campbell."* There was no love lost. The travellers stayed the night in a barn, sleeping on a bed of hay, and the next day they explored the ruins of the Nunnery, the Abbey, and what were called the monuments of the kings of Scotland, Ireland, Denmark, and France with little to be seen except some grave-stones flat on the earth with any inscriptions worn away by the weather. Boswell goes on to comment about the local economy stating that *"Iona is a fertile island. The inhabitants export some cattle and grain. They are industrious, and make their own woollen and linen cloth. They brew a good deal of beer, which we did not find in any of the other islands."*

On the evening of 20 October Johnson and Boswell sailed across to the mainland where they stayed with the Reverend Neil McLeod. The next day, they acquired horses for the journey to Lochbuie, riding through the Ross of Mull and Brolass which Boswell describes as *"the most gloomy and desolate country"*. They arrived at Lochbuie with its ancient Castle of Moy in the late evening, noting that the place took its name from the Gaelic for "yellow cake" which was the colour of the hills above the settlement.[4] They were welcomed at Lochbuie House by the 50 year old laird John Maclaine who apparently did not live up to his reputation as a *"great roaring braggadocio"*.[5] Instead, Boswell describes him as *"a bluff, comely, noisy old gentleman, proud of his hereditary consequence, and a very hearty and hospitable landlord"*. The following morning at breakfast, Hector's wife Isabel (the sister of Sir Allan Maclean) described her husband as a *"Dungeon of Wit"* being a Scottish expression to reflect a person of considerable intellect. Later in the morning of Friday 22 October, they took a ferry and by evening they had arrived at Oban where they found a tolerable inn. The next day they travelled overland to Inverary.

Felix Mendelssohn

Felix Mendelssohn Bartholdy was born in Hamburg in 1809, the son of a prominent banker Abraham Mendelssohn and his wife Lea Bartholdy. Bartholdy was adopted as part of the family name to demonstrate a break with their Jewish past which Abraham had renounced before Felix was born. Felix would eventually be baptised as a member of the Reformed Protestant faith and, in 1811, the family moved to Berlin where their home became a salon for intellectuals and musicians.

Felix had an interest and natural talent for music from an early age. He began taking piano lessons when he was six years old and later received tuition from Carl Zelter a teacher recommended by Sarah Levy who had been a pupil of the Bach family. Felix made his first public appearance as a pianist at the age of nine, and by the age of 12 he was composing string symphonies and chamber works. His first work, a piano quartet, was published when he was 13 and, in 1824, he composed his first symphony for full orchestra (Op. 11 in C minor). Aged 16 he wrote his String Octet in E-flat major, a work which marked the beginning of his maturity as a composer. This and his Overture to Shakespeare's *A Midsummer Night's Dream*, which he wrote a year later in 1826, are the best-known of his early works. Later, in 1843, he also wrote incidental music for the same play, including the famous "Wedding March".

Besides music, Mendelssohn's education included art, literature, languages, and philosophy. With a particular interest in classical literature, he translated Terence's *Andria* for his tutor Heyse in 1825 who had it published in 1826 as a work of "his pupil, F****". This translation qualified Mendelssohn to study at the Humboldt University of Berlin, where from 1826 to 1829 he attended lectures on aesthetics given by Georg Wilhelm Friedrich Hegel. In 1821 his previous tutor Zelter introduced Mendelssohn to his friend and correspondent Johann Wolfgang von Goethe. And, in 1829, with the backing of Zelter and the assistance of the actor Eduard Devrient, Mendelssohn arranged and conducted a performance in Berlin of Bach's *St Matthew Passion*.

Over the next few years Mendelssohn travelled widely, including ten visits to Britain where he lived for a total of 20 months. During his visits he won a strong following, and he composed, performed, and also edited for British publishers, the first critical editions of Handel's oratorios and the organ music of J. S. Bach.

During his first visit to Britain in 1829 Mendelssohn ventured up to Edinburgh, and Scotland inspired two of his most famous works. He began to write the overture *The Hebrides* (also known as *Fingal's Cave*) in December 1829 following his visit to Staffa. He was so impressed by the cave that he scribbled the opening theme of the overture on the spot, including it in a letter he wrote home the same evening. Subsequent performance of this work helped the natural landmark to become a tourist destination. On the same trip to Scotland in 1829 he began to write the *Scottish Symphony* (Symphony No. 3) which he eventually completed in 1842.

During this period, in March 1837, he married Cécile Jeanrenaud, the daughter of a French Reformed Church clergyman. The couple had five children. On his last visit to Britain in 1847, he appeared before Queen Victoria and Prince Albert as a soloist and was the conductor for a performance of the *Scottish Symphony*.

In all, Mendelssohn composed five symphonies, many concertos and chamber music, songs, organ works, choral works and operas. In the final years of his life, he suffered from poor health. A final tour of England in 1847 left him exhausted and ill, and the death of his sister, Fanny, on 14 May, caused him further distress. Less than six months later, on 4 November, and aged only 38, Mendelssohn died in Leipzig after a series of strokes.

The Livingstones

David Livingstone, the 19th century explorer and missionary, was born in Blantyre in Lanarkshire. He is rightly celebrated as a son of that town, but his family came from the island of Ulva, and their history illustrates the sad story of the clearances.

In the 18th century, and probably long before, the Livingstones were tenants of the Clan Macquarrie, and there are still remains of the stone house in which they lived on the southern slopes of the island. David's great grandfather, John Livingstone is known to have fought and died at the Battle of Culloden leaving behind a wife and son named Neil Mor Livingstone. Like so many tenants, the family's traditional way of life involved the tending of cattle and sheep and growing food for man and beast, but they also gathered seaweed which was used to make soap and glass and as fertiliser. This industry eventually collapsed, making it increasingly difficult to eke out a living. In the 1770s the landlord Lachlan Macquarie sold the island to settle mounting debts and subsequent landlords demanded higher rents which set in motion an exodus of the population.

So it was that in 1792 David Livingstone's grandfather Neil Mor left the island, moving to Blantyre in Lanarkshire to work in a cotton factory. At around the same time, other members of the Livingstone family left Ulva resettling in Canada and the United States. Happily settled in Blantyre, his grandfather would become a respected member of the community, was married and had a son named Neil who received a sound education and became a school teacher. He married a local girl named Agnes, and in 1813 their son David Livingstone was born in a tenement building constructed for cotton workers.

David Livingstone was brought up in a god-fearing household and acquired a strong religious faith, first as a Presbyterian but then as a member of the less strict Congregational church. At an early age he worked in the cotton mill whilst attending the local school in Blantyre. However, he had yearning to enter the medical profession and, in his teenage years, he began to save money for a university education. In 1836, he entered

Anderson's University in Glasgow to study Greek and Theology. He then acquired a tutor in Latin, knowledge of which was a requirement to enter medical school. Shortly after, he applied to join the London Missionary Society ("LMS") and became a student at the Charing Cross Hospital Medical School. During 1838 and 1840 he completed courses in medical practice, midwifery, and botany. During this period he also spent time on missionary training in London and in Ongar, Essex. Eventually he qualified as a Congregational Minister and, in late 1840, he also qualified as a Licentiate of the Faculty (now Royal College) of Physicians and Surgeons of Glasgow.[6]

Livingstone had hoped to go the China as a missionary, but in the early 1840s that country was in the grip of the first Opium War. Instead, he opted for Africa and arrived in Cape Town in March 1841. In 1843 he joined the missionary Roger Edwards to set up a mission station in Mabotsa Botswana. During his time there, he was injured by a lion and was nursed back to health by the daughter of another missionary, Mary Moffat. She would become his wife in January 1845.

Livingstone had always been an adventurous fellow and, with his religious zeal to save the local population from the impact of European "civilisation", he felt the need to venture further afield. In 1851, he struck out north up to the River Zambezi along which he travelled for the next two years risking life and limb. He eventually encountered the vast waterfall that he named Victoria Falls.[7] Being the first European to penetrate this part of Africa, this journey made him famous.

In 1856, Livingstone returned to Britain, and his work as a geographer was recognised by the Royal Geographical Society who presented him with their gold medal. Encouraged by the LMS, he then wrote up his journal which took the form of a travelogue, *Missionary Travels* that was published in 1857. The book included accounts of his field science, sympathetic descriptions of African people, and advocacy that missions and "legitimate commerce" by river into central Africa would facilitate the end of the slave trade.

Following his success, Livingstone had plans for further epic journeys. However, the LMS were not prepared to back him and he resigned. He was then appointed as Her Majesty's Consul with a roving commission to operate throughout the eastern coast of Africa. His remit also extended to the interior and, in January 1858, he led a second Zambesi expedition with six specialist officers. This venture had a chequered outcome, and he eventually return to Britain. However, in the 1860s he returned for several further trips including an expedition to find the source of the Nile. On one of his periods at home, he visited Ulva in the hopes of finding some evidence of his family but this was to no avail.

During yet a further trip in 1871, Livingstone's whereabouts became the subject of concern. In response, the New York Herald newspaper hired Henry Stanley to go and find him. In due course, he was successful, meeting Livingstone on the banks of Lake Tanganyika on 10 November 1871 which gave rise to the attributed famous words of Stanley - *"Dr Livingstone I presume"*. He died on 1 May 1873 at Chipundu, southeast of Lake Bangweulu in present-day Zambia, from malaria and internal bleeding due to dysentery.

Robert Louis Stevenson

Robert Louis Stevenson was born in Edinburgh in 1850, the son of Thomas Stevenson a leading lighthouse engineer. An only child, he was brought up in a devout Presbyterian household. In his early years, he had a chronically weak chest, a condition that would stalk him for his whole life. After attending a local school, with frequent home schooling, he eventually attended Edinburgh Academy. Although he received a broad education, from an early age he began to write, with his first piece entitled *The Pentland Rising: A Page in History* being published in 1866.

In 1867, Robert attended Edinburgh University to study engineering with his family expecting that he would follow the family profession. Each year during the holidays, as part of his training, he travelled to inspect the family's engineering works, and in 1870 this took him for three weeks to the island of Erraid to observe the building of the Dhub Artach lighthouse.[8] While on Erraid, he also visited the Skerryvore lighthouse on the isle of Tiree west of Mull.[9]

Despite this exposure to the family profession, Stevenson enjoyed the travels more for the material they provided for his writing than any interest in the lighthouses. Thoughts of writing were never far from his mind, and notes he kept on the 1870 trip refer to the voyage by steamship to the island of Iona, where he stayed at the Argyll Hotel, and trips to both Staffa and Erraid. Uncertainty about his career came to a head in April 1871 when he notified his father of his decision to pursue a life of letters. Though his father must have been disappointed it probably came as no surprise. To provide some security, it was agreed that Stevenson should read Law and be called to the bar which he duly accomplished. Thereafter, he began a long career in writing and publishing articles, essays, poetry and books.

Throughout the 1870s, and despite his intermittent health issues, Stevenson continued to be a frequent traveller. In 1874, he would again visit Mull and, in 1876, he visited Northern France where he met a married American woman named Frances (Fanny) Osbourne. When she went home to California, he kept in touch with her and, after she divorced her philandering husband, in 1879 Stevenson travelled to California to be with her. However, en route he fell ill. Fanny took him in and nursed him back to health. In the process they became engaged and they were married in San Francisco in 1880.

Following their marriage, the couple returned to Europe, shuttling back and forth between Scotland and the Continent. In 1884, they eventually settled in Westbourne in Hampshire where they lived in a house Stevenson named 'Skerryvore'. Notably, from April 1885 Stevenson had the regular company in Hampshire of the novelist Henry James who had moved to Bournemouth to support an ailing sister. At this point in his life, Stevenson was largely bedridden and described himself as living *"like a weevil in a biscuit."* Yet, despite his ill health, during his three years in Westbourne, Stevenson wrote the bulk of his most popular works - *Treasure Island*, *Kidnapped*, *The Strange Case of Dr Jekyll and Mr Hyde*, *The Black Arrow*, *A Tale of the Two Roses*, *A Child's Garden of Verses* and *Underwoods*.

In 1887, in search of a warmer climate, the Stevensons moved to Colorado and then to New York. Then, in 1888, Stevenson chartered the yacht *Casco* and the family set sail from San Francisco for a voyage of nearly three years through the eastern and central Pacific. During this period, he completed *The Master of Ballantrae*, and provided a record of his travels in the book entitled *In the South Seas* which was published posthumously. In 1890, he left Sydney, Australia, on the *Janet Nicoll* for his third and final voyage among the South Seas islands. He ended up in Samoa. On 3 December 1894, he was talking to his wife and straining to open a bottle of wine when he suddenly exclaimed, "What's that?" He asked his wife "does my face look strange?" and he collapsed. Aged 44, he died of a cerebral haemorrhage and, much loved by the locals, he was given a ceremonial burial on Mount Vaea.

There are references to Mull in three of Stenson's books. The island of Erraid was the model for a fictional island named Aros which figures in a short story published in a book called *The Merry Men and Other Tales and Fables* published in 1882. Mull and Erraid figure in *Kidnapped* published in 1886, and his personal impressions of Erraid are given in a book of sixteen essays entitled *Memories and Portraits*, published in 1887. His accounts of Mull are particularly striking in *Kidnapped*. At an early stage in the adventure, David Balfour (Balfour was Stevenson's mother's maiden name) finds himself stranded on Erraid because he thinks it is an island. He then spends a couple of cold and miserable days eating raw shellfish before he learns that it is actually an islet, with the ability to walk to the mainland when the tide is out. There is then an account of his journey through the Ross of Mull to Torosay with reference to features which still exist today.

Major General Sir Colin McVean Gubbins

In a much later time, but no less worthy, one of the most famous people who spent his formative years in Mull was the leader of the British Special Forces during World War Two. Colin Gubbins was born in July 1896 in Tokyo. His father was the Oriental Secretary of the British Legation to Japan, and his mother was Helen McVean the daughter of Colin McVean who had been a civil engineer working in Japan in the late 19th century. Helen was the grand-daughter of the Reverend Donald McVean who had been the minister of the Free Church for Iona and Mull and was married to Susan Maclean.

In 1885, Helen's parents returned to live in Mull and took up residence in Killiemore House which is in Kilfinichen to the north of Loch Scridain. Colin and his four siblings were sent to live with these maternal grandparents when he was a very young child.[10] He was educated locally, and came to love the island. In his teens, he was sent to Cheltenham College and then to the Royal Military College at Woolwich. Only 18 years old, he was an active participant in the First World War, fighting at Ypres and the Somme and winning the Military Cross. After the war, he then served in the Russian Civil War, before going into intelligence during the Irish War of Independence in the early 1920s. These engagements sparked his interest in "irregular" warfare.

After some years as a military officer in various diplomatic missions, and a time in documenting manuals for irregular warfare, at the beginning of the Second World War, Gubbins joined military intelligence and then saw action in support of the resistance in Poland, Czechoslovakia, France and Norway. In 1940, and now an acting Brigadier, he joined the newly formed Special Operations Executive ("SOE"). In the early days, amongst other things, he was responsible for establishing what was called "the Shetland Bus", which was a typical SOE operation ferrying insurgents between the Shetlands and Norway to resist German occupation. In 1943, he was appointed as SOE Executive Head with responsibility for the activities of resistance movements worldwide including the work of the author's father!

After the war, Gubbins became the managing director of a carpet and textile manufacturer. However, he remained in touch with people in many of the countries he had helped to liberate. He was also a co-founder of the Special Forces Club in Knightsbridge, London. A shooter and fisherman, he spent his last years at his home on the island of Harris. In 1976, he was appointed the Deputy Lieutenant of the Western Isles, and died on Stornoway on 11 February 1976.

Sorley Maclean

Sorley MacLean is one of the most important poets of the modern era, and played a significant role in sustaining Gaelic poetry. He was born on the island of Raasay in 1911 where his parents owned a small croft and ran a tailoring business. His father's family came from Mull, and the ancestors of both his parents had been evicted during the 19th century clearances. As he grew up, memories of those times were still fresh amongst family members. Sorley was raised as a Calvinist, with Gaelic as his first tongue. While still respectful of the church, as a teenager he abandoned religion and became a life-long socialist.

Educated on Raasay and at Portree High School on Skye, Sorley attended the University of Edinburgh studying English Literature but also taking classes in the Department of Celtic Studies. Already a poet, he was involved in literary circles, played for the university shinty team, and was associated with the Communist Party where he met Hugh MacDiarmid. In 1934, he obtained a job as a teacher at Portree High School, and in 1938 he took up a post at Tobermory High School. He spent a year on Mull, and the landscape and the devastation caused by the clearances had a profound effect upon him. He is reported as saying *"I believe Mull had much to do with my poetry: its physical beauty, with the terrible imprint of the clearances on it, made it almost intolerable for a Gael."* In 1939, Sorley moved to Boroughmuir High School in Edinburgh and became friends with many intellectuals of the era. During this time, as well writing many poems, he became a noted historian, and published two influential papers on nineteenth-century Gaelic poetry in *"Transactions of the Gaelic Society of Inverness."*

In 1940, Sorley joined the Royal Corps of Signals, and in 1942 he served in the North Africa Campaign where he was severely wounded. After recuperating back home in hospital, he resumed his teaching career in Edinburgh and in 1946 he married Renee Cameron with whom he had three daughters. In the early post-war years, he wrote his most well-known poem, *Hallaig*, which was published in 1954. This provides a supernatural representation of a village depopulated during the Clearances with the ghosts of evicted residents wandering through the adjacent woodlands. In 1956 Sorley took up a post as Head Teacher at Plockton High School and promoted the use of Gaelic. At this time, he was also active in politics and joined the Scottish Labour Party.

In 1972, Sorley retired and moved to his great-grandmother's house on Skye. Following the publication of his poetry into English and German, he was a frequent visitor to Europe to provide poetry readings and, between 1973 and 1975, he was *writer in residence* at the University of Edinburgh. In the early 1970s, he was instrumental in founding *Sabhal Mòr Ostaig* which is a higher education college located on Skye with teaching in Gaelic. Sorley died in Inverness in 1996.

ENDNOTES

1   Carl Linnaeus was a Swedish botanist, zoologist, taxonomist and physician who established the modern system for naming of organisms.

2   Access to the Journal was made possible through Project Gutenburg who provide digitised versions of selected books on line.

3   This is General Sir Allan Maclean, living in "the sticks", with Duart Castle lost to the Campbells and now very much a ruin.

4   In fact the name Moy is probably from the Norse word Moi meaning sandy plain.

5   Further information on these buildings, and the current Lochbuie House which post-dates the building which Johnson and Boswell visited, can be found in Chapter 25.

6   In January 1857, he was made an Honorary Fellow of the Faculty.

7   The local Kololo tribe called this waterfall 'Mosi-oa-Tunya' – 'The Smoke that Thunders'. Now in Zambia, Livingstone is commemorated with a statue inscribed with the words "Christianity, Commerce and Civilization".

8   The lighthouse sits to the southwest of Iona. It was designed by David and Thomas Stevenson, and was constructed between 1867 and 1872.

9   Skerryvore Lighthouse is the tallest in the U.K. and built by his uncle Alan Stevenson between 1838 and 1844.

10   Killiemore House was owned by the Duke of Argyll.

PART SIX

REBIRTH OF COMMUNITY

COMMUNITY LAW

I
t is a heartening fact for the people of Mull that, in the last two decades, the Scottish Parliament has enacted legislation that provides for land reform, community empowerment, and the development of a national plan to deliver a healthy and sustainable existence on Scotland's Islands. Taken together these Acts constitute significant social engineering, and reverse years of exploitation of both individuals and communities, in which individuals were free to pursue private gain at the expense of the public interest. The new laws provide for a radical change in the rights of ordinary citizens and communities to access and enjoy their environment, to acquire property for community purposes, and to be directly involved in planning decisions about assets that impact on a given local community. And they have the potential to radically re-energise Mull as a community-based society reflecting the age-old spirit of dùthchas.

Scottish Legal System

B
efore describing the current legal framework for community living in Scotland, it is worth noting the history of the Scottish legal system which developed quite separately from the rest of the United Kingdom.[1] It is strongly influenced by the concept of civil law based on codified statutes, compared with the concept of common law which relies on "case law" as recorded in published judicial determinations.

Until the 12th century, Scottish society existed without a documented rule of law. In places like Mull, temporal justice was mostly administered through custom and practice as determined by leading members of the community, while the church took care of spiritual and many domestic matters. With the Norman invasion of England in 1066, this would begin to change for many parts of Scotland, with the influx of a feudal system in which justice was determined by the crown. However, in the Northern and Western Isles, where clans were prevalent, the traditional community-based systems would largely prevail for another several hundred years.

The earliest documented Scottish "rule of law" was established by King David I in the mid-12th century. The Leges inter Brettos et Scottos specified codes based on ancient customs for addressing a range of civil and criminal matters including murder, honour, theft, and the right to bear arms.[2] There were also provisions for exemption to these codes, specification of heirs, the management of foster children, payments for hospitality, dowries for marriage, and the swearing of oaths. Issues arising would be determined by a range of temporal and clerical courts but, under the Davidian system, the crown also began to appoint sheriffs to act as royal administrators and tax collectors. During the next century, the power of these sheriffs would gradually be extended with the ability to hear a variety of civil and criminal cases, although the King's courts were mostly confined to dealing with cases of treason. In places like Mull, it was the custom and practice for clan chiefs and other family leaders to dispense justice. At the same time, ecclesiastical courts had jurisdiction over matters such as marriage, inheritance, legitimacy and contracts made under oath. Interestingly, unlike the royal courts, these clerical courts were generally staffed by men with a knowledge of both the Roman civil and ecclesiastic canon law which came into existence in the 12th century, and often offered a more equitable form of justice.

There is important documentary evidence of the rules applying in all these courts in the latter part of the Middle Ages, with a variety of written records still in existence including the Regiam Majestatem.[3] This seminal work from the early 14th century consists of four books, providing the basis for dealing with contracts, civil actions, crimes, and judgements, and is largely based on a number of older works embracing Roman, Celtic and English legal precedents.

By the 16th century, Scotland was beginning to develop a common rule of law that was distinctly Scottish. In part, this was triggered by the 1496 Education Act that required landowners to send their eldest sons to study Latin, law and the arts for at least three years at a Scottish university. This facilitated the development of a group of people with training that would become the basis of a legal profession with the ability to take responsibility for the centralised administration of the royal courts. Eventually, this new system would take precedence over the ecclesiastic courts and extend to all four corners of the kingdom. Initially, it operated in a hierarchical manner deriving its authority from the King's Council with a specialised group of councillors directly accountable to the King. However, eventually legal experts would codify, define and systematically update a commonly applicable Scots law which did not rely on royal prerogative. Of great significance, in May 1532, after consultation with the Pope, the Scottish Parliament established the Scottish College of Justice or Court of Session. This body consisted of 14 members (seven churchmen and seven laymen called senators), with the Lord Chancellor presiding. The College proceeded to establish written rules of practice and constituted a closed list of ten lawyers permitted to appear before them, six of whom had studied law in Europe. While recognising the traditional Scottish common law, this extended the influence of Roman law. As a consequence, the general practice during this period was to defer to specific Scottish laws where relevant recorded precedent was available, and to fill in any gaps with provisions derived from written civil and canon law.

In the years that followed, which included the Reformation, the power of ecclesiastic courts would continue to decline and, in 1640 Parliament determined that membership of the College of Justice should be restricted to laymen only. Then, in 1672, Parliament passed the Courts Act which introduced the High Court of Justiciary consisting of five members of the College of Justice. This would become the highest court in Scotland for the administration of criminal justice, working alongside the Court of Session that dealt with civil cases.

Interestingly, whilst the Act of Union of 1707 unified the kingdoms of Scotland and England under one Parliament, it also recognised the separate and independent legal system in Scotland. Article 19 of the Act confirmed the continuing authority of the Court of Justiciary, and the Court of Session. Appointment to the latter, as a "Lord of Session", required at least five years membership of the "Colledge of Justice". Furthermore, while the new British Parliament had the power to enact laws on public administration, Scottish law still had precedence on matters concerning private rights. Subsequently, the body of law specific to Scotland would continue to grow during the 18th and 19th century. Today, the Supreme Court of the United Kingdom usually has a minimum of at least two Scottish justices to ensure that some Scottish experience is brought to bear on appeals administered by that court which relate to Scotland.

Scottish Community and Land Law

In the last 150 years, significant progress has been made in addressing the long-standing social injustices arising from concentration of land ownership in Scotland. The first substantive legislation involved the largely ineffectual Crofters Holding Act of 1886 and, in the early 20th century there were then a number of further attempts which failed to shake the power and influence of the long-held vested interests of a small number of land owners. In reality, land reform did not begin in earnest until the 1950s with a succession of Acts designed to recognise and maintain crofters' rights. These were The Crofters (Scotland) Act 1955, The Crofters (Scotland) Act 1961, The Crofting Reform (Scotland) Act 1976 and The Crofter Forestry (Scotland) Act 1991.

As context for what the recently re-established Scottish Parliament has achieved in reversing the long history of exploitation, it is worth noting the following Scottish government statements. In identifying the problem, it was stated in a government publication in 2016 that:

"Scotland has the most concentrated pattern of private land ownership in Europe because of several historic factors, such as feudalism, succession laws, fiscal policies and agricultural support".[4]

In addressing this problem, in which the pattern of land ownership over several generations undermined community-based life through removal of people from traditional lands, the Scottish government identified a central objective as follows:

"To improve Scotland's system of land ownership, use, rights and responsibilities, so that our land may contribute to a fair and just society while balancing public and private interests".

With these sentiments in mind, the 21st century has seen a succession of Acts of Parliament which have sought to correct long term injustice. Amongst other things, by 2020, this had resulted in the transfer of over 1 million acres of land to community ownership.[5] The following is a brief summary of the land reform measures adopted by both the Scottish Parliament and the Westminster Parliament since 1999.

Scottish Land Fund 2000

In 1991, the Westminster Parliament established an organisation named Highlands and Islands Enterprise ("HIE") the aim of which was to facilitate projects designed to encourage economic development and to achieve sustainable and resilient communities in remote parts of the UK. The HIE began by establishing a land fund to which it allocated £250,000 for land purchases.

Building on this initiative, in 2000 the Scottish Parliament established the Scottish Land Fund ("SLF"), with responsibility for administration referred to HIE following a tender. The specific aim of the fund was to help communities buy land and related assets through access to what was called the New Opportunities Fund which was financed by proceeds from the UK National Lottery. Initially, the fund comprised £10 million, with grants of up to £1 million available between 2001 and 2006. The initiative triggered an enormous response from local communities and in 2003 the fund was increased to £15 million.

As a consequence of this modest beginning in reversing the concentrated pattern of land ownership, by June 2005 the SLF had assisted some 200 communities with land purchases of varying size. When this initial programme terminated in 2006, it was decided to continue the activity through access to funds arising from the Growing Community Assets programme of the Big Lottery Fund ("BLF"). This was also administered by HIE, but under new criteria determined by the BLF.

With the extension of the scheme, HIE undertook a detailed analysis of the initial programme which showed that during the period 2001–2006 support had been allocated to some very large purchases with five projects accounting for 50% of the money spent with a peak of £6.4 million in one year. With the aim of extending the reach to smaller projects, the programme was amended to involve a submission process that gave weight to some broad community-based criteria. The scheme also provided technical assistance in preparing applications, which were then assessed by a professional committee appointed by the government.

There is little doubt that, although modest, these initial schemes encouraged a major change in community thinking. And the impact was significantly enhanced by subsequent Land Reform legislation.

The Land Reform Acts

The next steps in this journey involved legislation to have a direct impact on the structure of land ownership. The Abolition of Feudal Tenure etc (Scotland) Act 2000 removed the centuries-old system of land ownership whereby 'vassals' could be restricted in activities on their land subject to payment of feu duties.[6] The Title Conditions (Scotland) Act 2003, modernised the types of interests and legitimate burdens that can be attached to land titles and provided default arrangements for land ownership where there were no title deeds. And the Tenements (Scotland) Act 2004 modernised the management of tenement titles, prescribing owner obligations and tenant rights.

However, by far the most important piece of legislation was the Land Reform (Scotland) Act 2003. This provided a statutory public right of access to land, and established a legal framework whereby bodies representing rural and crofting communities had a right to buy land. As we will see in later chapters, these provisions have had direct consequences in Mull where there are several examples of the implementation of the Act which has three parts.

Land Access

The first part of the 2003 Act codifies the right to universal access to land in Scotland. This encompasses a right to be on land for recreational, educational and certain other purposes and a right to cross land. Access rights apply to any non-motorised activities, including walking, cycling, riding and camping. The Act also allows access to inland waters for canoeing, rowing, sailing and swimming, and it prescribes a responsibility to exercise the right of access to land and waters in a responsible manner as specified in the Scottish Outdoor Access Code.

Community Right to Buy

The second part of the Act establishes the community right to buy land, allowing communities with populations of up to 10,000 to register an interest in land, and entitling them to first right of refusal should the owner put the land up for sale or register an intention to transfer ownership. To register such a community interest, citizens must establish a representative body which will undertake the acquisition and hold title to the land.

Crofting Community Right to Buy

The third part of the Act provides the right for a crofting community to acquire a piece of land in which they have a direct interest as a crofter. This differs from the community right in that it can be exercised at any time, regardless of whether the land has been put on the market, and even in the absence of a willing seller.

Outcome of 2003 Act

The initial response to these provisions and conversion of applications into full community land/asset acquisitions was limited but, with growing public awareness, it slowly gathered pace. By the end of 2018 there had been 236 registrations of interest from 120 community groups, with

24 approved while the remainder were either deleted or remained on the register as active registrations.

Despite a relatively modest uptake, the Act has motivated a number of buy-outs which did not rely on legislative enforcement. And it's generally agreed that the legislation has facilitated a shift of power away from a small number of private landowners towards communities consisting of many citizens.

Scottish Rural Parliament (2014)

In response to an initiative of the European Parliament, in 2011 the Scottish government provided for the establishment of a Scottish Rural Parliament to take place every two years.[7] Although not the subject of legislation, the government approved some broad objectives for the body based on principles established by the European Parliament as follows:

To strengthen the voice of rural communities, and to ensure that their interests and well-being are strongly reflected in the policies of the Scottish government,

To promote self-help, common understanding, solidarity, exchange of good practice and cooperation among rural communities throughout Scotland,

To enable rural people to play their full role in addressing the economic and political challenges which confront Scotland.

The first meeting of the Scottish Rural Parliament was convened between 6th and 8th November 2014 in Oban, and was attended by delegates from Mull. At the end of the sitting, the Parliament approved the following motion.

- Scotland needs new democratic structures decided, agreed upon and led by communities.
- Rural communities should be empowered to take action for themselves.
- Rural areas require their own set of outcome measures, monitoring arrangements and measures of deprivation.
- Rural businesses need to be effectively supported to survive, grow and thrive.
- Rural communities need to be well connected to services through integrated and affordable transport.

- Broadband and mobile phone signal are essential services which should be available to all.

This was powerful stuff that augured well for the development of democracy at a community level. However, it remained to be seen whether the Scottish Parliament and rural communities would succeed in meeting the fine aspirations. Subsequent gatherings were facilitated by an organisation called Rural Action Scotland, and Parliaments have been held in 2016, 2018, 2021, and 2023 to monitor achievement and review objectives. Their deliberations have certainly impacted subsequent legislation.

Community Empowerment Act 2015

The Community Empowerment Act is designed to enable people in rural areas to act collectively in pursuit of community goals, and to have a say in decisions about the local delivery of public services. The Act comes in eleven Parts which are worthy of a brief description to demonstrate the all-embracing nature of the legislation.

Part One requires that the government develop a statement that specifies national outcomes. Already completed, this has been the subject of an iterative development process involving public input and review.

Part Two mandates a community approach to local planning with public bodies such as Councils required to consult with the community affected by any proposals. Plans must reflect agreed priorities, identify the nature and purpose of improvements, and provide information on how and when they will be achieved.

Part Three prescribes how community involvement will take place. Public bodies are required to work with communities to ensure they meet community expectations and, if a community group has an idea to make services better, then it has the right to submit and explain its ideas. Afterwards, the public body must write a report indicating what was achieved and how the community group contributed.

Part Four is designed to consolidate the provisions of the 2003 Land Reform Act, giving community groups in both rural and urban settings a right to buy land that has been abandoned and/or neglected with a potential detriment to neighbours. The community group may pursue this objective even if the owner doesn't want to sell. To facilitate this process, community groups can apply to have land in which they have an interest to be registered on a national list. Then, if and when the owner decides to sell it, they are compelled to give the community group first refusal. A similar system has been established for sitting crofters.

Part Five extends the right to buy or lease assets to include property owned by public authorities in circumstances where the asset is unused or underutilised. This is subject to the making of a suitable case for alternative land use.

Part Six allows community groups to lease land from Land and Forestry Scotland if they want to grow trees and use or sell the wood.

Part Seven permits the government to require that supporters have a say in how their sports club is run.

Part Eight refers to property bequeathed to Councils for the "common good". If the Council wants to sell or make changes to such property, they have to tell people and ask for their views.

Part Nine modernises the law relating to allotments, clarifying the rights and administrative rules for Councils and citizens. It also puts an onus on Councils to expand the number of allotments to meet demand and facilitate food self-sufficiency.

Finally, **Part Ten** requires that Councils must consult with residents on a range of land use matters, and Part Eleven allows Councils to reduce rates for worthy community bodies.

The Act also established two new funds. The Investing in Communities Fund is a consolidation of several other funding bodies committed to the development of local community resilience, and the Aspiring Communities Fund is designed to provide financial support to associated community bodies and third sector organisations

Land Reform (Scotland) Act 2016

This Act consolidated the earlier legislation, including the legal provisions relating to tenant farmers, and is notable for granting the Scottish government the power to force the sale of private land to community bodies to facilitate sustainable development in the absence of a willing seller. The Act also established a Scottish Land Commission, with responsibility to consider the concentration of land ownership, land taxation, and the effective use of land for the common good.

Islands (Scotland) Act 2018

In 2013, Councils representing the Western Isles, the Shetlands Isles and the Orkney Isles launched what was called the "Our Islands – Our Future Campaign". The aim was to insert an island perspective into the public policy area. In response, in 2014, the Scottish Government published a document entitled Empowering Scotland's Island Communities, with the aim of promoting the voice of island communities, harnessing their resources, and enhancing their wellbeing. In turn, the UK government adopted a policy called Framework for the Islands requiring that legislation should take into account island circumstances, although this was not legislated. In the meantime, the Scottish government began to work on an Islands Bill and on 6 July 2018 the Bill for the Islands (Scotland) Act 2018 received Royal Assent. The Act introduces a number of measures designed to ensure that the needs and aspirations of islanders are accommodated in public policy. The following is an extract from the preamble.

"Islanders have a strong sense of community, freedom and safety. And they play an important economic role, whilst enjoying a spectacular natural environment and rich cultural heritage. They are not only resilient, but also innovative. While islands are great places to live, they have been, and in some cases remain, challenging. Towards the end of the 19th century, many islanders migrated, not entirely through choice. The clearances marked island communities with some long-lasting scars, including a sense that decisions were taken by people not living on the islands that overlooked the public interest in pursuit of private gain.

This is an historic piece of legislation, and one of the first provisions under the Act was the preparation of a National Islands Plan. This Plan was established in 2018, and provides a progressive framework for public investment in Mull and other Scottish islands. It makes compelling reading in terms of the commitment not only to economic development and material prosperity but also the concepts of building community and wellbeing. And the aims and intentions, process of implementation, and intended outcomes are worthy of a book in its own right! The following is a modified extract from the Plan, together with some comments on the process of implementation, which has involved extensive public consultation, and an indication of some initial outcomes.

The purpose of the Plan is to ensure improved outcomes for island communities arising from the operations and activities of a public nature. To this end, it requires that the government identify all the authorities that have an obligation under the Act and establishes that the intended outcomes for island communities will include:

- Increase in population levels,
- Economic development, improvement in the environment, health and wellbeing of islanders, and community empowerment,
- Improvement in transport services,
- Improvement in digital connectivity,
- Reduction in fuel poverty,
- Effective management of the Crown Estate,
- Enhancement of biosecurity, including the protection of islands from the impact of invasive non-native species.

There is also an imperative to address other issues of importance to island communities such as housing, climate change, energy, education and cultural heritage.

Having set these broad objectives, the government entered a period of extensive consultation to ensure a strong collaboration and partnership with local authorities, island communities, and all the other stakeholders involved. This was seen as an essential requirement to ensure that the Plan reflected "the distinctive geographical, natural heritage and cultural characteristics (including the linguistic heritage) of each of the areas inhabited by island communities". During the consultation, the government planning team visited 41 islands and organised 61 events which allowed them to engage face-to-face with almost 1,000 people. And the live events were complemented by online consultation during which nearly 400 responses were received.

In 2020, the government then published an Implementation Strategy designed to deliver a Plan that was Fair, Integrated, Green and Inclusive. Amongst other things, this aimed to encompass the objectives of a Local Governance Review which had been directed at enabling a better balance of power, responsibilities and resources between national government, local government, and communities. The definitions of the four characteristics above in italics are worth noting as they reflect the spirit of the exercise.

- A **fair** plan will strive towards equality across Scotland with a human rights approach that will support greater accountability and help ensure that rights are respected, protected and fulfilled,
- An **integrated** plan will promote joined-up services based on a cohesive, place-based and holistic approach to policy and will build economic, social and environmental considerations in an integrated approach to island policy,
- A **green** plan will harness and unleash the potential of a green (land) and blue (waters) economy in times of climate emergency, and
- An **inclusive** plan will promote genuine community empowerment at the local level enabling decisions to be taken as close as possible to where their impact will be felt.

In this whole process, the government was aware of the potentially disastrous impact of the British government's decision against the wishes of the Scottish people to leave the European Union. The EU has significant legislation that provides for cohesion and provisions for investment in and support for disadvantaged communities. To ensure that the benefits of this enlightened approach was not lost, the government determined to align the Plan with the spirit that has driven the EU cohesion policy over several years.

Finally, the Plan includes a set of quantitative and qualitative measures and indicators to identify the extent to which the proposed outcomes are actually achieved. To provide an indication of what all of this means for Mull, it is worth noting the Objectives which are follows.

Objective 1 is to address population decline and ensure a healthy, balanced population profile through repopulation, and through the retention of young islanders.

Objective 2 is to improve and promote sustainable economic development, working through HIE, the University of the Highlands and Islands, and other key stakeholders such as the Mull and Iona Community Trust.

Objective 3 is to improve transport services including development of plans for new ferries, improved ports, and reduced vehicle emissions.

Objective 4 is to improve housing on Scottish islands, through a long term building plan, targeted rental policy, and grants to crofters.

Objective 5 is to reduce the level of fuel poverty through supporting local generation of energy.

Objective 6 is to improve digital connectivity, by improving broadband services, and achieving full fibre rollout.

Objective 7 is to improve and promote health and wellbeing through providing equitable access to the NHS, use of digital systems to reduce need to travel, additional services for the aged, and improved sports facilities,

Objective 8 is to improve and promote environmental wellbeing and deal with biosecurity, including adoption of the Zero Waste programme, and initiatives to reduce the ecological impact of tourism.

Objective 9 is to ensure that Scottish islands are at the forefront of addressing climate change, including implementation of renewable energy programmes and support for expansion of forests.

Objective 10 is to empower communities through stronger local democracy, more devolution of powers, implementation of a tax on accommodation used by some short term visitors, and stronger emergency response organisations.

Objective 11 is to support arts, culture and language by investing in the creative talents of islanders, and supporting the use and visibility of Gaelic and Scotland's other indigenous languages and dialects.

Objective 12 is to promote and improve delivery of education through the University of the Highlands and Islands ("UHI") with the aim of broadening the options for young people, enabling equal access to those on the mainland, and supporting those from disadvantaged backgrounds.

Objective 13 is to ensure transparent implementation of the National Islands Plan, and to create of a Young Islanders Network to ensure that the Plan meets the interests and priorities of young people;[8]

Conclusion

In conclusion, this lengthy account of all that has been enacted in recent times should leave no doubt that the Scottish Parliament is fully committed to establishing a community-based society in places like Mull which is based on sustainability, well-being, and environmentally responsible development. Its legislation is also designed to remove obstacles to the development of healthy communities that were established and maintained over several centuries by vested interests in pursuit of personal wealth, and to empower people with public spirited aspirations to overcome those would seek to pursue that private interest at the expense of the public good. It is radical stuff, and it is a long term agenda with outcomes that will not be fully realised for many years. What is also clear is that the spirit and intentions of the legislation have broad acceptance within Scottish society. This reflects a culture and national character which is significantly different from some other parts of the United Kingdom, and more akin to Scotland's neighbours across the North Sea in Scandinavia. Given Scotland's history as an independent nation, this should not surprise the reader.

In the chapters which will follow, an account is provided of several examples of how the legislation identified in this chapter has been played out on the island of Mull. It is a record of great achievement by a people for whom community and the public interest are at the core of their existence.

ENDNOTES

1   The account which follows is based on articles available on Wikipedia.
2   Only a small fragment of the original document survives, describing the penalties for several offences committed by one citizen against another.
3   In 1291, the English King Edward I attempted to assert his feudal overlordship of Scotland by destroying all existing legal documents with the aim of enforcing English law. Following the Scottish Wars of Independence, and the Battle of Bannockburn in 1314, the Regiam Majestatem was assembled to provide a comprehensive digest of previously established Scottish law.
4   These words are taken from a report entitled "Impact of diversity of ownership on social, economic and environmental outcomes" published in July 2016 by the Scottish government's Agriculture and Rural Directorate following research into land ownership in rural areas of Scotland.
5   The total land area of Scotland is 19.252 million acres.
6   Scotland was one of the last places in Europe to abolish feudal tenure.
7   This is now called the Scottish Rural & Islands Parliament.
8   This Network got under way in 2021.

MULL & IONA
COMMUNITY TRUST

Although it is not a unique institution, over the last twenty five years the Mull & Iona Community Trust ("MICT") has been one of the most successful community organisations of its kind. Its story begins in 1996, when a philanthropic body named the Coram Trust engaged consultants to assess the potential for a community-owned entity in Mull dedicated to supporting the development of social capital, including facilities and services for local people, and businesses with a social purpose.[1] The consultants met with various interested parties, identified a range of potential activities, and identified several local issues. The results of their review suggested that the scope of an organisation should encompass a number of "sustainable well-being" objectives including the following:

- Prevention and relief of poverty,
- Support for the sick, aged and others with special needs,
- Provision of low budget housing for local people,
- Establishment of enterprises to service unmet local needs,
- Management of community land and associated assets,
- Facilitation of a community education programme,
- Support for environmental conservation projects,
- Provision of recreational facilities, and
- Organisation of local community events.

In response to the Coram Trust review, in 1997 community leaders established the Mull and Iona Community Trust ("MICT") which was constituted as a company limited by guarantee with charitable status.[2] The founders determined that this should be a *member* rather than a *shareholder* based organisation, and there are currently around 300 members, many of whom contribute through voluntary work. Membership is open to the public, with a joining fee for lifetime membership, and is not unreasonably withheld. Since 1997, MICT has slowly expanded from one employee to the current complement of around 30 staff. It is led by long serving General Manager, Moray Finch. The Annual Budget varies according to the financial status of certain key projects. In the early days, annual turnover varied between £500,000 and £1.5 million. By 2020, this figure had reached £1.9 million, with annual expenditure of over £1 million, and assets in excess of £7 million. Funding derives from multiple sources, including grants from various levels of government, income from managing various land, facilities, and services, grants from private investors, donations, and significant income from the Castaway Charity Shops run by MESS.[34]

MICT is based at the An Roth Community Enterprise Centre, which is located opposite the Craignure Ferry Terminal.[5] This building includes facilities that may be hired for the conduct of business meetings and training courses, and MICT offers a range of office services to local enterprises and individuals

Governance

Much of the success of MICT comes from a strong system of governance, with diligent oversight of performance and genuine accountability to stakeholders. The Board is elected by members at the AGM and comprises up to 14 volunteers who are accountable for setting strategy and oversight of operational activity. Typically, Board members are local residents, including representatives of other community organisations.

The Board, chaired by the long-serving local resident Sandy Brunton, operates in a highly inclusive manner. It holds open meetings, with an agenda item entitled

"Members Forum" which provides an opportunity for any member to provide input and raise concerns. In addition to its Annual Report, the organisation issues a Quarterly Newsletter providing an update on plans and activities.

The current organisational structure comprises the General Manager and his deputy, and six departments - the Ranger Service, Housing, the Ulva Ferry Development Program, the Ardura Forest Management Program, the MESS Project, and Financial Administration.

Strategic Plan

From the outset MICT implemented a highly professional approach to scoping and implementing its operations. In 2012, the Board and operational team completed a strategic plan which included an inspirational *Vision* to be *"An influential, respected and sustainable organisation"*, achieved by using the values of being *"democratic, accountable, and enterprising"*. At this stage, it also adopted a *Mission* and overarching *Strategy "To improve the quality of life in Mull and Iona"* by *"Working together to unlock the potential of the islands"*. Subsequently, this Plan has been updated every five years and, in the latest version for the period 2022-27, the Vision, Mission and Values Statements have been significantly extended to read as follows:

Vision

The current vision, which reflects a picture of what a healthy community should look like and has a strong focus on the interests of the family, is as follows.

- Children are educated close to where they live;
- Their younger siblings have access to childcare allowing their parents to work full time;
- Their older brothers and sisters enjoy real and worthwhile career opportunities;
- Families are able to live in homes they can afford, with full access to essential services and infrastructure;

- Older people are able to spend their later years properly cared for on the islands, with dignity and respect.

Mission

The current Mission statement is as follows: "To enable thriving and socially connected communities through high quality local services, housing and amenities, making use of our natural and human assets to sustain our economic, cultural and natural environment."

Values

In 2022, MICT adopted five core values which are manifest in a set of behaviours required of all those involved in the organisation as follows.

Community led and driven: It matters that MICT work is valued by the community and seen as benefitting the islands, with Board members from all parts of the island providing a range of views on the challenges we face.

Fair, ethical and transparent: MICT employs staff on terms that match best practice regarding wage levels, pensions and flexible working. Volunteers are treated with the same respect and appreciation.

Environmentally sensitive and conscious: Activities follow best practice to protect the natural environment. We promote emerging solutions and technologies to help others pursue environmentally sustainable economic development.

Respectful of the islands' cultures and heritage: Diversity is valued and development activities preserve local culture and natural heritage.

Collaborative and supportive: Relationships with partners on and off our islands are nurtured, with opportunities sought to work together for the benefit of everyone, and to use MICT experience, skills and expertise to support others with their activities.

Strategies

At the outset, MICT adopted four Strategic Areas for activity which continue to provide the framework for the work of the organisation.

a) Housing and Other Infrastructure

The aim is to facilitate effective infrastructure, with the construction of new and improved facilities. This includes a commitment to deliver the *Mull & Iona 2030 Initiative*, with its emphasis on affordable housing for local residents.

b) Affordable Community Services

The aim is to develop community-based capacity, by supporting the establishment and effective operation of community groups, and by providing advice on the preparation of business cases to attract funding for the delivery of new and improved local services.

c) Environmental and Cultural Heritage

The aim is to protect and develop the natural and cultural heritage of Mull, Iona and surrounding islands in harmony with community needs. This strategy includes the provision of a ranger service to work with other organisations in the protection of community parkland and waterways.

d) Economic Opportunity

The aim is to promote and contribute to the development of a *sustainable* island economy, through consolidation and diversification. MICT also seeks to deliver affordable financial services through the establishment of a local credit union.

Core Programmes and Achievements

Through the implementation of the above strategies, over the last twenty years, MICT has established a range of programmes with significant achievements in building the island's social capital, including the following:

Housing

There has been real progress in addressing the island's housing crisis.

- MICT has constructed six new houses for rent in Ulva Ferry and refurbished for rent an old schoolhouse in Pennyghael. They have also facilitated the construction of 14 new houses in Lochdon by West Highland Housing Association.
- MICT is working with the Argyll and Bute Council on two significant initiatives:
  - Development of a plan to refurbish a selection of abandoned houses on the island.
  - Establishment of a scheme to provide housing-related financial assistance to local people.
- A project has been established with a local builder to secure the construction of affordable housing in Dervaig.
- MICT has consulted with the owners of holiday rental properties to arrest and reverse the loss of houses for rent by local people.
- The establishment of a community-owned property management company is being evaluated, the role of which would be to establish an ongoing programme of social housing construction.

Infrastructure and Services

- In 2020, MICT commenced operation of the Nonhebel Light Industry Park which offers premises, self-storage, fenced compounds, and lock up units, for local business tenants.6 After its first 12 months, the site was 85% occupied, with all six business units and eight lock-up units tenanted. Further expansion of Nonhebel Park has become possible due to further grants from the Scottish Government's Regeneration Capital Grants Fund and from Highlands and Islands Enterprise.
- MICT has been a trail-blazer in founding the Garmony Hydro Scheme. This project started in 2010, with the establishment of Green Energy Mull to develop and operate a 400kw system, and was completed in 2015. Proceeds, which have reached over $200,000 per annum, are invested in the Waterfall Fund which awards grants to local community organisations and individual local people in need.
- MICT operates a community bus service connecting Calgary, Ulva Ferry

and Salen, and also provides a bus for primary school children to have access to gym facilities and swimming lessons. Electric Vehicles are available seven days a week with a door-to-door service anywhere in Mull.

- MICT has lobbied strongly for an improvement in broadband services.
- MICT is leading a drive to improve the insulation of housing to enhance sustainability and address fuel poverty.
- MICT has operates three Castaway Charity Shops which recycle a range of goods, and a programme called MESS which fosters environmentally responsible behaviour. MESS has facilitated the introduction of recycling bins, beach cleaning, and other recycling projects.
- MICT has established a network of public access to defibrillators some of which are installed in redundant telephone boxes.

Conservation

MICT operates a Ranger service based out of premises at Aros, with a team of up to four employees. The service is responsible for management of MICT interests in various pieces of land, delivery of a range of conservation projects, and engagement with the public to promote environmental awareness.

Community engagement involves the organisation of events and projects, including conservation programmes for local and visiting schools. Funding for the service comes from partnerships with Mull Eagle Watch, Scottish Natural Heritage, Forestry and Land Scotland, and the National Trust for Scotland, and from fees for services rendered.

Community Development, including Education and Support for Young Families

A key to the sustainability of local communities is the availability of viable primary school facilities and support services. Notable achievements are as follows:

- Significant progress has been made in regenerating the Ulva Ferry community. The construction of new affordable houses for rent at Ulva Ferry has contributed to the viability of the Ulva Primary School, and MICT has also facilitated the delivery of community facilities and the upgrading of on-shore boat access.

- The Scottish government has provided financial assistance for the completion on a trial basis of an Out of School Care Programme, including the operation of breakfast clubs, a child care agency, a mobile child-minding service, and emergency relief to families with urgent needs. An ongoing service is under active consideration.

Forest Resource Management

In 2019, MICT acquired the Ardura Forest from Forestry and Land Scotland.[7] This is a 200 hectares community property which includes 110 hectares of Sitka spruce and Japanese larch trees. Subsequently, MICT has completed the following activities:

- A long term forestry plan has been developed and approved by Forestry and Land Scotland.
- Commencing in 2021, 70 hectares of the spruce trees have been harvested. This resource has yielded significant revenue for future investment in community programmes and a further 40 hectares is available for future harvesting.
- MICT has a long term plan to deliver sustainability, and aims to reforest the property with native species that will provide a varied habitat for ground, tree, and air-living animal species, as well as plants. Further local collaboration will also enabled the creation of a community tree nursery to provide tens of thousands of seedlings.
- Management of the forest includes the reinstatement of forestry paths with assistance from Argyll and Bute Council.

Pandemic

MICT provided strong support to the community during the Covid 19 pandemic with the establishment of a home delivery programme during lock-down. The Argyll and Bute Council financed the cost of emergency food parcels, hot lunches, and delivery of groceries.

Current Activity and Future Plans

All of the operational programs delivered by MICT continue to expand and evolve. In particular, the Ranger Service is delivering a busy program of community-based projects and activities to encourage conservation, including events such as working parties that involve collecting rubbish on the beaches. In 2023, MESS and Island Castaways had a record year with a 50% increase in shop sales, and have held a highly successful fashion show. In the meantime, MICT continues to operate the community bus service, the industrial park which now includes a second phase, and all the other services mentioned earlier in this chapter. In the recent Quarterly Newsletters, the following new initiatives are of note.

a) **Hospital Helipad**

The ability of the island to provide emergency assistance to people with medical needs is significantly constrained. MICT is a major party to the construction of a Helipad on land donated by Andy and Naomi Knight. Funding for construction will be financed by a national charity and the facility will be owned, managed and maintained by a local operator.

b) **Craignure Daycare Nursery**

With 95 new houses in Craignure at planning stage, Community Enterprise have just completed a feasibility study for the establishment of a new facility to meet the growing demand for this service and this is under consideration

c) **Expansion of Nonhebel Industrial Park**

With all units occupied, MICT has obtained a further grant from the Scottish Government Regeneration Capital Grant Fund to expand the facility with four more units.

d) **Ulva Ferry Shore Facilities**

A new building with facilities for the local community and visitors to the Ulva Ferry area is under construction, with solar panels and a septic tank.

e) **Ardura Community Forest**

While intermittent work continues in re-wilding the forest, new signage is being installed, and tracks are being upgraded. A biodiversity plan is being including an assessment of the long term impact of forestry activity on flora and fauna. In the meantime, Mull Wildlife Group continue to undertake regular surveys of the bird population, with signs of an increasing number of species following the recent felling of non-native trees. Funding has been received from the Rural and Island Communities Idea into Action Fund for a review of the Ardura Community Well-being Project which is being undertaken with support from SKS Scotland.[8]

f) **Housing**

The possibility of establishing special accommodation for key workers is being assessed.

g) **People with Special Needs**

The provision of additional residential facilities for the elderly, to complement the existing Council-run facilities at Bowman Court, is under assessment.

Conclusion

Since its foundation twenty five years ago, MICT has had a major impact on life in Mull and contributed significantly to the regeneration and long term health of the community. During that time, the size and scope of activity has expanded significantly in terms of the people employed and the physical assets established and maintained. The organisation has also established a level of sustainability through revenue from its endeavours to maintain its own existence and support other community organisations and needy individuals. The nature and content of this success is absolutely in keeping with the original humanitarian aims of the Coram Trust with its roots in caring for the disadvantaged. The benefits deriving from its activities are evident in physical outcomes such as the building of houses and facilities, support for families, the establishment of new services, care for the less advantaged, and the expansion of the population. However, MICT has also delivered significant intangible benefits in terms of the well-being of the community living in Mull and neighbouring islands and the development of viable and sustainable communities in parts of the island where existence was previously marginal. Also, through the performance of its staff, the organisation has established a reputation for operating in a highly capable and professional manner, and this is reflected in the very large number of public and private funding agencies who provide financial support for MICT led projects.

Much of MICT's recognition and success is due to the unstinting efforts of a small team of dedicated staff, supported by enthusiastic volunteers, and the group of stalwarts who as Board members have had oversight of the work involved. In particular, since 2010, Moray Finch has led this organisation with distinction, showing great vision, dedication, compassion and resilience. These efforts, including a commitment to environmental sustainability in a time of global warming, are not only applauded by the local community, but have also been acknowledged further afield. When the Scottish Government established the National Island Plan in 2019, MICT was the model of choice for developing similar activity in other remote parts of Scotland.

ENDNOTES

1   The Coram Trust has a long history of supporting orphans and related social causes, and has a particular interest in the challenges posed by poverty and homelessness in remote areas such as the Highlands and Islands.

2   The Objectives identified in the Articles of Association largely reflect the scope identified in the Coram Trust Review.

3   Significant public funding has been received from the UK government, various branches of the Scottish government, Argyll and Bute Council and, until recently, the EU.

4   MESS stands for Mull and Iona Environmentally Sensitive Solutions.

5   An Roth is Gaelic for the wheel.

6   This facility is named after Andrew Nonhebel, a local businessman who initiated the concept.

7   Ardura Forest is located to the north west of Loch Spelve in the SE of Mull.

8   SKS Scotland assists volunteers in delivering community-based projects.

NORTH WEST MULL COMMUNITY WOODLAND COMPANY ("NWMCWC")

The NWMCWC is something of a phenomenon. Although it came into existence after the Mull and Iona Community Trust, it has been a pioneer of community-based development activity, in large measure facilitated by the re-establishment of the Scottish Parliament in 1999. It owes much of its success to a small group of enterprising residents who have worked with a passion to improve the well-being of the people and the health of the environment. Despite significant and inevitable bureaucratic hurdles, and the scepticism of some, their largely volunteer work manifests the very best tradition in the modern age of the traditional spirit of *dùthchas*.

Pioneering Phase (2006-2011)

In the early 2000s, there was an embryonic movement in Scotland which aimed to establish community-owned forests. The aims were to both conserve the environment and deliver access for the benefit of local people. In 2005, an opportunity to pursue this mission arose in Mull. What was then known as the Forestry Commission had decided to dispose of two properties adjacent to Dervaig on the Mornish peninsula.1 These were the Langamull forest (250 hectares adjacent to the road between Dervaig and Calgary) and the West Ardhu forest (420 hectares straddling the road between Dervaig and Torloisk). Disposal of the properties was largely driven by economic factors, with the forests seen as a relatively unproductive resource. Whilst the land was acknowledged as having tourist and conservation value, the growth, harvesting, and replanting of trees in that part of Mull was costly given the relatively remote location and poor local access roads. As noted in Chapter 17, in the early years of the 21st century the newly established Scottish Parliament had enacted ground breaking legislation that gave community-based organisations the right to acquire such properties. This right was triggered if and when a property came onto the market, with the government providing financial assistance to facilitate acquisition.

Getting wind of the impending sale of the properties in late 2004, local people living in the Dervaig district called a public meeting to discuss the possibility of a community purchase. With some 50 people attending, it was resolved to establish the North West Mull Community Woodland Group ("NWMCWG"), and subsequently this organisation commissioned a feasibility study. For this purpose, it was determined that "the community" who would be a party to the venture comprised the 250 people on the Dervaig Electoral Roll. This encompassed the main village of Dervaig, and residents living in Calgary, Croig, and along the roads leading towards Aros, and over the hill to Torloisk. The feasibility study was undertaken by a company named Margin in association with Ian MacLennan and Nick Marshall, and a report on the potential venture was issued in May 2005. This consolidated the results of extensive public consultation with the local community, as well as providing a detailed assessment of all the factors relevant to making a decision about acquiring the properties. The analysis encompassed the types of economic activity that the properties might sustain, including timber harvesting and wood-fuel, the potential for renewable energy, the establishment of forest crofts, construction of low-cost housing for sale or lease to local people, the benefits to the community in terms of employment, amenity, and recreation, and an evaluation of environmental factors. The consultants also considered the potential source of funding for purchase, and the likely costs and income arising from management of the property as a not-for-profit enterprise. In their conclusions, the consultants considered a range of options for acquiring either one or both properties, either as a business or an amenity owned and maintained by the community. They recommended that both woodlands should be purchased, with a company to be established that would manage the properties on an ecologically sustainable basis for the benefit of local people.

In late 2005, the NWMCWG considered the consultants' report, and it was decided to accept their recommendations. A project team was then established under the leadership of Colin Morrison, and this committee quickly produced an action plan. The first steps were to establish the North West Mull Community Woodland Company ("NWMCWC") as a private company limited by guarantee, to register with the government and the Forestry Commission the community's interest in acquisition of the land, and to launch a major fund-raising project to support the activity. The NWMCWC came into existence in July 2005, with an initial Board of ten volunteer directors

In the next six months, members of the company committed significant time to fund raising and to further evaluation of the scope of operations. The sum required for the acquisition from the Forestry Commission under the National Forest Land Scheme, was £340,000 plus professional fees. However, pending any income from managing the properties, substantial additional finance was required, not least to construct an access road suitable for logging vehicles and to acquire appropriate operational equipment. The Board approached various charitable and philanthropic foundations as well as completing an application for a grant from the newly established Scottish Land Fund. They also launched a local fund raising campaign and approached the banks for a loan. In the end, the funds for purchase and on-costs were found, with finance from the Scottish Land Fund, Highlands and Islands Enterprise, the Robertson Trust, the Hugh Fraser Foundation, contributions from local fundraising, and an interest free loan. With much local celebration, the purchase was concluded in May 2006.

With acquisition of the properties completed, the real work of this venture began. The Board completed its first Business Plan and, over the next five years, this became the blueprint for activity including the following:

- Establishment of the North West Mull Community Fund to which local people could apply to finance community projects and education opportunities,

- Preparation for the harvesting of the forest,
- Development of infrastructure to facilitate both business and recreational activity including construction of a forestry-linked haulage road,
- Completion of a feasibility study on development of a micro hydro-electric plant,
- Establishment of forest crofts for occupation by local people,
- Establishment of community facilities.

In the first few years, the Board committed significant time to assessing options for all these ventures, and implementing plans. However, initially, the top priority was to construct a sealed and all-weather haulage road connecting the forests to the C46 public road from Dervaig to Aros.

Haulage Road

This project involved the construction of a 16.5 km road and was a complex exercise, requiring negotiation with a number of local residents through whose land the road would run, and involving the installation of bridges, cattle grids, gates and fences. The total cost of this project was in the order of £2.4m, of which just under £700,000 was borne by the company in the form of an interest free loan to be paid back from the proceeds of harvesting the forest. Associated with this project, the team mapped out a series of walking and cycle tracks to provide property-wide public access. The timeframe for completion of this road project was five years commencing in 2006.

While this project was under way, the team gave initial thought to other activities as follows.

Forestry

The two properties had substantial forests with the Sitka Spruce being the dominant species. In terms of harvesting, the Langamull crop was around three years in advance of West Ardhu and, for both stands, the plan was to fell the trees, and transport the logs to pulping and saw milling plants on the mainland. To manage this operation as part of a long term cycle, the Board established a 20 Year Forest Design Plan (2009-29) which encompassed the selection and engagement of a number of specialist contractors.

A significant element, which in part determined the route of the haulage road, involved the identification of a suitable pulping and milling facility. The Board identified a company named UPM Tilhill located at Kilmallie near Fort William on Loch Linnhe. This operation had the benefit of access by water, as opposed to transit by circuitous roads on the mainland, with the logs loaded onto a transit ship at an existing temporary floating pier on the east coast of Mull.

Micro Hydro-Electric Power– Ardhu Burn

The West Ardhu property had a substantial stream flowing into Loch a' Chumhainn (Loch Cuin) and the slope of the terrain, not to mention the local rainfall, offered the opportunity for a hydro-electric scheme for generating renewable energy. The Board commissioned a feasibility study for a plant that would meet local power needs, with a transmission line connecting to the National Grid. This had the merit of providing a regular annual income that would potentially cover long-term overheads and running costs.

Crofts

In the Middle Ages right through to the 17th century, Mull had a large number of townships with the local people living and supporting themselves through small holdings of agricultural land, eventually called crofts. As we have seen in earlier chapters, this form of habitation was a vestige of the social contract under the clan system, in which there was a right of tenure in return for services rendered. Most of these townships and small holdings on the island had been swept away during the clearances of the 18th and 19th centuries, although the rights of crofters were belatedly legislated following the Crofters Commission in 1886. In the 21st century, the Scottish Parliament had legislated to facilitate the expansion of this kind of land tenure. On the NWMCWC lands there was the potential to establish several forest crofts, with crofters taking responsibility for clearing and revegetation, and the potential for constructing adjacent habitation. Like all NWMCWC ventures, the rules and regulations associated with this form of land tenure were considerable and implementation required extensive groundwork.

Archaeology

The Langamull estate included significant remains of previous human occupation in the form of derelict structures that had been the homes of crofters in a village called Kildavie. In 2004, three people from the village of Croig next to Loch Cuin had begun to excavate these kind of ruins in the district with an archaeological team called the *Croig Group*. Their investigations eventually revealed a much earlier human existence, commencing in the Mesolithic Age (c. 10,000 BCE to c. 4,000 BCE). Around the same time, archaeologists from Reading University were excavating adjacent Neolithic Age (c. 4,000 BCE to c. 2,000 BCE) remains and they linked up with the Croig Group. Working together, they established what became known as the Kildavie Project and, in 2007, their efforts were included in the long term plans of the Royal Commission on Ancient and Historic Monuments of Scotland ("RCAHMS"). With the advent of NWMCWC, the Kildavie Project became a significant community activity. The company made it a priority to improve access to the excavation, and an Archaeology Interest Group was established, to encourage wider community involvement in the excavation, and to educate local people about their heritage.

Newsletter

From the outset, the Board was keen to establish systematic accountability for its activities to the local community. In 2006, the organisation began to issue a quarterly newsletter to report on its work, and this communication continued for a number of years as the various projects reached fruition. (This form of communication has now been superseded by an actively-managed web site and a Facebook page).

Education and Training

The Board considered that a significant role for the organisation was to deliver a range of education and training opportunities for local residents. In addition to the archaeology programme, these included the following:

- The establishment of a Forest School where children from both the Dervaig and Ulva Primary Schools could be assembled and receive information about the natural world and their heritage,
- The provision of practical courses to train local people in the use of woodland equipment, and
- Provision of first aid training.

Tourism and Nature

The Board was mindful of the potential to generate income from eco-tourism, with visitors interested in nature walks and bird watching. The properties already included several walking tracks, and the Board determined to extend these tracks, and provide related infrastructure such as picnic areas. In the early days, a major focus was the appearance on the properties of white tailed eagles, and the organisation worked with the Royal Society for Protection of Birds to ensure responsible bird watching, with participants required to respect and protect nesting sites.

Social Events/Fund Raising

Given the considerable costs in implementing its many projects, a major activity for the Board in its first five years was the organisation of several social events and fund raising activities. These included a Race Night, regular sessions of Bingo, a 100 Club Draw (starting in 2011), Forest Fun Days, organisation of a local Producers Market, and a celebration on Bonfire Night.

Consolidation Phase (2011-2016)

About five years down the track, NWMCWC reached the end of its pioneering phase, with the completion of a number of initial projects and the termination of the initial five year line of funding from the Land Fund. The organisation was now well established as a viable local operation with significant community engagement. And, to take stock of the progress made, the Board commissioned an independently-facilitated Community Forum to continue and consolidate accountability to local people. This provided an opportunity for community members to receive an account of the journey to date, and to raise any queries they might have about the company's past, current and proposed future activities. A successful event was held in late 2011, when the Board was able to provide the following report on the company's achievements.

- 16.5 km of road had been constructed, and was now ready to take HGV traffic. Given that the road was special purpose, although foot traffic was permitted, it was not open to private vehicles. Enforcement of this condition would be a continuing issue.

- Several community crofts had been established in the forest. These were the first of their kind to be introduced anywhere in Scotland under current legislation and leases for two of them had been released in late 2011.
- Significant progress had been made in extending walking tracks, with signage, a visitor car park, and picnic tables.
- The company was now ready to proceed with harvesting of the forests.
- Numerous community-based facilities had been established to enable recreation, education and tourism.

The Board's report was well received, with largely positive feedback, helpful comments on existing projects, and a wealth of suggestions for future activity. Subsequently, with investment in essential infrastructure largely completed, the Board switched its focus to establishing the resources to finance operational activity and future projects.

Forestry

With the logging road completed, it was planned to begin harvesting with the Langamull cut in early 2012. However, due to some severe weather, the felling process was actually started in West Ardhu where a number of fallen trees were removed for safety reasons. Then the main Langamull project got underway, with logs felled by UPM Tilhill transported to a floating pier at Fishnish established and operated by TSL, a local building and haulage contractor. The first load of 700 tonnes was despatched on 14 May 2012, and delivered to BSW's pulping and saw mills in Kilmallie later in the day.

With the start of forestry operations, the Board was keen embrace the highest standards of industry practice and in 2013 it obtained accreditation under the UK Woodland Assurance Standard scheme. To streamline the logistics, it was planned to replace the floating pier at Craignure with a permanent structure that would handle larger and more economical loads. This came to fruition with the opening of a new pier on 16 December 2013, enabling the shipping contractor to optimise transport by linking with another haulage operation out of Pennyghael.

In 2014, the Langamull felling had been completed and operations switched to West Ardhu where logging continued until late 2016. Thereafter, both properties were laid fallow for several years before re-planting of the next crop of trees with a life cycle of up to forty years.

Micro Hydro-Electric Project

With the initial line of external funding coming to an end, a major focus of the Board was to secure a reliable source of income. Although forestry would generate a financial return, it was intermittent, and the supply of hydro-electric power to the community and to the National Grid was seen as a significant source of regular and reliable future income. The construction of this facility was a relatively complex matter, with the need for approval from several bodies including the water authority, the main supplier of energy to the national grid (SSEN), and the Argyll and Bute Council.[2] Following completion of a Feasibility Study, the Board entered negotiations with all the parties as well as engaging engineers and surveyors to effect construction. In mid-2014, the Scottish Environment Protection Agency ("SEPA") gave a licence to extract water, but planning permission from the Council was not obtained until mid-2015. To fund the project, the Board identified a company that worked on the basis of providing a loan which was repaid out of the operating income over an agreed term as operations went live. Initially, it was planned to achieve connection by May 2016. It would take quite a bit longer.

Forest Crofts

The public offer of nine crofting leases with local housing had generated a relatively slow response. To encourage uptake, the Board investigated the construction on crofting land of low-cost housing. A Housing Needs Survey was completed, and the Board then engaged with Rural Housing Scotland which already had several projects in Mull. A project to construct a prototype under the "Our Island Home" scheme was initiated and, to clarify the scope and obligations of a crofting lease, the Board established a standard plan to be followed by a crofter, which included a requirement to clear and replant 80% of the property. By 2014, permission to proceed with the remaining six leases had been given by the Crofting Commission and Land Court.

Local Housing

Based on the results of the Housing Needs Survey, the Board identified the potential for assigning some parts of the forestry properties to blocks for construction of low cost housing for rent or purchase by local people. Apart from addressing a serious local housing shortage, with many local houses purchased by people from the mainland for holiday lets, the financial return from such development also had the ability to earn significant income. Council planning permission was eventually received for two homes at Kengharair.

Education

From the outset, the Board had recognised the potential for community access by local primary school children with the establishment of a Forest School. There was already a shelter and seating for talks in Langamull and, in the consolidation phase, the Board sought to expand access. This involved the establishment of a fruit orchard in the West Ardhu forest to be tended by the school children as a vehicle for learning about food production.

Cemetery

At the Community Forum in 2011, it had been suggested that the Board should establish a woodland burial site. With a shortage of such amenities in Mull, this was broadly accepted by the community, and initially it was planned to allocate an area of two hectares on a site with views to the islands of Coll and Tiree, and a shelter and a toilet for those attending burials and visiting graves.

Wood Burning

With clear-felling under way, and the logging of both forests scheduled to take about five years, the Board identified an opportunity to supply wood for burning. This had the potential to deliver an additional stream of revenue, provide local employment, and ensure a long-term supply of wood fuel to local residents. The forest also offered seasonal access to Christmas trees. Eventually, the wood fuel operation would become a significant activity, with various cuts (including logs and kindling) sold by volume to local residents. The Board acquired a local operator called Crannich and rebadged the operation as Island Woodfuels. A wood-fuel operator was recruited in 2014 and, in 2015, a shed was established for storage of equipment.

Archaeology

After the initial flurry of activity, in the early 2010s, excavation was intermittent. This was very much the nature of archaeology projects, with funding not always available and many sites around Scotland competing for the attention of a small group of qualified people and associated enthusiastic volunteers. In the meantime, the company had established new access paths to the Kildavie Project site, new signage, and visitor facilities, and those responsible for the activity had also established a web site. In 2014, a significant excavation recommenced under the direction of the Heritage Archaeological Research Practice ("HARP") involving three staff and 15 university students, with assistance provided by local volunteers. This would be the beginning of a continuing programme.

Transformation Phase

By late 2015, most of the projects envisaged in the initial Business Plan had been completed, although the micro hydro-electric facility was not operational until March 2018. Mindful of a need for a new lease of life, and with an ambition to expand its activities beyond the main focus of forestry management, at the 2015 AGM the Board recommended a change to the organisation's name, dropping the "Woodland" in NWMCWC. At the time, the Board was mindful that new legislation was being enacted by the Scottish Parliament to enable community organisations to acquire properties through a process of compulsory purchase. For some reason, perhaps a fear that the organisation was over-stretching, the proposal met with opposition from some members of the organisation and was defeated. This did not deter the Board. The full story of diversification is provided in the next section of this chapter, with the advent in 2017 of the Ulva Project. This expanded vision would indeed *transform* the scope of the organisation. In the meantime, the Board continued with its knitting as follows.

- After a couple of years of lying fallow, the forests were ready for regeneration. Under the 20 year forestry plan, the Board were mindful of the need to improve the conservation value of the properties in terms of biodiversity. They therefore selected a range of mostly native trees for planting that was consistent with 44% of the forest reaching defined conservation targets by 2029.

- The company acquired a share in a mobile sawmill, enabling it to produce sawn timber to order in situ.
- The company continued to market wood fuel products, with management of a woodshed for storage and seasonal supply of Christmas Trees.
- All nine crofting properties were let, with management plans approved for each.
- The use of the woodland for recreation and educational purposes continued to expand, and plans were adopted to extend the initial set of footpaths for public access to the forests.
- With the properties having several important historical sites, the company had talks with the Mull Historical & Archaeological Society and Historic Scotland to participate in an *Adopt a Monument* scheme.
- The company continued to prepare two building blocks for rent or purchase.
- The Woodland Burials project was put on hold as the area initially allocated did not meet evolving regulations for the establishment and operation of cemeteries. However, bearing in mind a growing local demand for lairs, it was hoped that a new area could be identified.[3]

As recognition for all its work, in 2015 the UK Forestry Commission nominated NWMCWC for inclusion on the World Wildlife Fund website as a Case Study for outstanding community achievement.

The Ulva Project

In 2015 and 2016, the Scottish Parliament enacted significant new legislation, the Community Empowerment Act and the Land Reform Act, to further facilitate community ownership of private land. Amongst other things, Part Four of the Community Empowerment Act provided for communities to acquire land that had been abandoned or neglected, even if the owner did not want to sell. And the Land Reform Act extended this right to facilitate sustainable development, while establishing a Scottish Land Commission with responsibility to deliberate upon the effective use of land for the common good. At the same time, in 2017, another significant piece of land in the Mull area was about to come onto the market. This would facilitate the transformation of the NWMCWC as envisaged by the Board.

History of Ulva Island

Ulva, with its satellite of Gometra Island off the western shoreline, sits within Loch na Keal opposite the hamlets of Ulva Ferry and Lagganulva. It comprises around 5,000 hectares and measures 12 km by 4 km (compared with Iona's 5 km by 2.5 km). In the Livingstone cave which is located inland from the cliff face on the southern shore, archaeological excavation has revealed evidence of occupation since Mesolithic times (5,500 BCE), with standing stones 400 metres to the west of Cragaig dating from 1500 BCE. The island probably acquired its name from the Vikings who called it *Ulvoy* meaning "Wolf Island". Known as Ulbha in Gaelic, the island was part of the kingdom of Dál Riata and, before Scotland assumed control in 1266, it was part of the Norse Kingdom of the Isles. From the 13th century (and possibly well before), the island was the home of the Clan MacQuarrie within the Lordship of the Isles with a strong fealty to the Clan Macdonald. During those times, the MacQuarries also held sway over neighbouring islands and an adjacent part of Mull and the chief served as a member of the Lordship's Council. At its peak, the island is said to have had a population of 800.

During its history, Ulva has become a place of some renown. For many years, when travel by boat was the main means of transport, it was a staging post for those visiting Iona and Staffa. As noted in Chapter 16, in 1773 it was visited by Dr Samuel Johnson and James Boswell, and it was an inspiration for the 1815 narrative poem *Lord of the Isles* by Sir Walter Scott which covers the return of Robert the Bruce culminating in the Battle of Bannockburn.[4] It is also the birthplace (possibly at Ormaig) of the famed 19th century Governor of the Australian colony of NSW, Lachlan

Macquarie, and was the sometime home of the grand-parents of explorer David Livingstone. In many respects, this island has seriously *punched above its weight*!

For many centuries, Ulva life was based on the traditional clan system, with clansmen living in small communities tending cattle, growing their own food, and fishing in local waters. In the summer months, to enable arable land to recover, clansmen would take their animals to common land on the moors where they lived in temporary accommodation called shielings.[5] During the Lordship of the Isles, the community also provided a standing army to pursue the military campaigns of the dominant Clan Macdonald and their allies.[6] With the demise of that Lordship loyalties transferred to the Clan Maclean of Duart. When they were ousted by the Duke of Argyll the people of Ulva were largely left to their own devices, and continued in their traditional way of life led by chiefs of the Clan MacQuarrie until late in the 18th century.

The last and 16th Chief of the MacQuarries was Lachlan who was born around 1720. His father died in 1735 and did not have his title as chief confirmed until 1739. For much of his life he presided over a relatively prosperous community. However, he eventually ran up significant debts, and in 1777 he had to sell up. In relatively short order, the island passed through the hands of Dugald Campbell and then Charles Campbell before being acquired in 1785 by Colin Macdonald of Boisdale (known as "Staffa"). Staffa was very enthusiastic about his purchase and brought his family to live on the island. He was a wealthy man, much loved by the locals, and initiated the lucrative kelp trade. When he died in 1800, Ulva was inherited by his younger son Reginald (also known as Staffa) who would prove to be a great trustee of the island's heritage. He invested heavily, bringing Cheviot sheep and extending woodlands; he also acquired the neighbouring island of Gometra, Colonsay and parts of the Ardmeanach peninsula. With the continuing success of the kelp industry, his time saw the establishment of a regular ferry service to Mull. He also built Ulva House which was completed in 1815, and the prosperity of the community warranted the construction of a parish church and manse.[78]

Sadly, the younger Staffa eventually over-reached himself and began to run up debts. However, his wife Elizabeth was the daughter of the wealthy Dr Henry Steuart who, with the best of intentions, purchased the debts from Staffa's creditors.[9] Sadly, this proved to be a misguided venture and Dr Steuart decided to sell. At the time Sir Lachlan Macquarie and his brother Charles were in the market for land in the area, and Sir Lachlan was particularly interested in re-establishing the MacQuarrie heritage in Ulva. However, by the time Charles had concluded arrangements to buy the island in 1825 Sir Lachlan had died. Charles followed through with the deal, but struggled to make a go of the property. By the 1830s he had decided sell, but he then died, and in October 1835 the trustees of his estate sold the island to Francis Clark.

The purchase of Ulva by Francis Clark would bring a huge change to community life on the island. On acquisition, Clark inherited an economy that was booming with a population of over 600 people. Potatoes were the staple food, and the kelp industry was still thriving with the exported seaweed used for fertiliser, glass making and soap. However, in the 1840s, this economy was hit by two significant changes. The bottom fell out of the kelp market, and Ulva was hit by the potato famine as a consequence of a water-borne virus called *phytophthora infestans* which was probably brought to the island through the import of infected kelp. In any event, Clark was eventually driven to pursuing the same policy of clearances that was being implemented in Mull. Within a few years, more than 400 people had been driven from the island and, by the 1881 census, the population had dropped to 51. In the meantime, the Clark family proceeded to extend Ulva House which became their residence until it was burnt down.

The Clark family continued to own the increasingly impoverished island until 1945 when they sold it to Edith, Lady Congleton, for £10,000. Amongst other things, she was responsible for the construction of a new Ulva House on the same site as the mansion occupied by the Clarks. On her death in the 1970s Ulva was inherited by her daughter Jean Howard, with her son James (known as Jamie) employed as estate manager. On her death in 2014, Jamie inherited the island. By now there were only five residents.

The Project

In May 2017, Jamie Howard published a notice to sell Ulva and the NWMCWC Board was quick to respond. After consulting with people living on Ulva and adjacent parts of Mull, it was evident that there was substantial support for a community buy-out. In particular, if the island was community-owned, a number of local people saw the potential for re-population, increased economic activity, additional employment, and an increase in the number of school-children available to attend and sustain the Ulva Primary School located at Ulva Ferry. With this initial encouragement, the NWMCWC organised a petition in support of an application under the *Land Reform (Scotland) Act 2016* to register an interest in buying the island. As required under the Act, this petition was conducted as a vote of all the population on the electoral roll defined as the "NWMCWC Catchment", and received 66% support. Subsequently, the Board commissioned a Feasibility Study to assess the scope and finances of a community-managed buy-out and development programme, and then submitted an application. In July 2017, the Board issued the following public statements to indicate its intentions:

"The aim is to manage the estate to provide sustainable benefits, for the community in the short to medium term, and for future generations including the repopulation of the island in the long term."

"This sale marks a crossroads in the history of Ulva and north-west Mull and provides a golden opportunity to ensure the survival and bolster the development of a fragile and remote community, enabling a vibrant and sustainable future for generations to come. Sustainable community benefit is dependent on more people living and working year-round on the island itself, and the way to achieve this is for the land to be owned and managed by the community.

The default position would be continued private ownership with no assurance of significant community benefit. Indeed there is every chance of continued decline of economic activity and community participation in the event of Ulva becoming a private recreational estate for an absentee landlord – possibly with restricted or much more difficult access than at present. In this regard the selling agents' comments regarding the estate's international marketing and the estate's right of control over access to the piers are telling.

In its public pronouncements, the Board went on to provide an outline of its very considerable development proposals which included:

- Improvement in the housing stock and other buildings, including modernisation of existing houses and refurbishment of derelict houses.
- Improvement in infrastructure, including consolidation of the ferry terminal, better access for fishing boats, upgrade of tracks and footpaths for use on foot and by bike, and renovation of the church for religious and other purposes.
- Revitalisation of agriculture, including possible re-establishment of crofting-based activity.
- Implementation of sustainable forest management.
- Expansion in tourism, including an improved ferry service, security of tenancy for the associated restaurant, provision of self-catering accommodation, establishment of an artist's studio, and introduction of new activities such as pony trekking, mountain biking, sailing, canoeing, and sea fishing.
- Enhancement of biodiversity, and safeguarding sensitive habitats and species.
- Support for marine fishing and aquaculture.

Following its declaration of intentions, the Board established an Ulva Buyout Committee to have carriage of the application, including the completion of a Business Plan. Meanwhile, the government began the process of considering the NWMCWC application.

At this point, it began to emerge that some community members, particularly people living on the banks of Loch na Keal, were not entirely supportive of the application. In part this was because the people running the NWMCWC (who lived in and around Dervaig) were seen as outsiders, and the petition of local people to test local support for the buy-out did not include a wider demographic. There were also concerns that, as a forestry management organisation, NWMCWC did not have the skills to manage the very wide range of activities cited in the buy-out application to the government.

In the weeks before Christmas 2017, the concerns of some community members were voiced at a meeting of the Mull Community Council.[10] Consequently, this body adopted a motion opposing the buy-out because they believed that the project should be a "whole of Mull" matter, and subject to a vote of the whole island. Some also reiterated the view that the NWMCWC was not an appropriate or competent body to be pursuing such an objective. Yet others took the view that the legislation which facilitated this community buy-out proposal was a serious interference in the open property market with the potential to compromise a legitimate personal gain from sale of the property. In any event, in 2018 the Scottish government accepted the NWMCWC application to register an interest in the purchase of Ulva. It then suspended the sale of the island on the open market, and proceeded to consider the Ulva Buyout Committee's Business Plan.

In June 2018, the Government approved the NWMCWC buyout, and also determined to provide a grant of £4.4 million from the Scottish Land Fund ("SLF") to cover most of the cost of the purchase price of £4.5 million and £150,000 related expenses. The remainder of the funding was financed by an unrestricted donation of £500,000 from the Macquarie Bank in Australia and £100,000 raised through charitable donations and local events.[11] Included in the SLF funding was a two-year line of finance to employ a development manager and for related education and training. In announcing the decision, John Watt, the chair of the SLF, stated that it was a "momentous day" for local residents, and went on to say that *"I wish them every success as they go on to raise the remaining funds that will allow them to turn their dreams into reality."* The buyout was completed on 21 June 2018.

Following the buy-out, the Committee proceeded to employ a Development Manager, Wendy Reid who joined the organisation in mid-2019 and quickly took up local residence and turned her mind to the start of what was a very demanding long term project. In a report on the initial direction of her endeavours which she issued in late 2019, she made the following comments.[12]

"The master plan for the island involves making improvements to infrastructure, increasing the population, and implementing a return to farming. More specifically, it is intended to create jobs, to provide new affordable housing, and to tempt young Scots to make the island their home. There are a range of activities that will achieve this objective, with some initial progress already achieved including the following:

- *A campsite has been opened with a hostel and mini-hotel.*
- *With funding from Marine Scotland, initial repairs to the slipway and the connecting pier in Ulva Ferry have been completed. This will facilitate the annual visit of over 5,000 tourists and improve access for fisherman working out of the Sound.*
- *In early 2020, the renovation of six houses will be completed to enable the population to increase to 20 by 2024 and to 50 in the foreseeable future.*
- *Plans are in preparation to repurpose Ulva House, as a visitor centre with two self-catering flats.*
- *The oldest blackhouse on the island, which sits close to the ferry landing area, (Sheila's Cottage) has been restored including a new thatched roof.*[1314]

Subsequently, the organisation has completed a range of preparatory work to achieve the long term objectives as identified in the Ulva Project Master Plan. To exploit the potential for expanding the island's population, it is planned to construct of a mix of leasehold and owner-occupied houses including the option for new residents to undertake self-build. To protect the community's long-term interest in properties that are sold, occupants must commit to a minimum period of residency, and there is a pre-emptive right for the community to buy back properties coming up for sale. An initial survey in 2019 reflected interest from over 500 people.

As regards the island's long-term environmental health, a land-use assessment and habitat survey was completed, with the aim of getting the right balance between agriculture and conservation. Anticipating agricultural use, an application was submitted under the Agricultural Environment and Climate Scheme ("AECS") with the aim of introducing cattle. It was envisaged that this might involve either a single farm or a croft-based system. At the same time, the company determined to reduce the deer population of 400-500 to a sustainable level consistent with a viable venison business.

Following the upgrade of the ferry service and the publicity arising from the community acquisition, annual visitor numbers to Ulva initially increased from around 4,000 before the NWMCWC purchase to nearly 7,000. As part of a long term programme to make the island more attractive to tourists, the organisation installed 70 new signposts to assist walkers and mountain bikers, a group of volunteers commenced the rejuvenation of the walled garden adjacent to Ulva House, and extensive work was completed on culverts, drainage ditches, and potholes in roads.

In the meantime, considerable time was committed to reviewing options for the future use of the partially-derelict Ulva House. Whilst it was initially envisaged that the building could be used as a heritage centre with accommodation, it eventually became apparent that there were significant obstacles to implementing this plan (including onerous planning conditions for modifications to B Listed buildings, and escalating building costs), and it is possible that the property will be sold to a private buyer with a covenant to protect community interests.

Current NWMCWC Status and Future Plans

Since completing the Ulva Buy-out, the NWMCWC has continued from strength to strength. It faces significant challenges, but has developed a maturity to accommodate external threats, adapt to its environment, and reinvent itself with an appropriate skill set when the need arises. All of the projects relating to the initial acquisition of woodland properties have continued to evolve, and great strides have been made in implementing the business plan for the Ulva Project.

Forestry

As with all its activities, NWMCWC has continued to take advice from appropriate experts in the field, and is now working with an organisation named TreeStory who are experts in managing sustainable forests.[15]

At Langamull North, the land is now fully mounded in preparation for planting the new and diverse set of trees. Planting is underway, and the gestation period for much of the new forest is several decades. In the immediate years ahead, the main activity will be to maintain a healthy plantation in an uncertain future climate.

The Langamull South properties have been fenced, and planting there will proceed following completion of works at Langamull North. Meanwhile harvesting on the Kengharair side of West Ardhu property is ongoing and will provide the funds for future replanting.

Wood Fuels

Island Woodfuels remains the only supplier of woodchip products across the island with several domestic customers. The firewood market is at times challenging, but this will stabilise once replanting of the forests has been completed.

Micro Hydro-Electric Power

The micro hydro-electric scheme continues to generate an income for the company, helping to underpin the ongoing costs of operating the organisation.

Housing

The Argyll Community Housing Association is proceeding the construction of houses on the Potential Development Area at West Ardhu. This will not only provide much needed housing for affordable rent, but should allow the company access to further housing development sites. Currently, all of the existing nine crofts are let and, with strong public interest, NWMCWC hopes to expand this form of housing.

Environmental Regeneration

Peatland restoration remains an aspiration. In addition to restoring biodiversity, peat bog has the ability to trap carbon and address global warming. It is also a source of fuel for burning.

Cemetery

NWMCWC is seeking a new site to meet an established demand for lairs.

Community Facilities

Toilets have been installed at Dervaig.

The Ulva Project

It is still early days in a project which may take ten or more years to complete. But steady progress has been achieved as follows.

- A farm with 30 head of cattle has been established which covers the whole island, and land management practices have been adopted that protect and enhance natural heritage, improve water quality, manage flood risk, and mitigate/adapt to climate change. A farmer who has moved from the Isle of Harris is now the tenant. The land also supports a small herd of sheep and there are some feral goats. In 2022, a bull was introduced and in 2023 many calves were born.
- The company is testing the market for potential buyers of Ulva House with the building to be used for accommodation or for business.
- Refurbishment of the Manse and six other houses has been completed and the premises let to people working on the island.
- The company is working with the Argyll Community Housing Association to construct several new houses for occupation by people living and working locally.
- Ardalum House (originally a shooting lodge) which sits in the north-east of the island has been repurposed as a hostel.
- The Craigaig Bothy on the south side of the island has been restored with the help of local designer Banjo Beale, and Bearnus Bothy on the north-west side of Ulva has been repurposed and let.
- The ferry service continues to be run as a very successful operation by a couple who live in the Ferry House which is now leased from NWMCWC.
- The Boathouse Restaurant has been let to new tenants who have refreshed the menu and service.
- There are plans to replace petrol and diesel-engine quad bikes with all electric vehicles.
- As part of its environmental management plan, NWMCWC has implemented a programme to remove bracken and other weeds.
- The company has entered into a partnership with a stalker to manage the red deer population down to sustainable levels.

The NWMCWC Team

In the 15 years since its inception, over 40 people have served on the NWMCWC Board. This reflects extraordinary resilience for a community-based voluntary organisation. Since its inception in 2005, the Board was constituted as a team of up to 16 people, including up to 12 elected at the AGM, one appointed by the Mull Community Council, and up to three co-opted to enable an appropriate mix of skills and experience. The Articles of Association provide for three year terms, with retirement of a third of the Board each year. Directors may only serve two consecutive terms, after which they must stand down for at least one year. In reality, many Directors have served one or two three-year terms, but then returned after time out.

Over the journey, one person has demonstrated an amazing dedication to the cause. Colin Morrison was the inaugural Chairman and, subsequently, with appropriate retirement for a year after two consecutive terms, he has served as a member of the Board throughout the organisation's existence although he is no longer in the Chair. Colin's contribution cannot be over-estimated, but several others have provided long and distinguished service, including John Morrison who was an inaugural member and served as Treasurer for eight years. The organisation also owes much of its success to Ian Hepburn who served as Development Manager in the Pioneer phase. At the same time, for over five years Belinda Hale served as the organisation's administrator. During the Consolidation phase, John Addy, Iain Thomson, Andy Mayo and Ian Hepburn provided sterling service, with Chris Lidell taking on the role of Development Manager with a two year grant from the Scottish Government commencing in late 2014. He was succeeded by Malcom Ward. Since, the advent of the Ulva Project, membership includes two directors from that part of Mull, Anne Cleave who lives in Ulva Ferry and Andrew Primrose from Gometra.

Whilst most of the work has been undertaken on a voluntary basis, the organisation has established a complement of paid staff. The current team are:

Office Manager: Helen Murray
Administration Office: Alex Lane
Ulva Development Manager: Wendy Reid
Wood Fuels Operator: Duncan MacAry

Conclusion

In conclusion, the NWMCWC has proven to be a remarkably energetic, resilient and innovative organisation. The original woodland project proved to be a great preparation for a much expanded role and, given the evolving mix of experience and competencies, the whole venture has demonstrated what a determined group of community volunteers can achieve. Indeed, contrary to those who had doubts about the organisation's ability to diversify, it has acquired and applied a widening set of skills to embrace a much broader set of activities than those involved in forestry management. In the process, it has established a level of permanence and longevity which community organisations often fail to achieve. This prompts me to refer to the research into long-lived organisations undertaken many years ago by an employee of the Shell Company, Arie de Geus.[16] He identified four characteristics for the long-term success of a business organisation – a strong sense of identity and unity of purpose, tolerance of diversity at the margin, sensitivity to the environment in which it operates including stakeholders, and conservative financial management. Of all the community work that figures in this book, NWMCWC probably "takes the gold medal" for meeting these criteria in its work in Mull.

Looking to the future, the organisation faces a number of challenges. Not least, it needs to maintain a team of volunteers able to find the time, energy, and resilience to continue the pursuit of its organisational goals. However, it should have no fears about its ability to expand and develop the range of activity. Its achievements in an evolving environment are manifest.

ENDNOTES

1   The Forestry Commission is now known as Forestry and Land Scotland. With headquarters in Inverness, it is responsible for managing the country's forests and ensuring the continued provision of timber supplies to support the rural economy. It also seeks to enhance biodiversity, support tourism, and increase public access to the green spaces that will help enhance Scotland's physical and mental health.

2   SSEN is the Southern Scotland Energy Network.

3   In Scotland, the word lair refers to a burial plot.

4   In the days of Ronald Lord of the Isles, the Clan MacQuarrie provided a significant force in support of Robert the Bruce. In the poem, there is reference to the islands passed during the boat trip that Robert takes from Skye to the mainland including "The shores of Mull on the eastward lay, and Ulva Dark and Colonsay, and all the group of islets gay, that guard Staff round".

5   A shieling was a roughly constructed temporary hut, made of branches, with turf on the roof held down by stones.

6   A report on the availability of troops to support King James VI prepared by John Cunningham in 1596 indicates that Mull could provide 900 men, Ulva 60, and Gometra/Inch Kenneth 16 each. (David Caldwell)

7   Staffa Macdonald died in 1838, and his passing would mark the end of an era. Confronted with difficult economic imperatives, the new owner of Ulva would have a very different view about community life on the island.

8   This Presbyterian kirk built in 1826/27 was designed by Thomas Telford, and is still in use. The building sits in a cemetery, with an adjacent manse.

9   Dr Steuart was from Lanarkshire. After a military career, he was noted for pioneering work in land regeneration. As a classical scholar, in 1799 he was elected as a Fellow of the Royal Society of Edinburgh and in 1814 he was granted the baronetcy of Allanton. He died in 1836.

10   As noted in Chapter 22, the Mull Community Council is an elected body with around 15 members representing communities across Mull and Iona. They lobby Council and Government to obtain support for local projects. At the time, membership did not include a representative of North West Mull or Ulva.

11   The bank's donation was in recognition of its link to Lachlan Macquarie.

12   This is a modified version of the wording.

13   Sheila MacFadyen was the last resident, living there until the 1950s.

14   A blackhouse is a building with double dry-stone walls, a floor with flagstones, and a roof of wooden rafters and a thatch of turf with straw and reed. There us a central hearth. It was designed to accommodate animals as well as people.

15   TreeStory are a company dedicated to revitalising the landscape by offering holistic and sustainable forestry solutions that combine technical knowledge for managing forests with a commitment to biodiversity.

16   Arie de Geus was the head of Royal Dutch Shell's Strategic Planning Group and published a number of learned papers on his research into "the Living Company". He died in 2019.

DÙTHCHAS
LANDSCAPE AND COMMUNITY IN MULL AND IONA

SOUTH WEST MULL
& IONA DEVELOPMENT
(SWMID)

Whilst it may not have received the same kudos as some other community organisations in Mull, SWMID is a high performer with significant achievements during its decade-long existence in a sometimes overlooked corner of the island.

The genesis of community-based development activities in the south west of Mull was in 2010 when Highlands and Islands Enterprise ("HIE") identified Ross of Mull and Iona, including Brolass and Tiroran, as worthy of receiving support through a programme called Growth at the Edge ("GATE").[1] Initially, the organisation nominated as a local partner to receive funding for this activity was MICT and a development officer, Morven Gibson was appointed with oversight from a local team called the Ross of Mull and Iona Development Group. Following widespread consultation with the community, in 2011 this led to the creation of the Ross of Mull and Iona Community Plan which encompassed an analysis of the local people, infrastructure, economy and environment, and provided a vision and mission for future development. Despite this promising start, the logistics of supporting this activity from MICT in Craignure proved to be a challenge and, with local communities eager to have control of their own affairs, it was decided to create a separate entity for driving community development in the south-west. Consequently, in 2014, SWMID was established and registered as a community company limited by guarantee.

SWMID is governed by a Board and most of the members are elected at the AGM. However, there is the ability to co-opt additional directors to meet the competency profile. The current Board has nine elected members and one co-opted member and is chaired by Cameron Anson. It meets every month to six weeks. The Board appoints a CEO who has responsibility for operational activity, and there are currently seven other staff supporting a range of programmes and projects.

At present, the organisation is based in a building called the Columba Centre in Fionnphort that is owned by Historic Environment Scotland ("HES").[2] This building (originally called the St Columba Heritage Centre) was opened in 1997 as a museum providing information about Iona and the life of St Columba with a café and gift shop. This concept, particularly with the development of a separate historical museum on Iona proved to be difficult to sustain, and the building was subsequently re-purposed. Half of the building is now leased to SWMID and the other half is retained by HES as a base for their local maintenance work and for storing ancient stones which had previously been displayed in the heritage centre. SWMID have established their part of the building as their registered address with an office, a hot desk, and a community gym, and they sublet part of the building to an artists' collective called South West Mull Makers who use their space as a studio and retail facility.

Strategy

Initially, SWMID worked with the Strategic Plan developed through the GATE programme which had a long term timeframe and a wide range of potential activities. The Vision in this plan was that, in ten years' time, Ross of Mull and Iona would be a proactive community, developing practical ideas and opportunities to achieve a balanced, socially and economically viable, and prosperous population. The Plan then identified a range of potential projects and outcomes under four headings: People, Home, Economy and Environment. In 2023, this blueprint was substantially updated and replaced by a five year plan with the following structure.

Vision
A Thriving and Resilient Community.

Mission
To ensure the future sustainability of our community.

Strategic Directions
The plan identifies two strategic directions as follows:

- To deliver projects that achieve community goals and maintain SWMID's financial accountability.
- To engage with young people to understand from them what the barriers are to living here and, in collaboration with our young people, support measures to help them stay here.

Outcomes
In keeping with the framework established in the original Ten Year Plan, the 2023-2028 Plan provides a set of performance outcomes under four headings as follows:

People: A more diverse and demographically balanced population.

Home: Better, affordable housing provision in the area.

Economy: A wide range of business and employment opportunities, with more year-round employment and training.

Environment: A reduction in local carbon emissions and increase in biodiversity.

Operational Activity

Since 2014, SWMID has established a range of operational activity, gradually expanding to encompass a diverse range of programmes and projects. In implementing these programmes, the organisation continues to consult widely with the local community and welcomes input and participation by volunteers working in support of the professional staff.

Forestry

Shortly after SWMID was established, an opportunity arose to acquire the Tiroran Forest which was owned by what was then called the Forestry Commission (now Forestry and Land Scotland). This property on the Ardmeanach peninsula was on the market because the Forestry Commission considered it to be "unmanageable as a viable operation". In 2014, SWMID declared an interest in acquiring the forest, with acquisition to be financed by funding from the Scottish Land Fund, loan funding from Social Investment Scotland, and some additional grant support from HIE.[3] The Forest was purchased for £930,000 under the National Forest Land Scheme which gives communities the opportunity to buy forest land currently in Public Ownership. The acquisition was warmly welcomed by most local residents.

SWMID took possession of Tiroran forest in 2015. The property of 2,030 acres sits astride what is sign-posted as the "scenic route" from Pennyghael to Salen, and the current forest was planted in the 1960s with a mix of elm, hazel, oak, rowan, and sycamore trees. On assuming responsibility for the property, SWMID established an extensive felling and replanting plan with operating costs financed in part by a government carbon offset programme. Initially, logs were sent to the mainland for milling. However, following the Tiroran Timber Sawmill and Biochar project, and with support from the *Prince's Countryside Fund* and the *Rural and Island Communities Ideas into Action Fund*, some of this activity has now been brought "in-house". From March 2023, SWMID has taken ownership of a sawmill and the organisation supplies wood products such as cladding and fence posts to local customers, while the bark and other waste products is converted into biochar in a specialised kiln. Created by burning organic matter without oxygen, biochar sequesters CO_2 within the ground for hundreds of years and acts as a natural fertiliser.

Through ownership of this forest SWMID has established the Tiroran Community Forest as its flagship community project with a range of public access programmes. In addition to the re-establishment of a crofting community, of which more below, these programmes include a Nature Trail created by Bunessan Primary School children, an adventure playground facilitated by the Woodland Tribe, a shelter with information about wildlife in the forest, an outdoor sculpture gallery of willow figures created as part of a community art project led by local weaver Alexandra James, an eagle viewing hide for watching white-tailed eagles, and a conservation programme designed to conserve remnant Caledonian rainforest.[4]

Crofts and Housing

In 2020, with the help of Woodland Croft Partnership, SWMID developed plans to establish woodland crofts within the Tiroran community forest, a district which was once home to the crofting townships of Knockroy and Achonnaill. Despite some local opposition, in January 2024 the Crofting Commission approved six woodland crofts adjacent to the ruins of Achonnaill. SWMID has already received expressions of interest from a number of interested parties and, once the formal application process is established, it is expected that potential crofters will produce outline plans for actively managing their land. This may include growing food for sale, development of tree nurseries, and a range of other sustainable activities.

With the support of the West Highland Housing Association, and Argyll and Bute Council SWMID has also undertaken a feasibility study with the aim of enabling the provision of social housing for local people to rent. It is hoped to proceed with the acquisition of land for this purpose in the Bunessan area.

Kelp Farming

In recent times, SWMID identified the potential for a kelp farm and commissioned a feasibility study to assess the viability of such an operation. As we have seen from earlier chapters, this activity is not new to Mull, but died out in the 19th century because of limited demand for the kelp based products. The feasibility study suggested that this activity had the potential to provide a range of products including nourishing food for human consumption, fertiliser for soil regeneration, bio fuel, low methane-producing livestock feed, biodegradable packaging, and moisturising agents for use in cosmetics. It was also noted that growing seaweed contributed to the reduction of carbon emissions, sequestering greenhouse gasses, and acting as a carbon sink.

Based on the results of the feasibility study, which does not involve harvesting of old growth kelp which will be retained for biodiversity, SWMID developed a business case that helped to secure public and private investment, with a view to providing an operation which will complement the local fishing industry. A licence to operate off-shore from a six hectare base off the shoreline was then obtained and in 2021 the organisation established the Aird Fada Seaweed Farm.

Farming involves embedding seeds in lines attached to on-shore infrastructure, and collecting the plant for processing on a sustainable basis. In 2022, the first 6 km of seeded line delivered 60 tonnes of sugar kelp. At present the kelp is sent away for processing, but SWMID eventually hopes to establish a local processing capability at Bendoran.

The venture has been established with input from many specialists including the Scottish Association of Marine Science ("SAMS"), HIE, Argyll and Bute Council, Argyll Aquaculture Ltd and a local company called Inverlussa Marine Services. Until the departure from the EU, the project received financial support from the European Maritime and Fisheries Fund. Current operations are being funded by the Co-op Carbon Innovation Fund.[5]

Eco-Tourism

In the early 2020s, SWMID had the opportunity to acquire a two acre block of land next to the shoreline at Bendoran, with finance from the Scottish Land Fund. Bendoran is an inlet on the south of Loch Scridain with a sheltered mooring. The site has been developed as a multi-use facility, with a slipway established with funds from the Islands Green Recovery Fund, boat storage, and facilities for the Aird Fada seaweed operation.[6] Part of the site has been leased to Bendoran Watersports who offer sea kayaking and sailing, whilst the Bendoran Water Activities Club has also been established to provide access for local people to a range of water sports. In the longer term SWMID plans to continue developing the site's multi-use resources with facilities, employment, and training opportunities for local people and access for visitors and tourists.

In the meantime, SWMID has established an *aire* within Tiroran Community

Forest for self-contained motorhomes and campervans, and SWMID are also looking at building some off-grid log cabins for adventure eco-tourism.[7]

Bunessan Community Garden

SWMID has a strong link with the Ross of Mull Historical Centre in Bunessan the activities of which are covered elsewhere in this book. SWMID employs a gardener to manage the community garden and to provide advice to local people on gardening practice. The property generates some income through sale of produce.

Conclusion

Now in existence for ten years, SWMID has become a well-established and relatively mature organisation. In a relatively short time, it has achieved a proven track record with completion of a range of projects across a diverse set of activities. Led by a dedicated group of skilled and enthusiastic people, supported by a team of professional staff, with a commitment to fostering community engagement in an environmentally sustainable manner, it is a beacon of community-based activism and presents great prospects for the future.

For more information, their Web Site – swmid.co.uk – is a great read.

ENDNOTES

1   The GATE programme is now called Scottish Edge and aims to work with local organisations with investment designed to facilitate "whole of community" growth.

2   HES is the lead public body established to investigate, care for and promote Scotland's historic environment. It manages the Abbey Museum on Iona and Dunstaffnage Castle adjacent to Oban on the mainland.

3   Social Investment Scotland provide access to finance and support to help maximise the impact of community-based social enterprises.

4   The Woodland Tribe is a not for profit Community Interest Company promoting and supporting the establishment of adventure playgrounds through active engagement with community members in creating their own facility.

5   The Co-op Carbon Innovation Fund is financed by the Co-op Foundation which was established by the UK retail business The Co-op to reduce greenhouse gas emissions.

6   The Islands Green Recovery Fund was established by the Scottish government to operate in 2020/21, and has now been replaced by the Island Communities Fund as part of implementing the 2019 National Islands Plan.

7   An aire is an area for overnight parking of self-contained motor-vans. This is not a campsite, so awnings are not permitted, and visitors must take all waste away when they leave.

PART SEVEN

21ST CENTURY MULL & IONA

THE LAND AND SEAS

While Mull exemplifies remarkable community activism, the wider community also thrives. This part of the book provides a flavour of a rich and the rewarding life of current residents, using economic and demographic information derived from census reports and field research. This account includes some personal stories that illustrate the endeavour and achievements of some notable current residents.

As context, it should be noted that in 2020 the resident population of Mull and Iona was estimated to be around 3,000 permanent residents including 170 living on Iona. A majority of these people live in the five main towns of Tobermory (population 1,000), Salen (500), Dervaig (100), Bunessan (70), and Craignure (70). The remainder live in villages, on the main estates, or on individual rural blocks. Few people are registered as unemployed. Of those employed 74% work in the services sector, 11% in construction and related trades, and 7% in agriculture, forestry and fishing.

The Land

The history of the ownership and occupation of land in Mull has followed a pattern that is similar to many other areas of the Highlands and Islands. Over the last 300 years, with the agricultural revolution, clearances, and the proliferation of holiday homes, more and more land has been owned and occupied by fewer and fewer people with a steady growth in absentee landlords and a wholesale departure of traditional residents.

However, at the beginning of the 21st century, the tide of depopulation began to turn, with a slow increase in numbers facilitated by Acts of Parliament designed to encourage re-population. The full story of the slow dispossession of the many for the benefit of the few is told in several books including *The Scottish Clearances* by Professor Sir Thomas Devine and *The Poor Had No Lawyers* by Andy Wightman. In recent times, as a consequence of the legislation enacted by the Scottish Parliament since 1999, Mull has been in the vanguard of exploiting the opportunity to reverse this trend.

The total land mass of Mull, Iona and other immediately adjacent islands is about 221,000 acres. Most property is privately owned although, thanks to public policy which is encouraging the construction and renovation of property for letting to local people, there are a growing number of tenants in both public and private housing.[1] Around 40% of this land is owned by six absentee owners, and a further 15% is owned by two resident families. The main economic activities on these significant estates are farming tourism, and recreation. A further 13% of the land is owned by the Scottish government and other public institutions. This includes forests administered by Forestry and Land Scotland, public infrastructure such as schools which are managed by Argyll and Bute Council, and property owned by statutory bodies such as the National Trust for Scotland.[2] 4% of the land is owned by community based organisations. Of the remaining 28%, half is owned by eight families (four of whom are residents) and the balance is held by a large number of other resident and absentee owners. Many individual properties are leased to people who live and work locally, but a substantial number are let to tourists and/or used as a holiday home. Of particular note is the following:

- The biggest estate, Benmore, comprises around 32,000 acres in the centre of the island.
- The biggest resident landowners, the Corbett family, own about 21,000 acres which encompasses much of the traditional territory of the Clan Maclaine around Lochbuie.
- The Duke of Argyll continues to be a significant land owner in the south of Mull.

- The current Chief of the Clan Maclean owns an estate which includes Castle Duart.
- Iona is owned by the National Trust for Scotland.
- Substantial areas of forest are held by the community organisations NWMCWC, MICT, and SWMID, and NWMCWC owns the island of Ulva.

While there is unlikely to be a major shift in this pattern of land ownership in the near future, government policy on land reform may see an increase in community-owned land. It is also possible that the Council may choose to levy a higher rate burden on absentee owners that would release some property for purchase by local residents.

Agriculture

Mull is home to significant herds of cattle, sheep and deer and there are areas of arable land for growing a range of crops. There is a viable dairy industry, for milk and cheese, cattle for high quality beef production, and two piggeries.

There are various approaches for managing land used for agriculture and, from conversations with several landowners, there are several perspectives which will underpin how the future may unfold.

- It is likely that the current balance of land use will continue, with a mix of dairy, cattle, and sheep farming, and deer stalking.
- A number of estates embrace organic farming which seeks to re-establish and sustain the native soils, and encourage a healthy ecosystem.
- Community groups and some others support a return to crofting communities with sustainable farming on small holdings.
- There are landowners who wish to retain significant estates for private recreation.
- There is some support for the re-establishment of the original ecosystem including the Caledonian rain forest, following the model established in the Cairngorm Connect project.[3]

Bearing in mind this diversity of views, one of the most striking aspects of life in Mull is the remarkable enterprise shown by a number of individuals and families that have brought viable agricultural activity to the island while respecting the environment and enriching the local community. Apart from the larger agricultural estates such as Benmore and Lochbuie which are managed in a professional manner with the best interests of the community at heart, two notable examples on a smaller scale are the organic farms at Baliscate and Ardalanish the history of which is a microcosm of more enlightened agricultural activity on the island. The dairy farm at Baliscate is the main source of the island's milk supply as well as being the vehicle for other successful businesses such as Isle of Mull Cheese and the Island Bakery. The cattle and sheep farm at Ardalanish provides a range of organic meat products and woven woollen textiles.

Dairy, Cheese and Biscuits

In many ways, the Reade family epitomise the very best of what can come from people settling in Mull in modern times. Their story is presented here as an example of great endeavour and enterprise.

The Reade family story begins in the 1960s. After meeting on a cycling holiday, Chris Reade and her now late husband Jeff married in 1963 and acquired a dairy farm in Somerset. However, with difficult market conditions in the late 1970s, they opted for a change of scene. They had always been interested in Scotland because of its beautiful landscape and interesting people. So, in the spring of 1979, they ventured north on their first holiday in over 10 years, leaving the farm in Somerset in the hands of friends. Whilst travelling through northern England, quite fortuitously, Jeff found a notice for the sale of 40 acres in Tobermory. They decided to investigate and travelled up to Mull, camping in a beautiful spot next to a river and the ancient standing stones at Baliscate.[4] In the morning, looking across the valley, they spotted the ruins of a house on the hillside which turned out to be the property for sale, a small farm called Sgriob-ruadh.[5] Their hearts told them "This is the place!"

On returning to Somerset, Chris completed some due diligence which revealed that, with most of the local milk supplies coming from the mainland, there was an opportunity to establish a viable local dairy at Sgriob-ruadh. They despatched a bid in a sealed envelope and, ahead of the closing date, they travelled back to their camp site in Mull to await the outcome of the auction. On the allotted day, it did not look good because a company had put in a higher bid. However, under Scottish law the vendor is not compelled to accept the highest offer and initially no offer was accepted. A few days later, Chris and Jeff were invited to a meeting at the Tobermory Hotel and after a conversation with the vendor, they were told that the property was there's. Following settlement in late 1979, in early 1980 the Reades and their family of four sons (Brendan, Matthew, Garth, and Joe) moved to Mull.

On taking up residence at Sgriob-ruadh, the initial workload of fixing up the house and establishing a viable operation was enormous. With Chris and Jeff initially spending much of their time still running their farm in Somerset, they put the family's fortunes in the hands of their teenage sons. That was quite a big decision, but the Reades trusted their boys and felt assured that Mull was a relatively safe place with friendly people. Whilst completing their education at local schools, the boys did an amazing job, not only looking after the property, but milking what was initially a small herd of five cows, organising delivery of milk to retail outlets, and making all the other day to day decisions. They also quickly became friends with the local lads, who taught them how to ride motorbikes, and local women looked after them by providing food and mending clothes. In the meantime, Jeff was passionate about renewable energy and investigated the establishment of a hydro-electric scheme using the Tobermory River which runs through the property. After completing a survey, Brendan completed a project to install a water turbine to power the property.

In 1981, Jeff and Chris finally completed their exit from Somerset, and transported all their worldly goods to Mull in a 7 tonne truck. In 1982, Brendan at 18 became a full-time farmer, supported by his younger brother Garth.

Even from the early days, the farming business encompassed both the supply of milk and cheese making. This was because the dairy herd was geared to peak demand for milk during the tourist season and, during the rest of the year, there was a surplus. The mostly hard cheddar cheese was named after the island of Mull, taking on the character of the local pasture, and gradually acquiring a reputation for quality. Currently, this milk and cheese business now employs 17 people including Brendan and Garth, three grandchildren, and 12 other staff.

Amongst other things, Sgriob-ruadh is notable as a sustainable operation, producing its own electricity, and recycling waste products in several innovative ways. In addition to generating energy from both water and wind turbines, there is also a wood-chip burner. Also, when building a new dairy in 2000, a swimming pool was installed which operates as a heat sink as well as a community amenity. Following a family research project, the family has also established a distillery which produces Isle of Mull gin using the dairy by-product of whey, and herbs and fruits grown in the farm garden. The family also keep pigs which consume the waste from all the family enterprises.

The success of this family is not confined to their agricultural investment. Joe Reade, the youngest of Chris' children, has proved to be a highly successful entrepreneur, establishing a bakery and biscuit factory on the island. After graduating from Edinburgh University where he met his wife Dawn, and learning the trade with a local baker, in 1994 Joe established the *Island Bakery*. Working out of a garage, the couple quickly established a reputation for supplying quality bread and, in 1996 they acquired a shop on the Main Street of Tobermory which became the Island Bakery Delicatessen. In the early 2000s, they identified a niche market for producing "organic" biscuits and established *Island Bakery Organics*. This has proven to be a huge success, with the biscuits winning product quality awards and being sold through shops in Glasgow and beyond which are supplied by a family-owned depot in the city. By 2007, this biscuit business had become the mainstay of their enterprises, and it was decided to sell the Deli. In 2012, they then constructed a new bakery, which had the merits of being powered by renewable energy.

While the farming, cheese and biscuit businesses continue to be an important part of the Reade family's contribution to island life, the achievement of the fourth son should not be overlooked. Chris Reade describes her son Matthew as a free spirit with a strongly creative streak. Although he played a key role in the family's transfer to Mull, he had a passion for artistic activity. Eventually, he met and married Julia who was an artist, and they set up an art gallery in Calgary. This property includes a woodland walk and café and is a centre for the display and sale of local arts and crafts.

For the future, the Reade family are always looking ahead. Adjacent to Sgriob-ruadh farm they now operate a very popular café called the Glass Barn, and a shop which sells the company's cheese, biscuits and spirits. Who knows where their energies may take them next.

Unfolding over a period of 40 years, from days before the internet and modern communications, the Reade family story is nothing short of intrepid, bringing extraordinary enterprise and prosperity to Mull through creativity, hard work and dedication. The outcome today, in terms of establishing what has become a range of thriving enterprises employing many local people, is a tribute to two remarkable people, Chris and Jeff, and their brilliant family.

Beef, Sheep and Woollen Textiles

Ardalanish is a 1,500 acres farm, located on the southern side of the Ross of Mull peninsula. It is a windy spot, but has adequate top soils for growing pasture and crops. In the centre of the property, there is a fresh water loch with springs that provide ample water. At one time, there would also have been significant stands of trees, and there is an abundance of peat for heating.

Historically, this land was part of the territory controlled by the Clan Maclean. In medieval times, there were significant communities of tacksmen and crofters living off the land through growing crops and grazing sheep and cattle. The people would have sustained a reasonable living, whilst being bound to serve in the laird's intermittent military escapades. Eventually, this way of life began to change with the introduction of a tenancy system with rents paid to finance the increasing financial commitments of the laird. As we have seen earlier in this book, this system eventually brought significant financial pressure to all the parties, with the laird running up debts that he eventually could not repay. As a consequence, in the late 17th century, ownership of the land was transferred to the Duke of Argyll.

In the years that followed, this part of Mull was subject to the same practices as in other parts of the Duke of Argyll's estates. For a time, some crofters turned their endeavours to farming kelp for making soap, fertiliser, and salt peter. However this diversification had a limited life, and eventually the Duke imposed significant increases in the rents which drove out many of the tenants. Eventually there was wholesale eviction as people were replaced by sheep. According the Census of the time, in 1840 there had been as many as 191 people living on this property. And, as in the neighbouring community at Shiaba, evidence of the homes and agricultural endeavours of the people then living on the estate are easily identifiable in the modern landscape. This includes the foundations of houses and the furrows that mark their *lazy-bed* farming methods. Within twenty years, there were only one or two families left, looking after sheep. Eventually, the wool industry collapsed and the property became almost derelict.

After a long period when the only residents were a flock of sheep, in the late 20th century this property came up for sale. In 1994, a couple named Araminta (Minty) and Aeneas Mackay bought the estate including 600 sheep.[6] Minty had been born and brought in Tobermory while Aenaes grew up on the mainland, but both were from farming families. When they acquired the property, the couple pondered their options and decided to diversify in a way that would bring an environmentally sensitive approach to farming whilst adding value through weaving the wool into "organic" fibres and fabrics.

The sheep the Mackays inherited were mostly the small Hebridean blackface breed that has existed in Scotland since the middle of the 18th century, and these animals seemed well-adapted to the harsh conditions on this wind-swept corner of Mull.[7] However, the numbers were not really sustainable, and they determined that a flock of around 200 would be more viable. With the aim of introducing weaving, in 2005 they approached a local weaver, Bob Ryan. As it happened, he was about retire and was thinking about how to dispose of his antique looms. At first, Bob showed no interest in deferring his retirement, but it was agreed that his equipment would be stored in the Mackays' byre. However, Bob then changed his mind and started to reassemble the looms and, when the Mackays failed to find a weaver, he agreed to provide free training to apprentices and be a mentor to those that completed the course.

Thus began a journey that would see the Mackays become legends in their own life-time. In no time, Bob was training a series of enthusiastic trainee weavers, the wool was being sent off for spinning at a mill in New Lanark, and the local looms were then used to make a range of products including plaids, scarves, and woollen hats. The Mackays opened a shop for sale of their meat and woollen goods and pursued retail opportunities in Tobermory and further afield. The farm also became a centre of community activity, and a magnet for tourists. The fabrics, with hues that reflected the unique nature of the local environment in terms of subtle colours were also winning design awards. And the success of a farm run according to organic principles won the Mackays accreditation by the Soil Association.[8] As a consequence, their work came to the attention of the Prince of Wales who visited the property, and Bob Ryan was awarded an OBE!

After twenty years, Minty and Aeneas decided that it was time to pass the baton to a new couple. In 2011, they sold they farm to Anne and Andrew Smith who have taken the property and business from strength to strength. Today, Ardalanish supports 300 Hebridean sheep, and some highland and other cattle. Now in his 80s, weaver Bob Ryan still maintains a keen interest, providing advice about weaving and the operation of the looms. Nowadays, the property also includes a herbal garden where traditional plants are grown for colouring the wool, including woad (from granite) for blue hues. The business supports several staff including people from overseas and the on-site shop caters for both woollen goods and many fine cuts of organic meats. The Smiths also send their goods to a shop in Tobermory and to the Calgary Arts Centre. The whole property is now off-grid, and powered by wind turbines and solar panels with batteries.

The Abattoir

Until the early 1980s, there was no slaughterhouse on Mull, either to meet local demand or to facilitate outward trade. As was the custom for many years, cattle and sheep were herded onto vehicles and sent by ferry to Oban. Eventually, there was enough local demand to create a local kill-only facility on Mull and, in 1982, local farmers established a community owned slaughterhouse called Mull Slaughterhouse Ltd ("MSL").

MSL is operated under the Community Benefit Societies Act 2014 which provides for body corporate type organisations operating on a not-for-profit basis as either as a *co-operative* or a *community benefit society*. MSL is a community benefit society with sites at Calachally, Salen, Glenforsa, and Aros. It has shareholders with £10 shares, and is managed by a volunteer Committee of Management with a Director who is currently Flora Corbett.

The basic cycle of operation for this business involves slaughter of cattle, sheep and pigs (and deer in season) every week, followed by the full butchery of the carcass. It is a *one-stop* shop, meaning that the animals are killed, butchered and packaged at the one location. The company employs a licensed slaughterman, 2 full time butchers, a packer and an administrator. To maintain a viable structure, the company provides a service to farmers on Mull, the surrounding islands and mainland areas and around 60% of the throughput is "off-island". To some extent, this inter-island traffic is subsidised in that the ferry company CalMac only charges for trailers transporting animals. There is no charge for empty vehicles on return journeys.

The main customers for MSL are local farmers who then supply their product to local retail outlets, hotels, pubs, and farmers' markets. Fees for service are calculated on a basis designed to cover recurrent costs. Given the relatively small scale of operations and complex logistics, the end-products are more expensive than equivalent products from a city abattoir, but are still cheaper than would be the case if animals were transported to slaughterhouses on the mainland.

Given the not-for-profit basis of MSL, the financial objective of the company is to break even. However, the organisation does face significant challenges with a need for funding to finance the installation of modern equipment. If this essential operation were to close, Mull would have to go back to using facilities on the mainland which would drive up costs and prices. Strenuous efforts are being made to secure the same sort of on-going support from the Scottish government that is given to farmers.

Fishing

The fishing industry has always been a staple of human survival in Mull, with a range of species in local waters. However, it is not an easy life working in seas adjacent to the North Atlantic. In recent times, aquaculture based in the more protected waters provided by sea lochs has become an essential part of the economy with several salmon farms in southern Mull and a mussel farm in Loch Don.

There are a number of fishing operators based in Tobermory, including full time boats and several operating on a part time basis. In addition there is a scallop diver, some trawler/dredgers, and several creel boat operations based in Ulva Ferry and the Ross of Mull.

The fishing community consult with each other through membership of the Mull Fisherman's Association ("MFA"). This organisation lobbies for in-shore fishermen interests, including marine protection in the Sound of Mull, and liaises with the SSMEI (Scottish Sustainable Marine Environment Initiative) which has developed plans for securing sustainable creel fishing. To this end, the Sound of Mull has been the subject of an SSMEI Pilot Study, along with the Firth of Clyde, the Shetlands and the Berwickshire coast.

More broadly, the shellfish industry is a major part of the Scottish economy. Scotland is the biggest producer in Europe, and there is growing interest from China. Membership of the EU was an important aspect of sustaining this trade providing free access to a large market, with EU regulations providing for strict controls on numbers of fish and crustacea caught, although this did not extend to in-shore fishing. The MFA has supported the introduction of some limits for conservation, but most of the fishermen would prefer open slather.

The fishing industry in Mull is not without significant issues. Apart from the facilities provided for ferries, there are no permanent non-tidal piers. This is because local harbours mainly cater for tour operators and recreational fisherman. The industry is also under threat from plans to designate the waters around Mull as *Highly Protected Marine Areas ("HPMA")*.

HPMA status potentially involves the banning of both commercial and recreational fishing, collection of shell fish, kelp farming, renewable energy developments and the introduction of new piers. Not surprisingly, the MFA has been making strenuous representations to preserve the local industry from blanket bans on fishing activity.[9]

Tobermory Harbour Association ("THA")

Public harbours in the UK operate under the *1964 Harbours Act*, which is administered in Scotland by the Scottish Government. The THA was founded as a community organisation in 1983 to own, manage and maintain the harbour facilities within Tobermory Bay. It is a community company limited by guarantee and operates on a not-for-profit basis. In 2017, it was granted Statutory Harbour Authority status through a Harbour Empowerment Order under the Harbours Act.

THA is governed by a small Board and an Executive Committee. The Board is responsible for strategic planning, policy, and managerial oversight, and ensures compliance under the Port Marine Safety Code. The Executive Committee is responsible for oversight of operational activity and routinely briefs its members through notices on the tides, the weather, current works on infrastructure, changes to regulations, and local on-water and in-water activities such as diving.

ENDNOTES

1   Information on land ownership comes from the Scottish Government agency Registers of Scotland, data on the Web Site "whoownsscotland.org.uk", and local intelligence including material published by MICT.

2   Argyll and Bute Council covers the historic counties of Argyll (County town Inverary) and Isle of Bute (County town Rothesay), and the southern Hebrides.

3   The Cairngorm Connect project is a partnership of neighbouring land managers committed to a 200 year vision of establishing corridors of orginal habitat on a landscape scale in the Cairngorm National Park.

4   Baliscate was an early settlement predating Tobermory.

5   "Sgriob-ruadh" is Gaelic for red path.

6   Some of the material in this section is drawn from an article in an edition of The Scotsman published on 19 June 2011.

7   The Hebridean is a breed of small black sheep, sometimes known as the St Kilda. The now rare breed are particularly effective at scrub control, have a strong preference for grazing on bracken and heather, and are especially adept at living on wet ground.

8   The Soil Association is a UK charity. Founded in 1946, it has over 27,000 members, and its activities include the certification of organic food production, and campaigning to oppose intensive farming.

9   The Scottish government has the ability to designate waters as "highly protected" under the Marine (Scotland) Act 2010.

DÙTHCHAS
LANDSCAPE AND COMMUNITY IN MULL AND IONA

INFRASTRUCTURE & SERVICES

A significant challenge for remote locations is to retain a critical mass of population. This requires infrastructure and services sufficient to enable a healthy and enjoyable life regardless of age.

Transport

For much of Mull's history, people have moved around the island by foot and by horse, and some of the ancient pathways are still evident. Eventually, many tracks were improved sufficiently to allow the passage of wagons, traps, and even carriages for the privileged few. However, from the very early days, the quickest way to get around was by boat, and Mull's history is full of stories relating to passage by sea. Nowadays, travel by smaller boats still forms an important part of transport around the island, while access from the mainland is dominated by ferries crossing the Sound of Mull.

Travelling Across the Island

The construction of sealed roads in Mull started in the 19th century. Initially, these mostly consisted of parallel concrete lanes, a few of which are still evident in the more remote parts of the island. Eventually, fully sealed single track roads were built, commencing within towns and villages and then extending to cover travel between communities.

In the modern era, the island has an adequate system of sealed roads, and there are sections of dual carriageway adjacent to the ferry terminal at Craignure and on the approaches to Tobermory. Outside the main towns, local people are largely content with the one way system, which includes clearly identified passing places. These are marked by poles, most of which have black and white hoops that are spaced out at 50-100 metre intervals. As a consequence, the average speed for longer journeys is around 50km per hour. This moderates the pace of life, but the locals learn to estimate their travel times accordingly.

There are no immediate plans to extend or upgrade the road network. Although some people would like the roads between Tobermory, Craignure and Fionnphort to be fully two way, there is significant local opposition to such works. Also, the terrain in the north east of the island does not easily lend itself to the widening of roads.

Maintenance of the existing road network is a never ending programme. In 2019/20 Argyll and Bute Council allocated £963,000 for road maintenance, and a further £38,250 for footpaths. Future plans, which mostly seem to reflect a need to accommodate the needs of tourists, include the following improvements.

- Strengthening main road surfaces to accommodate heavier vehicles all year round.
- Construction of more passing places, with improved, uniform and clearly worded signage.
- Construction of more substantial laybys with the ability to accommodate several vehicles at once.
- Regulation of the types of tourist vehicle allowed in some parts of the island.

To complete the picture, we should not forget Mull's dalliance with railways. The Mull and West Highland Railway opened in 1983, with a small-gauge line that ran 2 km from the ferry terminal at Craignure to Torosay Castle. The line was closed in October 2010, and the track lifted in October 2012.

Connecting with the Mainland

Communication with the outside world has for many centuries depended on travel by sea. The key bodies of water are the Sound of Mull, the Firth of Lorn, and the North Atlantic waters which flow between Ardmore Point on Mull and Kilchoan on the Ardnamurchan peninsula. In the modern era, the main system for travel from the mainland by boat involves harbours for drive-on ferries at Tobermory, Craignure, and Fishnish.

The fastest connection between Mull and the mainland is by a small ferry taking up to 23 vehicles between Fishnish and Lochaline with a "first come, first served" crossing that takes twenty minutes. Although it's a slow road on the other side of the Sound, leading down the banks of Loch Linnhe towards Fort William, it's the fast route to Edinburgh. Travelling north, there's a ferry taking up to 18 cars from Tobermory to Kilchoan on the Ardnamurchan peninsula. The crossing takes around an hour, with the road on the mainland initially single track.

The main link between Mull and the Scottish mainland is via Oban and the A85 road which goes east to connect with the A82 going north and south. Until the 1960s the car ferry service from Oban went to Tobermory. However, the main route is now between Oban and Craignure, with a journey across the Sound of Mull that takes around 45 minutes. This route has in fact been in existence for 150 years, commencing with a mail service following completion of the train line from Glasgow to Oban in July 1880.

There has been a pier at Craignure since 1894 which was originally on the south side of the bay. However, a pier on the west side of the bay was opened in 1964 with a project financed by the Council and a significant contribution from a businessman named Cameron Sunderland who owned a shop at Craignure and clearly saw the benefit of the passing traffic! Originally, the project included a two way road from Craignure to Tobermory, but only part of the route was completed because of local concerns about the environmental impact, not to mention the cost. Unfortunately, the current location of the terminal's slip way is far from ideal. Northerly winds blowing down the Sound hit the boats side on, and the service is therefore prone to suspension particularly in winter. Sixty years after its original construction, the current pier is now in need of significant refurbishment.

The main operator of ferries in Scotland is a company called CalMac Ferries Ltd ("CalMac") and it is easy to take this organisation for granted as it operates services in most weathers throughout the year. The company was founded in 1851 by the Hutcheson brothers to provide a steamer service from Glasgow to Oban and Fort William and then on through the Caledonian Canal to Inverness. In the late 1870's ownership was passed to David MacBrayne, and he developed the business, with mail boats from Skye to Islay, Harris and North Uist, and an Outer Isles service from Oban to Barra and South Uist. As new railways began to reach the West Coast - at Fort William, Kyle of Lochalsh and Mallaig, new ships and operations were added to the schedule including services to Mull. Following the First World War, MacBrayne's operations went into decline and eventually the mail service was taken over by the London Midland Scotland ("LMS") Railway Company with the ferry operation managed by a new company named David MacBrayne Ltd.

In 1948 LMS was nationalised and, in 1953, the state owned Scottish Transport Group was formed to operate not only MacBrayne's services but also other services including ships on the Clyde and buses. Soon after, the shipping companies were amalgamated and renamed Caledonian MacBrayne Ltd. This company eventually adopted the red lion in the yellow disc in the centre of the red funnel which can be seen today, and the roll-on roll-off ferries were introduced in the 1960s.

In 1990, Caledonian MacBrayne Ltd became wholly owned by the Secretary of State for Scotland and, from 1999, this responsibility transferred to the Scottish government. In 2006, they decided to split the company, with, Caledonian Maritime Assets Ltd (CMAL) now owning the ports and ferries, and CalMac Ferries Ltd (CalMac) operating the ferry service.

As a government entity, CalMac operates with significant community-based policies and, since 2015, the cost of carriage has been heavily subsidised under the Road Equivalent Tariff ("RET") system. This links ferry fares for residents and tourists to the cost of travelling an equivalent distance on land for passengers and vehicles, with a subsidy that is equivalent to around 50% of the actual operating cost. CalMac also have enlightened policies towards not-for-profit organisations such as stock carriers, charging them only for journeys when they are carrying animals, with back journeys free of charge.

Despite some frustrations in recent times, with a failure to replace aging ferries in a timely manner, and a poorly executed upgrade of the booking system, the importance of this great public service is greatly appreciated by most local people and there is a lovely ditty that reflects their position in the spirit of the isles which goes as follows.

"The Earth belongs unto the Lord
And all that it contains
Except the Kyles and the Western Isles
And they are all MacBrayne's"

Finally, although a commercial air service is not viable, the island does provide the capacity to travel by plane, with an airfield run by Argyll and Bute Council located at Glenforsa.[1]

Mull & Iona Ferry Committee ("MIFC")

Every major island in the Hebrides has a ferry committee and, as it says on their Web Site *"the Mull & Iona Ferry Committee is there to represent users and ensure that your voice is heard"*. On the face of it, this might seem a relatively straightforward matter. However, it's actually quite complicated because there are several agencies involved in providing the service. While CalMac runs the ferry service and CMAL owns the ships and most of the on-shore facilities, Argyll and Bute Council owns and maintain the piers at Craignure, Fionnphort and Iona. So, the MIFC has to liaise with a number of organisations as well as local Councillors and Scottish Parliament MSPs.

The MIFC includes representatives of many of the community groups identified in this book. The team is never short of business, including advocacy for the upgrade of the Craignure pier, and the replacement of the main and ageing ferry the MV Isle of Mull. However, the whole future of how to deliver the ferry service is also the subject of strategic debate. Future options have been considered in a review undertaken by Pedersen Consulting, and the government is also reviewing the options for future delivery of the service in what is called Project Neptune.

At an operational level, the MIFC:

- Provides information on the status of various ferry services,
- Advocates for resident-sensitive operating policies, such as the adoption of a medical protocol to assist residents in gaining priority for transit to attend medical consultations on the mainland,
- Considers ways of educating tourists about how to use roads and other services on the island,
- Assesses the potential impact of proposals such as the installation of barrages in the Sound of Iona,
- Provides community responses to CalMac proposals for changes in regulations,
- Fields complaints from the public, with advice on how to pursue individual cases with the various authorities.

Energy

For most of its history Mull has survived without electricity. On the mainland, the first homes to be connected to a public electricity supply were in Glasgow in around 1880, with such connections extended more widely after World War One when the first hydro-electric scheme in Lanarkshire was completed. The first move to provide a regular electricity supply to the Highlands and Islands was instigated in the *Hydro-Electric Development (Scotland) Act 1943*, and the first glimmer of an electric light bulb in Mull appeared during World War Two when an underwater cable from the mainland was installed to enable military activity.

In the modern era, the underwater cable from the mainland is still the main source of power in Mull, with Iona connected by a cable across the Sound of Iona. The system is managed by the Scottish and South Eastern Electricity

Network. However, with global warming, and the need to reduce our carbon footprint, there are now numerous renewable energy projects many of which have been initiated by community organisations. They include hydro-electric schemes, and systems involving solar panels and batteries, wind, and geothermal technology. The potential for wave power is also under review.

Housing

Housing in Mull represents a major challenge. At its peak in the 17th century the population reached at least 10,000. At that time, whilst some of the gentry lived in substantial mansions, the vast majority of people lived in single storey stone and wooden houses with straw roofs. With the clearances, most of these ordinary homes were abandoned and the ruins of houses which mostly date from the 19th century can be seen scattered across the modern landscape.

In the 21st century, the island has a housing crisis. In particular, some 30-40% of the current housing stock now consists of non-resident holiday homes and properties bought by absentee owners for let to tourists. As a consequence, the price of the houses is beyond the reach of someone on the Scottish living wage. The lack of affordable accommodation has led to both migration from the island and an inability to bring people to the island to take up local jobs.

A number of community organisations, and the owners of some of the larger estates, are endeavouring to address this issue, working with organisations like the Scottish Housing Fund who provide low interest mortgages. In particular, MICT has made significant progress in supplying affordable housing, and NWMCWC has made provision for crofting houses on their forestry properties, and for renovation of houses on Ulva. Some of the larger estates are also building houses for local rent, and there are plans to reclaim derelict properties in some parts of the island.

Finally, to increase the availability of housing stock, it is conceivable that the authorities will introduce policies such as higher rates for non-resident property owners with the potential for sale to local people. This has been done in some other parts of Britain such as Torquay, but it is easier said than done.

Education

A key element in retaining the current population in Mull is the provision of education facilities that meet young and growing families. At present, there are six Primary Schools (providing education for children between 4 and 12) which are strategically located so as to provide ease of access anywhere on the island. These are located at Bunessan (11 pupils in 2023), Dervaig (22), Lochdonhead (10), Salen (25), Tobermory (60), and Ulva (16). Notably, the facility at Salen includes a unit providing tuition in Gaelic.

The provision of secondary education is a major issue, for which there is no easy solution given current public funding constraints. For many years Mull has had its own secondary school located in Tobermory and this has served residents in the north of the island very well. Given the relatively small population, investment in a second secondary school in the south has never been an option. Consequently, with the logistics of travelling to Tobermory, it has become the practice for children from the south of the island including Iona to attend Oban High School on the mainland.

Given these constraints, the Council has established policy which provides clarity for secondary education access. Children who live to the north of Glen More, including those in the south east corner of the island, are in the catchment area for Tobermory High School which accommodates 130 students, and they receive free transport to attend. Children who live to the west and south of Glen More, are in the catchment area for Oban High School which accommodates 900 students. Funding is provided for them to travel to Oban on a daily basis, or to stay in Oban for the whole week with accommodation at the Glencruitten Hostel. This facility accommodates 80 students in single, double or triple bedrooms, has study and games rooms, and is a short walk from the school.

The consequences of this education policy are significant for people in all parts of the island, with the potential for disruption to family life. In particular, for some families living in the south they may not wish to send their children away and may feel the need to move north or leave the island altogether. The same thinking may deter people from applying for work in the south, which has the potential to lead to a labour shortage in that part of the island. On the other hand, some parents may actually welcome the travel of teenage children to Oban because it helps them to become independent. Also, with a much bigger catchment population, Oban High School is able to offer a wider curriculum.

The division in the secondary education system potentially also has wider consequences, impacting on the unity of the island. Children from the south develop a view of the world in which Oban is the centre of their economic and social world. They tend not to go to the north of the island at all, except for a few "all of island" events, and the habits of tripping over to the mainland becomes an entrenched way of life which undermines the viability of businesses in the north.

In recent times, all these issues have come to a head. Tobermory High School is bursting at the seams and the facilities are in need of a serious upgrade. The current site does not lend itself to expansion, and there are at least two options for meeting future requirements. A new school could be built in or around Tobermory which would suit a majority of islanders living in the north. However, the school could be moved to a site in the centre of the island which would address the logistical and other issues experienced by people in the south. An obvious location is the Craignure district which has relatively good connections in all directions (20 miles to Tobermory and 30 miles to Bunessan). Of course, the downside of this option is that a move of any distance from the current site in Tobermory will present a disadvantage for those people living in the north of the island.

Before the pandemic, there was talk of significant funding being available to finance a project that would assess these and other options. Subsequently, the government has been under financial pressures and has delayed a full evaluation. In the meantime, there has been lengthy speculation about the options, with Community Councils testing public opinion. The views of local parents are far from clear, with some seeing the advantage of a bigger school like Oban with a wider curriculum, while others wanting their children to be educated on the island; and many parents are uncomfortable about saying what they really think through fear of offending organisations with which they have previously been associated. This debate is far from resolution.

Finally, residents also have access to the Argyll College of the University of the Highlands and Islands ("UHI") based in Inverness. UHI provides a very wide range of courses from degrees through trade certificates, available on site or on-line.

Kinder and Day Care

There is an extensive system in Mull of Day Care for parents on a routine and emergency basis.

Health and Welfare

Mull has three primary care clinics in Tobermory, Salen and Bunessan. There is a pharmacy in Tobermory, but the clinics carry certain common types of medication for dispensing with a script. There is a dental practice in Tobermory.

There is a 24 hour Accident and Emergency hospital at Craignure, to deal with bone and eye injuries, paediatric issues, and tele-medicine (including X Rays). However, the island does not have surgical facilities, an optician, or (since 5 years ago) a mid-wife. The latter is a significant omission with pregnant women having to go to the mainland for the birth of their children. Usually this involves a stay with family or friends before having their baby at the Lorn & Islands General Hospital in Oban.

Mull is fortunate to have a Council run facility called Bowman Court which accommodates the aged and people with special needs.

Emergency Services

Mull is served by four police stations, at Tobermory, Salen, Craignure and Bunessan and there is a fire station at Salen. The RNLI operate a lifeboat out of Tobermory, from a station established in 1937. For ten years, it operated with notable success but, after the war, the service struggled to find the staff to maintain the service and operations were suspended. However, in 1990 it was re-opened, and in 2000 a new alongside berth was completed. In 2003, with funds from a bequest, the service acquired a new all-weather Severn Class lifeboat which serves to this day. The station responds to calls for assistance from up to 150 km away.

Mull Community Council

Many of the key services on which Mull relies are provided by Argyll and Bute Council (A&BC). This body, which is a unitary authority based in Lochgilphead, was established following the reorganisation of local government under *The Local Government etc (Scotland) Act 1994*. In return for payment of rates, residents receive significant services. These include planning, public secondary and primary school education, social welfare, waste management, road maintenance, maintenance of Craignure Pier and local management of the Scottish government subsidy of the ferry service, street lighting, provision of sports and leisure facilities, and licensing. In providing these services, the Council is obliged to consult with the network of community councils, including the Mull Community Council and the Iona Community Council (the activities of which are covered in Chapter 24). In Mull, there are also Council-maintained and community-managed halls in Craignure, Dervaig, Fionnphort, Pennyghael and Tobermory (Aros Hall).

Community Councils were established in Scotland following the *Local Government (Scotland) Act 1973*. Their purpose is to provide a voice for local people to local government and other public bodies as applicable. They have a statutory right to be consulted on planning applications, and a responsibility to demonstrate that the views they express are representative of the community. They are also required to brief the community about their deliberations, and encourage public participation.

Mull Community Council ("MCC") has been in existence since the 1970s. Membership comprises a group of up to 12 Councillors who are elected by public vote for four-year terms in a process that is managed by the A&BC. MCC Officers are elected at the AGM. MCC also has the ability to co-opt up to a further three members to provide expertise in fields relevant to the community's activities and services. Monthly meetings held at the An Roth building in Craignure are open to the public and are usually attended by several local A&BC Councillors and representatives of other community organisations. Although the organisation endeavours to draw representation from all parts of Mull, it sometimes struggles to find people from the southern part of the island and this deficiency is met in part by enabling participation by internet and by maintaining regular contact with the separately constituted Iona Community Council. MCC receives an annual grant from the A&BC to cover administrative expenses. It also applies for and receives grants for specific local projects and derives income from local fund-raising events to support a range of community activities and services.

MCC has no shortage of business and, at the time of publishing this book, the following were amongst the issues of significance for local people.

- Provision of secondary school education.
- Issues relating to the ferry service, including matters raised by the Mull & Iona Ferry Committee.
- Government plans to designate waters around Scotland as Highly Protected Marine Areas.
- Delivery of health and welfare services, including the management of the Bowman Court sheltered accommodation facility for the aged and "in-need".
- Reports from the police on recent crime and incidents, and plans for management of public events.
- The inadequate mail service arising from the privatisation of the Royal Mail, with insufficient funding to recruit staff and maintain delivery vehicles.
- Replacement of the Recycling Plant which has reached capacity limits.
- The possibility of charging higher rates or a tourist tax for properties that are used as holiday homes and/or tourist lets.
- Road safety measures, including speed limits.
- Stocking of local produce in local shops.

CONCLUSION

Finally, it is evident from the many conversations undertaken with local people in the course of field research that the provision of public services in Mull tends to suffer from what one might call "silo" thinking. And there is a need for an integrated approach to providing appropriate and sufficient social infrastructure for housing, education, health, transport and other services. Suffice it so say, given the multiplicity of levels of government and agencies providing these services, this is easier said than done. The problem is symptomatic of life in a remote location and hopefully this will be addressed under the impending Highlands and Islands Plan.

ENDNOTES

1   Built to complement the hospital in Salen, Glenforsa Airfield began life as Mull's only fixed-wing air ambulance evacuation facility. It is currently owned by Argyll and Bute Council, and managed by the Glenforsa Hotel.

CULTURE, SPORTS & TOURISM

The history of Mull reflects a rich diversity of language and culture. In modern times, the island has also attracted a great of range of people whose artistic endeavours provide for a vibrant creative society.

Language

Over the last 2,000 years the language used by local people in Mull has been through several phases. In the Middle Ages, while the dominant language across most of the mainland was Pictish, in the Hebrides Scots Gaelic became the main language, deriving from Irish settlers. When Pictish was replaced by Gaelic on the mainland, some in Mull were speaking Norse. However Gaelic eventually prevailed and, as late as 1500, the royal court was still speaking that language. Gaelic continued to be the main language amongst ordinary folk in Mull until the early 17th century when King James VI promoted the use of Scots English; and, by the middle of the 18th century, Gaelic was regarded by many in government as a primitive tongue spoken by backward people.

In 21st century Mull, with so many migrants, most local people in Mull now speak either English or Standard Scottish English ("SSE"). SSE consists of a distinctive vocabulary with many words drawn from Gaelic and Norse and expressions that derive from distinctive Scottish institutions. Typically the locals switch between the two depending on the circumstances. However, there are still many Gaelic speakers on the island.

Interestingly, the accent you will hear in Mull is softer to the ear than is found in places like Glasgow. This is because, going back a hundred years and more, many people in Mull spoke Gaelic at home and learnt their English at school from migrant teachers who were not acquainted with the local vernacular. This difference in accent is very evident across Scotland, with a significant Gaelic speaking diaspora living in Scottish cities.

Religion

Life in Mull and Iona continues to harbour a strong spiritual quality through the presence and activities of the Church of Scotland, other Christian denominations, and several other faiths. There is also the inter-denominational Iona Community about which there is more information in Chapter 24. The islands are endowed with a rich heritage of active, repurposed and derelict religious buildings.

Church of Scotland

The Church of Scotland continues to be a pillar of Scottish society with well-established institutions in all corners of the country. At the parish level, the church comprises a minister (elected by the congregation), local elders, members, and others attending worship. As well as administering to the spiritual needs of the community, ministers and elders take it in turn to attend meetings of the General Assembly which operates as "the sovereign and highest court" of the church and is chaired by a non-executive Moderator. The General Assembly administers the church, determines doctrine, and organises missionary activity. Although there is no hierarchy, longer serving and more experienced members are appointed as "elders". Notably, while the monarch swears an oath to secure the Protestant Religion, they are not a member of the body but appoint a non-voting High Commissioner to attend General Assembly meetings.1 A notable past holder of that position was the 27th Chief of the Clan Maclean, Lord Charles Maclean.

Previously part of the Presbytery of Argyll, from January 2024 the local Church of Scotland community became part of the newly created Clèir Eilean Ì Highlands and Hebrides Presbytery.[2] Within the local Presbytery, there has also been some recent consolidation with the creation of two "charges". Iona and the Ross of Mull (including Pennyghael) now operate as one parish (Kilfinichen and Kilvickeon have now been dropped from the name), while the rest of Mull is a single congregation named North Mull, comprising what were previously four parishes with four buildings as follows.

- Tobermory
- Salen and Ulva
- Kilninian & Kilmore (Torloisk and Dervaig)
- Torosay and Kinlochspelve (Craignure)

Although regular attendance at services has declined in recent times, the church in Mull currently has around 200 registered members, and is active in encouraging others to join the fold. At the time of writing, there are significant changes in the leadership and organisation of the local church. In 2023 the Minister for the two southern parishes, the Rev Jenny Earl, retired and in mid-2024 the Parish Minister for North Mull, Rev Liz Gibson will also retire. Liz came to the island in 2013, not expecting to continue as a parish minister, but took up the role following the sad death of the Rev Johnny Paton. In late 2024, she and her husband Martyn will resume life on their croft, growing organically certified produce. In future, all of Mull and Iona will share one minister.

Other Christian Denominations and Faiths

Although the Church of Scotland is the main Christian church in Mull and Iona, other denominations do have an active presence and are permitted to have use of Presbyterian churches for services. The Scottish Episcopal Church has its own places of worship at Gruline (St Columba Church), and at Lochbuie (St Kilda Church) which is owned by the Lochbuie Estate. Roman Catholics have a church in Tobermory (Our Lady Star of the Sea) and a "House of Prayer" on Iona and also make use of the Church of Scotland facility in Craignure. There is a Free Church in Tobermory which is still active, and local Quakers meet regularly online and at various venues around the island. Another part of the local Christian community is an organisation called the Door Trust (An Dorus). This is based in Salen and operates as a Christian Resource Centre providing opportunities for worship, discussion and fellowship. It has a library, accommodation for those who wish to study on site, and meeting rooms.

From time to time, other faiths have surfaced including an assembly for members of the Bahá'i community.

The Arts

If you visited Mull fifty years ago, cultural activity was largely limited to traditional musical gatherings, a small number of individual artists and craftsmen working in isolation, and occasional displays in galleries. In the 21st century, the blossoming of organisations and events involving music, theatre, writing, arts, and crafts is quite extraordinary for such a small community. The following gives a taste of what the community has to offer, enriching the local community as well as attracting visitors from other parts of Scotland, the UK and overseas. The Mull and Iona Arts and Crafts Trail identifies more than eighty individuals and groups who are active in ceramics, drawing, film-making, glassware, jewellery, literature, painting, photography, podcasts, poetry, pottery, printing, sculpture, and textiles. There are also a range of live performers.

An Tobar and Mull Theatre

Mull is fortunate in having an organisation called An Tobar and Mull Theatre the aim of which is to foster the promotion, provision, appreciation and understanding of the arts.3 Formed in 2013, this is a not-for-profit charitable organisation with around 10 staff led by Chief Executive and Artistic Director Rebecca Atkinson-Lord. The organisation receives a multi-year grant from Creative Scotland, with the level of funding geared to a plan submitted by the organisation.4 Access to the live venues are partly financed by ticket sales.

An Tobar in Argyll Terrace Tobermory was originally the island school but, with the reorganisation of education in the 20th century, the Council-owned property fell derelict. In the 1990s, an American author named Mary Norton Scherbatskoy visited Mull. She was taken with the island and engaged with the arts community to raise funds to finance the repurposing of the derelict school into an Arts Centre. There was significant public subscription, with the balance of funds required for building works coming from various public grants. The facility was opened in 1997, with occupation subject to a pepper-corn rent.

An Tobar operates as a music venue and has galleries for the display of paintings, ceramics, knitting and other arts and crafts. There are around 50 annual events including gigs, shows and exhibitions. The music venue has a stage with seating for up to 60, and hosts performances by bands and musicians across a range of genres bringing an eclectic programme of exceptional music to Mull. The art gallery aims to present exhibitions that reflect the diversity of the community and visitors, showing a wide range of visual art and craft disciplines. It hosts three or four curated exhibitions each year selected from a broad spectrum, including internationally recognised artists to emerging artists starting their careers with their first solo exhibition. Works exhibited have ranged from highly technical installations such as Graham Fagen's *The Slave's Lament*, or Yulia Kovanova's *Colony* exhibition, to the intricate silver sculptures in Lucy Woodley's *Ultima Thule* or the exuberance of the wall hangings in Eve Campbell's *Vestige*. The An Tobar facility has a café and a bar, with a balcony overlooking the harbour.

Mull Theatre started life as Mull Little Theatre in Dervaig in 1963, and is currently located in a production centre at Druimfin to the south-east of Tobermory which was opened in 2008. It commissions, supports, develops, produces and presents theatre and performance of all kinds including plays, musicals, dance, opera, circus, contemporary performance and comedy. It produces theatre in-house and tours it nationally and internationally, with an emphasis on small scale touring to remote highlands and islands communities, and acts as a key receiving house for national and international touring companies. It also conducts residencies for creating new works, and is home to Mull Youth Theatre which runs an extensive outreach programme in schools.

Although active throughout the year, most of the live acts at An Tobar and Mull Theatre are organised to take place in the tourist season. In the other months, the main focus is art shows in the galleries.

Arts and Crafts Galleries

In Mull, there are a range of retail outlets and facilities where the public can access the results of local artistic endeavour. Apart from craft shops in Tobermory, of particular note are the Calgary Arts Centre with its nature walk, the South West Mull Makers Art and Craft Centre in Fionnphort, Oran Creative Crafts on Iona, The Old Byre Heritage Centre and the Willow Workshops in Dervaig, Lip na Cloiche Crafts at the gardens and nursery in Ulva Ferry, Islands Castaways run by MICT in Tobermory, Aosdana jewellery on Iona, and the Knockvologan residency and study hub for art, literature, field research, and nature preservation in Fionnphort.

Festivals

The **Mull and Iona Mod** (called Mòd Ionadach na Dreòlluinn) was established in 1938 and is a celebration of Gaelic culture.5 Held in Tobermory in September, it encourages the use and development of the Gaelic language and music through solo, choral, oral and instrumental competitions. The **Tobermory Book Festival** is held in October at An Tobar and other locations over three days, with authors talking about their latest works all of which have Highlands and Islands themes. Inspired by the composer's love of the Hebrides, the **Mendelssohn in Mull Festival** of chamber music is held in September. It involves free concerts and workshops held at a wide variety of venues in Mull and Iona including Duart Castle, Creich Church near Fionnphort, and Iona Abbey. In particular it brings together young musicians who are mentored by more experienced players. The free **Mull Music Festival and Fiddle Week** takes place over a weekend in April and features folk groups, Scottish dance bands, traditional musicians and singers. The separate **Mull Fiddle Week** in August is a festival for young people aged from 5 to 25, making music in creative sessions for all playing levels. The **Eats Fest** is held in Tobermory in mid-summer and is an opportunity to taste a range of local produce.

Tourism

A major industry on Mull is tourism. In recent years, whilst interrupted by the pandemic, the number of visitors to the island has grown enormously bringing significant income to the economy and providing access for people from all over the world to an outstanding landscape, a wide range of flora and fauna, the offerings of a vibrant artistic community, and the delights of local food. Given the climate, the high season is relatively short from late spring to early autumn. However, with over 200,000 visitors annually, at its peak the population of the island grows to over 10,000 with traffic on the roads at bursting point. This seasonal influx of visitors does not come without some problems. "Wild camping" on non-designated sites, with accumulation of rubbish and wild roaming of dogs which worry livestock, is not welcome but does occur. Also, the roads are unsuitable for some tourist vehicles, with the behaviour of some visitors sometimes inconsiderate. However, in the main these issues are born without rancour by the locals.

The number of tourist operators on Mull are too numerous to provide a comprehensive account in this book. This includes the operators of local hotels, the arts and craft galleries mentioned earlier in this chapter, boat trips to neighbouring islands, and a very wide range of nature-related organisations which enable lovers of flora and fauna to obtain responsible access to nature. The island also provides the ability for visitors to let houses and cottages, and bring camper vans which tour the island in large number during the summer months.

The endeavours of one family, the Morrisons, provide an insight into the development of tourism. The matriarch of the family, Mary MacRae was born in Skye in 1911. During the Clearances in the 19th century, her grandparents and her then nine-year old father had been evicted from a croft at Suisnish in the south of Skye, and the memory of those difficult times are part of the family's heritage. As a young adult the Gaelic-speaking Mary trained as a teacher and, in 1933, she took up a job in Mull where she met her husband Colin Morrison who was a local tenant crofter whose family had lived on Mull for a good many generation. They set up home at the family's croft at Penmore Mill near Dervaig and in 1947 Iain was born.

After completing his education, Iain Morrison joined the merchant navy and, for more than ten years, he was a deck officer travelling all over the world. However, in the early 1970s he settled back into civilian life in Mull, and met his wife-to-be Patricia at a dance in Craignure. It was love at first sight, and they were soon married. Before long they were raising a family and, with tourism beginning to develop and Iain on extended leave, in 1973 they established a company originally called Croig Cruises, (a name which they changed to Turus Mara in 1982), operating wildlife tourist boat trips to Staffa, the Treshnish Islands, and Iona.6 Returning permanently from the sea in 1976, for Iain this was not only a career that made use of his maritime skills, but also enabled him to share with visitors the wonders of the outer islands which he had explored and enjoyed as a boy.

Turus Mara now operates two boats out of Ulva Ferry, *Hoy Lass* and *Island Lass* and, as mentioned earlier in this book, the company's tours are famed for their "Puffin Therapy". The daily trips to the Treshnish islands are a way of life for the Morrison family, operating in fair weather and foul, with Iain's son Colin now also a member of the team. After graduating from Strathclyde University where he studied history under Professor Sir Tom Devine, Colin initially joined the business as a crew member and eventually became a skipper in 1998. In 2009, the business expanded with the opening of a "top notch" restaurant named the *Am Birlinn* which is housed in a contemporary wooden building with soaring windows reminiscent of the nautical name, and internal décor that includes a taste of local art and crafts.[7] The company also offers cottages for holiday lets.

Through their endeavours, the Morrisons provide employment for several local people including their newly appointed skipper Fergus Reade, the grandson of Chris Reade whose story appears in Chapter 21. Also, as mentioned in other chapters, Colin Morrison has been a leader in community activism through his work with the NWMCWC and his role with the local branch of the SNP. The Morrisons reflect all that is best in Mull society.

Sports Activity

Mull has a number of sports facilities including swimming pools, golf courses, and several sports grounds. The annual calendar includes events which bring people together from all parts of the island and from further afield. Amongst the most important are the following.

The Mull Highland Games

The earliest references to athletic contests in Scotland come from the 11th century with events used for selection of King James IV's bodyguards. Subsequently, competitions involving music, dance and athletics have been a persistent feature of Scottish life. The move to establish a "Games" began in the late 18th century with the establishment of Highland Societies committed to reviving certain aspects of Scottish culture that had been suppressed following the Jacobite rebellions. In 1821, the St Fillan's Highland Society sponsored a full-scale games with athletics, dancing and piping.[8] This led to similar events throughout the country, and a full blown Games came to Mull in 1923 with the Chief of the Clan Maclean of Duart as its patron.

In current times, the Mull Highland Games is held in July in Tobermory. It is run by volunteers and consists of a number of programmes as follows:

- Athletic events including open and local races over a mile, half mile, 440 yards, 220 yards, and 100 yards. There are also High Leap, Long Leap, and Hop Step & Jump competitions and a cross country race.
- An Art Competition for adults and children.
- Dancing competitions, including the Sword Dance (Gille Chaluim), Highland Fling, Old Trousers (Seann Triubhas), and various Reels, Jigs and Hornpipes.
- Competition in several styles of piping.
- Traditional heavy events, including tossing the caber, hammer throw, shot put, and tossing "over the bar".

The Games begins with the assembly of a pipe band in Tobermory Main Street, and a march around the town and up to Erray Park which is located to the west of the town at the Tobermory Golf Club.

Mull Car Rally

The Mull Car Rally was the brain-child of an Englishman named Brian Molyneux who was chairman of the Mullard Car and Cycle Club in Lancashire.[9] In 1969, he convinced local enthusiasts to embrace the idea of an overnight event. This had 57 participants and centred on the A848 between Tobermory and Craignure. Subsequently, the route was extended to include stages through forestry in Dervaig, Fishnish and Lettermore and, eventually, it became a "whole of island" event, over two days starting on a Friday night. In 1990, the Rally became a closed road event which was the first of its kind in the UK.[10] However, this would eventually come back to bite the organisers with insurance concerns that resulted in a hiatus in 2017 and 2018 while new *Closed Road Motor Sports* legislation was enacted. In the meantime, a modified form of the Rally was held off the main roads using private land and forest tracks.

Since 2010, the event has been run by the Mull Car Club, and is scheduled for October well after the tourist season. Given the disruption to normal traffic, the Club undertakes extensive consultation with the community on the timing of road closures.

Rugby Sevens

Apparently, the first game of rugby was played on the public park in Tobermory on 30 July 1978 in a match between locals and a team from a visiting Royal Navy frigate. Thanks to the noble efforts of one John Rutherford, the home team won.[11] The Mull Rugby Club was established shortly thereafter on 5 September. In those days, Mull had no public sports facilities, and games were played on the fields of local farms and on the air strip at Glenforsa. Rugby became popular because it was played by local boys attending secondary schools on the mainland, and this extended to girls in 1992.

Eventually the Mull Rugby Club launched a fund-raising campaign to establish local facilities and acquired land at Garmony. This proved to be very successful with sufficient funds to finance the construction of Club Rooms, changing rooms, two pitches and a car park. Subsequently, lights were established for training and, in 2011, a new Club house was completed which has recently been refurbished by Banjo Beale. This facility is available for all sports and has been used for football, athletics, hockey, school sports, and shinty.

A key driver in developing the Rugby facilities has been local interest in Rugby Sevens. A local competition was first organised in 1985, and was the first in the world to include females. It has been played every year since (apart from cancellation in 2023 due to ferry issues) and is a major event over a weekend in May attracting teams from all over Scotland including other island communities and the major universities. It is known as the World's Most Sociable Sevens.

On Water Activity

In 2009, the Oban Yacht Club decided to establish a **Round Mull Yacht Race**, and this has been held annually ever since. In recent times it has scheduled for late June or early July over a three-day weekend, with sections between Oban, Tobermory, Bunessan and Oban. It attracts entries from all over Scotland and further afield. The competition comprises a number of classes, the Bank of Scotland Trophy for best overall points in amalgamated classes, and a trophy for the fastest circumnavigation of Torran Rock.

In August each year, the RNLI runs a fund-raising **RNLI Lifeboat Day** with events in Tobermory and Fionnphort. Meanwhile, in the Ross of Mull there is an annual event called **The Uisken Games.** This is held in August on Uisken Beach (near Bunessan) and encompasses a raft race and beach games.

Tobermory Horticultural Society

The Tobermory Horticultural Society was founded in 1890. The annual Show is held at Aros Hall and includes competition for flowers, vegetables and baking.

Environmental Conservation and Research

Scotland is fortunate in being home to some of the more pristine environments in the British Isles, and is the subject of significant conservation and research programmes

The Hebridean Whale and Dolphin Trust ("HWDT")

The HWDT is a marine conservation charity that takes action through a range of community based research and education programmes. The organisation regards itself as a change agent, conducting research that underpins the future safeguarding of whales, dolphins and porpoises. Its work includes the training of volunteers to become citizen scientists who participate in marine sighting networks. It also provides educational experiences in the dedicated Discovery Centre in Main Street Tobermory, on the organisation's boat *Silurian*, and by visiting schools around the whole of the Hebrides to educate young people about their marine heritage.

Mull Otter Group

One of the delights of visiting Mull, if you know where to look along the 300 km of coastal habitat, is the observation of Eurasian Otters which are classified as a vulnerable species. The Mull Otter Group is a registered charity with the notable wild life photographer James Buchanan as its Patron. The organisation aims to educate the public about the conservation needs of otters, and is responsible for the following activities:

- Research into the biology and ecology of the species, including otter mortality.
- Education of local residents and visitors about responsible otter watching.
- Implementation of road and other safety measures to limit mortality arising for otter movements.
- Operation of an otter rescue service, including the management of a rehabilitation programme in liaison with SSPCA and IOSF.

On-Line Community

Mull has a very active Facebook Page that provides a host of useful information about day to day life on Mull. There are a range of specialist offshoots covering various special interest groups.

ENDNOTES

1   There is a provision for this in the 1707 Act of Union.
2   Clèir Eilean Ì represents over 100 churches across 40% of Scotland's landmass.
3   An Tobar is Gaelic for the well, to reflect its role as a source of creativity.
4   Creative Scotland allocates funds to more than 100 organisations, with Regularly Funded Organisations receiving grants every five years.
5   Mod is a Gaelic word for meeting. An Ionadach means local, and Dreòlluinn is a name for Mull.
6   In Gaelic, Turus Mara means a "journey by sea".
7   Am Birlinn comes from the Norse for "long boat" which is reflected in the architecture of the restaurant.
8   St Fillan was an Irish monk who migrated in the 8th century and whose relics were cherished by Robert the Bruce as contributing to the Scottish victory at te Battle of Bannockburn in 1314.
9   Brian Molyneux died in 1996.
10 The Closed Road event require an Act of Parliament which was the subject of a Bill in 1988 and was passed in 1990.
11 John Rutherford, known as Rud or Ruddie, was born in Selkirk in 1955 and became a highly decorated member of the Scottish Rugby team playing at Fly Half and winning 42 Caps. He was a founding member of the Mull Rugby Club.

IONA COMMUNITIES

For such a small island, raising its modest head above the eastern reaches of the North Atlantic Ocean, Iona is a very special place with a history of spiritual community spanning nearly 1,500 years. In the modern era, the island is in the care of the National Trust for Scotland, and the Abbey church and related buildings are owned by the Iona Cathedral Trust and managed by Historic Environment Scotland with an admission fee for public access.[1]

Heritage

While it is generally accepted that Christianity was first brought to Scotland by St Ninian in the late 4th century, Iona can reasonably claim to be the cradle of Christianity in Scotland, and the life and times of St Columba provide a spiritual legacy for both Iona and Mull. According to legend, St Columba was born into a noble family in County Donegal in Ireland in CE 521. He was educated by monks at the Movilla monastery and, as a young adult, he continued his studies under a bard named Gemman, before joining a monastic order at Clonard Abbey.[2] At Clonard, he studied under a sage named Finnian who was a follower of St David, and eventually he became a monk and then an ordained priest. As an adherent of Celtic Christianity, St Columba proceeded to found a number of monasteries in Ireland before setting out on a pilgrimage to Jerusalem.[3] This was cut short in France and he returned to Derry.

There is some disagreement about the next part of St Columba's life. However, it is said that he was involved in a dispute between the local clergy and clan leaders in Derry that led to the death of several people. Although he was eventually absolved of any blame, in the aftermath he moved to another part of what had become the Gaelic kingdom of Dál Riata. In CE 563, he travelled with twelve supporters to settle on Iona which King Conall mac Comgill had offered him as a base.

In the next few years, St Columba established a place of study and learning. Apparently, he was a tall and well-built man, who spoke with some authority about his beliefs. In time, he became respected as a local mediator between warring factions both within Dál Riata and beyond; he was also capable of holding his own in battle and is said to have gained the upper hand in a skirmish with King Brude of the Picts who was eventually converted to Christianity. St Columba is said to have provided prophecies and performed a number of miracles, including one in which he vanquished a great beast to the depths of the River Ness after it had killed a local Pict![4]

As the years unfolded, St Columba turned his monastery at Iona into a school for missionaries, with the main focus being the conversion of the Pictish tribes on the mainland of Scotland. He also founded several churches around the Hebrides. Noted as a scholar, he wrote a number of books and hymns, and Iona became a centre of learning for all of Dál Riata. According to tradition, he died and was buried in the Abbey on 9 June CE 597. His benediction is not documented, but he has been generally acknowledged as a saint since the early Middle Ages.

Following St Columba's death, the religious institution which he founded flourished for many years, acting as a centre of faith, learning, healing and hospitality and a place of pilgrimage. Iona also became a burial place for the first and several subsequent kings of Scotland. Indeed, the cemetery is reputed to hold the bones of 48 Scottish, eight Norwegian and four Irish kings.[5] However, with its international reputation as a repository of antiquities, in the 8th century the island was the subject of incursions by the Vikings who repeatedly sacked the community. Consequently, in CE 849 the St Columba's remains were removed, with some parts sent to

Downpatrick in Northern Ireland and the remainder sent to Dunkeld. The surviving monks retreated back to Ireland.[6] Nothing remains of the mostly wooden original buildings apart from earth works. However at least one building in stone remains from the 9th century.

Like the rest of the Western Isles, in the late 9th century Iona became part of the Norse Kingdom of the Isles. In the mid-12th century, Somerled launched a revolt in which he established control over the southern Hebrides and became a patron of Iona with St Oran's Chapel constructed as a family burial place.[7] In 1203, Somerled's son Ranald re-established the monastery as the Benedictine Abbey and sometime after he built the neighbouring Augustine convent of which his sister, Bethoc, was the first Prioress.[8] This period must have been a time a great spiritual renaissance in which Iona once again became a centre of Christian learning.

In 1266, the Hebrides became part of Scotland, with Mull and Iona part of the autonomous Lordship of the Isles. Over the next two hundred years, the Abbey was expanded and Iona continued to flourish as a religious centre within territory controlled by the Clan McKinnon. Indeed, several members of that clan became Abbots of the Abbey, although ownership of the island was eventually taken over by the Clan Maclean.

Like so many religious institutions, during the Reformation in the 16th century, the Abbey and Nunnery went into decline and were eventually abandoned with their treasures removed. The buildings were left to fall into ruins, although the main cemetery (with St Oran's Chapel) continued to be in use, as was the Nunnery for the burial of women.

In the years that followed, control of Iona and the neighbouring part of Mull fell into the hands of the Dukes of Argyll who had evicted the Clan Maclean family in the late 17th century. Over the next two centuries, the Dukes had no special interest in the island or its religious heritage and largely left the islanders to their own devices. Notably, on a visit in 1773, Samuel Johnson wrote that *"the island, which was once the metropolis of learning and piety, now has no school for education, nor temple for worship"*.

Thankfully, that is not the end of the story. In 1899, the 10th Duke of Argyll transferred ownership and management of the Abbey and Nunnery to a charity called the Iona Cathedral Trust ("ICT") which between 1900 and 1910 undertook extensive works to restore the Abbey church.[9] In the 1930s, and under the auspices of the Iona Community founded by the Reverend George Macleod, the architect Ian Lindsay (working with Reginald Fairlie as his mentor) undertook other restoration works the initial phase of which was completed in 1938. Subsequently, as the main users of the Abbey church and its immediate environs, the Iona Community rebuilt many of the monastic buildings, creating a home for their community work (see a separate section below), and in 1957 Ian Lindsay restored St Oran's Chapel.

In 1979, the Argyll family sold the rest of Iona to the philanthropist Sir Hugh Fraser who then donated the island to the people of Scotland, with the National Trust for Scotland acting as trustees. In the meantime, the ICT have established a museum which sits to the north of the Abbey church, making use of the old infirmary.

Finally, although the current Abbey is a reconstruction of the medieval building, it reflects the physical and spiritual presence established in the Middle Ages, and there are many reminders of the ancient heritage scattered across the site. These include the 9th century St Martin's Cross, which stands at the entrance to the Abbey.

The Landscape and People

Iona is not a *"chip off the old block"*. Its physical composition is quite distinct from that of Mull. In fact, a majority of the island shares its geology of gneissic rocks with the neighbouring islands of Coll and Tiree which date back 2,000 million years.[10] Remnants of the related pink granite can be found in the south west corner of the island. Associated with younger rock formations along the eastern coast, the island is also famed for its green marble, with remnants of quarrying visible along the south- east shore. The island is about 5km long by 2.5km wide with the highest point, Dùn I, being 101 metres above sea level. The weather is highly changeable and global warming is taking its toll through more frequent and more violent storms that damages roads, piers and buildings.

When you take the brief ferry trip across the Sound of Iona from Fionnphort, and walk up the hill from the jetty through the town of Baile Mor to the Abbey, it's difficult not to feel a presence that transcends the modern world and links you to 1,500 years of human existence. Apart from its religious heritage, the island has several sites reflecting older human occupation including the remains of a hill fort at *Cuil Bhuirg* and some caves along the western coast.

The island currently has a population of around 170 permanent residents. The majority live in the main settlement known as "the village" which is located at St Ronan's Bay. In recent times, the demography has changed significantly with more young people and families taking up residence.

For its size Iona is a vibrant community, and the modern society is a far cry from the sad and neglected population found by Dr Johnson in the late 18th century. This renewal reflects the impact of the re-construction of the Abbey in the 1930s. In the current era, the main occupations of the locals are linked to administration of the Abbey and other heritage sites, tourism (hotels, restaurants, and craft centres), farming, and fishing.[11] There are also several retail outlets serving the local community, emergency workers, and a range of tradesmen serving local needs. The island maintains a volunteer fire brigade, but the main medical facilities and police are based at Bunessan.

Iona Community Council

Iona is administered by Argyll and Bute Council ("AB&C"). Given its relatively remote position and its status as a location of significant religious heritage, the residents have their own Community Council which advises the A&BC on local issues.

The Iona Community Council ("ICC") comprises a group of up to 8 Councillors who are elected at the AGM for four-year terms. This team comprises a Convenor, five Councillors, and up to a further three members who are co-opted for their relevant expertise. Representatives of the Iona Community also attend. The body meets at least quarterly, and meetings are usually attended by one or more of the four local A&BC Councillors. The organisation receives an annual grant of around £500 from the A&BC to finance administrative expenses. It also receives specific-purpose funding from grants secured by other island organisation, and derives income from local fund-raising events to support a range of community activities. The declared aim of the ICC is as follows:

- To identify community views on current issues, and fairly express the diversity of local opinions to the A&BC and other organisations as appropriate;
- To take such action in the interests of the community as are desirable and practicable;
- To promote the well-being of the community and to foster community spirit;
- To be a vehicle for local people to voice their opinions on any matter affecting their lives.

In recent times, the ICC has had no shortage of business which has included the following.

Village Hall

Pride of place on the island, and dominating the upper slopes at the top of the hill from the main slipway at St Ronan's Bay, is a new community hall which was opened in May 2021 and replaced a much loved 90 year old building. The construction project was managed by the Iona Village Hall Community Trust with a committee comprising mainly younger volunteers who live on the island. Works were undertaken by Corramore Construction Ltd, and the construction was financed through funding from the National Lottery, several other charitable trusts, and numerous local fund-raising activities. Equipment was financed by the A&BC. The Hall is not only a meeting place but acts as a centre for a wide range of community activity including art classes, and a Gaelic language programme. It is also a venue for recitals by the Mull Gaelic Choir.

Education

While Iona has its own primary school, the future of secondary education is very much a live issue on the island. The ICC has been consulted on A&BC proposals to replace the existing facility at Tobermory, with future options including a new school in Tobermory, or the development of a school in the more central Craignure area. While the latter would have some benefits for children from Iona through reducing their travel time, the catchment area would still be relatively small compared with Oban High School which is able to provide a wider curriculum than Tobermory High School.

Housing

Iona has an acute housing problem, with insufficient houses to meet local needs. Not least this is because a growing number of houses have absentee owners who may only live on Iona for a few weeks each year and let their houses to tourists. Also, when houses come up for sale, the price is beyond local residents.

In response to this issue, ICC has supported a Housing Project which has recently seen the completion of 5 community houses for local people to rent. These were built by the Iona Housing Partnership and are managed by the West Highland Housing Association.

Energy

The ICC is committed to a transition to renewable energy and the decarbonisation of the economy. To this end, it has facilitated the Iona Renewables Project, with support from the Scottish government's *Strengthening Communities Programme* and the *Investing in Communities Fund.* The aim of the Project is that, within 15 years, and hopefully sooner, a community owned asset will be established with the following benefits.

- Alleviation of fuel poverty through cheaper energy,
- Reduction in carbon emissions as a contribution to the reduction of global warming,
- Improved knowledge amongst residents of responsible and efficient use of energy at home and work,

- Creation of employment for management and maintenance of the power system, and
- Generation of income for local investment.

The vehicle for delivery of the community-owned electricity supply and "heat network" will be a company named Iona Energy Limited, and all viable options for energy generation, storage and transmission are under consideration, including solar, wind and wave. Initially the main source of power will be a biomass geothermal system, with access through bore holes.

Fishing

The Scottish government has announced proposals to reserve 10% of the coastline through the declaration of *Highly Protected Marine Areas* which potentially include waters around Iona. ICC has liaised with residents and represented their concerns about the impact on the local economy, including the fishing industry and tourist boat operations. Further representations are pending.

Pier and Facilities

A major issue for the island is the status of the pier at St Ronan's Bay which is vital infrastructure for the ferry service to Mull. The pier is managed by A&BC, and there are continuing problems with the condition of the slipway. In the meantime, the non-functioning public toilets next to the pier are in need of A&BC funding for renovation and currently present a poor welcome for visitors to the island.

Breakwater Project

In winter there are a lot of ferry cancellations due to adverse weather and rough seas, and there is a major project in prospect to establish two breakwaters in the Sound of Iona on either side of the ferry crossing. This proposal has met with some opposition because of the impact on the beauty of the landscape. However, the A&BC has listened to these concerns and intends to use red granite to soften the visual impression.

The Iona Community

The Iona Community ("the Community") was founded in 1938 by the Reverend George MacLeod. The Community was established to promote ecumenism, social justice, and peace, and is constituted as a charitable trust with its headquarters in Glasgow. The Community has around 300 "Members" who elect a Council as the governance body. There is also a wider community of around 2,000 associate members and friends. Members are people who have been "Hallowed" following a period of two years training in which they study the vision and mission of the organisation, undertake one or more community projects, complete a written examination, and otherwise prove themselves to be worthy of admission.[12]

The organisation is self-funded, with occasional grants from the government and A&BC to fulfil Health and Safety and other regulations. A significant amount of the organisation's funds comes from the Members (up to £1 million per annum) and, in becoming a Member it is a requirement to give at least 10% of personal income to charity, 40% of which must go to the Community. To this end, Members are expected to provide an annual statement of how they have conducted their lives including income, living expenses, and work activity. The Community's income is largely used to finance the salaries of staff and the upkeep of the buildings.

This is essentially a Christian organisation, with Members coming from all denominations, although they are unlikely to be evangelical. They live and work throughout the world, with a third in Scotland, a third in England and Wales, and the remainder in Germany, the Netherlands, Switzerland, USA, and Australia. There are associated organisations in a number of countries, including the USA, Germany, the Netherlands, Australia, and Northern Ireland.

Although women were at one time excluded, current the Membership has approximately equal numbers of men and women. The form of their involvement varies, depending on their particular interests, with only a few at any one time resident on the island to perform administrative tasks and lead island-based programmes. Notably, the Community is not a missionary organisation, but is a vehicle for campaigning on a very wide range of social and political issues, both on an individual basis and sometimes collectively. The Members also form what are called "Family Groups" in which individuals living in a particularly district seek to convene as a local group.

From its base on Iona, the Community operates two main activities, the Visitor Programme, and Camas which involve the employment of around 20 professional staff, on contracts which are no more than three years in length. The staff are rarely Members, but have a skill set and personality that enables interaction with participants in the programme.

The Visitor Programme is run at the community facilities on Iona and lasts for a week. It is not a "retreat", in terms of requiring periods of silence in tune with monastic traditions. There are certain set features such as two religious services each day, and sometimes there is a theme for the week with guest speakers. Attendance at the services is not compulsory, but promotional material suggests that *"we hope you will attend"*. As a general rule, these services are significantly different from normal church services, as they include an opportunity for those present to participate in discussions about a very wide range of topics. Apart from this structure, there is plenty of free time and there are no organised groups although, in any one week, a group can be formed by people with common interests. In fact, attendees have many agendas. Some just want to get away from every-day life and enjoy the landscape and some agreeable company. Others want time to enjoy the peace and quiet, have a think, and embrace the "spirituality" of the place.

This Programme brings in around 1,500 people per annum and attendees encompass people from all backgrounds, beliefs, and demographics. Applications to attend are nearly always accepted. Each visitor pays fees to cover the costs of food and lodging, and is expected to contribute to the day to day operation of the facilities. This includes making their bed, cleaning their room, and taking their turn in cleaning bathrooms! They do not cook their own food, but they take turns to wash up and there are no facilities for self-catering.

Camas is a programme designed to help and support teenage children from deprived backgrounds.[13] Most of the children come from Glasgow and similar urban environments. This is a core activity in keeping with the mission of the Founder George McLeod, and is run by staff with specialist skills who volunteer their time for a whole season in return for board and lodging. Initially, the programme was based in a building called the MacLeod Centre on Iona. However, in the absence of facilities that meet modern expectations, interest declined to the point where it was no longer a viable operation and it is currently closed.[14] Instead, the Community established a somewhat different "outward bound" type of operation, with activities based at a property which lies between Fionnphort and Bunessan, down a 2 km track that is reached by foot. The accommodation consists of two converted 200 year old quarryman cottages next to a bay. It is off-grid, and there are no access to telephone or Wi-Fi. The young people come for a week and live together working through their issues with expert support to facilitate constructive interaction.

In addition to these main activities, the Community owns a company called Wild Goose Publications, which produces material on social justice, the promotion of world peace, holistic spirituality, healing, and some innovative approaches to worship. Output includes books, tapes, CDs, scripts for the performance of plays, and material for personal reflection and group discussion. It also operates a Welcome Centre and shop mostly run by volunteers.

ENDNOTES

1   The National Trust for Scotland was established in 1931 and is a charity with responsibility for managing ancient buildings and historic sites.

2   Movilla Abbey lies to the east of Belfast. Clonard is in the centre of the city.

3   Prevelant in the early Middle Ages, Celtic Christianity had a strong emphasis a love of nature, with an optimistic view of human nature. Following the Synod of Whitby in 664, it was subsumed by Roman Christianity (with its leadership in Rome) with a focus on obedience, prayer and silence.

4   This is one origin of the tale of the Loch Ness monster, Nessie, from a written account in 565 AD.

5   There are no markings on the gravestones, but recorded royal burials include Kenneth I, Donald II, Malcolm I, Duncan I, Macbeth, and Donald III.

6   It is said that the monks took with them an incomplete illustrated manuscript of the gospels. This eventually became the Book of Kells which is now in Trinity College Library in Dublin.

7   Oran is said to have been St Columba's uncle.

8   According to Martin Martin, a 17th century antiquarian, until the 19th century, there was a stone on Iona with a Gaelic inscription (not now legible) which read Bethoc, daughter of Somerled.

9   The trustees include a majority nominated by the Church of Scotland, but include nominees of the Roman Catholic Church and Episcopal Church of Scotland, and the Iona Community Council.

10 These rocks which are typical of what is called the Lewisian complex.

11 The annual number of passengers on the ferry service (130,000) suggests an annual influx of over 100,000 visitors.

12 After completion of the training, admission is a formality, although candidates must commit to the values and policy of the organisation.

13 Camas is Gaelic for bay.

14 Reinstatement of the original Camas operation is currently under active consideration with a project which would involve refurbishment of the Macleod Centre.

TRUSTEES OF HERITAGE

Mull is a treasure trove of culture and history. In this chapter we acknowledge the contribution of those who are guardians of the island's heritage.

Mull Historical and Archaeological Society ("MH&AS")

MH&AS was established in the 1970s as Mull Historical Society, and adopted its current name to avoid confusion with a local band.1 The aims of the organisation are to promote knowledge of the archaeology and social history of the island, and foster related research. It has over 100 members, including a significant number of non-residents, and provides a busy annual programme of events which includes visits to sites of interest and meetings addressed by notable archaeologists and historians. Through its website (mull-historical-society.co.uk), MH&AS also provides information on a range of publications, the latest results of research, and selected writings on social history.

The current Chair of MH&AS is Anne Cleave and her personal story reflects a significant contribution to life on the island over the last 30 years. Anne comes from Yorkshire and is a librarian and archivist by inclination and interest. Through involvement with publishing, she became a member of the Society of Indexers and this brought her into contact with the author Eve Eckstein. In part payment for services rendered, in 1985 Eve invited Anne and her husband Colin to stay at her cottage on Mull. They fell in love with the place and, a few years later they moved to the island. In those days, this was easier said than done because the Council wanted incoming residents to work on the island. Fortunately, at the time, a local publishing company in Tobermory was up for sale and in 1995 they lodged a successful bid. They moved to the island in 1996 and they later acquired a property in Ulva Ferry.

Anne got involved with the MH&AS in the late 1990s, taking on a variety of roles including treasurer, secretary and, in 2017, Chair. In 2003, she and her husband sold the publishing business, but retained responsibility for a number of community-related activities, including production of the island's Red Book Directory, publication of the local newspaper called *Round & About*, and management of the Salen Agricultural Show. Over the last 20 years, Anne has undertaken a number of archival research projects for several local people including the Clan Maclean, and has facilitated the applications for grants for the stabilisation of Moy Castle on the Lochbuie estate. Sadly, in 2017 Anne's husband Colin died, but she has continued a wide range of community activities and in 2020 joined the board of NWMCWC.

The Mull Museum

The Mull Museum was founded in 1972, at a meeting chaired by Duncan MacQuarrie in which local interested parties shared a variety of historical artefacts. Subsequently, a temporary display was mounted in the old Baptist church which is now the Masonic Hall, and in 1980 a constitution for the organisation was formally adopted. Then, in 1986, three sisters, Daisy and Jesse Craig, and Ena Sutherland donated premises in the Columba Building on Main Street in Tobermory to act as a full time Museum. This facility now comprises a permanent historical exhibition, a reference library of books and other archival material, a store, and offices.

The exhibition area of the Museum is open to the public on most days of the week and displays a range of historical items including prehistoric tools, artefacts from the Spanish Armada vessel sunk in 1588, and items from both World Wars. The library, for which there is access for research by appointment, contains over 900 books donated to or bought by the Museum. The collection includes the archives of the *Clan MacLean Association* and working papers for Jo Currie's book *Mull, the Island & its People*.

The Museum has sponsored several projects, through funds from various heritage grants and donations. These have included *Scotland's Rural Past* which focussed on research into deserted rural settlements, several archaeological digs such as the Baliscate Chapel in Tobermory in 2012, the Lephin dig at Glengorm between 2019 and 2022 which uncovered various medieval artefacts, and the Kildavie Project which is an ongoing activity now located within the lands owned by the NWMCWC.

While the Museum caters for recording and presenting the history of the whole of Mull and its surrounding islands, it has a significant focus on Tobermory. Its contribution is supplemented by museums in Bunessan (The Ross of Mull Historical Centre) and on the island of Iona (The Iona Abbey Museum). The Museum is mostly run by volunteers, but there is a part time archivist whose focus is to foster social history research, maintain the archives, and respond to public enquiries. Further information is available through the web site www.mullmuseum.co.uk and Mull Museum on Facebook.

The contents of the Library come from many sources, but worthy of a special mention is the work of Christine Leach, who has compiled significant records for the Ardmeanach and Brolass districts and has undertaken several local research projects. Originally a teacher in England, Christine first came to Mull in the 1980s on holiday, and became enchanted with the island. In 1987 she acquired a small cottage for holiday visits at Ballachmore in Gribun, and in 1992 she then moved to Mull to take up a job as Warden of a YMCA facility at Tavool. For the next ten years Christine lived in a tied rented cottage on the Tavool estate, with a more than full time job in the tourist season, while the quieter winter months were spent in various creative pursuits. When the YMCA eventually closed its operations, Christine acquired her current home at Balevulin which was originally the miller's homestead attached to the local township of Camus. This property, located in Tiroran, includes a studio where she now works, and houses the *Pennyghael in the Past Historical Archive* ("PPHA") and library.

During the last 20 years, PPHA has undertaken considerable research into the history of all the local farms in the study area of Ardmeanach and Brolass. The field work has included extensive interviews of local people, and a significant outcome is the production of booklet for each farm some of which are in the Mull Museum. Amongst other things, the PPHA library contains books and pamphlets published by a number of other local historians including a history of the area entitled *"Ardmeanach – A Hidden Corner of Mull"* by Jackie LeMay (better known to local people as Jackie Bradfield) and a monograph *"Glen More: A Drive Through History"* which Jackie produced with Joanna Gardner.[2]

Christine now has restricted mobility, but remains very active. She receives frequent historical queries about the area via email or through visitors to the PPHA. Also, she and three colleagues (Andrea Cameron, Elizabeth Carter, and Miek Zwamborn) have recently published a book on the Beaton family of doctors who lived for many years in Brolass (*Hebridean Healers – The Beatons of Mull*)."

Ross of Mull Historical Centre ("ROMHC")

As you travel through Brolass and the Ross of Mull, you can't fail to notice the many archaeological remains in the landscape, which reflect the painful history of depopulation through clearances. In 1997 the local community established a working party to survey evidence of human habitation and publish related material. After several years of careful work, and periodic exhibitions of material collected, it was decided to establish a permanent facility as a repository for items of historical interest. Fortuitously, in 2001 Historic Scotland had acquired the old water mill and Millbrae Cottage on the edge of Bunessan and had undertaken significant renovation. In 2007, it was agreed that this site would make an appropriate home for the ROMHC. The project to establish the facility was financed by a grant from the Heritage Lottery Fund and others, and it was opened in 2009.

In addition to the existing administrator, the committee subsequently appointed local writer, illustrator and environmentalist John Clare who carried out several projects including a survey of the Kilpatrick Estate in which he identified some 142 historical remains, helped produced interpretation panels, and recorded burial monument inscriptions and other records to enable publication of booklets for the four local burial grounds: Kilpatrick, Suie, Kilvickeon and Fionnphort. John also acted as a local guide, provided workshops and talks, and subsequently joined the management committee.

The ROMHC is currently managed by a board of voluntary directors, supported by volunteers. In addition to its historical displays, it has an extensive archive which accommodates ancestry research, hosts events, provides linkages with other bodies, publishes newsletter, retails a variety of publications, and takes on other activities with relevance to local history. It has also undertaken several projects which include the following:

Discover the Ross

In August 2004 the organisation published a series of booklets on local walks with a focus on introducing walkers to local historical sites.

Caring for Kilvickeon

The remains of the only medieval parish church on the Ross of Mull are at Kilvickeon which is to the south-east of Bunessan. Despite its age, many structures and artefacts have survived and, in 2013, Historic Scotland committed £39,000 to finance emergency repairs. Then, in 2015, a further £87,871 was allocated to consolidate the works. In the course of related excavation, a surprisingly uneven 'floor' was discovered and a valuable and intricately carved artefact dating from the 16th century and known as the "Mariota Stone" was uncovered. This has been restored to its original position inside the church.

Focus on Ardchiavaig

In 2017, an archaeological survey of the deserted rural township of Ardchiavaig was undertaken and subsequently a digital documentary was produced.

Further information on current ROMHC activities and projects, including the Community Garden and a Feasibility Study to renovate the Mill building, may be found on the ROHMC Website (rohmc.org.uk).

Iona Abbey Museum

Adjacent to the Iona Abbey is a museum which makes use of what used to be the Abbey infirmary. This building was restored by the Iona Cathedral Trust in 1964 and is now the home of a history of life on Iona since the arrival of St Columba. The museum includes many artefacts, including carved stones and remnants of St John's Cross, which were uncovered in a series of excavations over the last twenty years. A walk through the presentation is accompanied by haunting music.

The Lochbuie Estate

One of the most significant properties in Mull, owned by the Corbett family, is the Lochbuie Estate ('the Estate") in the south east corner of the island adjacent to the head of Loch Buie. The properties that make up the Estate approximate a substantial part of the lands held by the Clan Maclaine from the time that Hector Maclean was granted title by the Lord of the Isles in the 14th century, and include a modern-day farm.

The Estate encompasses several significant man-made structures of historical importance. By far the oldest structure is a circle of stones dating from the Bronze Age which stands in the fields to the north of Lochbuie House and is accessed by a pathway from the main road into the village. From the Middle Ages, the oldest buildings are Moy Castle constructed in around 1400, and two Maclaine mausoleums one of which goes back to around 1200 and was consecrated in 1500 for St Kenneth (the patron saint for shipwrecked sailors). After living in the castle for several centuries, in the 18th century the 17th Chief John Maclaine built a more comfortable dwelling called Moy House into which the family moved in 1752. This building is noted for the visit in 1773 by Dr Johnson and James Boswell as recorded in the inscription above the lintel of the front door. Subsequently, the 19th Chief Murdoch Maclaine built Lochbuie House which was occupied by his family in 1790. The final building of historic importance, which sits in the approaches to Lochbuie House, is the St Kilda Episcopal Church which the Clan Maclaine completed in 1876.

The Clan Maclaine retained control of most of this Estate for more than 500 years. However, for financial reasons following the First World War, the 24th Chief Kenneth Maclaine relinquished ownership which transferred to Sir Stephen Gatty. Subsequently, in 1922, it was acquired by Sir Richard Garton who appointed a local manager for a total holding which at this stage was around 29,000 acres. In 1934, Sir Richard died and the Estate was inherited by his daughter Dorothy who was married to the Reverend Lionel Corbett. They handed the management of the Estate to their son John Corbett who, following the death of his father in 1946 and his mother in 1967, eventually inherited the Estate. During this period, part of the Estate was acquired by Richard Gatty, who was the son of Sir Stephen, and his sister Hester who was married to the poet Siegfried Sassoon.

In the years that followed, John Corbett continued to manage what was now an Estate of around 21,000 acres and, on the passing of his mother in 1967, he inherited the properties. However, as the years caught up with him, in 1979 his son James Corbett (Jim) moved north with his wife Patience to manage the Estate based at Laggan Farm. When John died in 1998, ownership was divided between his children and Jim agreed to continue running all of the properties, and Jim and Patience moved into Lochbuie House. In 2011, Jim's son Thomas, who was raised on the Estate, came back to live at Lochbuie, taking up residence with his wife Flora at Laggan Farm. Tom now runs the farm, while Flora has opened a very successful café on the site of the old Lochbuie Post Office. As Noted in Chapter 21, Flora also runs the Mull Abattoir.

In the modern era, the main activity on the Estate continues to be agriculture. There is a herd of 120 cattle and 2,200 sheep, and the family also has stalking and fishing rights. In addition to the historic structures, the properties include several houses which are occupied by family members, farm employees and self-catering tenants.

The notable Moy Castle is a fort house constructed to withstand attack from inland and the sea, with a small stone slip for mooring boats which for many centuries were the main form of transport to other parts of the island and beyond. It is accessed by a footpath from the public car park in Lochbuie village. The building has several levels including a dungeon, a still active well on the ground floor, and rooms which would have served as a chapel, a banqueting room and personal quarters. At the top of the structure there are significant defensive parapets. When the Corbett family acquired the Estate, the Castle was a ruin with unstable parapet walls and, given the cost of remedial works, the castle remained in that state for some time. However, since taking on responsibility, Jim has done his best to maintain all of the ancient buildings. In 2003, he commissioned a survey under the auspices of Historic Scotland with the building registered as a national monument. Initial works were then undertaken to stabilise the parapet walls. In the 2010s, Jim commissioned further works to maintain the structure and, at the time of writing, further grants are being sought to finance the re-construction of the entrance and repointing of stonework.

Finally, Jim Corbett's contribution to Mull society has not been confined to running the Lochbuie Estate. He has also been active in the community, serving for several years as a member of the Mull Community Council. He is also accommodating to members of the Clan Maclaine who visit as individuals or for periodic gatherings of the whole Clan.

The Maclean Heritage

As living members of the Clan will tell you, Mull is a Maclean island. This is not an idle claim and, as I have frequently found, famous people with the Maclean surname nearly always have Mull ancestors. As we have seen in earlier chapters, Lachlan Lubanach Maclean and his wife Mary took up residence in Duart Castle in the 14th century and the Clan became established as the dominant family for a the next 350 years. A history is provided in Chapter 8. In the late 17th century, for a while, the Dukes of Argyll and the Campbells inserted themselves. However, the presence of the Clan Maclean was never expunged and, following the repossession of Duart in the 20th century, they resumed their rightful place.

Before the arrival of Lachlan Lubanach in 1367, there were already substantial buildings on Mull constructed in the 13th century by the Clan MacDougall. At that time, Aros Castle was the administrative centre, but Lachlan and his wife took up residence in Duart Castle. At that time, Duart was already a substantial building with thick stone walls and a deep ditch on the inland side. In the next twenty years, Lachlan extended the fortifications to include a four storied tower house. In the years that followed, further works were undertaken to consolidate and maintain the castle. However, the next major development was until the 16th century when Hector Mor the 12th Chief strengthened the eastern ramparts and constructed the main gatehouse which is the modern entrance to the castle.

As we know from earlier in this book, Duart Castle would figure in history on a number of occasions, not only in the local military escapades of the Clan Maclean during the Lordship of the Isles, but also in national events as the Clan Maclean supported the royalist cause in subsequent centuries. It was visited by one of the ships of the Spanish Armada blown off course during the aborted invasion of England in 1588, and the castle would figure in the Civil War when Oliver Cromwell used it to station troops. In 1692, following a financial default by the 20th Chief Sir John Maclean, the Duke of Argyll took possession of the Castle and proceeded to partly dismantle the main structure leaving the rest to fall into disrepair. Subsequently, much of the Clan Maclean estate associated directly with Duart Castle was sold off and the Castle and its immediate grounds were left as a ruin. The wider estates controlled by the Clan also passed into the hands of the Dukes of Argyll.

In 1910, all of this changed when the 26th Chief of the Clan Maclean, Sir Fitzroy Maclean, purchased title to Duart Castle. The property included several acres of surrounding land including access to the local road system. Following his acquisition, Sir Fitzroy restored the Castle, and installed modern facilities such as electric power, plumbing, and heating. With the building now habitable, in the remainder of the 20th century, the Chiefs of the Clan again had a base to which members of the Clan from across the globe could look as the ancestral home.

In the 21st century, Duart Castle is the home of Sir Lachlan Maclean CVO who became 28th Chief in 1990. During his tenure, he has acted as both leader of the clan and trustee of the heritage. The maintenance of the building requires considerable financial resources. However, Sir Lachlan and his family have raised the funds to regularly maintain the building and secure its long term future through regular maintenance. To finance some of this expenditure, the family has established Duart Castle as a major tourist venue with streams of visitors arriving daily.

In addition to his responsibility for maintaining the physical integrity of Duart Castle and the adjacent estate, Sir Lachlan also commits significant time to the community of which he is the world-wide leader, including the Clan Maclean Heritage Trust and several other related organisations.[3] He sees this as a very important part of his day to day existence, and receives a steady stream of enquiries from people who are seeking a sense of attachment and belonging to the history and heritage of the family's connection with the island. Like many Scottish clans, there is a well-supported clan society (the Clan Maclean Association) which welcomes all those who claim an association with the clan and fosters research into the activities of the clan since the Middle Ages. Periodically, the society organises a gathering on the island attended by the diaspora from across the world. The most recent was in 2023.

Aros Castle

Given the strategic position looking both north and east, it is likely that there was some form of fortification at the head of the cliffs at Aros Mains in Viking times. The current Aros Castle was constructed by the Clan MacDougall in the 13th century and, for several hundred years, it would be the administrative centre of the island. When the Clan Maclean arrived in the 14th century, although they would take up residence in Duart Castle, it would continue to have an important role as a place for gatherings, and as a barracks for troops. While it slowly declined in importance, it was still in use in the 17th century and, as late as 1608, King James VI summoned clan chiefs to meet there. Subsequently, it continued to be used as a barracks, with the Duke of Argyll housing troops in the castle in the 1670s when he was attempting to seize control of Maclean lands. However, in the late 17th century it slowly fell into disuse and, with lack of maintenance, by the 1690s the writer Martin Martin was describing the castle as a ruin.

Nowadays, with only a few of the main walls standing and no roof, Aros Castle stands as a haunting and picturesque reminder of medieval times. It is maintained by Historic Environment Scotland with public access by footpaths adjacent to precipitous cliffs.

Cairn na Burgh Castle

Cairn na Burgh Castle in the Treshnish Islands has figured in the history of the people of Mull for many centuries. Now a ruin, the structure of the castle straddles two islands which are only a few metres apart, Cairn na Burgh Mor and Cairn na Burgh Beag. The buildings are sited on top of steep cliffs making it virtually impregnable. The location was of strategic importance as it controlled the western approaches to Mull.

The origins of the castle are not entirely clear, although it is said that the Vikings established a fortress there called Kiaranaborg. It is first recorded as a castle in the time of Somerled, and was a Clan MacDougall fortification during the mid 13th century. As happened with other property held by that clan, following the conflict between the Balliols and Robert the Bruce in which they backed the losing side, in the 14th century ownership passed to the Clan Maclean.

In subsequent years, the castle was on several occasions a refuge for senior members of the Clan Maclean, and figured in several conflicts. Following the abolition of the Lordship of the Isles, in 1504, it was unsuccessfully besieged by King James IV following the decision of Lachlan Maclean to continue support for the Clan Donald. During the Reformation, it was used as a safe haven for manuscripts moved from Iona. In the Wars of the Three Kingdoms, when the local clans sided with the royalist cause, the castle was attacked and taken by a Covenanter Army, and subsequently Oliver Cromwell put the castle to the torch. In the process, several of the Iona manuscripts stored there were destroyed.

Following the annexation of Clan Maclean territory in the late 17th century, the castle was attacked on several occasions by the Clan Campbell anxious to deny refuge for the Macleans. In the 18th century it was used to house government troops during the Jacobite rebellions of 1715 and 1745. Thereafter, it fell into disuse and disrepair. It is now owned and maintained by the Hebridean Trust and has been the subject of archaeological investigation by Glasgow University.[4]

Other Significant Estates

Most of Mull is owned by a relatively small number of people many of whom do not live on the island. This is entirely consistent with the pattern of land ownership across much of Scotland. From a community point of view, this is not necessarily a bad thing. It is not who owns the land that matters so much as what the owner sees as their mission and responsibility. Fortunately, Mull has a number of land owners who are active in managing their estates as successful and environmentally sensitive businesses providing employment to local people and mindful of their heritage.

ENDNOTES

1   The Mull Historical Society is a band established by Colin MacIntyre in 2000. Born in Mull in 1971, he formed his first band called The Love Sick Zombies when he was a student at Tobermory High School. After university and several other careers, in his twenties he became a full time musician.
2   Ardmeanach – A Hidden Corner of Mull, by Jackie Le May, was published by Iona Press in association with the Mull Historical Society in 1995.
3   A charming and self-effacing man, Sir Lachlan has lived at Duart Castle for several years. He maintains a modest existence, and is not beyond sweeping the courtyard of the castle!
4   The Hebridean Trust was established in 1982 to regenerate island communities, restore and maintain historical monuments, and preserve the natural environment. It is a charitable organisation funded by public donation, the National Lottery and Historic Scotland.

FUTURE OF COMMUNITY

When I started this book, my aim was to tell the story of a remarkable place and community. With a somewhat superficial knowledge of Scottish and local history, at the beginning of my journey I had naively imagined that the islands of Mull and Iona would resound with echoes of the clan-based culture of the Middle Ages. In pursuing my research, and thanks to the wise counsel of the local cognoscenti, it soon became apparent that this was fanciful. Apart from the relatively unchanged landscape, the society in 21st century Mull and Iona has only a tenuous connection with the clan-based social contracts of the bygone era. Instead, there is a different explanation for the strength of the current community. There is still evidence of a special kind of spirit that drives free spirits to come together in confronting adversity in remote places. However, the well-being of the modern community reflects a current population who demonstrate some very special qualities of enterprise, resilience, community action, and commitment to sustainability.

Before concluding this book with some final words about this model of a decent society that offers hope to the world, it is first worth reminding ourselves of how in the 21st century the human species has got itself into something of an existential crisis, which makes the achievements in Mull all the more remarkable.

The Challenges of the Modern Age

As a consequence of our technological advances, over the last 250 years we have achieved amazing progress in improving the quality of life of a majority of the human species. However, this progress has come at a mounting cost to the delicate balance of life and the health of the biosphere. Our progress has been driven by two self-destructive forces – our lust for relentless economic growth regardless of the finite nature of the Earth's resources, and our insatiable appetite for energy through consumption of fossil fuels. Personal greed in the pursuit of wealth is an abiding part of the human condition which is unlikely to be abandoned any time soon! However, slowly, and reluctantly, most rational people have come to recognise that we can no longer depend on fossil fuels for energy, with global warming having the potential to make life on Earth unbearable.

Whilst the huge threat to our existence posed by environmental factors should be uppermost on our agenda for survival, the human species faces other crises. In the last few years, we have been reminded of our vulnerability to new viruses. For a time in the 20th century, it seemed that we were headed for a world in which we would be able to eliminate virtually all the threats to our physical health. The Covid-19 virus quickly changed that fantasy. The ingenuity shown in our response is a cause for hope, but the turmoil arising from the pandemic is a huge reality check on our apparent invincibility.

Another significant concern is the resilience of our systems of government and the rise of populist-based libertarianism. Since the age of the enlightenment in the 16th century, when reason prevailed over superstition, "the West" has settled into a range of regimes that are broadly termed "liberal democracies". These various forms of delivering a civil society are characterised by representative government based on free elections, an open media, and an independent judiciary which deliver a civil society and the rule of law. However, there are conflicting views about what constitutes justice, and there are significant forces who are opposed to the pursuit of a community-based approach where individual freedoms are tempered by policies designed to seek the common good and protect the less advantaged. It is the libertarian belief that governments should confine themselves to securing rights to the pursuit of wealth almost regardless of the impact on the public good. This counter-community ideological view is not a recent invention. It is based on centuries of philosophical reflection and is deeply rooted in our body politic. The positive manifestations of this philosophy are legislation such as a Bill of Rights that guarantee freedom of speech, a free press, and free association. However, there is an anti-social down-side that has become a cancer in the modern world. Nowadays, there is a minority in every western country who pejoratively characterise any attempt to foster the interests of the community, and "pander" to minority interests and the disadvantaged, as "socialist", "communist", or "woke".[1] Such anti-social forces have infected conservative political parties through populist appeals to self-interest at the expense of the common good. The agenda in terms of "anti-community" policy includes a commitment to small government, unregulated markets even though they may be dominated by self-serving and exploitative oligopolies, privatisation of essential public services and infrastructure, low taxation which denies the ability to invest in essential infrastructure, "trickle-down" economics in which the poor benefit from the largesse of the rich, "freedom" to say what you like despite the impact on others, intolerance of diversity, and the ability to carry guns as a means of personal protection. This line of thinking, putting individual freedom ahead of the common good, poses a huge threat to the maintenance of healthy communities and a civil society.

If the libertarian threat wasn't bad enough, in current times we are also beset by our fair share of autocratic government in many parts of the world. Following the end of World War Two, there was a period when it seemed that forms of "democracy" were spreading to every corner of the globe with a culmination in the fall of the Berlin Wall in 1989 which delivered a temporary euphoria. However, the ugly spectre of dictatorship never actually disappeared and has recently been spreading, bringing war to Eastern Europe and looming hostilities in Eastern Asia. Such regimes serve to entrench the power of the privileged few at the expense of the many, mostly have little regard for the finite nature of the world's resources, and disparage the need to respect diversity or care for the disadvantaged.

Then there is the impact of religion. This is not to deny either the importance of spirituality for our mental health, or the values derived from religious faith that underpin civil society in many parts of the world. However, in the 21st century, we have been hit by the resurgence of fundamentalist beliefs, and it takes many forms. In particular, some adherents of the main religions from the Middle East embrace literal interpretations of their ancient holy texts which drives them to deny the knowledge derived from science, to belittle women, and to embrace the violent elimination of opponents.

Finally, in the 21st century, there is the epidemic of lies and misinformation available on the internet, provided by fools and rogues to drive fear, ignorance and anti-social behaviour. Facilitated by monolithic international companies operating beyond the reach of regulation by nation states, this phenomenon goes virtually unchecked. The disinformation confuses and misleads huge numbers of people who are driven to adopt irrational anti-social beliefs and embrace numerous conspiracy theories which undermine social cohesion. This stream of invective against supposed threats to the good life also leads to the support of populist leaders who appeal to the dark side of human nature.

Community-Based Living in the 21st Century

Despite this somewhat depressing view of the present world, the message from this book is that there is the prospect of securing a more palatable future for mankind and the environment of which we are a part. Within our society there are people building a future based on all the good things that we have learnt from our historical experience whilst taking advantage of modern science and technology. And the endeavour of many people living in Mull and Iona is a prime example of a work-in-progress which stands as a beacon for others to follow and a counterpoint to societies driven by privilege and greed.

At the core of this renaissance is a commitment to the concept of community. At the beginning of this book, we noted that this basis for a healthy society relied on the following inter-connected characteristics:

- Identification with a geographical location.
- Living in a functional relationship with each other.
- Having opportunities for individual self-fulfilment.
- Sharing a sense of identity and/or unity of purpose.
- Commitment to a common destiny.

The establishment of a society in which these characteristics prevail is really not too much for us to ask of ourselves and those with whom we share the world; and it's an aspiration that has driven significant reform before. In the 1940s, Sir William Beveridge identified an agenda to counter what he called the five evils of the age which still resonate today: Want (poverty), Disease (inequality of access), Ignorance (misinformation), Squalor (housing), and Idleness (unemployment).[2] The Beveridge Report of 1942 was a blueprint for building Britain's welfare state which underpinned civil society for a generation until it was disrupted by the libertarianism of recent times.

In the case of Mull and Iona, the renaissance of community since the turn of the 21st century is not a dream; and there are significant factors that have driven the development of a healthy and civil society. To begin with, one should not underestimate the fact that local citizens are blessed with a landscape, flora and fauna which command respect for the environment and provide daily inspiration to all regardless of their personal wealth and status. Love of country is a vital element in developing a sense of belonging and common identity, and an appreciation of the delicate balance of nature drives a wide spread commitment by local people to sustainable living.

A second and very important factor is the character of people who choose to live in Mull and Iona. The current community encompasses a diverse set of peoples, native born and migrants, most of whom share values which lead them to work together for the common good. As noted in Parts Six and Seven of this book, this propensity is manifest in the people and organisations that are committed to community activism, and to sustaining a range of organisations and activities that add value to every-day existence. To these notable endeavours should be added a real commitment to value and cherish the history and heritage of Mull and Iona, which is a vital element in defining identity and belonging, and an amazingly vibrant artistic community which treasures and promotes creative endeavours.

Whilst much of this progress has been achieved through the diligent efforts of local people and organisations, we should not forget the context in which this flourishing of community has taken place. An important factor in enabling all of this to happen is the renaissance of what it means to be Scottish including the re-establishment of the Scottish Parliament. The legislation that the Parliament has enacted for land reform, community empowerment, and resurgence of the Highlands and Islands, has been a vital vehicle for much of what has been achieved at the local level.

Finally, if the contents of this book have told us anything, it is perhaps that the time-worn ethos of dùthchas, sustainable living through mutual support on the land that we share, really does live on. In modern terms, Mull is a community that values its natural environment, encourages human enterprise, thrives on team work, appreciates its history and heritage, celebrates artistic endeavour, acknowledges the need to live within the constraints of its resources, and respects/ensures provision for the needs of the least able. These are the true measures of what constitutes a civil society in the 21st century. The world should take note.

ENDNOTES

1   The word "woke" derives from the Afro-American vernacular, meaning alert to discrimination, but is now used sarcastically to describe progressive and empathetic views.
2   Sir William Beveridge was a British economist and UK Liberal politician (1879-1963). The Beveridge Report issued in 1942 provided a vision for Britain's recovery following World War II.

ACKNOWLEDGEMENTS

I n writing this book, I owe a great debt to a large number of people who have contributed in many and diverse ways. At the start of my adventure, I was fortunate to meet several residents of Mull who were extremely helpful in sharing with me their knowledge and experience and introducing me to others. In particular, both Mary Phillips of the MH&AS and Sue Hawkes of MICT have been stalwarts in helping me throughout the project, and Anne Cleave and Christine Leach have been generous in sharing their insights and experience. Alisdair and Georgia Satchell have also been good friends in supporting and encouraging me, as have David and Priscilla Fell.

In preparing a number of chapters, I am grateful for input from a number of people with specialist knowledge. Jim Westland provided very helpful comments on the account of Mull's geology, Professor Sir Tom Devine was generous with his time in reviewing my take on modern Scottish history and providing insights and suggestions for further reading and research, Gordon Maclean and Calum Hall were very helpful in sharing their knowledge of the artistic life of the island, Liz Gibson provided valuable insight into the history and current life of the church, and John Dale of the Iona Community and Jane Martin of the Iona Community Council gave me great insights into life on that blessed isle. In preparing the material on the work of current community organisations, I am especially grateful to Moray Finch of MICT, Colin Morrison of NWMCWC, and Cameron Anson of SWMID. I am also indebted to Jim Corbett for sharing his knowledge and experience on the history and heritage of Lochbuie, and Sir Lachlan Maclean for his insights into the history of the Clan Maclean and the role of the clan in the modern era.

In addition to all those mentioned above, I am especially grateful to all those people who, during my two periods of residency in 2019 and 2023 agreed to meet and share with me their personal life stories. Finally, I would like to thank a number of people who have provided generously of their time in reviewing and editing the manuscript. As always, I am also very grateful to my publisher Simon Hepworth and his team for completing yet another lengthy tome, Cameron Duncan for his sterling work in designing the presentation of the book, and Wendy McCann for the design of the map of Mull.

ACKNOWLEDGEMENTS

DÙTHCHAS
LANDSCAPE AND COMMUNITY IN MULL AND IONA

GLOSSARY

A&BC	Argyll and Bute Council
AECS	Agricultural Environment and Climate Scheme
BLF	Big Lottery Fund
CMAL	Caledonian Maritime Assets Ltd
CSA	Campaign for a Scottish Assembly
EU	European Union
HARP	Heritage Archaeological Research Practice
HES	Historic Environment Scotland
HIE	Highlands and Islands Enterprise
HPMA	Highly Protected Marine Area
HWDT	Hebridean Whale and Dolphin Trust
ICC	Iona Community Council
ICIA	Island Community Impact Assessment
JNCC	Joint Nature Conservation Committee (of UK Parliament)
LMS	London Missionary Society
MCC	Mull Community Council
MEP	Member of European Parliament
MESS	Mull and Iona Environmentally Sensitive Solutions
MFA	Mull Fishermen's Association
MH&AS	Mull Historical and Archaeological Society
MICT	Mull and Iona Community Trust
MIFC	Mull and Iona Ferry Committee
MSL	Mull Slaughterhouse Ltd
NHS	National Health Service
NPS	National Party of Scotland
NSW	New South Wales, a State in Australia
NWMCWC	North West Mull Community Woodland Company
RCAHMS	Royal Commission on the Ancient and Historical Monuments of Scotland
RET	Road Equivalent Tariff
RNLI	Royal National Lifeboat Institution
SAMS	Scottish Association of Marine Science
SEPA	Scottish Environment Protection Agency
SLF	Scottish Land Fund
SNP	Scottish National Party
SOE	Special Operations Executive
SP	Scottish Party
SSE	Standard Scottish English
SSMEI	Scottish Sustainable Marine Environment Initiative
STG	Scottish Transport Group
SWMID	South West Mull and Iona Development
THA	Tobermory Harbour Association
UHI	University of Highlands and Islands
YMCA	Young Men's Christian Association

BIBLIOGRAPHY
& SOURCES

Author	Title	Publisher	Place	Date
Boswell, James	Journal of a Tour to the Hebrides with Samuel Johnson, LL.D.			1786
Caldwell, David	Mull & Iona: A Historical Guide	Birlinn	Edinburgh	2018
Clare, John	Various booklets on the environment, archaeology and culture of Mull			
Collins, Ronald W	The Genealogy of the Clan Maclean	Collins	New York	2017
Crossman, Ashley	Understanding Functionalist Theory	ThoughtCo	New York	2020
Currie, Jo	Mull: The Island and its People	Birlinn	Edinburgh	2010
Devine, Prof Sir Tom	The Scottish Nation, a Modern History	Penguin	London	2012
Devine, Prof Sir Tom	Independence or Union – Scotland's Past and Scotland's Present	Penguin	London	2016
Devine, Prof Sir Tom	The Scottish Clearances – A History of the Dispossessed	Penguin	London	2019
Harari, Yuval Noah	Sapiens, A Brief History of Humankind	Penguin	London	2015
Houston, I	Memories of Mull.	Ross of Mull Historical Centre	Mull	2003
Jenkins, David	Mendelssohn in Scotland	Chappell	New York	1978
Le May, Jackie	Ardmeanach: A Hidden Corner of Mull	New Iona Press	Iona	1995
Le May & Gardner	Glen More: A Drive Through History	Brown & Whittaker	Leeds	2001
Littlewood and Jones	Wild Mull – A Natural History of the Island and Its People	Pelagic Publishing	London	2021
MacCormick, John	Island of Mull; Its History, Scenes & Legends	Hannan	London	1923
Macinnes, Allan I	Clanship, Commerce and the House of Stuart	Tuckwell	East Lothian	1996
Mackenzie, Ann	Island Voices: Traditions of North Mull	Birlinn	Edinburgh	2002
Maclean, Sir Fitzroy	The Isles of the Sea	Collins	London	1986
Maclean, Ian	Celebrating the Clan Maclean	Lulu Press	London	2023

Author	Title	Publisher	Place	Date
Maclean, J P	A History of the Clan Maclean	Robert Clarke & Co	Cincinnati	1889
Martin Martin	A Description of the Western Islands of Scotland Circa 1695	Cornhill	London	1703
McKirdy, Alan	Mull, Iona, and Ardnamurchan – Landscapes in Stone	Birlinn	Edinburgh	2017
McNab, P A	Highways and Byways in Mull & Iona	Luath Press	Edinburgh	1988
McWhinney, Sarah	Mouth to Ear Memory			1992
Mithen S, & Wicks C	Proceedings of the Prehistoric Society	Cambridge University Press	Cambridge	2018
Munro and MacQuarrie	Clan MacQuarrie – A History	NWMCWC	Dervaig	2023
Offer, John	Herbert Spencer, Sociological Theory and the Professions	Ulster University	Coleraine	2019
Oram, Richard D	Lordship of the Isles	Brill	Leiden	2014
Plant, Marjorie	Domestic Life of Scotland in the 18th Century	Edinburgh University Press	Edinburgh	1952
Riddoch, Lesley	Blossom – What Scotland needs to flourish	Luath Press	Edinburgh	2013
Schutte, Dr de Wet	Community Development and Social Engineering	University of Western Cape	Cape Town	2015
Stephenson, Dr David	Mull & Iona: A Landscape Fashioned by Geology	Scottish National Heritage	Perth	2011
Stevenson, R L	Kidnapped	Cassell & Co	London	1886
UK Government	Joint Nature Conservation Committee: Report On Region 14	HMSO	London	1995
Wegener, Alfred	The Origins of Continents and Oceans	Dover Publications	USA	1915
Whittaker, Jean	Mull Monuments and History	Brown & Whittaker	Tobermory	1993
Wightman, Andy	The Poor Had No Lawyers	Birlinn	Edinburgh	2015
	Argyll: An Inventory of the Monuments Volume 4: Iona. RCAHMS			1982
Whyte, Alisdair C	Settlement Names and Society	University of Glasgow	Glasgow	2017

DÙTHCHAS
Landscape and Community in Mull and Iona

INDEX OF SIGNIFICANT PEOPLE

INDEX OF SIGNIFICANT PEOPLE ...*CONTINUED*

INDEX OF SELECTIVE SUBJECT

INDEX OF SELECTIVE SUBJECT ...*CONTINUED*

ABOUT THE AUTHOR

Gavin Wigginton was born in Nottingham in 1945. He is a sometime graduate of the Universities of Wales (in Swansea) and Hull. In the late 1960s he commenced a career in the private sector of British industry, with roles as an internal consultant, HR manager, corporate planner, and company secretary.

Since 1986, Gavin has lived in Australia. After a time with the National Companies and Securities Commission, he was for 15 years a senior manager with the Australian Red Cross Society's blood service. In 2005 he was awarded the Society's Distinguished Staff Award. More recently, he has been a management consultant specialising in governance and risk analysis and has served on the board of a number of not for profit organisations.

Gavin has been an active environmentalist for most of his adult life, and for ten years served as Honorary Secretary and a board member of the Australian Conservation Foundation. He is an Honorary Life Member of the Foundation.

Nowadays, Gavin is an author, specialising in biography and social history.